EDEXCEL AS/A-LEVEL FIFTH EDITION

UK GOVERNMENT AND POLITICS

NEIL MCNAUGHTON

DYNAMIC LEARNING

HODDER EDUCATION
AN HACHETTE UK COMPANY

KT-546-996

In order to ensure that this resource offers high-quality support for the associated Pearson qualification, it has been through a review process by the awarding body. This process confirms that this resource fully covers the teaching and learning content of the specification or part of a specification at which it is aimed. It also confirms that it demonstrates an appropriate balance between the development of subject skills, knowledge and understanding, in addition to preparation for assessment.

Endorsement does not cover any guidance on assessment activities or processes (e.g. practice questions or advice on how to answer assessment questions), included in the resource nor does it prescribe any particular approach to the teaching or delivery of a related course.

While the publishers have made every attempt to ensure that advice on the qualification and its assessment is accurate, the official specification and associated assessment guidance materials are the only authoritative source of information and should always be referred to for definitive guidance.

Pearson examiners have not contributed to any sections in this resource relevant to examination papers for which they have responsibility.

Examiners will not use endorsed resources as a source of material for any assessment set by Pearson.

Endorsement of a resource does not mean that the resource is required to achieve this Pearson qualification, nor does it mean that it is the only suitable material available to support the qualification, and any resource lists produced by the awarding body shall include this and other appropriate resources.

Hachette UK's policy is to use papers that are natural, renewable and recyclable products and made from wood grown in sustainable forests. The logging and manufacturing processes are expected to conform to the environmental regulations of the country of origin.

Orders: please contact Bookpoint Ltd, 130 Park Drive, Milton Park, Abingdon, Oxon OX14 4SE. Telephone: (44) 01235 827720. Fax: (44) 01235 400454. Email education@bookpoint.co.uk

Lines are open from 9 a.m. to 5 p.m., Monday to Saturday, with a 24-hour message answering service. You can also order through our website: www.hoddereducation.co.uk

ISBN: 978 1 4718 8931 8

© Neil McNaughton 2017

First published in 2017 by

Hodder Education,
An Hachette UK Company
Carmelite House
50 Victoria Embankment
London EC4Y 0DZ

www.hoddereducation.co.uk

Impression number   10 9 8 7 6 5

Year   2021 2020 2019

All rights reserved. Apart from any use permitted under UK copyright law, no part of this publication may be reproduced or transmitted in any form or by any means, electronic or mechanical, including photocopying and recording, or held within any information storage and retrieval system, without permission in writing from the publisher or under licence from the Copyright Licensing Agency Limited. Further details of such licences (for reprographic reproduction) may be obtained from the Copyright Licensing Agency Limited, Barnard's Inn, 86 Fetter Lane, London EC4A 1EN.

Photos reproduced by permission of: **p. vi** Alain Le Garsmeur 'The Troubles' Archive/Alamy Stock Photo; **p. ix** Chris Whiteman/Alamy Stock Photo; **p. xiii** White House Photo/Alamy Stock Photo; **p. xx** mbruxelle/Fotolia; **p. 2** Adam Eastland/Alamy Stock Photo; **p. 5** Jeff Gilbert/Alamy Stock Photo; **p. 7** Anna Stowe/Alamy Stock Photo; **p. 12** George Olney/Alamy Stock Photo; **p. 21** Arch White/Alamy Stock Photo; **p. 25** Bjanka Kadic/Alamy Stock Photo; **p. 30** REUTERS/Alamy Stock Photo; **p. 42** Russell Hart/Alamy Stock Photo; **p. 45** Paul Davey/Alamy Stock Photo; **p. 50** Paul Davey/Alamy Stock Photo; **p. 57** Erica Guilane-Nachez/Fotolia; **p. 61** Malcolm Park Editorial/Alamy Stock Photo; **p. 65** Arzt/AP/REX/Shutterstock; **p. 68** REX/Shutterstock; **p. 70** alpegor/Fotolia; **p. 72** Steve Parkins/REX/Shutterstock; **p. 81** Ken McKay/ITV/REX/Shutterstock; **p. 90** Tim Rooke/REX/Shutterstock; **p. 98** Heartland Arts/Fotolia; **p. 100** Della Batchelor/Alamy Stock Photo; **p. 105** Claudio Divizia/Fotolia; **p. 106** Anthony Collins/Alamy Stock Photo; **p. 110** Ady Kerry/Alamy; **p. 118** Paul Swinney/Alamy Stock Photo; **p. 123** Keith Morris/Alamy Stock Photo; **p. 124** Jeffrey Blackler/Alamy Stock Photo; **p. 127** Keith Morris News/Alamy Stock Photo; **p. 136** Mark Harvey/Alamy Stock Photo; **p. 139** Lenscap/Alamy Stock Photo; **p. 142** Andrey Burmakin/Fotolia; **p.152** bbourdages/Fotolia; **p. 154** Roger Parkes/Alamy Stock Photo; **p. 161** REUTERS/Alamy Stock Photo; **p. 165** REUTERS/Alamy Stock Photo; **p. 171** Martin Bond/Alamy Stock Photo; **p. 180** Stephen Barnes/Alamy Stock Photo; **p. 183** Paul Davey/Alamy Stock Photo; **p. 186** Sipa Press/REX/Shutterstock; **p. 196** norbel/Fotolia; **p. 198** Heritage Image Partnership/Alamy Stock Photo; **p. 203** Cliff Hide PR/Alamy Stock Photo; **p. 207** John Fryer/Alamy; **p. 216** Duncan Bryceland/REX/Shutterstock; **p. 222** PA Wire/Press Association Images; **p. 225** PA Wire/Press Association Images; **p. 229** Kirsty Wigglesworth/PA Wire/Press Association Images; **p. 234** REX/Shutterstock; **p. 238** REX/Shutterstock; **p. 242** Mark Thomas/REX/Shutterstock; **p. 247** Gavin Rodgers/Alamy Stock Photo; **p. 251** Meibion/Alamy Stock Photo; **p. 256** REX/Shutterstock; **p. 257** 360b/Alamy Stock Photo; **p. 258** REUTERS/Alamy Stock Photo; **p. 259** Alan D West/Alamy Stock Photo; **p. 266** REX/Shutterstock; **p. 270** chrisdorney/Fotolia; **p. 273** REUTERS/Alamy Stock Photo; **p. 274** Justin Kasez12z/Alamy Stock Photo; **p. 278** Michael Tubi/Alamy Stock Photo; **p. 280** ifeelstock/Fotolia; **p. 287** Isopix/REX/Shutterstock; **p. 289** Anthony Collins/Alamy; **p. 292** Josemaria Toscano/Fotolia.

Cover photo reproduced by permission of Tim Ellis/Alamy

Typeset in India by Aptara Inc.

Printed in India

A catalogue record for this title is available from the British Library.

Get the most from this book

This new edition of our best-selling textbook covers the key content of the Edexcel government and politics specification for teaching from September 2017.

Special features

Objectives
A summary of the learning objectives for each chapter.

Synoptic link
Page-reference links between concepts that occur in more than one area of the specification.

Key terms
Concise definitions of key terms (in the specification and for understanding) where they first appear.

Study tip
Revision advice such as common mistakes, pitfalls and key points to remember.

Knowledge check
Short questions to assess comprehension of the subject.

Debate
The two sides of a controversial question set out to hone evaluation skills.

Discussion point
Interesting questions to be used as the basis for class discussions or homework.

Key concepts in this chapter
A summary of key concepts used throughout the chapter.

Summary
A summary at the end of the chapter against which students can check their knowledge.

Further information and web guide
Websites, books and articles that are relevant to the chapter.

Practice questions
Revision questions at the end of each chapter.

Contents

Introduction and background   vi
What is politics?   vii
What is government?   xi
The state and the government   xiv
Branches of government   xv
The evolution of the UK political system   xvi

Component 1 Participation   1

Chapter 1 Democracy and participation   2
Two forms of democracy   3
The nature of representative democracy in the UK   6
How democratic is the UK?   10
Political participation in the UK   14
Suffrage   19
Pressure groups   22
Rights in context   31

Chapter 2 Political parties   42
Principles of political parties   43
Established political parties   55
Emerging and minor political parties   71
Consensus and adversary politics   75
UK political parties in context   77
A summary of the role of parties in the UK   83

Chapter 3 Electoral systems   90
Different electoral systems   91
Referendums   103
Electoral outcomes   109

Chapter 4 Voting behaviour and the media   118
Social class and other social factors   119
Voting trends and theories   132
The media and opinion polls in politics   138
Three election case studies   144

Component 2 UK government 151

Chapter 5 The constitution ... 152
What is a constitution? ... 153
The development, nature and theory of the UK Constitution ... 154
The sources of the UK Constitution ... 159
Constitutional reform in the UK ... 162
Devolution ... 175
Current debates on further constitutional reform ... 182

Chapter 6 Parliament ... 196
Background ... 197
The House of Commons and House of Lords ... 201
Comparing the powers of the House of Commons and House of Lords ... 210
Legislation ... 212
How Parliament interacts with the executive ... 214
A general assessment of Parliament ... 225
Reform of the House of Lords ... 228

Chapter 7 The prime minister and executive ... 234
The role, powers and structure of the core executive in the UK ... 235
Ministerial responsibility ... 244
The power of the prime minister and cabinet ... 247
The relationship between prime minister and cabinet ... 252

Chapter 8 Relations between institutions ... 266
Background: the nature and role of the judiciary in general ... 267
The judiciary (especially the Supreme Court) and Parliament ... 275
The judiciary (especially the Supreme Court) and the executive ... 277
The Supreme Court and rights ... 279
The European Court of Human Rights ... 279
The independence of the judiciary ... 281
How powerful is the Supreme Court? ... 283
The relationship between the executive and Parliament ... 284
The UK and the European Union ... 287
Sovereignty ... 290

Index ... 298

Answers to the knowledge check boxes and the
practice questions at the end of each chapter can be found at:
www.hoddereducation.co.uk/EdexcelPolitics

Introduction and background

Children in Belfast in the 1970s during The Troubles

Objectives

This introduction will inform you about the following:
- ➔ The nature of politics
- ➔ The nature of government and the state
- ➔ How government and politics relate to each other
- ➔ Many of the key concepts which are relevant to government and politics in the UK
- ➔ The historical development of the UK political system
- ➔ The basic principles that underlie UK government and politics today

What is politics?

The term 'politics' has come a long way since it was coined by the classical Greeks. Originally it was little more than a description of how states were governed. In the modern world, however, 'politics' suggests *conflict* — that is, conflict between ideas, conflict between sections of the community and conflict between individuals.

The alternative to peaceful political activity can involve physical conflict. This may take the form of general disorder and/or terrorist activity (as in Northern Ireland from 1968 to the mid-1990s, in the Middle East or racial tensions in American cities), revolution (as in Russia in 1917, Libya in 2011) or civil war (China in the 1930s and 1940s; Syria, Somalia and Sudan more recently). Such violence can be viewed as a *failure* of politics. If conflict cannot be resolved peacefully within political institutions and processes, groups often resort to violence. In Northern Ireland in the 1990s and 2000s, for example, successive British governments and leaders sought to persuade political leaders — even those who led extreme groups such as Sinn Fein and the Democratic Unionists — to renounce violence and pursue their goals through conventional, peaceful politics instead. In the event, peaceful politics was finally and happily restored to the province after 2007.

Professor Bernard Crick, in his celebrated work *In Defence of Politics* (4th edn, 1992), summed up the meaning and importance of politics thus:

> Politics arises from accepting the fact of the simultaneous existence of different groups, hence different interests and different traditions, within a territorial unit under a common rule.

So we can summarise that the term 'politics' refers to three main activities concerning the state. These are the conflict of ideas, the conflict of interests and the struggle for power. Below we examine each of these in turn.

The conflict of ideas

Modern politics would not be politics unless those who take part in it adopt and promote ideas as to how the state should be run and how society should be shaped. When individuals go to the polling station they generally have political ideas in their minds, however mild and unformed these may be, when they vote. The ordinary members of political parties presumably join their party in the first place because they have political ideas and hope to further them through their chosen party. Politicians themselves, whether they be local councillors, members of regional assemblies, national Members of Parliament (MPs) or ministers, are continuously involved in promoting political ideas. At all levels of politics, therefore, we see and hear the clash of ideas. Indeed in 2015–16 the UK was engaged in perhaps the biggest clash of ideas in its modern history — whether to leave or stay in the European Union (EU). This was politics at its most intense.

On a grand scale, political ideas become ideologies. An **ideology** can be defined as a collection of ideas that propose social change and include some 'blueprint' for a future idealised society. These ideas are also based on one or several specific principles such as equality, common ownership of property or individual liberty. Ideologies are often radical, and so those who support them usually flourish on the extremities of moderate Western politics. The most influential and successful ideologies have included, for example, socialism, fascism, feminism and radical forms of liberalism and nationalism. Conservatism is also often described as an ideology, although many

> **Key term**
>
> **Ideology** A coherent set of well-established ideas that propose specific changes in society and which imply some kind of vision of what kind of society is desirable. Ideologies are also based on certain fixed values and principles such as freedom, equality, order and justice.

people who call themselves conservatives are *opposed* to change. When ideologies come into conflict, politics can become extremely volatile. This occurs because ideologically motivated groups tend to have firmly held views and are especially determined to bring about their political goals. It is for this reason that ideological conflict often breaks out into violence, as described above.

A good example of *ideological* conflict occurred within the UK Labour Party in 2015. Having suffered two consecutive election defeats, the party needed to elect a new leader to succeed Ed Miliband. To everyone's surprise Jeremy Corbyn, a radical socialist candidate, emerged as a front runner. The leadership election within the party became a bitter ideological conflict. Corbyn won, so socialism triumphed in this case against a more moderate form of social democracy that had dominated the Labour Party since the mid-1990s.

On the whole, however, in the stable, well-established 'democracies' of the world, politics remains a more moderate, and certainly peaceful, activity. Most political activists wish to create changes in society which are not fundamental. Jeremy Corbyn and his followers were an unusual exception to this reality. Such moderate changes may be based loosely upon ideological thinking, but they may also be viewed as ways of improving the general welfare and security of the people. Table 1 identifies a number of political ideas that have emerged in the UK in recent years, together with their opposing beliefs.

Activity

Research the following current political issues. What are the main points of conflict?

- Policy concerning energy generation in the UK
- Policy concerning conflicts in the Middle East
- How the government should tax the very wealthy

Table 1 The conflict of ideas – some political conflicts in the UK in 2016–17

Proposal	Opposing idea
Britain should renew its Trident nuclear submarine fleet despite its very high cost.	Britain should abandon its nuclear deterrent on the grounds of both cost and morality.
A system of selective grammar schools should be introduced in various areas to allow the most able pupils to study in a more challenging environment.	All schools should be open to pupils of all abilities and be genuinely comprehensive.
The level of income tax should be systematically reduced to create more disposable wealth and create more incentives to growth in incomes.	Income taxes should be relatively high, especially on the wealthy, to reduce the income gap between rich and poor and to be able to pay for better public services.
Immigration should be strictly controlled to protect jobs and public services in Britain and to avoid social conflict.	Britain should remain open to immigration to boost the economy and make society culturally more diverse.

The conflict of interests

When we use the term 'interests' we mean sections of the community that have an interest in their own concerns. Various groups may feel they need special protection, that they do not receive their fair share of the national wealth, or are not treated fairly by government. The nature of such groups, or interests, varies considerably. They may be occupational groups, such as firefighters, students or junior doctors; they may be regional, such as those who live in the countryside, or inhabitants of regions that are economically depressed; they may be representatives of industries such as tobacco manufacturing, brewing or horse-racing. An 'interest', as far as politics is concerned, is any group that seeks to act to achieve some improvements in its own circumstances. Most groups believe that politics can provide a solution to their concerns.

Junior doctors on strike in Nottingham, April 2016

Interests use the political system and members of the political community to further their own cause. They sometimes attach themselves to a political party. Trade unions, in particular, used to work closely with the Labour Party (indeed, Labour emerged from the trade union movement at the start of the twentieth century). More recently the Countryside Alliance, which defends the interests of members of rural communities, saw the Conservative Party as its most traditional supporter. In more general terms, interests will use a variety of methods to further their aims. This may involve public demonstrations, internet and media campaigns, influence in Parliament and so on. Their methods will be explored further in Chapter 1.

So, part of politics is about the clash of such interests. Often their aims conflict with each other and, when this happens, politics becomes the process of resolving these conflicts. Examples of the conflict of interests are shown in Table 2.

Table 2 Examples of the conflict of interests, 2016–17

Interest(s)	Counter-interest(s)
Business groups and the North of England region support the development of HS2, high-speed rail links between London and the north.	Environmentalists oppose the destruction of the countryside, while rural communities on the routes fear they will suffer.
Oil companies seek government permits to allow 'fracking' in various locations.	Environmentalists and local communities oppose fracking on the grounds that it may be dangerous.
Current old-age pensioners wish to preserve the value of their pensions.	Younger people believe their living standards are being eroded to pay for the older generation and so wish to see a more balanced provision between them and the older generation.
Junior NHS doctors opposed reform to their working hours.	Groups representing patients wished to see a more comprehensive, 7-day health service.
Representatives of poorer sections of society support a more generous welfare benefits system.	Representatives of taxpayers resist higher benefits to keep down the tax burden.

In cases like those described in Table 2, politicians face the difficult task of mediating between conflicting interests.

The struggle for power

Arguably, the desire for power is a natural human characteristic. This is a contentious view and some ideological groups, anarchists in particular, may deny it. However, we need not concern ourselves with psychology or philosophy here. What matters to us in our study of political behaviour is that modern society clearly produces many people who do have a drive to achieve and exercise power. Many will say, of course, that their motives for achieving power are altruistic. They have a desire to improve society in some way and must therefore gain power to be able to do so. Yet some may seek power *for its own sake*. Whichever is true — and perhaps both are true — there can be no doubt that politics is about the struggle for power between individuals and groups.

This struggle takes many forms, some of which are shown below:

- Parties compete against each other for power at national, regional and local elections.
- Individuals compete at elections to become representatives in local councils, regional assemblies or the Westminster Parliament itself.
- Individual politicians compete to be appointed to senior positions, either in the government or on the opposition front bench.
- At the very highest level of power, there is a struggle to be prime minister within the governing party.

These struggles for political power are what many of us think of when we use the term 'politics'. This is partly because the media tend to concentrate on such issues when reporting on politics and partly because the struggle for power does, to some extent, reflect the other conflicts we have described. Clearly, which party wins an election will determine to a degree which political ideas become dominant and which interests are more likely to be favoured.

When Margaret Thatcher was elected leader of the Conservative Party in 1975 the policy direction of her party began to change and the nature of British society was transformed during her premiership in the 1980s. The election to power of the Labour Party in 1997 after 18 years of Conservative government also began to change the balance of power in the UK. Under Thatcher, for example, financial and business interests found themselves more influential, while trade unions lost much of their political impact. Under Labour, after 1997, Britain became more closely integrated within the EU and the interests of the poor were more favoured.

In 2010 a new kind of struggle emerged when the UK saw its first coalition government since the Second World War. This meant that the struggle between parties was taking place both *inside* and outside government. The two coalition partners — Conservatives and Liberal Democrats — were forced to compete with each other to have their policies adopted.

The struggle to become party leader is also a permanent feature of British politics. When David Cameron resigned as Conservative leader and prime minister in 2016, following his defeat in the EU referendum, there was an immediate contest to replace him within the Conservative Party, ultimately won by Theresa May. Jeremy Corbyn replaced Ed Miliband as Labour Party leader in 2015 and Tim Farron replaced Nick Clegg as Liberal Democrat leader in the same year.

So, when individuals seek political power, the effects of the outcome can be far reaching. At the same time, however, the struggle for power is, to some extent, merely a reflection of a natural desire of some individuals to gain status and influence.

Activity

Research the following former prime ministers. In each case establish why they lost power and who replaced them:

- James Callaghan
- Margaret Thatcher
- Tony Blair

What is government?

Before we attempt definitions of government and the state, it may be useful to consider a number of concepts that are related to such institutions. In particular, it is important to understand the principles that lie behind the activity of governing. These are legitimacy, power, authority and sovereignty.

Legitimacy

Here we are asking the question: what gives any government the *right* to rule? This refers both to the *system* of government — for example, monarchy, single-party rule, parliamentary democracy etc. — and to the individuals who hold office within the government. It is a difficult question to resolve because it has a number of answers, all of which are plausible.

There are several possible ways in which legitimacy can be claimed.

- **Tradition** is the first option. It suggests that a system of rule is legitimate if it has existed for a long period of time. This is a form of legitimacy often claimed by hereditary monarchies. Such monarchies still flourish in the Gulf States in the Middle East.
- **Force** is a more controversial basis for rule. The argument here is that *any* government, no matter how it is constituted, could be seen as legitimate if it is able to maintain peace and security within a country. This is sometimes described as 'might is right'. In the democratic world, however, this kind of legitimacy is not normally acceptable.
- **Consent** has become the most important criterion for legitimacy. Indeed, where power is exercised with the broad consent of the people, expressed specifically through elections, we can describe it as **democratic legitimacy**. The principle itself is simple: if a regime enjoys the broad consent of its people, it can be considered to be legitimate. Consent can be shown by widespread peaceful participation in politics as well as by a lack of open dissidence.

Power

In a general sense, *power* can mean the ability to make other people or groups do what one wants them to do, even if this is against their will. But this is too simple a definition. We use the term 'power' to signify a whole variety of means by which one individual or institution is able to exert its will over others. In particular, we need to consider different *levels* of power. These are set out below.

- **Coercive power** is the strongest form. This can also be described as *force*. Coercion involves the use of physical force, or at least the threat of physical force. In extreme cases, coercion can involve the use of execution, torture, terror and imprisonment of opponents, as has occurred in many totalitarian regimes. Of course, most states do not need to go to such extremes. It is sufficient to reserve the use of force against those who refuse to conform to the laws or who threaten the security of the state itself.
- **Political power** is perhaps how we generally understand the concept of power. This is the power exercised by members of the political community, including parties, their leaders and other institutions. Political power includes the ability to persuade, but it normally involves the use of rewards and sanctions. Thus prime ministers in the UK have power because of their use of patronage. Since a prime minister controls the appointment of all ministers and many other senior positions

Key terms

Consent In democratic politics consent means that government is founded upon the authority of the people. Normally consent is demonstrated in free elections. However, it can also be indicated by widespread support for the institutions of government.

Democratic legitimacy A key principle in modern democratic life — government may be considered legitimate if, first, it is elected and, second, it is accountable to the electorate. In this way the consent of the people is implied.

Synoptic link

This section on power should be revisited when you read Chapter 7, where the sources of prime ministerial power are explored.

in the apparatus of the state, such as top civil servants and judges, he or she is able to exercise power. This is particularly true when we consider the way in which the party whips in Parliament are able to control MPs. By making it clear that loyalty to the party line may improve an individual's career prospects, power is effectively being exercised.

The strongest form of political power, however, is that which is granted by Parliament — the ultimate source of all political power in the UK. Thus, government departments, their ministers, devolved governments in Scotland and Wales, local authorities and other public bodies have all been granted powers by Acts of Parliament. The powers of the prime minister, meanwhile, have been established largely by tradition or *convention*, as such traditions are often known. This means that a prime minister exercises power simply because everybody in the political community accepts that he or she has the traditional right to do so.

- **Influence** is the weakest form of power. We often use the word 'power' when we really mean influence. Thus it is said that the newspapers have power, or that public opinion is powerful, or that trade unions have power within the Labour Party. In each of these cases it is *influence* that is being referred to. In such examples, the press, the people and the unions may have some influence over what government and Parliament do, but they cannot enforce their wishes. In 1974 Steven Lukes also identified three forms of political power which mirror these distinctions. The first is power is exercised *openly* (through cabinet and parliament, for example); the second is *secretive* power (behind closed doors in negotiations among ministers, officials and outside parties); and the third is *manipulative* power (which involved persuasion and the use of incentives). Both secretive and manipulative power may involve links between decision makers and the media, as described in Chapter 4 of this book.

Authority

Key term

Authority Authority is the right to exercise power. It is closely associated with the idea of legitimacy. In a democracy, authority is normally granted by the electorate or by the legislature.

Authority is a more difficult term than power. Often the terms 'power' and 'authority' are used interchangeably, but in politics it is essential to distinguish between them. Put simply, authority is the *right* to exercise power, it is not power itself. When we say a teacher has authority, for example, we mean that he or she has been granted power over the students by the head teacher and, more indirectly, by the parents and the wider community. Thus, the source of the authority allows the teacher to exercise power.

In pure democracies all political authority has its source in the people. The situation in the UK, however, is more complex. While it is true that many of those working in the political system exercise power because they have been directly or indirectly elected by the people, this cannot be said of either the prime minister or the monarch. Their sources of authority have been described as *charismatic* or *traditional*. The ruling party, meanwhile, rules because it has won a general election. This is known as *elective* or *rational* authority. The German sociologist Max Weber (1864–1920) clarified the nature of political authority by identifying its nature in three ways:

- **Traditional authority** The right to govern exists because authority has existed over a long period of time. This applies particularly to hereditary monarchies, such as the sheikhdoms of the Middle East. It can be assumed that if the people have allowed such monarchies to exercise power over a long period of time, they are, by implication, consenting to such rule.
- **Charismatic authority** The term 'charisma' refers to an individual's ability to inspire and persuade, and attract a following, by the force of their personality.

Members of the Saudi Royal family enjoy traditional political authority

Here authority is granted by acclaim, because the people wish to be governed by a particular leader. Charismatic authority is typically combined with other forms and so increases the quantity of authority, allowing more power to be exercised. We can say, for example, that President John F. Kennedy in the USA enjoyed charismatic authority in addition to his elective authority (US presidents are directly elected, so enjoy direct elective authority). Donald Trump was elected US president in 2016 to some extent because, to his supporters at least, he was a charismatic figure.

- **Legal–rational authority** This refers to any rational way of granting authority. In practice, in modern democracies, this is always by election and so is best described as 'elective authority'. In current politics, elective authority is the most powerful justification for the exercise of power.

Table 3 shows the relevant sources of authority of four UK governing institutions.

Table 3 Sources of authority in the UK

Parliament	The authority (which is limited) of the House of Lords is traditional. The Commons' main source of authority is by election and, therefore, the people. However, the fact that Parliament as a whole is sovereign has its origins in tradition.
The government	Clearly the government's authority is elective.
The monarch	Though the power of the monarchy is very limited, the Crown enjoys considerable traditional authority.
The prime minister	Much of the PM's authority is traditional, but he or she also enjoys indirect elective authority in terms of being the leader of the ruling party. Some prime ministers, such as Winston Churchill and Margaret Thatcher, were also said to enjoy charismatic authority to reinforce the other two sources.

Key term

Sovereignty Ultimate power that cannot be overruled. Sovereignty can be either legal or political, depending on whether it is legally enforceable or whether it is a political reality.

Sovereignty

Before we examine the meaning of **sovereignty**, it is important to note and avoid a point of potential confusion. The monarch of the UK is sometimes described as the 'Sovereign' or even the 'Sovereign Lord'. This appears to indicate that the monarch holds supreme power. While in the past, historically, the monarch was indeed the sovereign power, a situation which held true up to the seventeenth century, it is no longer the case. However, although the term is no longer valid, it is often still used out of tradition. We must, therefore, ignore this anomaly.

It is useful to divide sovereignty into three main types — legal, political and popular:

- **Legal sovereignty** means the ultimate source of all legal authority. In practice, it amounts to the ultimate source of all laws and of all legal power.
- **Political sovereignty** refers to the location of real political power. Instead of thinking only about where legal power lies in theory (*de jure*), political sovereignty allows us to consider who ultimately makes political decisions *in reality* (*de facto*). Thus, at elections, the people are politically sovereign because they decide who will form the next government. Between elections it is more realistic to think of the prime minister and the government as being politically sovereign.
- **Popular sovereignty** is a form of political sovereignty. It relates to those occasions when the people themselves seem to be making ultimate decisions. At elections, the people become sovereign for a day, when they choose governments and representatives, and grant a mandate to a government. Referendums are another obvious example. With the increasing use of internet polls and petitions, it could be argued that a new form of popular sovereignty is in the early stages of development. The UK's momentous decision to leave the EU in the 2016 referendum was a perfect example of popular sovereignty at work.

Synoptic link

The concept of sovereignty is explored in Chapter 8.

A note on the role of the monarchy

We cannot leave government without referring to the position of the monarchy in the UK. Historically, of course the monarch *was* government in England and indeed Scotland. This was the case until the seventeenth century. Since then, gradually but inexorably, the monarch has ceased to be the government and has ceased to have any political role at all. Yes, the monarchy and all that goes with it *seems* to be important, but, in a political sense, it is not. How does this come about?

The answer is that everybody in the political system pays lip service to the authority of the monarch out of traditional respect, but everybody also understands that this does not really mean anything. The monarch exercises no power and is not permitted to involve herself in politics at all. She is a figurehead who represents the *idea* of the United Kingdom, but not the substance, a symbol of unity and strength, but not of political direction.

The state and the government

As with many political concepts, the terms 'state' and 'government' can be misunderstood and used as if they have the same meaning. In reality they are very different and should be employed with great care.

The state

If we refer to '*a* state' or '*the* state' we mean different things. *A* state is a country, a territory within which sovereignty can be identified and is widely recognised both within the country and abroad. There is no doubt that France, Italy, the USA and Nigeria are 'states'. Other countries recognise them as states and understand who represents their government.

When we say '*the* state', however, we are referring to institutions within the country. *The* state normally refers to the permanent collection of institutions that administers a territory. Normally we would include the following within the state:

- The armed forces and the security and intelligence establishment
- Law enforcement agencies, including judges, courts, the police and the prison service
- The bureaucracy or civil service — politically neutral bodies which may stay in office even when political governments change
- Other institutions that may or may not be parts of the permanent apparatus of the state, depending on the arrangements within the country (in the UK, the National Health Service, most educational organisations, the BBC and the Benefits Agency are all parts of the state; in the USA, healthcare is largely in the private sector and there is no state-run broadcasting; in France, the railways are part of the state, while in the UK they are not)
- Bodies that exist at sub-central level, such as local authorities and devolved administrations

So, we can make two assertions about the state: first, it is normally politically neutral and, second, it is permanent.

Government

The government is a collection of individuals and bodies that are political in nature and that are not permanent. In the UK the government consists of the prime minister, cabinet, junior ministers and political advisers. Should the governing party lose power, all these individuals will cease to be the government and will be replaced by a new team. Normally we expect the government to give political direction to the state. Indeed, the senior members of the state are usually appointed by members of the government.

MPs, peers and Parliament in general do not fit neatly into either the 'state' or the 'government'. Instead they form the legislature (see below), whose role is to provide consent and accountability to government.

Branches of government

It is customary to divide the activity of government into three branches.

Legislature

In broad terms the legislature means the law-making body. However, this can be misleading, especially in the UK. Parliament, the UK's legislature (known as Congress in the USA, the Chambre de Députés in France and the Bundestag in Germany), does not normally make law. This is the responsibility of the government. In the UK, the legislature is primarily concerned with providing formal consent to

> **Synoptic link**
>
> Parliament, the UK legislature, is described and analysed in Chapter 6.

proposed laws — an activity known as 'promulgation'. Parliament also has limited powers to amend proposals and may, on rare occasions, reject proposed legislation. Legislatures in other countries sometimes *do* develop their own laws, notably the US Congress, but governments are usually more significant than legislatures in this law-making role.

Executive

The executive branch has three main roles.

- The first is to develop new legislation and present it before the legislature for approval (this includes identifying the need for new legislation and drafting the laws themselves).
- The second is to arrange for the implementation of the laws.
- Finally, the executive runs the state and so administers the country, making decisions when they are needed and organising state-run services.

Synoptic link

The UK executive branch is described and analysed in Chapter 7.

Judiciary

The judiciary refers to the legal system and the judges in particular. Most of the judiciary is not concerned with politics but rather with criminal matters and disputes between individuals and organisations. But at the high levels of the judiciary — in the UK this includes the High Court, the Court of Appeal and the Supreme Court — some legal cases involve politics. When there are disputes about the meaning of laws, when citizens' rights are in jeopardy, or when there are disputes concerning the behaviour of the government or the state, the judiciary has political significance. Nevertheless, as we shall see below, judges are expected to adopt a neutral stance, even though they are concerned with political matters.

Synoptic link

The UK judiciary is described and analysed in Chapter 8.

The evolution of the UK political system

Magna Carta, 1215

Though Magna Carta is an ancient document it was an important landmark in the development of the political culture and constitution of the UK. This was the establishment of the rule of law — in particular, the principle that the monarch (the government in modern times) cannot act above the law. Though often abused in the centuries since 1215, the rule of law still persists as a cornerstone of UK democracy.

Activity

Research Magna Carta. Identify any rights referred to in it that are still relevant today.

The Glorious Revolution and the Bill of Rights, 1688–89

In 1688 the unpopular Catholic king, James II, was removed from the English throne. He was replaced by the Dutch Protestant prince, William of Orange, and his wife Mary. It was known as the 'Glorious Revolution' though it was largely peaceful. Part of the price to be paid by William and Mary for the throne was a number of restrictions on their power. These were contained in the **Bill of Rights** of 1689.

Five terms of the bill, which was an Act of Parliament, were especially important:

- that the king would rule alongside a *permanent* Parliament
- that Parliament would be the result of *regular, free elections*
- that members of Parliament would enjoy *freedom of speech*

Key term

Bill of rights A general name given to any codified set of citizens' rights. Many countries have a bill of rights attached to their constitution. The most famous bill of rights is made up of the first ten amendments to the US Constitution. The UK Parliament passed a bill of rights in 1689, but this was mostly concerned with the rule of law together with the sovereignty of Parliament and freedom of speech for its members.

- that the monarch would require the *consent* of Parliament to levy taxes
- that the monarch would *not* have the power to repeal or set aside any laws without the *consent* of Parliament

As well as establishing parliamentary government and constitutional monarchy, the Bill of Rights was the main practical result of the political ideas of the great English philosopher and early liberal thinker, John Locke (1632–1704).

The events surrounding the Glorious Revolution also saw the early development of the traditional two-party system in England. The supporters of monarchical power were described as Tories, while the Protestant supporters of parliamentary power were called Whigs. Most Tories were members of the aristocracy and landed gentry while the Whigs tended to be members of the new capitalist middle classes. By the nineteenth century most Tories formed the Conservative Party, while most Whigs turned into Liberals.

Students of the government and politics of the USA should also note that several of the principles established in the English Bill of Rights were replicated in the American Constitution, written a century later. In particular, two clauses were almost exactly reproduced in the early amendments to the US Constitution in 1791, both of which remain controversial to this day. These are the *right of the people to bear arms* (second amendment), and the protection of the people from *cruel and unusual punishment* (eighth amendment). Certainly the English Bill of Rights of 1689 can be seen as a precursor of the US Constitution of 1787.

The Great Reform Act 1832

It is fair to say that, in the early eighteenth century, general elections in the United Kingdom ranged from being irregular at best to corrupt at worst. Constituencies varied in size, with some so small — just a handful of registered voters (mainly wealthy property owners) — that it was a simple task for a wealthy candidate to buy enough votes to win. These were often described as 'rotten boroughs'. Many of the small rural seats were effectively in the hands of wealthy members of the aristocracy, who controlled the voters. The rural parts of the country were over-represented, while urban, newly industrialised parts still had few constituencies. In short, representation in Britain was corrupt and uneven.

This had the effect of bringing the House of Commons into disrepute. Far from representing the people, the Commons was full of wealthy members of the upper and middle classes, many of whom saw being an MP as a useful status symbol rather than as a civic duty. Real power lay in the hands of the monarch, his or her courtiers, plus a few wealthy members of what was known as the 'governing class'. Many MPs rarely attended the chamber and few were concerned with the interests of their constituents. Britain was a parliamentary democracy effectively in name only.

Following a long campaign, mostly fought by the Whigs, a bill was finally brought before Parliament in 1832 to try to eliminate these problems. After fierce debate it was passed. Among its many clauses, two stand out:

- The franchise (right to vote) was extended. There was a qualification to voting which involved ownership and tenancy of property. This restricted the electorate to about 500,000. The Act reduced the property qualification to allow a further 3% of the population to vote. This may not seem radical, but it did begin the

Synoptic link

John Locke, who influenced the Glorious Revolution, is a key figure in the history of liberalism. Indeed, Locke is seen as one of the founding fathers of liberalism. He will become a key element in the study of liberalism in the 'political ideas' section of this A-level specification.

Key term

Suffrage Suffrage means the right to vote. Universal adult suffrage, finally established in the UK in 1928, means that all adults 18 and over have the right to vote unless disqualified on the grounds of criminality or insanity.

process of widening the right to vote (the right to vote is known as **suffrage**). Once the principle was established, it was inevitable that, before the end of the century, all adult men would have the right to vote.

- The Act redrew the electoral boundaries so that the rotten, or very small, boroughs were removed and parts of the country which were previously under-represented (mostly industrialised areas) were awarded new constituencies. This meant that few parliamentary seats could now be 'bought' and there was more even representation of the people.

The development of the two-party system

We saw above the development of an early two-party system during the Glorious Revolution of 1688–89, with Whigs and Tories emerging. However, it was not until the nineteenth century that anything like the modern two-party system arrived.

- During the second half of the century, the Conservative Party emerged. Many historians count Sir Robert Peel as founder of the party. He was prime minister in both the 1830s and 1840s. This party tended to represent the interests of the wealthier 'gentrified' classes and stood for good order, the preservation of traditional institutions and values, and opposition to the new radical ideas being promoted by liberals and socialists. Though the Conservatives (still often described as 'Tories') were usually members of the wealthy classes, they claimed to represent the interests of the mass of the working people against the evils of the growing capitalist system.
- The Liberal Party was largely formed from politicians described as Whigs and other radical thinkers. The date of its founding is a little vague but is generally put at 1859. Its first leader was Lord Henry Palmerston, who was prime minister twice between 1855 and 1865. Liberals were mainly made up of members of the fast-rising middle classes. They represented small independent farmers, merchants, tradesmen, industrialists and the professions. They campaigned to extend democracy, to preserve free markets and free trade, and to pursue the interests of small property owners and the business classes in general.

The two-party system that emerged in the nineteenth century reflected the division of society into two ruling classes — the upper classes and the middle classes. At that time, the working classes, though numerically superior to the other classes, were not represented by a political party of their own. In the nineteenth century there was no sizeable socialist party in the UK. The principal reason was, of course, that the working classes did not have the right to vote for most of the century. They had no property and so were excluded from the franchise. Propertyless male members of the working class had to wait until 1884 for the right to take part in elections.

Knowledge check

From the results of elections between 1992 and 2010, in what ways did the two-party system begin to erode?

The electoral system

The electoral system was a second factor in the formation and retention of a two-party system. The first-past-the-post system makes it difficult for smaller parties to establish themselves, so the Conservatives and Liberals were able to dominate general elections until the emergence of the Labour Party in the early twentieth century.

The early Labour Party was led by a charismatic figure, Keir Hardie. As the party developed and began to gain parliamentary seats in the early years of the twentieth century, it found it difficult to make headway because the electoral system discriminated against it. The party won just two seats in 1900 and this had increased only to 42 by 1910. In 1922, however, when it won 142 seats, the Labour Party finally demonstrated that it was about to replace the Liberals.

It had taken time for the newly enfranchised working classes to realise their interest lay in voting for Labour rather than one of the two established parties. When they did, in the 1920s and 1930s, the Liberal Party was doomed to decline. Instead of a three-party system developing, as was occurring in the rest of the European democracies, the Liberals were largely replaced by Labour so a new two-party system arrived to replace the old one.

Two reasons are usually suggested for this. One is the electoral system, while the other is the division of British society in the twentieth century into two distinct and cohesive classes, middle and working, each represented by its own political party.

The creation of the welfare state, 1940s

In the 1940s, at the end of the Second World War, the Labour government that won the 1945 general election set out to create a system of state-run, publicly-financed welfare that was so extensive it became known as the **welfare state**.

The welfare state was a comprehensive system, to be financed from taxation and run by the state, both central and local government, covering people's needs 'from the cradle to the grave'. At its centre lay the National Health Service (NHS), set up in 1946, but the welfare state also included a system of benefits covering such needs as unemployment, disability, income support, sickness, maternity and care of the elderly. The state old-age pension was extended to all, and an increasing quantity of subsidised rental housing was made available through local government.

Issues surrounding the welfare state, how it is financed and run, what it should include and whether the private sector should be involved in supplying its services, have dominated British politics ever since. It has affected government and politics in a number of ways, including the following:

- The scope and powers of the UK state were expanded greatly. Put simply, government became bigger; it became responsible for a whole range of new services.
- The welfare state raised many political issues, often the centre of conflict between the parties. These have included how much should be spent on services, who should be entitled to benefit from them, how they should be run and who should run them.
- In recent decades the issue of which services can be supplied by private-sector organisations, as opposed to the state, has become a matter of intense political conflict.

Britain joins the European Community, 1973

At the end of the Second World War many European politicians put their minds to the future of the continent. They were mainly concerned with two issues — economic reconstruction and the preservation of continental peace.

Key term

Welfare state A collective title given to those services that are run by the state and financed out of general taxation, and to which all citizens are entitled, mostly free of charge at the point of delivery. It includes the state education system, the NHS, social care services, the benefits system, subsidised local authority housing and state pensions.

Activity

Research the Beveridge Report. What were the five great evils that Beveridge identified and that his scheme was designed to address?

Synoptic link

The details of UK membership and its significance are described in Chapter 8.

The main plan to deal with postwar Europe was based in France and was developed by two politicians there, Jean Monnet and Robert Schuman. This was the European Community (EC), which has since become the European Union (EU).

The plan was to invite European countries to form a customs union or free-trade area so that trade would grow and, with it, economic cooperation. The longer-term plan was to turn this economic union into a political one. At first just six countries were members, but in the years since it has grown to 28 members in 2016. The UK joined on 1 January 1973.

Flags in front of the European Union building in Brussels

Activity

Study the historical section of this introduction. Identify which historical events and developments have shaped the following:

- The establishment of the rule of law
- The establishment of parliamentary sovereignty
- The rise in the status and importance of the House of Commons
- The growth in the responsibilities of the state
- The erosion of parliamentary sovereignty
- The restoration of some parliamentary sovereignty

UK membership has had a number of influences on government and politics, including the following:

- The very issue of whether the UK should remain a member has twice created a major rift in British politics. At various times both the Conservative and Labour parties have been internally divided on the issue. On two occasions, in 1975 and 2016, this issue was settled by referendums, in 1975 to remain and in 2016 to leave.
- Because EU laws and regulations are binding on members, all government decisions must take European law into consideration.
- The UK Parliament was no longer fully sovereign. It had to comply with European law.
- UK courts had to enforce European law.

In general, therefore, Britain, while remaining an independent state, had to accept that it was also part of a wider political community. Following the 2016 referendum, UK membership of the EU is now coming to an end (see below).

The UK leaves the European Union

The historic referendum vote of 23 June 2016 that began the process of bringing the UK out of the EU changed the landscape of UK politics. It saw the end of the career of a prime minister — David Cameron — and caused a major upheaval within the Labour Party. More permanently, though, it changed the whole nature of parliamentary sovereignty and the way in which UK government goes about making policy. How it will affect the UK economy and society remains to be seen, but the very masonry of UK politics has been severely loosened by the event. The formal process of leaving begins in 2017 and is expected to be completed in 2019.

Summary

Having read this introduction, you should have knowledge and understanding of the following:
→ The fundamental nature of politics
→ The fundamental nature of government in the UK
→ The distinctions between government and state
→ The main principles behind the status and operation of government in the UK
→ How the UK system of government and politics has evolved, with key historical landmarks
→ An appropriate vocabulary to be used when discussing government and politics

Practice questions

AS and A-level

These are not necessarily exam-style questions, but they will help to reinforce what you have learned. Write answers to the questions, using the approximate number of words suggested in each case.

1 Distinguish between the concepts of government and the state. (50 words)

2 What is democratic legitimacy and how can it be achieved? (100 words)

3 The UK monarch has no political power. Why, therefore, is it so crucial to the way in which government operates? (100 words)

4 How and why is Parliament sovereign in the UK? (100 words)

5 In what ways is politics about conflict? (150 words)

6 What are the main historical events that have shaped government and politics in the UK? (500 words)

COMPONENT 1

PARTICIPATION

1 Democracy and participation

The Greek philosopher Plato believed that 'the people' would not respect decisions made by their peers, i.e. what many think of as the process of 'democracy'. For Plato, it was desirable that people should be ruled by their superiors. Authority granted to a leader, he thought, would be more respected than popular decision making. Lack of respect would lead to disorder. Furthermore, left to making their own decisions, people would fall prey to rabble rousers and demagogues. Plato also noted that democracy treats everyone as equal, in terms of knowledge and understanding, when, in reality, they are not equal.

The democratic process continues to prove problematic. Concerned voices are growing louder, voices suggesting that representative democracy is failing many sections of society, that it serves the interests of the majority and leaves minorities behind. This has led to new calls for the return of popular democracy, including referendums. Populist leaders have emerged all over the democratic world, telling us that democracy is no longer working.

Even so, democracy remains a popular form of government. It is assumed in most of the world to be a 'good thing'. The question remains, however, what form of democracy is most desirable?

The history of democracy in the UK has been concerned with how to convert the political system from being the preserve of an elite to being a popular exercise in which the mass of the people can take part in an orderly manner. In practical terms, this has meant spreading democratic practice by extending the franchise, by improving the extent and accountability of representative democracy and by introducing elements of direct democracy through the increasing use of referendums and digital democracy. This chapter will explore the nature of these developments.

Plato (wearing red) in Raphael's fresco 'The School of Athens'

Objectives

This chapter will inform you about the following:
→ The meaning of the term 'democracy' and the different types of democracy
→ The ways in which people participate in politics in the UK and trends in that participation
→ The historical development of democracy in the UK
→ The nature and importance of e-democracy
→ The development of the franchise in the UK and current issues concerning the future of suffrage and voting
→ The means by which we can make an assessment of how democratic the UK political system is
→ What pressure groups are, how they work, how their activities are changing and their place in a democracy
→ Forms of political influence other than pressure groups and parties
→ The nature and context of rights in the UK and their relationship to obligations
→ Issues concerning rights in the UK, including how effectively they are protected
→ The claims of collective rights versus individual rights
→ A review of organisations concerned with rights

Two forms of democracy

Direct democracy

We normally divide the concept of democracy into two main types. These are **direct democracy** and **representative democracy**. Direct democracy was how the idea was first conceived in ancient Greece, mainly in the city state of Athens in the fifth century BC. Hence it is sometimes described as 'Athenian democracy'.

The assembled free citizens would make important decisions, such as whether the state should go to war or whether a prominent citizen who had committed anti-state acts should be exiled. Laws were also made in this way, and the officials who ran the state were elected in the same fashion. In between examples of direct democracy, therefore, a form of representative democracy took over, running the day-to-day affairs of the state. But it is the direct form of democracy that we tend to remember today.

After Athenian democracy declined in the fourth century BC, direct democracy, with a few exceptions, disappeared as a democratic form until the nineteenth century. The Swiss have used forms of direct democracy throughout their history and still use it extensively to this day, but the idea did not spread. Some communities in the early life of the USA conducted local government by direct democracy (largely through 'town meetings') but these were also rare exceptions.

Today direct democracy has returned in the form of the referendum, now relatively common in Europe and some states of the USA. However, direct democracy cannot replace representative democracy completely. Rather, it is an *addition* to representative democracy. Some decisions are considered so vital, and also so unsuitable for representatives to make them, that they are left to the people.

Direct democracy has its critics as well as its supporters. Table 1.1 summarises the main advantages and disadvantages of direct democracy.

Key terms

Direct democracy A form of democracy where the people themselves make key decisions. In modern societies this usually takes the form of holding referendums.

Representative democracy A form of democracy where the people elect or somehow choose representatives who make political decisions on their behalf. It also implies that representatives are accountable for what they do.

Table 1.1 Direct democracy — is it desirable?

Advantages	Disadvantages
It is the purest form of democracy. The people's voice is clearly heard.	It can lead to the 'tyranny of the majority', whereby the winning majority simply ignores the interests of the minority. Elected representatives can mediate between the interests of the majority and minorities.
It can avoid delay and deadlock within the political system.	The people may be too easily swayed by short-term, emotional appeals by charismatic individuals. (The great philosopher Plato criticised direct democracy on these grounds.)
The fact that people are making a decision gives it great legitimacy.	Some issues may be too complex for the ordinary citizen to understand.

Representative democracy

Representative democracy is the most common model to be found in the democratic world today.

The basis of this type of democracy is that the people do not make political decisions but, instead, choose representatives to make decisions on their behalf. The most common way of choosing representatives is to elect them. (In parts of ancient Greece, representatives of the people were sometimes chosen through a lottery!) Indeed, if representatives are not elected, it calls democracy into question. Elections are, in other words, what we first think of when we consider representation. But it is not only elections that characterise representative democracy. Those elected also need to be accountable.

Accountability is essential if representatives are to act responsibly and in the interests of the people. It is at election time that accountability is most striking. Both individual representatives, such as MPs in the UK, and the government as a whole are held accountable when the people go to the polls. During the election campaign, opposition parties will highlight the shortcomings of the government and will offer their own alternatives. At the same time the government will seek to explain and justify what it has done in an effort to be re-elected. Similarly, individual representatives will be held to account for their performance — how well they have represented their constituents and whether their voting record in the legislature meets the approval of those same constituents. In between elections accountability is less certain. The legislature can hold government to account regularly, but the individual representatives are normally safe until the next election.

Having said that representatives in a democracy will be elected and will be accountable, we need to explain the concept of representation in general. It can have different forms and meanings.

Social representation

Social representation implies that the characteristics of members of representative bodies, whether they be national parliaments, regional assemblies or local councils, should be broadly in line with the characteristics of the population as a whole. In other words, they should be close to a *microcosm* of society as a whole. For example, close to half should be women, a proportion should be drawn from ethnic or religious minorities and there should be a good range of ages and class backgrounds in representative bodies. Of course this is difficult to achieve and the UK Parliament certainly falls short. This is explored further below when we discuss the state of representative democracy in the UK specifically.

> ## Key term
>
> **Accountability** This means that those who have been elected in a representative democracy must be made responsible for their policies, actions, decisions and general conduct. Without such accountability, representation becomes largely meaningless.

Representing the national interest

Though representatives may be elected locally or regionally, if they sit in the national Parliament they are expected to represent the interests of the nation as a whole. Sometimes this may clash with the local constituency they represent, so they have to resolve the issue in their own way. For example, an MP representing a constituency near a major airport may be under pressure to oppose further expansion on the grounds of noise and pollution, but may see it as in the *national* interest to expand that airport. Fortunately not all issues concerning the national interest cause such a dilemma. For example, foreign policy issues usually do not have local effects.

Local MP Zac Goldsmith protesting against the third runway at Heathrow Airport

Constituency representation

The locality that elects a representative in UK national politics is known as a constituency. In other countries different names are given. In the USA, for example, congressmen and women represent congressional districts. Wherever this kind of representation exists, though, it concerns *local* interests. It can imply three things:

1 It can mean representing the interests of the constituency *as a whole*. Should the building of a new railway be opposed? How can funds be extracted from central government for the redevelopment of a town centre? Will high levels of immigration into the area adversely affect the social balance? These are all examples of the kind of issue that might arise locally.

2 It can also mean representing the interests of *individual* constituents. This is often described as the **redress of grievances**. Has a constituent been unfairly treated by a public body such as the NHS or the taxation authorities? Is an asylum seeker not receiving a fair and speedy hearing? Has a person been the victim of a miscarriage of justice? These are typical examples dealt with by elected representatives.

3 Finally, it can simply mean that a representative listens to the views of his or her constituents when deciding about a national issue. This can lead to another dilemma. What happens if the elected representative does not personally agree with the majority of the constituents? This becomes a matter of conscience that has to be resolved by the individual concerned. This often occurred during the EU referendum campaign.

Party representation

All modern democracies are characterised by the existence of political parties. Furthermore, the vast majority of those seeking and winning election are members of a political party. It is unusual in modern democracies to find many examples of *independent* representatives who do not belong to a party. Parties have stated policies. At election time these are contained in a **manifesto**. It follows that members of a party who are seeking to be elected will campaign on the basis of the party's manifesto. This means that they are representing their party and the voters understand that they are.

Activity

Find out which parliamentary constituency you live in. Access the site of the local MP. What local issues are currently prominent in your area?

Key terms

Redress of grievances The practice, adopted by many elected representatives, of taking up the case of an individual constituent who feels they have suffered an injustice, usually at the hands of government or an agency of the state.

Manifesto A statement of a party's agreed policies produced during an election campaign to inform the public about the political platform upon which its candidates are standing. Candidates for the party are expected to support the manifesto and usually do so in the UK, though there may be exceptions.

It should be said that, in the UK, candidates for election do generally adhere closely to the party manifesto. In some political systems, notably the USA, party candidates may vary in their political stance from their party's manifesto or agreed policies. In such cases party representation is weaker.

Functional representation

This refers to the fact that some elected representatives will represent not only their constituency or region, but also a particular occupational or social group. For example, those who support and are supported by trade unions will often pursue the cause of groups of workers; others may represent professions such as doctors or teachers. This function can also apply to social groups such as the elderly, those with disabilities, members of the LGBT (lesbian, gay, bisexual and transgender) community or low-income groups. Of course, groups like this are also represented by interest groups that may be *outside* the parliamentary system, but functional representation can still flourish within elected legislative bodies.

Causal representation

Here representative bodies are not representing people so much as ideas, principles and causes. In a sense this represents the *whole* community, in that the beliefs and demands involved are claimed to benefit everyone, not just a particular group in society. Typical causes concern environmental protection, individual rights and freedoms, greater equality and animal rights. Though elected representatives often support such causes and principles, most causal representation is carried out by pressure groups.

Debate

Which is more desirable and effective: direct or representative democracy?

Advantages of direct democracy

- It is the purest form of democracy. It is the voice of the people.
- Decisions made directly by the people will have more authority.
- Decisions made by the people are more difficult to be changed or cancelled by future governments.
- Direct democracy can help educate the people about political issues.

Advantages of representative democracy

- Elected representatives may have better judgement than the mass of the people.
- Elected representatives may be more rational and not swayed by emotion.
- Representatives can protect the interests of minorities.
- Elected representatives may be better informed than the general public.

The nature of representative democracy in the UK

Having explored the concept of representative democracy, we are now in a position to consider how representative democracy operates in the UK and, having done that, to evaluate how effective it is. Before making that assessment it is necessary to examine the various ways in which people are represented in the UK.

At the outset we should note that the whole administration of representative democracy is regulated by the Electoral Commission. This body ensures that representation is fair, that all those entitled to vote can register to vote and that the parties do not have any undue influence through spending. The spending of political parties is now tightly controlled in the UK so that the process is even-handed. It can be said that representation in the UK today is fundamentally uncorrupted, fair and honest. Exceptions to this remain minor.

Levels of representation in the UK

First, we can see that the people are represented at different *levels* of government. Table 1.2 demonstrates how this works in the UK.

Key term

Decentralisation
The process of spreading power away from the centre (i.e. central government) both towards devolved governments in the national regions and to local government.

Table 1.2 Levels of representation

Level	Jurisdiction
Parish or town councils*	The lowest level of government. Only a minority (about 20%) of people come within the jurisdiction of a town council. They deal with local issues such as parks and gardens, parking restrictions, public amenities and small planning issues.
Local councils*	These may be county councils, district councils or metropolitan councils, depending on the area. They deal with local services such as education, public transport, roads, social services and public health.
Metropolitan authorities*	This is big city government such as in London or Manchester. These bodies deal with strategic city issues such as policing, public transport, arts funding, environment, large planning issues and emergency services. They normally have an elected mayor and strategic authority.
Devolved government	The governments of Wales, Scotland and Northern Ireland. They have varying powers, but all deal with health, social services, education, policing and transport. All three have elected representative assemblies (Parliament in Scotland).
National government	This is the jurisdiction of the UK Parliament at Westminster and the UK government.

* England and Wales

So we can see that all citizens of the UK are represented at three levels at least and that many enjoy four or five levels of representation. It is also clear that representation has become increasingly **decentralised** with the advent of devolution and the delegating of increasing powers to city administrations.

Synoptic link

The impact of devolution on representation is also discussed in Chapter 5.

Forms of representation in the UK

Having established at what levels of government we are represented, we can now examine what forms of representation flourish in the UK.

Constituencies

It is a cornerstone and an acknowledged strength of representative democracy in the UK that every elected representative should have a constituency to which they are accountable and whose interests they should pursue. These constituencies may be quite small, such as a parish or a local ward, and they may be very large — regions represented by Members of the European Parliament (MEPs) until the UK's exit in 2019, or in the London Assembly — but the same principle applies to all. This principle is that individuals in the constituency should have their grievances considered, that the interests of the *whole* constituency should be given a hearing in a representative assembly

The Welsh Assembly: an example of regional representation

and that the elected representative is regularly made accountable to their constituency. The levels of constituency in the UK, from smallest to largest, are shown in Table 1.3.

Table 1.3 Levels of constituency in the UK

Level	Representatives
Ward or parish	Parish and local councillors
Parliamentary constituency	MPs
City region	Assembly members
Metropolitan authority	Elected mayors
Devolved assembly constituency	Members of the Scottish Parliament (MSPs) or members of the Welsh and Northern Ireland assemblies
European parliamentary region and country	Members of the European Parliament (MEPs)

Activity

Research your own area, where you live. How many levels of representation does your area have and what are they?

Parties

The UK is unusual in that parties play a much more central role in representation than in most other democracies. This is for two reasons:

- First, in some systems parties are rather loose federations of members whose political outlook may vary a good deal. This is especially true of the USA. In the US system, representatives may call themselves a Republican or a Democrat, but this does not tell us exactly what their political views are, merely a *tendency* in one direction or another. In the UK, by contrast, a representative's party label tells us a great deal about their beliefs and *most* (though not all) representatives from the same party hold similar views. So UK parties are tighter, more united bodies.

- Second, it is usually the case that one single party governs in the UK. There was an exception between 2010 and 2015, when a coalition ruled, but the *norm* is for single-party government. After the June 2017 general election, however, an entirely new situation arose. There was a hung parliament and no party had an overall majority. The Conservatives decided, with the approval of the Queen, to form a minority administration. In order to ensure its survival, the government reached a formal agreement (not a coalition) with the Democratic Unionist Party of Northern Ireland (DUP), whose ten seats, added to the Conservatives' 318, formed a majority. In return for an extensive investment in Northern Ireland infrastructure and public services, the DUP agreed to support the government on key votes. Even so, the new government had to abandon many of its 2017 manifesto commitments. What kind of mandate the government, as formed in June 2017, actually had, was left in some doubt. Nevertheless, two parties had combined to put together a legislative programme.

These two factors place parties at the centre of representation in the UK. Their role is also connected to the doctrine of mandate and manifesto (see below).

Mandate and manifesto

Successful representation in the UK depends on this doctrine. The principle is this: each party produces a manifesto in the run-up to a general election. This statement of policy intentions is followed by the party's candidates. If that party wins power, it is said to have a **mandate** to carry out *all* the policies contained in the manifesto. In other words, it is granted the democratic *authority* to carry them out. It does not matter if the party only scrapes home in the election by one seat or wins well below 50% of the popular vote — it can claim such a mandate. All those who work in the UK political system accept this principle, however flawed it may appear to be. The great strength of the doctrine is that

Key term

(Electoral) mandate
The principle, operating in the UK, whereby a party that has been elected to government has the authority of the electorate to carry out its manifesto commitments.

everyone, people and politicians, knows where they stand; they know which policies have a democratic mandate and which ones do not. Furthermore, it provides a guide to the voters when they are called on to judge a government at a general election; voters can ask themselves how well and how accurately the government has carried out its mandate. In between elections MPs and peers can also call government to account on the basis of its electoral mandate.

The system does, however, have its faults, as shown in Table 1.4.

Table 1.4 The strengths weaknesses of the doctrine of the mandate

Strengths	Weaknesses
It grants a clear authority to an incoming government and so strengthens its legitimacy.	Parties in the UK today are always elected with less than 50% of the popular vote, so their mandate can be called into question.
It allows Parliament and the voters to judge the performance of government effectively.	Those who voted for the governing party do not necessarily support all its manifesto commitments.
It demonstrates clearly when a government may be overstepping its elective authority.	It is not clear whether the government has a mandate to carry out policies *not* contained in its last election manifesto.

One other aspect of this doctrine should be examined. This is the idea of the so-called 'doctor's mandate'. This relates to the practice of doctors having to gain the permission of a patient to do whatever is necessary to treat them for something unexpected while an operation is in progress. In other words, the patient is asked to trust the doctor to do the right thing while he or she is in no position to grant authority. In some senses the government in the UK can claim the same kind of mandate. Once a government is elected, unexpected events will arise. As long as it is the legitimately elected government, it can argue that it has the authority to take whatever action is deemed necessary. This applies in military matters or when an emergency or crisis emerges. Unlike the doctrine of manifesto and mandate, however, Parliament may feel more authorised to challenge such a claim by government if it thinks it is doing the wrong thing. The doctor's mandate, in other words, is not a blank cheque.

Government representation

The people as a whole are also represented by the elected government. As we shall see again below, it is a mark of a true democracy that the winning party or parties should govern on behalf of the *whole* community and not just those sections of society that typically support it. While it is true that there will be a *tendency* to support some groups more than others, this does not alter the fact that the elected government represents the whole nation.

Pressure groups

Pressure groups in the UK (and indeed in other democracies) are representative bodies in three ways.

1 They may behave rather like political parties in that they may have formal memberships and clear supporting groups and represent their memberships by pushing policies that will benefit them. This applies to sectional pressure groups such as the British Medical Association (BMA), the National Farmers' Union (NFU), the Automobile Association (AA) and the Taxpayers' Alliance. This was also described above as functional representation.

Discussion point

How valid is the doctrine of mandate and manifesto? Refer to Table 1.4.

Activity

Research the Conservative Party's 2017 election manifesto. In what ways did it seek a mandate for the following issues?

- Setting the level of the minimum wage
- Controlling energy prices
- Introducing selective grammar schools
- Negotiating the UK's exit terms from the European Union

Key term

Civil society A collective name for all the various associations, including parties, pressure groups, religions, voluntary organisations, charities etc. to which citizens belong and in which they may become active. Civil society acts as a vital counterbalance to the power of government.

2 Some pressure groups do not have formal memberships. They may represent a section of society but do not have direct means of determining what demands there are. They represent various groups but not in a very direct way. Examples of this include Age UK, Stonewall (for the gay community) and the British Drivers' Association (the BDA has a small membership but represents what it believes to be the interests of millions of motorists). This is also functional representation. Many of these groups are also local, though some have national concerns and take local action (Frack Off and Plane Stupid).

3 Pressure groups are engaged in causal representation. Here they represent a set of beliefs, principles or demands which they believe will benefit the whole community. They are promotional groups rather than sectional groups. Typical examples are Friends of the Earth (FoE), Action on Smoking and Health (ASH), Liberty (human rights campaigning) and Unlock Democracy.

All such pressure groups represent us in various ways. Whatever we believe, whatever we do and whatever our occupation, there is probably a pressure group working in our interests. It is all part of a *pluralist democracy* and a healthy **civil society**. The role of pressure groups in the UK is further explored later in this chapter.

Knowledge check

Which section of society is represented by each of these groups?

- The NUT
- The RCN
- The RAC

How democratic is the UK?

If we are to attempt an assessment of democracy in the UK, we need to establish what we mean by the term 'democracy'. More precisely, we should ask two questions:

1 What constitutes a democratic *political system*? A word of caution is needed before this assessment. Democracy is a contested term. There is no single, perfect definition. Therefore, the elements described below add up to a guide, a collection of the most commonly accepted features of a true democracy.

2 What constitutes a democratic *society*? This is a broader question and is explored below.

A democratic system defined

The following criteria commonly apply.

The peaceful transition of power

This is a feature often taken for granted in democracies but it is not guaranteed in many societies. It means that those who lose power by democratic means accept the authority of those who have won. If they do not, politics breaks down and non-peaceful conflict is likely to take over.

Free elections

Elections are a cornerstone of democracy. Without them it is impossible to imagine democracy working in any meaningful way. Indeed it is probably the first thing we look for when assessing whether a system is democratic or not. The description

Activity

Research the Gettysburg Address, delivered by President Abraham Lincoln in 1863 during the American Civil War. What was Lincoln's definition of democracy given in that speech?

'free' means that all adults (however that is defined) are free to vote and to stand for office. This is described as 'universal suffrage'. If significant groups are excluded (for example, women could not vote in any country, with the exception of New Zealand, before the twentieth century), the elections are not truly free and democracy is flawed. It also *implies* that there is a secret ballot. If there is not, votes can be bought and sold and voters can be coerced into voting a certain way.

Fair elections

This is a more difficult criterion. There is a narrow and a broad definition.

- The narrow definition is that 'fair' means that everyone has one vote and all votes are of equal value. It also suggests that there are safeguards in place to avoid electoral fraud and ballot rigging.
- The broader definition, however, concerns the electoral system used. Is it fair? This is more difficult. Does it mean the outcome of the election should be proportional, i.e. seats awarded to parties in proportion to votes cast? Most would say yes, in which case the UK fails as its electoral system (plurality in single-member constituencies, commonly known as 'first past the post' or FPTP) does not produce a proportional result. Instead it favours some parties over others.

Study tip

Many people loosely describe general elections in the UK as 'free and fair'. However, while they are certainly free, many argue they are not fair. So be careful not simply to run the two terms together uncritically.

Widespread participation in politics

It is important for the health of a democracy that a large proportion of the population participate in politics. A well-informed and active population can prevent government becoming too dictatorial.

Synoptic link

The whole issue of elections is explored fully in Chapter 3. The question of how free and fair elections in the UK actually are is analysed there.

Freedom of expression and information

In George Orwell's novel *Nineteen Eighty-Four*, the author describes a dystopia in which the all-powerful state controls the flow of all information to the population. It even changes accounts of history to suit its purposes. Orwell was illustrating, in a dramatic way, how access to independent information is vital if democracy is to survive. The alternative leads to dictatorship. This requirement implies a free media and no government censorship or interference. The development of the internet has helped enormously as it allows free access for all.

Freedom of association

Linked to freedom of expression is freedom of association. In terms of politics, this means the freedom to form parties or pressure groups, provided their aims and methods are legal. Parties and pressure groups are such vital vehicles for representation that, if they did not exist, or were suppressed, democracy would be almost impossible to sustain.

Protection of rights and liberties

Linked to freedom of expression and association is the idea that the rights and liberties of citizens should be firmly safeguarded. This implies that there should be some kind of enforceable 'Bill of Rights' or 'Basic Laws' to protect rights and liberties in such a way that the state cannot erode them. The European Convention on Human Rights (ECHR) is just such an example, enforced in 47 European countries, as is the US Bill of Rights, the first ten amendments of America's constitution.

Study tip

Be careful not to confuse the European Court of Human Rights (ECHR), which is *not* an EU institution, with the European Court of Justice, which is and which enforces or interprets EU law.

Key terms

Limited government
A feature of democracies with a constitutional safeguard is that the power of the government should have strict limits and that these limits will be enforced by the judiciary and the legal system in general. The only exceptions would involve emergency power.

Democratic deficit
A collective term for the features of the political system which do not conform to, or fall short of, the normal criteria for a true democracy.

The rule of law

This is the basic principle that all citizens should be treated equally under the law and that the government itself should be subject to the same laws as its citizens. It is linked to the concept of **limited government**, as described below.

Independent judiciary

The existence of the rule of law implies one other feature — an independent judiciary. It is a key role of the judiciary in a democracy to ensure that the rule of law is upheld. In order for this to happen, the members of the judiciary (the judges) must be independent from government and the whole process of politics. In this way they will ensure that all individuals and groups in society are treated equally under the law and that the government does not exceed its authority. It also means, of course, that the rights and liberties of citizens are more likely to be upheld.

Limited government and constitutionalism

Democracy is at risk if there are not firm limits to the power of government. Without these, there is a possibility that government will set aside democratic principles for its own purposes. We expect this to happen sometimes in times of warfare and emergency, but not normally. The usual way to set the limits of government power is to define them in a constitution which will be enforced by the forces of law. This is known as constitutionalism.

How democratic is the UK political system?

We are now in a position to assess the extent to which the UK political system is democratic in order to consider how it might be reformed. How well does it conform to the criteria described above?

Table 1.5 shows a 'balance sheet' in favour of the view that the UK has a healthy democratic political system. However, there remain a few serious flaws. Collectively, these are described as a '**democratic deficit**'. The main examples of the UK's democratic deficit can be summarised thus:

Speaker's Corner in London, where anyone can express their views

- The FPTP electoral system for general elections produces disproportional results, renders many votes wasted and elects governments with a relatively small proportion of the popular vote. It discriminates against small parties with dispersed support.
- The House of Lords has considerable influence but is an unelected body.
- The sovereignty of Parliament, in theory, gives unlimited potential power to government.
- The powers of the prime minister are largely based on the authority of the unelected monarch.
- The European Convention on Human Rights is not binding on Parliament, so individual rights and liberties remain under threat.

Table 1.5 How democratic is the UK political system?

Democratic feature	Positives	Negatives
Peaceful transition of power	The UK is remarkably conflict free.	None
Free elections	All over 18 can vote. There is little electoral fraud and there exist strong legal safeguards.	The House of Lords is not elected at all, nor is the head of state (monarch).
Fair elections	There are proportional systems in place in Scotland, Wales and Northern Ireland and for European parliamentary elections.	The first-past-the-post system for general elections leads to disproportionate results and many wasted votes. Governments are elected on a modest proportion of the popular vote.
Widespread participation	There is extensive membership of pressure groups, which are free and active. There is also a growing level of participation in e-democracy.	Turnout at elections and referendums has been falling. So too has party membership, especially among the young. However, membership of some parties began to rise in 2015 and turnout at general elections recovered considerably in 2015 and 2017. It is still below levels experienced in the 1950s though.
Freedom of expression	The press and broadcast media are free of government interference. Broadcast media maintain political neutrality. There is free access to the internet.	Much ownership of the press is in the hands of a few large, powerful companies such as News International.
Freedom of association	There are no restrictions on legal organisations.	Some associations are banned but this is because they are seen as based on terrorism or racial hatred.
Protection of rights and liberties	Strong in the UK. The country is signed up to the ECHR and the courts enforce it. The House of Lords protects rights, as does the judiciary.	Parliament is sovereign, which means rights are at the mercy of a government with a strong majority in the House of Commons. The ECHR is not binding on the UK Parliament.
The rule of law	Upheld strictly by the judiciary. The right to judicial review underpins this. The judiciary is independent and non-political.	None
Limited government and constitutionalism	Parliament and the courts do ensure the government acts within the law.	There is no codified UK Constitution so the limits to government power are vague. Parliamentary sovereignty means the government's powers could be increased without a constitutional safeguard. The prerogative powers of the prime minister are extensive and arbitrary.

A democratic society defined

The term 'democratic society' looks beyond the narrow confines of the political system, referring instead to the whole of society. It is still an important political feature, but it looks beyond institutions and processes. Before considering it, we need some thought about the concept of *power*. So far we have looked at political power, but the term is broader than that. There is, for example, *economic power*, which is the influence wielded by those who have wealth or businesses that account for large amounts of employment and income. There is also *social power*. This relates to people and groups who have influence over how people live and how they think.

If we place political, economic and social power together, therefore, we can consider how it is distributed within society; who has power and who does not; and how the distribution of power is shifting. If some people and organisations have more power than before, where did that power come from? Who has less power as a result? These questions help to determine whether a whole society is more, or less, democratic.

Pluralism/Pluralist democracy The idea that a wide variety of beliefs, lifestyles, religions etc. can flourish in a society and be tolerated. It also refers to the fact that there are likely to be many parties and associations active in society, that power is widely dispersed and that the people have access to many different channels of independent information. Finally, it can mean that there is 'open competition for power'. A pluralist democracy is one which displays these characteristics.

Elitism A description of a society or political system where power and influence are concentrated in the hands of a few people and organisations.

A number of qualities that make for a democratic society can be suggested:

- The political system is democratic (see above).
- Power should be distributed widely in society and not concentrated in a few hands. This is an important aspect of **pluralism**. Where power is concentrated, it is often described as **elitism**.
- There should be free information available to all. In other words, neither government nor any elites should control the flow of information to the people.
- There should be tolerance of different beliefs, lifestyles, religions and movements, provided these do not threaten the state and/or behave illegally.
- People should be free to form legal associations, including political parties and pressure groups. Such associations are known collectively as civil society. A flourishing civil society is another aspect of pluralism.
- There is widespread participation in political activity. A passive, uninformed people does not make for a healthy democracy.

No society can conform to all of these qualities to the full, but they are a useful set of criteria for making judgements about democracy.

Activity

This task can be undertaken by a whole class or individually. Study the criteria for a democratic society shown above. Decide where the UK ranks with each criterion, on a scale from 0 to 10 where 0 is not at all and 10 is excellent. Add up the total 'democratic score' for the UK. Compare your score with other members of the class. If you are studying the USA later, you might score the USA in the same way and compare the total with that of the UK.

Political participation in the UK

The term 'participation' covers a variety of forms of political activity. Most citizens participate in politics in one way or another. However, there are two variables involved:

- What kind of participation?
- How intensive is that participation?

The first question can be answered by detailing the various ways in which it is possible to participate in political processes. The second can be answered by placing these forms of participation into some kind of order that expresses the degree to which they require intense activity. They are described below in order of intensity.

1 **Standing for public office** This is the most intensive. Many local councillors are part-time, but they do have to give up a great deal of their lives to attending meetings, campaigning, meeting constituents, reading information and making decisions. It goes without saying that full-time politicians have to immerse themselves in the job. Even those who stand for office unsuccessfully have to devote a considerable amount of time to the effort of trying to get elected.

2 **Active party membership** Many people join political parties, but only a minority of these are active members, also called 'activists'. Activists are fully engaged with the party they support. This may mean attending local meetings of the party, voting for officers, campaigning in the community and canvassing at election time to try to ensure as many party supporters vote as possible.

3 **Active pressure group membership** Like party activists, these pressure group supporters may be full members, helping to raise both money and awareness of the

cause they support. Often it means attending or even organising demonstrations and other forms of direct action.

4 Passive party membership This means being enough of a supporter to join the party, but to take relatively little active part. Such members often confine their activities to help at election times.

5 Digital activists Since the growth of social media and the internet this has become a common form of participation. It requires only that the individual should take part in campaigns and movements that happen on the internet. In other words, participation is possible without leaving one's home. It normally involves such activities as signing e-petitions, joining social media campaigns, expressing support for a cause on social media etc. Media sites such as Change.org and 38 Degrees have greatly facilitated such activity.

6 Voting Voting is the most fundamental and yet the least taxing form of political participation. It has become especially convenient with the growing use of postal voting. Even with local, regional and national elections, plus referendums, most citizens have to vote only once a year at most.

We have seen above that high levels of participation in political processes are essential to a healthy democracy. If citizens are passive and do not concern themselves with politics, the system becomes open to the abuse of power. In other words, popular political participation helps to call decision makers to account and to ensure that they carry out their representative functions.

The ways in which people participate are changing. Some also claim that political participation is in decline, especially among the young. Both these phenomena are examined below.

Changing forms and levels of participation

Political parties

There is no doubt that party activism is in decline in the UK. In the 1940s and 1950s membership of all political parties rose to over 3 million, mostly Conservatives. If one were to add trade union members affiliated to the Labour Party, this figure was several million higher. Since then there has been a steady, accelerating decline. Of course those high figures did not mean that the mass memberships were politically very *active*, but they gave an indication of mass engagement with politics at some level. Figure 1.1 demonstrates this decline.

Activity

Figure 1.1 shows a small rise in party membership after 2010. This is largely due to a rise in membership of the Labour Party. Research the way Ed Miliband changed the method of electing a new party leader in 2014 (see page 16). Establish what the connection was between the new leadership election rules and party membership.

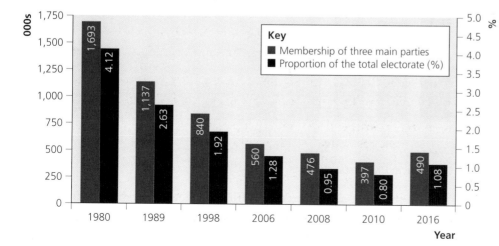

Source: Mair, P. and van Biezen, I. (2014) 'Party membership in Europe', *Party Politics*, Vol. 7, No. 1

Estimate and including over 300,000 new Labour Party members recruited for the 2015 leadership election plus new UKIP and SNP members

Figure 1.1 Party membership in the UK

It is clear that parties are no longer the main vehicle by which most people wish to participate in politics. There are, though, exceptions:

- There was a surge in Labour Party membership in 2015 when, under new rules established by the then leader, Ed Miliband, it was possible to join the party for just £3 (normal subscriptions to a party are much higher). This was to enable a wider section of Labour supporters to vote in leadership elections. A largely young new cohort in the Labour Party elected Jeremy Corbyn and thus changed the whole direction of the party. This was political activism of a fundamental kind, but it was possibly only a temporary phenomenon.
- Following the 2014 referendum on Scottish independence, membership of the Scottish National Party (SNP) surged, and it claimed to have over 100,000 members in a population of only just over 5 million.
- There was an increase in membership of UKIP in the run-up to the 2015 general election. Nearly 50,000 had signed up to the party by the time of the election, making UKIP the fourth largest party in the UK in terms of membership. After the 2015 election and in the run-up to the 2017 election membership of the Liberal Democrat and Green parties also rose.

These three examples that buck the trend of declining party membership suggest that people will still see parties as a vehicle for political action if they are proposing some kind of *radical* change. When it comes to more conventional politics and established parties, however, declining membership is continuing.

Voting

The act of voting, in an election or a referendum, is the least intensive form of participation and also the most infrequent, yet it is also the most important for most citizens. The level of turnout — what proportion of registered voters actually does vote — is, therefore, a good indicator of participation and engagement with politics. If we look at general elections, the picture is somewhat worrying. Figure 1.2 shows the turnout at general elections since 1979.

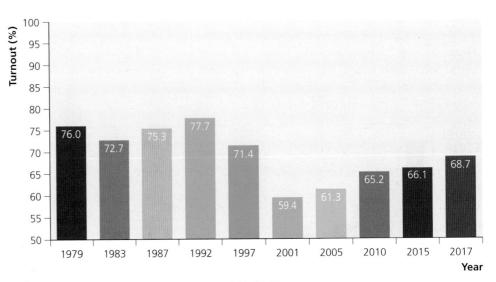

Figure 1.2 Turnout at UK general elections, 1979–2017

Synoptic link

The importance of turnout figures is also discussed in Chapter 4 on voting behaviour.

We can see that there is a general trend of falling turnout, though there has been a small recovery since 2010, a trend that was extended into the 2017 general election. The figure of two-thirds could be viewed as disappointing but also not serious in terms of democratic legitimacy. It is useful to compare turnout in the UK with that of other democracies. Figure 1.3 shows comparative figures for the two most recent general elections in other countries.

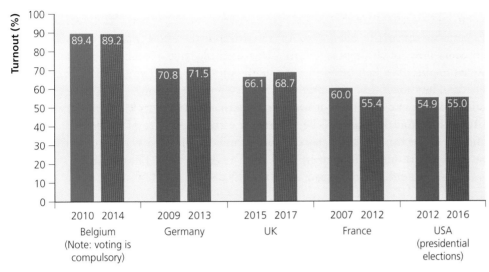

Figure 1.3 Comparative general election turnouts

Synoptic link

The reasons for variations in turnout, as well as its impact on the outcome of elections, are explored in Chapter 4 on voting behaviour.

Figure 1.3 shows that the UK stands in the middle of the 'league table'. This reflects the wider picture. It is interesting that the USA, often described as the purest democracy in the Western world, displays the lowest turnout figures in this selection, and one of the lowest in the democratic world.

Turnout in referendums is rather more volatile in the UK. Table 1.6 shows turnout in a number of key referendums.

Table 1.6 Referendum turnouts in the UK

Year	Subject of referendum	Turnout (%)
1998	Should London have an elected mayor?	34.1
1997–98	Devolution to: • Scotland • Wales • Northern Ireland	60.4 50.1 81.0
2011	The introduction of the AV electoral system	42.2
2014	Scottish independence	84.6
2016	British membership of the EU	72.2

We can see that referendum turnouts vary from 34.1% concerning local government in London up to 84.6% in the Scottish independence referendum. Turnout is, of course, a reflection of how important voters consider an issue to be. Voters are certainly becoming more used to having a say on single issues and it is noteworthy that turnout in the two most crucial referendums — EU membership and Scottish independence — turnout was higher than in recent general elections. As a comparison, in Switzerland, where referendums are common, the turnout tends to vary between 40% and 60%. High turnouts may occur because there is more than one question on the ballot at a time, so interest will be higher.

Key term

e-democracy A name used to describe the growing tendency for democracy to be carried out online in the form of e-petitions and other online campaigns.

E-petitions and e-democracy (also known as digital democracy)

E-petitions are a fast-growing form of participation. Indeed they have become so common the term '**e-democracy**' has come into use. Such referendums are part of the wider spread of digital democracy, where campaign groups use social media and the internet to promote their causes.

E-petitions have the advantage of requiring little effort and it is immediately apparent how much support a particular issue may have. Combined with the use of social media, they can build interest in an issue very rapidly, causing a bandwagon effect. They are often criticised as a form of participation as it requires so little effort to take part and there is no guarantee that participants know much about the issue. Nevertheless, they are becoming an established part of modern democracy and do, from time to time, have some influence. The site was temporarily closed in 2016 but is due to reopen in 2017 with revised rules. These will be shown on **www.parliament.uk** some time in 2017 or 2018.

Table 1.7 includes some of the most important e-petitions of recent times, and demonstrates how much impact they have had.

Table 1.7 E-petitions in the UK

Year	Subject	Signatures	Outcome	Platform
2007	Against a plan to introduce charges for using roads	1.8 million	The government dropped the plan.	Downing Street site
2011	Calling for the release of all documents relating to the Hillsborough football disaster of 1989	139,000	Following a parliamentary debate, the papers were released and a new inquest was launched.	Downing Street site
2016	Should there be a second EU referendum?	3.8 million	A parliamentary debate was held on the issue but no second referendum was allowed.	Parliamentary site

Pressure groups

As membership of and activism in political parties have declined, they have been partly replaced by participation in pressure groups. In terms of sectional groups, which represent a specific section of the community, this is nothing new. Many millions of people and organisations have formed themselves into pressure groups. Trade unions and professional associations have been particularly prominent. For many, such participation may be minimal, but some are activists in these organisations and help with political campaigning. The position with promotional groups, on the other hand, is changing.

Promotional groups pursue a particular political issue or a cause. Rather than relying on mass memberships, these groups seek mass activism, in other words they rely on mass active support rather than a large formal membership. This kind of participation is growing in the UK. The range and activities of pressure groups are explored fully on pages 22–28.

Social media and the internet

The importance of blogging, tweeting and general social media campaigning is growing. A campaign on a current issue can be mounted in just a few hours or days. Information about various injustices or demands for immediate action over some kind of social evil can circulate quickly, putting pressure on decision makers and elected representatives. Sites such as 38 Degrees and Change.org help to facilitate such social movements. Typical campaigns concern proposed hospital closures, opposition to road-building projects, claims of miscarriages of justice in the courts and demands for inquiries into the behaviour of large companies.

The conclusion we have to reach is that political action is more widespread than ever before. It may be less intensive and it may place less of a burden on people's time, but the fall in voting turnout and party membership has been largely overtaken by the growth of alternative forms of political participation.

Activity

Access the 38 Degrees and/or the Change.org site, and select two local and two national campaigns included in the sites.

- Describe the nature of the campaigns.
- Describe the methods being used to further those campaigns.

Suffrage

The term 'suffrage' refers to the right to vote in free elections. A second term related to this is the '**franchise**'. The UK has always led the world in widening the franchise and in the establishment of universal adult suffrage. The main stages in the extension of the franchise in the UK are shown in the timeline (Figure 1.4).

The battles for suffrage in the UK are now largely over (with the exception of some issues described below). The women's suffrage movement in the early part of the twentieth century was the last great struggle, with many women willing to go to prison following a campaign of civil disobedience. One woman, Emily Davison, lost her life when she fell under the king's racehorse in the Derby in

Key term

The franchise (also known as **suffrage**) The term 'franchise' essentially means the same as 'suffrage' — that is, the right to vote. The franchise has been gradually extended in the UK since 1832 to include all adults over 18 (over 16 in Scotland) with a few exceptions, such as prisoners currently serving a sentence.

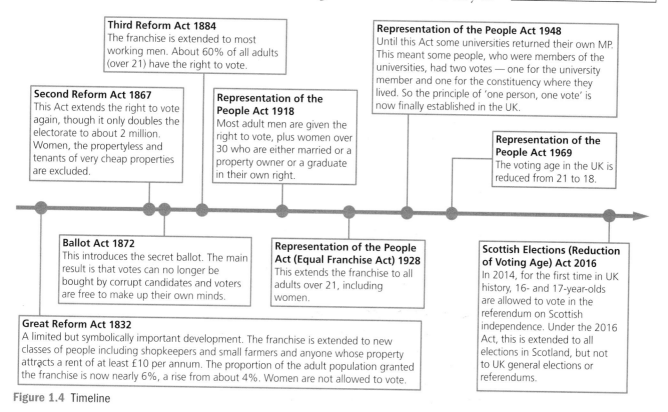

Third Reform Act 1884
The franchise is extended to most working men. About 60% of all adults (over 21) have the right to vote.

Second Reform Act 1867
This Act extends the right to vote again, though it only doubles the electorate to about 2 million. Women, the propertyless and tenants of very cheap properties are excluded.

Representation of the People Act 1918
Most adult men are given the right to vote, plus women over 30 who are either married or a property owner or a graduate in their own right.

Representation of the People Act 1948
Until this Act some universities returned their own MP. This meant some people, who were members of the universities, had two votes — one for the university member and one for the constituency where they lived. So the principle of 'one person, one vote' is now finally established in the UK.

Representation of the People Act 1969
The voting age in the UK is reduced from 21 to 18.

Ballot Act 1872
This introduces the secret ballot. The main result is that votes can no longer be bought by corrupt candidates and voters are free to make up their own minds.

Representation of the People Act (Equal Franchise Act) 1928
This extends the franchise to all adults over 21, including women.

Scottish Elections (Reduction of Voting Age) Act 2016
In 2014, for the first time in UK history, 16- and 17-year-olds are allowed to vote in the referendum on Scottish independence. Under the 2016 Act, this is extended to all elections in Scotland, but not to UK general elections or referendums.

Great Reform Act 1832
A limited but symbolically important development. The franchise is extended to new classes of people including shopkeepers and small farmers and anyone whose property attracts a rent of at least £10 per annum. The proportion of the adult population granted the franchise is now nearly 6%, a rise from about 4%. Women are not allowed to vote.

Figure 1.4 Timeline

Key term

Suffragettes
Campaigners in the early part of the twentieth century advocating votes for women, who used both parliamentary lobbying and civil disobedience as their methods.

1913, trying to attach a suffragette banner. Once women had equal voting rights after 1928, the attention of the women's movement turned to campaigning for more women being adopted as candidates for public office. The Labour Party, in particular, has made arrangements to ensure fair gender representation and the Scottish National Party has had great success in recruiting more successful female candidates for office.

There is no doubt that the issue of female suffrage has been the most important development in the field since the Great Reform Act of 1832. It demonstrated the power of concerted action by a united social movement and it had the effect of galvanising the woman's movement, which later became known as feminism. Women's suffrage also led the way in creating gender equality in a host of other fields.

Suffrage issues

A few suffrage issues remain to be resolved. It is not clear, for example, which UK citizens living abroad will be allowed to vote at home after the UK leaves the EU. There has also been a long-running battle between the UK Parliament and the European Court of Human Rights over whether prisoners should have the right to vote. But these are relatively minor, short-term issues, compared to other pressing concerns.

There are three remaining major franchise and voting issues in the UK. These are votes at 16, compulsory voting, and improving registration to vote and innovations in methods of voting. These are largely a response to low turnouts at election (see Chapter 4 on voting behaviour).

Votes at 16

Although 16- and 17-year-olds in Scotland were given the vote after 2014, the issue has not been settled in the UK overall. It remains a balanced argument.

It seems inevitable that 16- and 17-year-olds will one day gain the right to vote. However, this may have to wait until a party comes to power that feels it will benefit from younger people having the vote. This is likely to be a more radical party of the left.

Debate

Should 16- and 17-year-olds be given the right to vote?

Arguments in favour

- With the spread of citizenship education, young people are now better informed about politics than ever before.
- Voting turnout among the 18–24-year-old age group is very low. This may encourage more people to vote and become engaged with politics.
- The internet and social media now enable young people to be better informed about politics.
- If one is old enough to serve in the army, get married or pay tax, one should be old enough to vote.
- The radicalism of the very young could act as a useful balance to the extreme conservatism of elderly voters.

Arguments against

- People of 16 and 17 years old are too young to be able to make rational judgements.
- Many issues are too complex for younger people to understand.
- Few people in this age group pay tax so they have a lower stake in society.
- It is argued by some that the very young tend to be excessively radical as they have not had enough experience to consider issues carefully.

The Scottish Referendum vote of 2014 drew an enthusiastic response from many young people

Compulsory voting

Compulsory voting exists in about a dozen countries, though in many it is possible to 'opt out' of voting before the election and so avoid a fine. In some countries the government does not enforce compulsory voting, though it exists in law. In Australia, compulsory voting *is* enforced and a significant fine can be levied. Voters there do not have to vote for any candidate(s) but must attend the polling booth and mark a ballot paper in some way. Some 'spoil' the ballot paper to avoid a fine. The turnout in Australia, not surprisingly, is above 90%, and it is close to 90% in Belgium. In Italy, voting was compulsory until 1998 when turnout was typically close to 90%, but since voting has been no longer compulsory turnout has fallen (75% in 2013). So, there can be no doubt that compulsory voting has a dramatic effect on turnout. The relatively low turnouts at UK elections, especially at local and regional levels, have led to calls for compulsory voting. The arguments for and against are well balanced.

Debate

Should the UK introduce compulsory voting?

Arguments for

- It may force more voters, especially the young, to make themselves more informed about political issues.
- By increasing turnout it will give greater democratic legitimacy to the party or individual(s) who win an election.
- By ensuring that more sections of society are involved, decision makers will have to ensure that policies will address the concerns of all parts of society, not just those who typically vote in larger numbers.
- It can be argued that voting is a civic duty so citizens should be obliged to carry out that duty.

Arguments against

- It is a civil liberties violation. Many argue it is a basic right *not* to take part.
- Many voters are not well informed and yet they will be voting, so there will be ill-informed participation.
- It will involve large amounts of public expenditure to administer and enforce the system.
- It will favour larger parties against small parties. This is because less informed citizens will vote and they may have heard only of better-known parties and candidates.

Attention tends to centre on young voters in the UK because they typically vote in smaller numbers than older people. Turnout figures at UK general elections among the 18–24 age group are typically about 35%, while over 80% of the over 60s tend to vote. This may result in governments favouring the older generation against the young when making policy. However, civil rights campaigners are against compulsory voting, while the Conservative Party is unlikely to support it as the young tend to be more left wing than older people, so forcing the young to vote would favour Labour and other left-of-centre parties.

Registration reform and making voting more convenient

In 2014 the system for registering to vote in the UK was changed. Before the change there was *household registration*, which meant that one householder could register anyone living in the property on their behalf. Even those who were temporarily away from home, such as students, could still vote. This was replaced by *individual voter registration*, which meant that each individual was responsible for registering themselves at whatever address they considered to be permanent. It is estimated that about 1 million voters lost the right to vote in 2015 because their household registration was not transferred to individual registration. The main concern here is that most of the 'missing voters' were students and young people who do not have permanent addresses. Attention has therefore shifted from encouraging such people to vote to encouraging them to register in the first place.

Registration is a bigger issue in the USA than in the UK. This is because members of ethnic minorities in the USA typically do not register in as large numbers as the white population. In the UK it is hoped that the new system will settle down and, with easier online registration, the imbalance will correct itself. At the same time there have been demands to make voting more convenient. In particular, there have been proposals to introduce online voting or voting at post offices and even supermarkets. Online voting is the most popular proposal, not least because we are becoming increasingly used to taking part in online surveys and polls or e-petitions, giving rise to the term '**clickocracy**'. Voting in elections would be an extension of such practices. It is hoped that the young in particular will be encouraged to register and then vote online. Weekend voting has also been proposed. The main problem with such proposals is that they may open the door to fraud.

> ### Key term
>
> **Clickocracy** The increasing practice of taking part in surveys, petitions and political campaigns by registering one's opinion online. The 38 Degrees site is a prominent example of this.

Pressure groups

A pressure group can be defined as an association whose aim is to influence policy making at local, regional, national or European level without actually seeking power. Some collective organisations such as large companies and multinationals, media organisations, academic bodies and trade are not, strictly speaking, pressure groups, but they are so large and have such a vested interest in political outcomes that they behave *as though* they were pressure groups. They can therefore be treated and evaluated in the same way as pressure groups.

Pressure groups have a variety of aims and employ different methods but they all have in common a desire to influence government without becoming government itself. If a pressure group decides it wishes to exercise power, it becomes a political party. This happened when the trade union movement helped to form the Labour Party in the early twentieth century, when the Ecology Party became the Green Party in 1990 and when the UK Independence Party (UKIP) began to put up candidates at parliamentary elections after 1993.

The functions of pressure groups are as follows:

- To represent and promote the interests of certain sections of the community who feel they are not fully represented by parties and Parliament
- To protect the interests of minority groups
- To promote certain causes that have not been adequately taken up by political parties
- To inform and educate the public about key political issues
- To call government to account over its performance in particular areas of policy
- On occasions to pass key information to government to inform and influence policy
- To give opportunities to citizens to participate in politics other than through party membership or voting

In addition, pressure groups are a vital part of civil society, ensuring an active and informed citizenry and so helping to ensure that government is not able to become over-powerful. Without an active and effective civil society, governments are able to control the lives and the ideas of citizens excessively. Parties and Parliament also perform this function but pressure groups are a vital reinforcement.

Classifying pressure groups

It is normal to classify pressure groups into two main types in order to help us understand how they operate. These types are **promotional groups** (sometimes called 'cause' or 'issue' groups) and **sectional groups** (sometimes called 'interest groups'). The main characteristics of each are as follows.

Promotional (cause or issue) groups

As their name suggests, promotional groups are seeking to promote a particular cause, to convert the ideas behind the cause into government action or parliamentary legislation. The cause may be broad, as with groups campaigning on environmental or human rights issues, or narrow, as with groups promoting local issues such as the protection of green spaces or opposition to supermarket openings in high streets. Here are some prominent examples of promotional groups operating in the UK:

- Greenpeace
- Friends of the Earth
- Liberty
- Unlock Democracy
- People for the Ethical Treatment of Animals (PETA)
- Campaign for Nuclear Disarmament (CND)

Sectional (interest) groups

These groups represent a particular section of the community and so constitute part of the *functional representation* community in the UK. Sectional groups are self-interested in that they hope to pursue the interests specifically of their own membership or of those whom they represent.

Some sectional groups may be hybrid in that they believe that, by serving the interests of their own members and supporters, the wider community will also benefit. For example, unions representing teachers or doctors will argue that the interests of their members are also the interests of all of us. Better-treated and better-paid teachers or doctors and medical staff will mean better education and health for all, they argue.

It must be emphasised that large corporations such as Google, Starbucks and Amazon are so big and influential that they qualify as a kind of sectional pressure group on their own. They resist proposed legislation that might hinder their operations, and seek to emphasise the positive role they play in the national economy. As they employ high numbers of people and account for a large proportion of economic activity, they have a *strategically* important place in the economy. This gives them great insider influence.

> ## Key terms
>
> **Promotional group**
> An association whose goal is to promote a particular cause or set of beliefs or values. Such groups seek to promote favourable legislation, prevent unfavourable legislation or simply bring an issue onto the political agenda.
>
> **Sectional group**
> An association which has an identifiable membership or supporting group. Such groups represent a section of society and are mainly concerned with their own interests.

A particular example is successful resistance to popular calls for such companies to pay more in UK taxes on their profits. Firms and industries such as alcoholic drinks manufacturers have campaigned against price controls proposed to reduce excessive drinking. In a similar way, the confectionery industry has resisted attempts by the government to reduce the sugar content of its products in an anti-obesity drive.

Prominent examples of sectional groups are:

- Age UK
- British Medical Association (BMA)
- Muslim Council of Britain
- Taxpayers Alliance
- Confederation of British Industry (CBI)
- The MS [Multiple Sclerosis] Society

The features of promotional and sectional groups are summarised in Table 1.8.

Table 1.8 Features of pressure groups

Promotional groups	Sectional groups
They are altruistic in that they serve the whole community, not just their own members and supporters.	They are largely (not always) self-interested in that they serve the interests of their own members and supporters.
They tend to concentrate on mobilising public opinion and putting pressure on government in that way.	Although they seek public support, they tend to seek *direct* links with decision makers (insider status).
They often use 'direct action' in the form of public demonstrations, internet campaigns and sometimes civil disobedience.	Their methods tend to be more 'responsible' and they often take the parliamentary route to influence.
They seek widespread support.	They usually have a formal membership.

Insiders and outsiders

We can also classify pressure groups as 'insiders' and 'outsiders'. This distinction tells us a good deal about their methods and status. Insider group are so called because they have especially close links with decision makers at all levels. Collective organisations, as described on page 22, are, effectively, insider pressure groups. The main ways in which insider groups operate include the following.

- They seek to become involved in the early stages of policy and law making. This means that they are often consulted by decision makers and sometimes can offer expert advice and information.
- Some such groups employ professional lobbyists whose job it is to gain access to decision makers and make high-quality presentations of their case.
- Government at different levels uses special committees to make decisions about policy. Some groups may find themselves represented on such bodies and so have a specially privileged position. The National Farmers' Union (NFU) and the Institute of Directors (IOD) have advised government on these committees, as have trade unions and professional bodies representing groups of workers and members of the professions.
- Sectional groups may be called to testify before parliamentary committees, both select and legislative. Although they attend mainly to give advice and information, it is also an opportunity to have some long-term influence.

Outsiders are those groups which do not enjoy a special position within governing circles. This may be because decision makers do not wish to be seen to be too close to them or because a group itself wants to maintain its independence from government. Greenpeace, which is a radical environmental issue group, will have nothing to do with government and government does not wish to be associated with it. The typical characteristics of outsider groups are listed below.

- They are usually, but not always, promotional groups. Sectional groups with identifiable memberships and support groups are a useful ally in policy making, but promotional groups have less certain legitimacy.
- Their typical methods include public campaigning, in recent times often using new media to reach large parts of the population very quickly. They seek to influence not through direct lobbying or ministerial contacts, but by demonstrating to government that public opinion is on their side.
- Outsiders do not need to behave in such a responsible way as insider groups, so they often use civil disobedience, mass strikes and publicity 'stunts'.

Greenpeace campaigners at a demonstration against climate change

Methods used by pressure groups

Access points and lobbying

The ways in which groups seek to promote their cause or interests depends to some extent on the access points they have available to them. Insiders who are regularly listened to by decision makers will sit on policy committees at local, regional, national and even European level. They will also often keep permanent offices at their point of access. While the UK is still a member of the EU, for example, large groups and organisations have maintained offices in Brussels and Strasbourg. When the UK finally leaves the EU, these organisations will have to move their operation back to the UK. Even at local level, groups will seek to foster special relationships with councillors or with the mayoral office. Of course, if groups do not have such access points available to them, they must look elsewhere for their methods.

Public campaigning

Groups without direct access to government tend to mobilise public opinion to promote themselves. Public campaigning ranges from organising mass demonstrations, to creating and publicising e-petitions, to using celebrities to gain publicity, to acts of civil disobedience. Some examples of such campaigns are described in Table 1.9.

> **Key term**
>
> **Lobbying** An activity, commonly used by pressure groups, to promote causes and interests. Lobbying takes various forms, including organising large gatherings at Parliament or council offices, seeking direct meetings with decision makers including ministers and councillors, and employing professional organisations to run campaigns.

Table 1.9 Campaigning methods

Group	Aims	Methods
Plane Stupid	To prevent airport expansions	• Invading airports and blocking flights • Occupying airport terminals • Blocking entrances to airports • Delaying Heathrow expansion with a judicial review case • Organising e-petitions
British Medical Association (BMA)	To force government to withdraw a new contract for junior hospital doctors in 2016–17	• Regular withdrawal of labour for routine operations and treatments
Countryside Alliance	Among other issues, the restoration of fox hunting	• Local and national large-scale demonstrations
Greenpeace	Various environmental issues	• Civil disobedience such as destroying genetically modified crops, disrupting whaling and oil exploration in the Arctic

Synoptic link

Examples of the use of judicial review by pressure groups can be found in Chapter 8.

Study tip

When answering questions about pressure groups, use real-world examples. Be sure to learn the characteristics, experience and aims of a range of groups.

Activity

Research the following pressure groups. In each case identify their main concerns and the main methods they are proposing to promote their cause or interest:

- Mencap (**www.mencap.org.uk**)
- Article 19 (**www.article19.org**)
- Campaign for Real Ale (**www.camra.org.uk**)

Other methods

These can include the following.

- It is common for groups to make grants to political parties as a means of finding favour for their cause or interest. Trade unions have long financed the Labour Party. Many business groups and large companies send donations to all parties, but mostly to the Conservative Party. In this way they hope to influence policy.
- Parliamentary representation is very important. Most MPs and peers promote the interests of one group or another, raising issues in debate or lobbying ministers directly. They are sometimes able to influence the content of legislation, proposing or opposing amendments, if they sit on legislative committees.
- Media campaigns can be important. Groups may hope that the press, TV or radio will publicise their concerns. Although the broadcast media in the UK are politically neutral, some programming may publicise an issue to the benefit of the cause. Groups may help to finance such programmes. Press advertising can also be used.
- Some groups have resorted to illegal methods. This is sometimes a last resort when all else has failed, but they are also useful as a means of gaining publicity. Greenpeace, for example, has destroyed genetically modified (GM) crops to publicise the dangers, while members of Plane Stupid, wishing to demonstrate the dangers of airport expansion, have trespassed at Heathrow and disrupted flights.
- On some occasions a pressure group can pursue an issue through the courts if it feels government or a state body has acted contrary to the rule of law and has discriminated against a group in society.

Factors in the success and failure of pressure groups

Why are some pressure groups more successful than others? This is an important question because it can go some way to explaining the direction of policy. To some extent the fortunes of pressure groups will change with time and with the changes in government, but there are also several permanent factors.

Success factors

- **Size** The more supporters a group has, the more pressure it can place on decision makers. Politicians do not like to fly in the face of public opinion because they will regularly face the need for re-election. Size is no guarantee of success, as the anti-war coalition discovered in the lead-up to the 2003 Iraq war, but it is usually significant. Age UK, which campaigns on behalf of the elderly, has had many successes, not least because it represents such a large proportion of the population. What is more, older people vote in larger numbers than the young, so politicians tend to listen to them.

- **Finance** Wealthy groups can afford expensive campaigns, employ lobbyists, sponsor political parties and purchase favourable publicity. The banking industry and business groups such as the IOD and CBI have considerable funds and have, in recent years, secured favourable treatment from governments. As with size, finance is not always decisive. Trade unions, for example, give large donations to Labour but this has not resulted in much favourable legislation, save for rises in the minimum wage. Similarly, as public opinion has turned against the finance industry, its wealth may cease to be of any use.

- **The strategic position of a particular sectional group** For example, companies and industrial groups have a great deal of leverage because they are so vital to the economy. This is especially true if they can threaten to take their investment overseas. The banking and motor industries are in this position. Teachers, emergency services and medical professions are also strategic, though they face the danger of losing the support of public opinion if they use their position too often and too radically.

- **Public mood** The combination of public sentiment and strong campaigning can be successful in bringing an issue to the attention of decision makers. This has been the case with ASH — which campaigns on smoking and health — where anti-smoking feeling combined with a successful lobbying campaign in the last two decades has resulted in a raft of anti-tobacco legislation. The same is true of groups campaigning on behalf of the LGBT community. Success (notably over gay marriage) has been largely due to changes in public attitudes towards 'alternative' forms of sexuality.

- A variable factor concerns **the attitude of government itself**. Both promotional and sectional groups are bound to be more successful if they combine with a sympathetic government. During the coalition of 2010–15, for example, the influence of the Liberal Democrats in government helped to ensure that groups campaigning on behalf of the poor, such as Child Poverty Action Group (CPAG), were successful in reducing the tax burden on low-income workers.

Failure factors

- **Campaign groups which are too small and have limited funds** Typical among these are groups that represent people with rare medical conditions, local action groups that campaign for action by national or regional decision makers (such as campaigners against hospital closures) and groups which have only recently emerged and have not yet had time to make an impact. This problem is also related to a new phenomenon known as **hyperpluralism**. This makes government decision making very difficult but also means that smaller, less powerful groups find their voice drowned out by the noise of excessive **group politics**.

- **Unsympathetic government** Trade unions have problems influencing Conservative governments while Labour is usually unsympathetic to groups that seek to oppose social reform, such as anti-abortion campaigners or anti-gay groups.

- **Powerful countervailing groups** Forest, a pro-smoking campaign group, for example, has been regularly defeated by the anti-smoking lobby that has public opinion and government on its side. Plane Stupid, trying to hold back airport expansion proposals, is well organised and supported but faces opposition from the powerful air transport lobby as well as business groups.

Synoptic link

As pressure groups are part of a representative democracy, this section should be viewed in conjunction with the section on representation above on pages 8–12.

Key terms

Hyperpluralism A modern phenomenon describing the rapid growth in the number of interest and campaign groups operating in modern democracies. It is feared that the growth in numbers and influence of such groups makes government extremely difficult, as so many different demands and interests have to be satisfied.

Group politics A term that refers to the idea that political decision making involves mediating between the competing demands of different groups. It also implies that different groups have open access to decision-making individuals and bodies and that the demands of different groups are heard.

- **Public opinion can be a decisive factor**. Groups that are supported by public opinion are at a huge advantage, and the opposite is true. Groups that are conservative in nature, i.e. are seeking to hold back social and cultural change, often fall foul of public sentiment.

Knowledge check

What do the following initials of pressure groups stand for?

- CPRE
- CRAE
- ALF

Case study

ASH

Name of group

Action on Smoking and Health (ASH)

Founding and objectives

- Founded in 1967 by academics and interested parties
- Its objectives include the spreading of knowledge about the harmful effects of tobacco use and to press governments to adopt policies and laws to reduce tobacco use.

Methods

ASH conducts research and publicises existing research into the effects of tobacco. It shares this with governments and the public. For example, it has sponsored research into the effects of passive smoking and on the effect of e-cigarettes. It is largely an insider group, concentrating on lobbying lawmakers and governments, mainly using scientific data to underpin its case.

Successes

There are many examples of success, including:

- restrictions on advertising tobacco products and tobacco sponsorship
- health warnings on cigarette packs
- persuading government to increase tax on tobacco to deter consumers
- restricting point-of-sale advertising and promotion
- successfully campaigning for the law banning smoking in public places
- successfully persuading government to develop a law banning smoking in cars carrying children

Failures

ASH would like to go further on smoking bans and is now concerned that e-cigarettes may be harmful. As yet it has not succeeded in changing government policy in these areas.

Why is it successful?

It helps government to make policy by providing evidence and information. It acts responsibly and has built up a network of supporters within government and Parliament.

Pressure groups, society and democracy

The UK is a representative democracy. Political parties, social media and pressure group activity are the main components of a *pluralist democracy*. This term refers to the idea that there are multiple means by which different groups and sections of society can have their voices heard and that they have opportunities to influence government at all levels.

Pressure groups also form an important barrier between government and the governed. Citizens often feel that their influence through elections, referendums and political parties is too weak. Parties cannot represent a wide enough range of interests and causes, while elections and referendums are relatively infrequent. It is, therefore, important that there are alternative means by which citizens can constantly communicate with government. Pressure groups supply that channel of communication. Without them, citizens might feel powerless and ignored, which is a dangerous situation for a democracy.

Activity

Undertake a thorough case study on two pressure groups, one a promotional (cause) group, the other a sectional group. In each case, explain the following:

- The main aims of the group
- The typical methods used by the group
- The successes and failures experienced by the group

Debate

Do pressure groups enhance or threaten democracy?

Ways in which they enhance democracy

- Pressure groups help to disperse power and influence more widely.
- Pressure groups educate the public about important political issues.
- Pressure groups give people more opportunities to participate in politics without having to sacrifice too much of their time and attention.
- Pressure groups can promote and protect the interests and rights of minorities.
- Pressure groups help to call government to account by publicising the effects of policy.

Ways in which they may threaten democracy

- Some pressure groups are elitist and tend to concentrate power in too few hands.
- Influential pressure groups may distort information in their own interests.
- Pressure groups that are *internally undemocratic* may not accurately represent the views of their members and supporters.
- Finance is a key factor in political influence, so groups that are wealthy may wield a disproportionate amount of influence.

Think tanks, lobbyists and celebrities

Pressure groups are not the only external influence on decision makers. There are also organisations commonly known as '**think tanks**', lobbyists and, more recently, celebrities, who seek to influence policy and decisions. Some organisations have been set up *by* government itself to advise on policy. The King's Fund, which advises on health policy and expenditure, is a key example, as is the Office of Fair Trading, which helps to protect the interests of consumers. The Health and Safety Executive is also a semi-independent arm of government, advising on possible legislation in its field.

Think tanks

Some prominent examples of think tanks are listed below.

Neutral think tanks
- **ResPublica** — general policy issues
- **Chatham House** — international affairs
- **Centre for Social Justice** — policy on welfare issues
- **Demos** — current political issues

<table>
<tr><td>

Key term

Think tank An organisation whose role is to undertake research into various aspects of public policy. They are financed either by government or by private sources or both and they are used by decision makers to inform their policy deliberation. They may be neutral or have a political axe to grind.

</td></tr>
</table>

'Left-wing' think tanks

- **Fabian Society** — issues concerning social justice and equality
- **Institute for Public Policy Research** — various left-wing policy ideas

'Right-wing' think tanks

- **Adam Smith Institute** — promoting free-market solutions to economic issues
- **Centre for Policy Studies** — promoting ideas popular in the premiership of Margaret Thatcher

'Liberal' think tanks

- **Liberty** — promoting issues concerning the protection of rights and liberties
- **Reform** — concerning policies on welfare, public services and economic management

Lobbyists

Lobbyists are far from neutral. They exist to promote a particular interest. Sometimes called lobby groups, they are also described as public relations companies or public affairs agencies. They operate round EU institutions, Westminster, central government departments and devolved administrations, hoping to further the cause of those who employ them. Very often they employ former politicians who know their way around access points and can offer personal contacts in the political system. Sometimes they are criticised for being the 'hidden face' of influence or for being representative only of wealthy interests.

Celebrities

In recent years it has increasingly been the case that celebrities are used to promote a cause. Celebrities give opportunities for media attention and attracting public support. They have the particular advantage of offering influence without any great expense. Below are some examples of celebrity involvement.

- Former James Bond film star Joanna Lumley took up the case of the Gurkhas (Nepalese soldiers serving in the British army). The Gurkha Justice campaign sought to gain the right to residence in the UK for the Gurkhas. In 2009 the campaign was successful and these soldiers were allowed to settle in Britain.
- Chef Jamie Oliver has campaigned for many years for healthier eating, especially among school children. He constantly lobbies government to take action against child obesity.
- Former cricket star Sir Ian Botham has lent his support to the Countryside Alliance in its dispute with the Royal Society for the Protection of Birds (RSPB) over the issue of whether shooting birds is good for conservation.

Joanna Lumley celebrating with Gurkha activists following their successful campaign

Pressure groups and parties

It is important to distinguish between parties and pressure groups. While both seek to influence politics and political decision making, there are important distinctions. The main differences are as follows.

- Parties seek to gain power at various levels, whereas pressure groups do not. Some pressure groups do put up candidates for election, but they do not aspire to government.
- For that reason, parties are willing to make themselves accountable for their policies. Pressure groups do not.
- While parties develop policies across the whole range of government responsibilities, the concerns of pressure groups are narrow. They are interested in one cause or interest, or a cluster of causes.

It is for these reasons that pressure groups can never be as central to democracy as parties. The lack of accountability of pressure groups means they lack legitimacy.

Table 1.10 Group politics – the pressures on government: a summary of the various ways in which groups can influence government

Type of group	Example	Nature of pressure
Insider pressure groups	Age UK	Close links with decision makers, lobbying ministers and Parliament, participation in policy committees
Outsider pressure groups	Greenpeace	Demonstrations of public support, publicity campaigns, civil disobedience, digital campaigning
Social movements	Occupy campaign	Demonstrations, civil disobedience, online campaigning including e-petitions
Single-issue campaigns	Campaign against a third Heathrow runway	Illegal obstruction of the airport, digital campaigns, media representatives including celebrities, lobbying Parliament, recruiting sympathetic local MPs
Trade unions and professional associations	British Medical Association	Strikes, non-cooperation and demonstrations, lobbying Parliament, using sympathetic MPs
Companies and industries	Starbucks	Negotiating with government for favourable treatment

Rights in context

Rights and civil liberties

The terms 'human rights' and 'civil liberties' are often used interchangeably, but they mean slightly different things. In particular, human rights is a broader idea than civil liberties.

Civil liberties refers to the protections citizens have against government and the state, as well as those rights that are *guaranteed* by the state. In other words, they

Key term

Civil liberties The rights and freedoms enjoyed by citizens which protect them from unfair and arbitrary treatment by the state and government. They are also those freedoms that are guaranteed by the state and the constitution. Civil liberties are sometimes referred to as 'civil rights', especially in the USA.

are rights and freedoms in relation to the state itself. Prominent examples of civil liberties in the UK are:

- the right not to be imprisoned without trial
- the right to a fair trial if accused of a crime
- the right to vote and stand for election
- the right not to suffer discrimination on the grounds of colour, ethnicity, gender, sexual orientation, age etc.
- the right to form associations for peaceful ends

Human rights are broader and are not always guaranteed by government. They include most civil liberties but can go further. Human rights can also extend to having a decent standard of living, access to good healthcare and education, perhaps even the right to work. We also refer to the right to free expression, freedom of association, of belief and of movement. These are both rights and civil liberties.

The development of rights and formal equality in the UK

Common law rights

The traditional status of rights in the UK has been that every citizen was assumed to have rights unless they were prohibited by law. These rights were sometimes referred to as residual rights. For example, it was assumed that people had freedom of movement unless there was some legal obstruction, such as if a person was convicted of a crime and sentenced to custody.

In addition, rights were sometimes specifically *stated* as a result of a court case when rights were in dispute. In these cases a judge would decide what was the *normal* or *traditional* way in which such disputes would be settled. Having made his or her decision, the judge would declare what he or she understood people's rights to be. In doing so the judge was declaring **common law**.

Let's take the example of a married or cohabiting couple. If they were to split up, there might be a dispute as to how to divide their possessions, in other words what *rights* the couple had against each other. If there were no statute law to cover the situation, a judge would have to state what the common law was. Once a judge had declared what the common law was under a particular circumstance, he or she created a judicial precedent. In all similar cases, judges had to follow the existing judicial precedent. So a great body of common law and common law rights was created over the centuries.

The Human Rights Act 1998

The main terms and status of the Human Rights Act (HRA) are described in Chapter 5. Here we can offer a brief description. The HRA brought into effect the European Convention on Human Rights (ECHR), which was first established by the Council of Europe in 1950. The UK helped to draft the Convention but did not accept it as binding on its government — not until 1998, that is.

The ECHR establishes a wide range of rights to replace the patchwork of statute and common law rights in the UK. It is binding on all public bodies other than the UK Parliament (and it is politically binding on Parliament even if not legally binding —

Key term

Common law Traditional conceptions of how disputes should be settled and what rights individuals have. Common law is established by judges through judicial precedents when they declare what traditional, common law should be. It is sometimes described as 'judge-made law', although common law judgements can be found in law books or in digital form.

Parliament will rarely ignore it). It is also enforced by all courts in the UK, so that laws passed at any level should conform to its requirements.

The Freedom of Information Act 2000

Citizens in the UK had never enjoyed any right to see information held by public bodies, whether it related personally to them or not. By the end of the twentieth century, however, it was clear that the UK was out of step with much of the modern democratic world in this respect. In many countries, including the USA, legislation had been passed, first to allow citizens to view information held about them — for example, by the tax authorities, or social security or schools — and then to view information held by these bodies which it would be in the public interest to see. Governments were too secretive, it was widely contended, and this was a barrier to making them accountable. The Labour government which came to power in the UK in 1997, therefore, decided to redress this situation.

Since the Act was passed it has proved an invaluable tool for social and political campaigners, for MPs and for the media, allowing them to discover information never available in the past. It has helped to improve such services as the health service, the police, the civil service and educational establishments by shedding light on their activities and helping to promote reform.

The Equality Act 2010

There had been two parliamentary statutes prior to the Equality Act that established **formal equality** in the UK. The **Race Relations Act 1965** outlawed discrimination of most kinds on the grounds of a person's race or ethnicity. In 1970 the **Equal Pay Act** required employers to offer equal pay to men and women doing the same job. Important though these developments were, they failed to establish equality in the full sense of the word and missed out important groups in society who have suffered discrimination, notably those with disabilities and members of the gay community. Under the management of Harriet Harman, a Labour minister at the time, therefore, the **Equality Act** was passed in 2010.

The Equality Act requires that all legislation and all decision making by government, at any level, must take into account formal equality for different sections of society. Put another way, the Act outlaws any discrimination against any group. Equality is required and discrimination is outlawed on the following grounds:

- Age
- Disability
- Gender reassignment
- Marriage or civil partnership
- Race
- Religion or belief
- Sex
- Sexual orientation

In theory, *any* kind of discrimination is unlawful under the Act, but in practice it tends to apply to the following circumstances:

- Employment and pay
- Government services (local, regional, national)
- Healthcare

Study tip

Remember that the European Convention on Human Rights (ECHR) has nothing to do with the European Union. It is a product of the Council of Europe. So, if and when the UK leaves the EU, the ECHR will still be in force in the UK.

Key term

Formal equality The term 'formal equality' refers to aspects of equality that are established by law. The rule of law, in particular, establishes formal equality under the legal system — all must be treated equally by the courts and Parliament. Formal equality may also refer to equal treatment for different sections of society, established in law. This is also often described as 'equal rights'.

- Housing (sales or renting)
- Education
- Financial services
- Policing and law enforcement

Equality of the kind described above is especially important in relation to group politics and a healthy pluralist democracy. By establishing equality, both formal and informal, between different groups and sections of society, it is more likely that their demands and interests can be taken into account.

Rights and responsibilities

Rights in the UK

The first and perhaps most important truth about rights in the UK is that all citizens have equal rights. Long before the 2010 Equality Act this was a principle of UK law, but the Act finally confirmed it. This means that no individual and no group can be discriminated against as far as the law is concerned.

The second issue we should raise is: how well are rights protected in the UK? There is no doubt that they are more protected today than at any time in the past. The passage of such legislation as the Human Rights Act, the Equality Act and the Freedom of Information Act has ensured that rights are enforceable. Nevertheless, there are also weaknesses. The main issue is the fact that the UK Parliament remains sovereign. In practice this means that Parliament has the ultimate power to create rights or to take them away. In other words, it is not possible in the UK to create a codified set of rights that is binding on successive Parliaments. Furthermore, the rights pressure group Liberty has pointed out that legislation alone does not guarantee rights. It is ultimately up to parliament to ensure they are protected.

Activity

Research the European Convention on Human Rights. Outline what it says about the following issues:

- Family life
- Privacy
- Conscience and religion
- Servitude

Knowledge check

What rights were established by the Freedom of Information Act 2000?

The passage of the Human Rights Act did *appear* to establish binding right in the UK, but this was an illusion. The UK Parliament can, and occasionally has (for example, over anti-terrorism laws), ignored the European Convention on Human Rights. That said, Parliament remains reluctant to contradict the ECHR and all other public bodies must abide by its terms. It must also be said that the UK retains an international reputation for respecting human rights. It is one of the reasons so many migrants, asylum seekers and refugees are attracted there. Compared to many countries in the world, the UK is a haven for citizens' rights.

It is also true that rights in the UK can be suspended under special circumstances. All countries have such a provision, as it is necessary in times of crisis or emergency. Perhaps the best example occurred in the 1970s when the UK government introduced internment in Northern Ireland. Internment is the imprisonment, *without trial*, of suspected terrorists (people of German origin were interned in the UK during the Second World War for fear they might provide intelligence for the Third Reich or become subversives). This was done in Northern Ireland in order to remove as many potential violent political activists from the streets as possible. In the early part of the twentieth century, too, Parliament allowed the government to hold suspected terrorists for long periods without trial (though not indefinitely) as a result of the Islamic terrorist threat after 9/11.

Table 1.11 compares the strengths and weaknesses of rights protection in the UK.

Table 1.11 Rights in the UK: strengths and weaknesses

Strengths	Weaknesses
There is a strong common law tradition.	Common law can be vague and disputed. It can also be set aside by parliamentary statutes.
The UK is subject to the European Convention on Human Rights.	Parliament remains sovereign and so can ignore the ECHR or can even repeal the Human Rights Act.
The judiciary has a reputation for being independent and upholding the rule of law even against the expressed wishes of government and Parliament. The principle of equal rights is clearly established.	There is increasing pressure on government, as a result of international terrorism, to curtail rights in the interests of national security. The right to privacy, the right of association and expression as well as freedom from imprisonment without trial are all threatened.

Study tip

It is vital to understand the relationship between rights and the sovereignty of the UK Parliament. Full and equal rights can never be permanently guaranteed in the UK because Parliament is sovereign and can amend or remove them.

Responsibilities of citizens

The responsibilities of citizens have never been codified in the UK, but there is no doubt that they exist. With the increasing amount of immigration into the UK, the issue of what responsibilities or obligations citizens should have, especially new or aspiring citizens, has become more acute. It has been argued that rights can only be earned if they are matched by responsibilities, though this principle has never been firmly established. We can, however, identify a number of citizens' responsibilities which are widely accepted, and responsibilities that *may* exist, but could be disputed. These are shown below.

Clear citizens' responsibilities	Disputed citizens' responsibilities
<ul><li>To obey the laws</li><li>To pay taxes</li><li>To undertake jury service when required</li><li>Citizens have a responsibility to care for their children</li></ul>	<ul><li>To serve in the armed forces when the country is under attack</li><li>To vote in elections and referendums</li><li>To respect the rights of all other citizens</li><li>To respect the dominant values of the society</li></ul>

It should be noted that the clear responsibilities are enshrined in law. If a citizen does not accept those responsibilities, they run the danger of prosecution. The responsibilities that are in dispute may well be enforceable but many citizens will question them.

Collective versus individual rights

Although it is widely acknowledged today that the establishment and protection of individual rights are vital in a modern democracy, it also has to be accepted that the community *as a whole* has rights too, as do various *sections* of society.

Synoptic link

The role of the Supreme Court in protecting rights, as well as its relationship with other branches of government, is explained and analysed in Chapter 8. There are also important examples of key rights cases in Chapter 8.

Problems can arise where the rights of individuals clash with the collective rights of the community or sections of the community. Very often there is no solution to these conflicts but politicians are called upon to adjudicate. Occasionally, too, such conflicts may end up in the courts for resolution. Table 1.12 shows some examples of these kinds of clashes.

Discussion point

How would you resolve the conflicts between individuals' rights and collective rights as listed in Table 1.12? There are no right or wrong answers to these questions. As with so much in political life, they are matters of judgement.

Synoptic link

The issue of how rights are protected and how disputes over rights are adjudicated in the courts is further explored in Chapter 8.

Table 1.12 Individual rights v collective rights

Individual rights	Conflicting collective rights
Freedom of expression	The rights of religious groups not to have their beliefs satirised or questioned
The right to privacy	The right of the community to be protected from terrorism by security services that may listen in to private communications
The right to press freedom	The right of public figures to keep their private lives private
The right to demonstrate in public places (right to association and free movement) and thus cause disruption	The right of the community to their own freedom of movement
The right to strike in pursuit of pay and employment rights	The right of the community to expect good service from public servants who are paid from taxation

Key concepts in this chapter

Accountability This means that those who have been elected in a representative democracy must be made responsible for their policies, actions, decisions and general conduct. Without such accountability, representation becomes largely meaningless.

Civil liberties The rights and freedoms enjoyed by citizens which protect them from unfair and arbitrary treatment by the state and government. They are also those freedoms that are guaranteed by the state and the constitution. Civil liberties are sometimes referred to as 'civil rights', especially in the USA.

Civil society A collective name for all the various associations, including parties, pressure groups, religions, voluntary organisations, charities etc. to which citizens belong and in which they may become active. Civil society acts as a vital counterbalance to the power of government.

Clickocracy The increasing practice of taking part in surveys, petitions and political campaigns by registering one's opinion online. The 38 Degrees site is a prominent example of this.

Common law Traditional conceptions of how disputes should be settled and what rights individuals have. Common law is established by judges through judicial precedents when they declare what traditional, common law should be. It is sometimes described as 'unwritten law', although common law judgements can be found in law books or in digital form.

Decentralisation The process of spreading power away from the centre (i.e. central government) both towards devolved governments in the national regions and to local government.

Democratic deficit A collective term for the features of the political system which do not conform to, or fall short of, the normal criteria for a true democracy.

Direct democracy A form of democracy where the people themselves make key decisions. In modern societies this usually takes the form of holding referendums.

e-democracy A name used to describe the growing tendency for democracy to be carried out online in the form of e-petitions and other online campaigns.

(Electoral) mandate The principle, operating in the UK, whereby a party that has been elected to government has the authority of the electorate to carry out its manifesto commitments.

Elitism A description of a society or political system where power and influence are concentrated in the hands of a few people and organisations.

Formal equality The term 'formal equality' refers to aspects of equality that are established by law. The rule of law, in particular, establishes formal equality under the legal system — all must be treated equally by the courts and Parliament. Formal equality may also refer to equal treatment for different sections of society, established in law. This is also often described as 'equal rights'.

The **franchise** (also known as **suffrage**) The term 'franchise' essentially means the same as 'suffrage' — that is, the right to vote. The franchise has been gradually extended in the UK since 1832 to include all adults over 18 (over 16 in Scotland) with a few exceptions, such as prisoners currently serving a sentence.

Group politics A term that refers to the idea that political decision making involves mediating between the competing demands of different groups. It also implies that different groups have open access to decision-making individuals and bodies and that the demands of different groups are heard.

Hyperpluralism A modern phenomenon describing the rapid growth in the number of interest and campaign groups operating in modern democracies. It is feared that the growth in numbers and influence of such groups makes government extremely difficult, as so many different demands and interests have to be satisfied.

Limited government A feature of democracies with a constitutional safeguard is that the power of the government should have strict limits and that these limits will be enforced by the judiciary and the legal system in general. The only exceptions would involve emergency power.

Lobbying An activity, commonly used by pressure groups, to promote causes and interests. Lobbying takes various forms, including organising large gatherings at Parliament or council offices, seeking direct meetings with decision makers including ministers and councillors, and employing professional organisations to run campaigns.

Manifesto A statement of a party's agreed policies produced during an election campaign to inform the public about the political platform upon which its candidates are standing. Candidates for the party are expected to support the manifesto and usually do so in the UK, though there may be exceptions.

Pluralism/Pluralist democracy The idea that a wide variety of beliefs, lifestyles, religions etc. can flourish in a society and be tolerated. It also refers to the fact that there are likely to be many parties and associations active in society, that power is widely dispersed and that the people have access to many different channels of independent information. Finally, it can mean that there is 'open competition for power'. A pluralist democracy is one which displays these characteristics.

Promotional group An association whose goal is to promote a particular cause or set of beliefs or values. Such groups seek to promote favourable legislation, prevent unfavourable legislation or simply bring an issue onto the political agenda.

Redress of grievances The practice, adopted by many elected representatives, of taking up the case of an individual constituent who feels they have suffered an injustice, usually at the hands of government or an agency of the state.

Representative democracy A form of democracy where the people elect or somehow choose representatives who make political decisions on their behalf. It also implies that representatives are accountable for what they do.

Sectional group An association which has an identifiable membership or supporting group. Such groups represent a section of society and are mainly concerned with their own interests.

Suffrage Suffrage means the right to vote. Universal adult suffrage, finally established in the UK in 1928, means that all adults (currently over 16 in Scotland, over 18 in the rest of the UK) have the right to vote unless disqualified on the grounds of criminality or insanity.

Think tank An organisation whose role is to undertake research into various aspects of public policy. They are financed either by government or by private sources or both and they are used by decision makers to inform their policy deliberation. They may be neutral or have a political axe to grind.

Summary

Having read this chapter, you should have knowledge and understanding of the following:
→ How democracy in its various forms works in the UK
→ The distinctions between direct and representative democracy
→ The extent to which the UK is truly democratic
→ The nature of political participation in the UK, whether there is a participation crisis and possible ways in which it could be combated
→ The growing importance of e-democracy
→ The nature of representation in the UK
→ The nature of suffrage, how it developed in the UK and the issues surrounding changes to the franchise
→ The nature and activities of pressure groups in the UK
→ Issues concerning the operation of pressure groups in the UK
→ The general nature of political influence in the UK
→ The nature of rights in the UK and how they are protected
→ The conflicts between collective and individual rights

Further information and web guide

Websites

The most important think tank and campaign organisation concerning democracy in the UK is possibly Unlock Democracy. Its site contains discussion of many issues concerning democracy: **www.unlockdemocracy.org**.

The main rights pressure group is Liberty. Its site discusses current issues concerning rights: **www.liberty-human-rights.org.uk**.

The two main sites for campaigning on issue local and national are:

38 Degrees: **home.38degrees.org.uk**

Change.org: **www.change.org**

Further information on specific pressure groups can be found on their sites. A selection of interesting pressure groups is as follows. Websites can be easily accessed through a search engine.

- Age UK
- British Medical Association
- Friends of the Earth
- National Farmers' Union
- National Union of Students
- Action on Smoking and Health (ASH)
- Plane Stupid
- Frack Off
- Confederation of British Industry (CBI)
- British Banking Association

On the issue of rights in the UK, other than Liberty (see above), it is worth looking at the website of the Supreme Court: **www.supremecourt.uk**.

Books

A new book reviewing the development of democracy from its inception in ancient Greece to the modern day is Cartledge, P. (2016) *Democracy: A Life*, Oxford University Press.

Not new, but containing very good descriptions of democratic *principles*: Cole, M. (2006) *Democracy in Britain*, Edinburgh University Press.

This book is excellent concerning issues of participation: Flinders, M. (2012) *Why Democracy Matters in the 21st Century*, Oxford University Press.

AS

1 Describe the main features of representative democracy. (10)

2 Describe any three measures that have been proposed to increase political participation in the UK. (10)

3 Using the source, explain the distinctions between parties and pressure groups and why the distinctions are becoming blurred.
In your response you must use knowledge and understanding that are only in the source. (10)

> ### Pressure groups and parties
>
> It used to be the case that political parties were at the centre of policy development, but all this is changing. Increasingly, pressure groups in the UK are driving the political agenda. However, there are important distinctions between parties and pressure groups.
>
> The main distinction is that pressure groups do not seek power and cannot be held publicly accountable for what they do. Furthermore, parties have to develop policies across the full range of government responsibilities. Pressure groups, on the other hand, concentrate on single issues or clusters of related issues. These may concern, for example, the environment or human rights or equality issues.
>
> It is also true that parties operate largely *within* the political system, while pressure groups are often seen as *outsiders*, who concentrate on mobilising public support and putting pressure on decision makers from the outside. Of course, there are also insider pressure groups, usually sectional groups, which do have influence from the inside. It can be argued that the distinction between parties and pressure groups is becoming blurred.

4 'The UK Parliament is no longer a truly representative body.' How far do you agree with this statement? *In your answer you must refer to at least two views of representation and consider this view and the alternative to this view in a balanced way.* (30)

5 'The UK is suffering from a democratic deficit.' How far do you agree with this statement? *In your answer you must refer to at least two elements of democracy and consider this view and the alternative to this view in a balanced way.* (30)

A-level

1 Using the source, evaluate the view that the UK is suffering from a participation crisis. *In your response you must compare the different opinions in the source and use a balance of knowledge and understanding both arising from the source and beyond it to help you analyse and evaluate.* (30)

Turnout at elections

Low turnouts in UK elections and referendums have become a serious cause for concern. Many argue that democracy will decline if people do not participate in large numbers. One proposed solution is to introduce compulsory voting. This has been done in Australia and turnouts there are now above 90%. Compulsory voting reflects the idea that voting is a civic duty, so we can justify forcing people to vote. It is also probably true that larger turnouts will produce a more representative electorate. As things stand in the UK, it is the elderly who vote in large numbers, while the young tend to stay at home. This distorts the outcome of elections and referendums.

Falling turnout has accompanied a significant reduction in party membership and increasing disillusionment with party politics.

However, it can also be said that low turnouts are not as important as we think. Those who do not vote, it could be said, have voluntarily opted out of the democratic process. It may also be said that non-voters are likely to be ignorant about political issues. It is also true that wider political activity is actually on the increase. What is happening is that increasingly large numbers of people see pressure group activity and participation in social media campaigns as more meaningful forms of activity.

2 Evaluate the use of referendums to determine important political and constitutional issues. *In your response you must compare the different opinions in the source and use a balance of knowledge and understanding both arising from the source and beyond it to help you to analyse and evaluate.* (30)

The 2016 referendum on the UK's membership of the EU

The 2016 referendum on the UK's membership of the European Union was perhaps the most important democratic exercise in the history of the country. The question was important, of course, but the fact that many millions of voters took part in making such a momentous decision was most impressive. It certainly settled the issue after many years of political conflict, and people who felt they did not have a voice were now listened to. The vote created both legitimacy and public consent for the decision.

But behind the euphoria there were also serious concerns. The referendum campaign was dogged with controversy about misinformation and lack of clarity. The press were also accused of bias, with most popular tabloids campaigning relentlessly for a 'Leave' vote. Perhaps more importantly, some sections of the community felt they had been steamrollered into a decision against their will. Younger voters, the Scots and Londoners were all groups who voted strongly to remain within the EU, but they were overwhelmed by the national majority. The result was also very close — hardly a decisive outcome.

But, however much we may analyse the result, in the end the people had spoken and democracy had been served.

3 Evaluate the extent to which pressure groups enhance democracy in the UK. *In your answer you must refer to at least three pressure groups.* (30)

4 Evaluate the various ways in which rights are protected in the UK. (30)

2 Political parties

Two quotations illustrate the difficulty we have when judging the role and importance of political parties. The first is by John Adams, the second president of the USA. Near the end of the eighteenth century, on the eve of the development of the US Constitution, Adams wrote this:

> There is nothing I dread so much as a division of the republic into two great parties, each arranged under its leader, and concerting measures in opposition to each other. This, in my humble apprehension, is to be dreaded as the greatest political evil...

By contrast, the nineteenth-century British prime minister Benjamin Disraeli is quoted as saying to a colleague, 'Damn your principles, stick to your party.' Disraeli's remark suggested to MPs that their own ideas had to be put aside if they conflicted with their party's policies.

What we are seeing here is an ambivalent attitude to parties, which persists to this day. On the one hand, we must recognise that it is parties that make the whole political system work. Parties take people's ideas and beliefs, convert them into policies, convert those policies into practical programmes and, if they win power, convert programmes into action. Without parties, voters would find it difficult to differentiate one candidate for office from another and would not be able to make sense of political conflict. In other words, when it comes to voting we tend to vote for a party rather than an individual...but, on the other hand, we can also understand Adams' fears, as we shall see in this chapter.

Jeremy Corbyn at the 2016 Labour Party conference

Objectives

This chapter will inform you about the following:

→ The nature of political parties and what their functions are

→ Why manifestos are important and how they relate to the doctrine of the political mandate

→ How to distinguish between the terms 'left wing' and 'right wing'

→ How parties are funded and the nature of the political controversy over party funding, including proposals for reform

→ The origins of the Conservative, Labour and Liberal Democrat parties and the core beliefs of the three parties

→ The current policies of the three parties and the main factional differences in policy ideas that exist within the parties

→ The nature and impact of small parties in the UK

→ The nature and importance of consensus and adversarial politics

→ The nature of the term 'party system' and other party systems that exist within the UK

→ Factors that affect the success or failure of parties at election

Principles of political parties

Features of parties

We should start by offering a definition of a political party, at least in a modern democratic society. Here is a working definition:

> A political party is an organisation of people with similar political values and views which develops a set of goals and policies that it seeks to convert into political action by obtaining government office, or a share in government, or by influencing the government currently in power. It may pursue its goals by mobilising public opinion in its favour, selecting candidates for office, competing at elections and identifying suitable leaders.

Although we might argue about this definition, or add to it, it is a good enough summary that describes most organisations which we consider to be parties.

This definition also helps us to identify the features of political parties in the UK. These include the following:

- The members of parties share similar political values and views.
- Parties seek either to secure the election of their candidates as representatives or to form the government at various levels (local, regional, national).
- They have some kind of organisation that develops policy, recruits candidates and identifies leaders.

This is not a long list as the nature of political parties can vary in different parts of the democratic world. Typical variations in the features of parties include these:

- Some are mass membership parties with many adherents (UK Labour Party); others may have a small leadership group who seek supporters rather than members (the main US parties).
- Some parties may be highly organised with a formal permanent organisation (German Christian Democrats), while others have a loose, less permanent organisation (US parties that only organise fully during elections).

Activity

Research the organisation of the UK Conservative and Labour parties. Outline the main features of their structure and identify the main differences.

- Some parties may have a very narrow range of values and views, and are intensely united around those views (left-wing socialist parties); others have a very broad range of views and values, and so may be divided into factions (UK Conservative Party).
- Some parties are very focused on gaining power (main parties in the UK and the USA), while others recognise they will not gain power but seek merely to influence the political system (Green parties).

Functions of parties

Making policy

Perhaps the most recognisable function of a political party is the development of **policies** and political programmes. This is a role that becomes especially important when a party is in opposition and is seeking to replace the government of the day. Opposition parties are, therefore, in a fundamentally different position to the party in power. When a ruling party controls the government, its leadership *is* the government; there is virtually no distinction between the two. Therefore, the policy-making function of the ruling party *is the same as* the policy-making function of the government. It involves not only political leaders but also civil servants, advisory units and committees, and private advisers. Of course, the rest of the party — backbench MPs and peers, local activists and ordinary members — have some say through policy conferences and committees, but their role remains very much in the background. Most policy in the *ruling* party is made by ministers and their advisers.

In opposition, the leadership of a party is not in such a pre-eminent policy-making position. True, the leadership group will have most influence, the leader especially, but it is when in opposition that the general membership of the party can have most input into policy making. Through various conferences and party committees, the membership can communicate to the leadership which ideas and demands they would like to see as 'official' policy and therefore likely to become government policy one day. This kind of influence occurs at local, regional and national level.

The policy-formulating function is also sometimes known as **aggregation**. This involves identifying the wide range of demands made on the political system, from the party membership, from the mass of individuals in society as well as many different groups, and then converting these into programmes of action that are consistent and compatible. Aggregation tends to be undertaken by the party leadership group as these are the people who may one day become ministers and will have to put the policies of the party into practical government.

Representation

Parties claim to have a representative function. Many parties have, in the past, claimed to represent a *specific* section of society. For example, the UK Labour Party was developed in the early twentieth century particularly to represent the working classes and especially trade union members. The Conservative Party of the nineteenth century largely existed to protect the interests of the landed gentry and aristocracy. This has, however, changed in the contemporary UK because all the main parties argue that they represent the *national* interest and not just the interests of specific classes or groups. So, when we suggest that parties have a representative function, we mean today that they seek to ensure that all groups in society have their interests and demands at least considered by government. Of course, in reality, we understand that parties will tend to be biased towards the interests of one section of society or another.

Key terms

Policy A set of intentions or a political programme developed by parties or by governments. Policies reflect the political stance of parties and governments.

Aggregation A process, undertaken by political parties, of converting policies, demands and ideas into practical policy programmes for government. This involves eliminating contradictions and making some compromises.

Synoptic link

These functions of political parties should be studied in conjunction with Chapter 3 on electoral systems, as political parties are a key element in the electoral process.

Protesters at an anti-racism rally in London

One new phenomenon that has emerged, and which needs to be taken into account as far as representation is concerned, is the emergence of **populist** parties. Populist parties tend to emerge rapidly (and often disappear equally quickly). Typically they represent people who feel they have been ignored by conventional parties, in other words that they are *not* represented *at all*. The appeal of populist parties is usually emotional or visceral and plays on people's fears and dissatisfactions. They generally take root among the poor who feel they are left behind. These parties may be **left wing** and so propose socialist ideas, or **right wing** in which case they propose policies which are normally anti big government, anti taxation, anti big business. Right-wing populist parties tend to take a strong position on law and order and are socially conservative. A more detailed explanation of left- and right-wing ideas can be found on pages 49–51.

Table 2.1 shows some prominent populist parties that have emerged in various countries.

Table 2.1 Modern examples of populist parties

Country	Party	General political stance
UK	UKIP	Right wing
USA	Tea Party (part of the Republican movement)	Right wing
Greece	Syriza	Left wing
Greece	Golden Dawn	Right wing
Spain	Podemos	Left wing
Austria	Freedom Party	Right wing
France	National Front	Right wing

We are also seeing the rise of 'issue parties' that represent a particular cause. Green parties are the best example, but increasingly we are also seeing new parties dedicated to advancing women's rights in parts of Europe. Having said this, most contemporary parties in modern democracies still lay claim to representing the national interest.

Key terms

Populism A political movement, often represented by a political party, that appeals to people's emotions and which tends to find supporters among sections of the community who feel they have not been represented by conventional politics and politicians.

Left wing A general description of policies that conform to 'socialist' principles. Typical left-wing ideas include the redistribution of income from rich to poor through both taxation and welfare, public ownership and state control of key enterprises, the elimination of privilege and its replacement by equal rights and the promotion of equality of opportunity.

Right wing Policies often associated with conservatism. Typically they may include the promotion of individualism in contrast to left-wing ideas of collectivism, the withdrawal of the state from economic and social control, low personal and company taxation, a strong, authoritarian position on law and order and a stress on patriotism and nationalism.

Selecting candidates

Parties spend a great deal of their time and effort selecting candidates for office at all levels. They need to find prospective local councillors, elected mayors in those localities where such a position exists (notably London and other major cities), members of the devolved assemblies and the Scottish Parliament, candidates for the European Parliament (soon to be removed) and, most prominently of all, for the UK Parliament. This is mostly done at local and regional level, through party committees staffed by activists. The national party leaderships do have some say in which candidates should be chosen, but it is in this role that local constituency parties have the greatest part to play.

Identifying leaders

Parties need leaders and, in the case of the main parties, this means potential government ministers. They therefore have procedures for identifying political leaders. It is in this area that the established party leaders play a key role. For the ruling party, the prime minister completely controls the appointment of ministers. In opposition parties, the leader will choose a smaller group of 'frontbench' spokespersons who form the leadership. But despite the dominance of party leaders in this field, potential leaders cut their teeth to some extent in internal party organisations and committees. The formal organisations of parties give opportunities for members to become 'trained' as leaders.

The issue of political leadership was thrown into focus within the Labour Party in 2015–16. Following the party's 2015 election defeat, the former leader, Ed Miliband, resigned. This left behind a power vacuum. In finding a successor, the party ran into a huge controversy. The party membership voted overwhelmingly to elect Jeremy Corbyn. However, Corbyn's political views were far to the left of most of the Labour MPs and peers. He was the party leader, but the Labour MPs in Parliament refused to acknowledge him as *their* leader.

In contrast, the Conservative Party, which had lost its leader, David Cameron, in 2016 after his defeat in the EU referendum, had no such problems finding a successor. Theresa May was overwhelmingly the favourite among Conservative MPs and it became clear that most ordinary members of the party (who have the power to elect their leader) agreed with the MPs, so much so that all her opponents withdrew from the leadership contest.

So, finding leaders may not be as easy for parties as it might appear. One truth, though, is clear — a united party has an easier task in recruiting leaders than a divided party. Both the main UK parties discovered this after 2015–16.

Activity

Research the leadership elections of Labour in 2015 and 2016 and the Conservative leadership election of 2016. Answer these questions:

- Why did the leadership elections take place?
- What were the processes involved?
- What were the main controversies surrounding the elections in the Labour Party?
- Were there any controversies concerning Theresa May's election?

Knowledge check

Who are the current leaders of these UK parties?

- The Scottish National Party
- UKIP
- The Green Party
- The Democratic Unionist Party (Northern Ireland)

In addition:

- What is unique about the Green Party leadership and how does the party justify this?
- How many *female* UK party leaders can you identify?

Organising elections

At election time parties play a critical role. Apart from supplying approved candidates, the party organisations form part of the process of publicising election issues, persuading people to vote and informing them about the candidates. Without the huge efforts of thousands of party activists at election time, the already modest turnout at the polls would be even lower. Representatives of the parties are also present when the counting of votes takes place, so they play a part in ensuring that elections are fair and honest.

Political education

It is not only at election time that parties have an educative function. They are also continuously involved in the process of informing the people about the political issues of the day, explaining the main areas of conflict and outlining their own solutions to the problems that they have identified. Part of this process involves educating the public about how the political system itself operates.

This function is becoming less important. To some extent the media have taken over in supplying information to the public, but the growth of the internet and social media has also marginalised the parties. Pressure groups, too, have played an increasing role in informing the public. Even so, parties do present the electorate with clear choices in a coherent way.

Reinforcing consent

Finally, parties also have a 'hidden' function, but a vital one nonetheless. This can be described as 'the mobilisation and reinforcement of consent'. All the main parties support the political system of the UK — that is, parliamentary democracy. By operating and supporting this system, parties are part of the process that ensures that the general population consents to the system. If parties were to challenge the nature of the political system in any fundamental way, this would create political conflict within society at large. Parties that challenge the basis of the political system — those of the far left and right wing of politics — are generally seen as extremists and only marginal elements in the system.

Mandate and manifesto

The doctrine of the mandate

The doctrine of the **mandate** is a major feature of the UK political system. It is central to the relationship between the electorate, parties and government. The term 'mandate' can be described as consent, in that a mandate implies the consent of one person, allowing another to do what they feel is necessary for their welfare. In politics, therefore, a mandate represents the consent of the people, allowing a political party to do what it feels is necessary in the national interest if it succeeds in being elected to government.

The doctrine of the political mandate operates thus: when a party wins an election and forms the government of the UK or of one of the devolved administrations in Scotland, Wales and Northern Ireland (see Chapter 3 for detailed information on such devolved elections), it has a mandate to carry out all the policy commitments contained in its election manifesto.

It follows from this that the existence of **party manifestos** is vital to the operation of the mandate. The significance of the mandate doctrine is as follows:

- Electors can feel confident that they understand which policies they are consenting to when they cast their vote. This does, of course, assume that they have read and understood the party manifesto. If they have not, they are giving their consent in

Study tip

When answering questions on parties, be sure not to confuse *features* with *functions*. Features are the main characteristics of parties, while functions concern their roles and objectives.

Key terms

Mandate A term referring to the consent granted to a political party at election time by the electorate. The mandate gives legitimacy to all the winning party's manifesto commitments.

Party manifesto A collection of beliefs, aspirations, commitments and promises presented to the electorate by parties at election time. The manifesto forms the basis of the winning party's electoral mandate and allows parliaments or regional assemblies and the public to hold government to account.

ignorance. Even so, the doctrine does assume that electors have full knowledge of the manifestos and so can make a rational judgement.

- The mandate strengthens government, in that the winning party gains legitimacy for its policies. In 2017 the Conservatives sought an electoral mandate for its Brexit negotiation stance.
- The mandate means that Parliament (or devolved assemblies) can call government to account on the basis of the governing party's manifesto. If a government strays from its electoral mandate, Parliament and assemblies can feel justified in challenging the government.
- The mandate also gives electors the opportunity to judge the performance of government when election time comes round. They can ask the question, 'How successful was the government in delivering its mandate?'
- All the MPs from the winning party who are elected are 'bound in' by the mandate, as most voters vote for a party manifesto rather than an individual. Party leaders can therefore maintain discipline among members by emphasising to them that they were all elected on the same mandate.

The doctrine of the mandate does have some problems. Among them are these:

- It depends upon a single party winning an election outright. When there is a coalition, as occurred in the UK election of 2010 and has happened in Wales and Northern Ireland, two or more parties are involved and the actual content of the mandate is unclear as one party's manifesto no longer applies. Similarly, if no party wins an overall majority — as occurred in June 2017 — and a minority government is formed, the government cannot legitimately claim a mandate.
- It is clear that voters who have opted for one party do not necessarily agree with *all* its manifesto commitments. However, the mandate doctrine does assume the electorate has given its consent to the *whole* manifesto.
- Circumstances may change after a party takes power. This means they will have to amend their policies or abandon some or develop new policies. A governing party does not have a mandate for such changes.
- Some manifesto commitments may be rather vague and open to interpretation. This makes calling the government to account on the basis of its manifesto difficult and open to dispute.

Party manifestos

Since 1945 manifestos have become increasingly specific and detailed. They still contain the broad beliefs of the party, but there are also many very particular intentions. In 2017 the Labour Party manifesto, for example, was extremely specific. Its commitments included the following:

- People earning over £123,000 per annum should pay 50% income tax, while those earning above £80,000 should pay 45%
- Tuition fees for university students to be abolished and maintenance grants restored
- The total amount that elderly people pay for social care to be capped
- £100 billion to be invested in infrastructure projects such as railways, roads, housing, schools and hospitals
- Old age pension increases to be protected
- 2% of Gross National Income to be paid in overseas aid
- Arms sales to Saudi Arabia to be ended
- Build 300,000 homes a year for 5 years

Activity

Look at these examples of Labour manifesto commitments in 2017. Which policies can be said to:

- be economic in nature?
- concern welfare provision?
- affect education?
- concern foreign policy?

The development of such precise manifestos has improved the accountability of government and has gone some way towards improving the public's knowledge of political issues.

Right-wing and left-wing politics

The terms 'left' and 'right' should be treated with some caution, although they are commonly used in everyday political discussion to describe an individual's or a group's political stance. They are not very precise expressions.

It is because they are so vague that we need to be careful using these terms. In fact, it is usually best to avoid them altogether for the sake of clarity. It should also be noted that left and right descriptions of politics will vary considerably from one country to another. Nevertheless, we can construct a scheme that gives a reasonable picture of the left–right divide in the context of UK politics. Many issues do not fall easily into a left–right spectrum, but we can usefully consider economic issues and social issues to illustrate the distinctions. These are shown in Table 2.2 and Table 2.3.

Table 2.2 The left–right divide in UK politics: the economy and related issues

Left	Centre-left	Centre	Centre-right	Right
State economic planning and nationalisation of all major industries State to regulate large industries which exploit consumers or workers Relaxed approach to government borrowing, so much state investment in infrastructure	Elements from both centre and left	Largely free-market economy with some state regulation Pragmatic approach to government borrowing to stimulate economic growth	Elements from both centre and right	Strong support for totally free markets No state intervention in the economy
Redistribution of income to create more economic equality Strong trade unions, and protected rights for workers Protectionism for domestic industries Anti EU	Elements from both centre and left	Pro free trade Mild redistribution of income, with some poverty relief Pro EU and in favour of the so-called 'soft Brexit' option	Elements from both centre and right	Very low levels of taxation Avoidance of excessive government borrowing to stimulate growth Protectionism for domestic industries Free labour markets, with weak protection for workers Anti EU and in favour of the so-called 'hard Brexit' option

Table 2.3 The left–right divide in UK politics: social issues

Left	Centre-left	Centre	Centre-right	Right
Strong support for the welfare state Stress on equal rights and protection for minority groups Tolerance for alternative lifestyles such as same-sex marriage, surrogate motherhood Liberal attitude to crime and its remedies	Elements from both centre and left	Welfare state to concentrate on the most needy Support for multiculturalism Mixed attitudes to crime — typically a liberal attitude to minor crime but a hard line on serious crime The state should promote individualism	Elements from both centre and right	A more limited welfare state, with caps on the total amount of benefits available to families and tougher criteria for the claiming of benefits Anti immigration — support for strict controls Opposed to multiculturalism A traditional attitude to moral and lifestyle issues Stress on patriotism and national interest

We can now ask the question: how does this kind of analysis apply to UK parties in 2017? The general picture looks like this.

Conservatives

Theresa May, when she took over as prime minister in July 2016, sought to pull the Conservative Party back towards the centre of the political spectrum. Despite having a personal reputation as a right-winger, she declared that both economic and social policies would be directed towards the less well off. However, there is a large right-wing faction within the Conservative Party. These are members who look back to the policies of the party under Margaret Thatcher in the 1980s. This faction would severely reduce the scope of the welfare state, and insist that the state should not interfere in the workings of free markets. In the 2017 general election May stressed the concept of stability rather than reform, a right-wing tendency.

Labour

In 2016 the Labour Party was split. There were three main factions. The left, led by Jeremy Corbyn, came to prominence following his election as leader in 2015. Most MPs and peers, however, were in the centre (often described as 'Blairites' as their views are close to those of former prime minister Tony Blair, 1997–2007) or the centre-left. Corbyn's unsuccessful 2016 challenger for the leadership, Owen Smith, declared himself centre-left. In the 2017 general election, the party manifesto (see page 48) was based very much on left-wing ideas.

Liberal Democrats

The party is difficult to characterise, especially after its near destruction in the 2015 general election. However, what is left of the party straddles the centre ground. There are centre-left, centrist and centre-right members. The party does unite around issues concerning rights and multiculturalism, but is divided when it comes to economic policies. In 2017 the party concentrated on the idea that the UK should remain a part of the European single market, a centrist belief.

Tim Farron, the centrist Liberal Democrat leader 2015–17

Other parties

Smaller parties in the UK do not always fit neatly into the left–right spectrum. Many of them have one overriding policy issue which tends to mask the others. Nevertheless, as these smaller parties have gained ground in the twenty-first century they have tended to develop wider policy positions. Table 2.4 demonstrates where small parties stand in the spectrum, as well as showing what their main policy preoccupation is.

Study tip

When discussing party policies always remember to include policy differences *within* parties and not just *between* parties.

Table 2.4 Where smaller UK parties stand in the left–right spectrum

Party	Main policy position	Left–right position
UK Independence Party (UKIP)	Bringing the UK out of the EU and anti immigration	Right
Scottish National Party	Independence for Scotland	Centre-left
Green Party	Environmental issues	Left
Plaid Cymru	More autonomy for Wales	Centre-left
Democratic Unionist Party (Northern Ireland)	Retaining strong links with the UK	Centre-right
Sinn Fein	Re-uniting Ireland	Centre-left

The funding of UK political parties

How parties are funded

The position on party funding is a complex one. This is because UK parties have multiple sources of finance. The main ways in which parties are funded is as follows:

- Collecting membership subscriptions from members
- Holding fundraising events such as fetes, festivals, conferences and dinners
- Receiving donations from supporters
- Raising loans from wealthy individuals or banks
- The self-financing of candidates for office
- Up to £2 million per party available in grants from the Electoral Commission (see below for detail).

It is immediately apparent that the larger parties have better access to funds than their smaller counterparts. While the Conservative Party attracts large donations from wealthy individuals and business companies (other parties do too, but on a much smaller scale), Labour receives generous contributions from trade unions. These amounted to about £11 million in 2014–15, nearly 60% of the party's total income. This figure may well fall in years to come, however, as the rules for union donations are changing, essentially making it easier for individual union members to opt out of contributing to the party.

Smaller parties, by contrast, have no such regular sources of income. Add to this the fact that they have small memberships and we can see their disadvantage. It is understandable that donors are less likely to give money to parties whose prospects of ever being in power are remote. Those donors who do give to small parties are essentially acting out of idealism rather than any prospects of gaining influence.

Activity

Look up the websites of several parties. Compare the membership subscriptions charged by each party.

The funding of parties was regulated in 2000 by the **Political Parties, Elections and Referendums Act**. Among other regulations, this made the following stipulations:

- People not on the UK electoral roll could no longer make donations (thus reducing foreign influence).
- Limits were placed on how much could be spent on parliamentary elections.
- Donations over £500 have to be declared.
- Donations over £7,500 were to be placed on an electoral register.

Thus regulation stressed transparency rather than any serious limits on the amounts being donated. State funding was rejected as a solution at that time, and election spending controls were extremely generous.

Why party funding is controversial

Before looking at the issues surrounding party funding, we should consider how much parties actually receive. Figure 2.1 shows the income of significant UK parties.

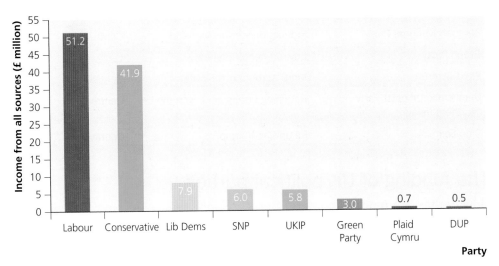

Source: Electoral Commission

Figure 2.1 Income of parties reported in December 2015

These figures illustrate immediately the first issue. This is the fact that funding is hugely biased towards the two biggest parties. When we consider that smaller parties are also disadvantaged by the UK electoral system at general elections, this funding shortfall represents a double problem. However, the question of party funding has a number of issues which are even more serious. The controversies include the following:

- As we have seen, the major parties are put at a huge advantage and, conversely, small parties are put at a great disadvantage, especially when it comes to fighting elections. Current party funding therefore promotes political inequality.
- Funding by large donors represents a hidden and unaccountable form of political influence. Parties are not allowed to change specific policies or propose legislation as a direct result of donations, but donors must expect some kind of political return for their investment. This might be true of trade unions and the Labour Party and business interests and the Conservatives.
- Aspects of funding may well verge on being corrupt. It is suspected that some donors may expect to receive an honour from party leaders such as a peerage or knighthood in return for their generosity. This is sometimes known as 'cash for honours'. It cannot be proved that it exists, but suspicions are strong.
- The steady decline of party memberships has meant that parties are even more reliant upon donors, which further opens up the possibility of corruption and the purchasing of political influence.

Key term

Cash for honours A phrase used by the media to describe the suspicion that some donations to parties are made in the hope and expectation that the giver will receive an honour such as a peerage or knighthood. The practice is considered to be unlawful but is difficult to prove.

The Electoral Commission, which monitors the income of political parties in the UK, has reported examples of large donations to parties. Some of the interesting examples are these:

- Between 2015 and 2017 the Conservative Party received £11.3 million from prominent figures and companies in the financial sector.
- In the same period the Conservatives received £3.6 million from property companies.
- One individual — hedge fund proprietor Angus Fraser — donated £1,137,400 to the Conservative Party during this period.
- The Unite trade union gave £657,702 to the Labour Party early in 2017.
- At the same time UNISON, the public service union, donated £376,242 to Labour.

So, such individual donations are not only seen as undemocratic forms of influence, but often carry some other kind of controversy. Similarly, trade union donations to Labour have been criticised on the grounds that members of unions are not given a clear enough choice as to whether their subscriptions should be spent in that way. It is also said that Labour is unduly influenced by union leaders because so much of their income comes from them.

Alternative funding structures and restrictions

Most commentators and many politicians agree that the way in which parties are funded in the UK is undemocratic and that it is in need of reform. The problem, however, is that there is no agreement about what to do. There are four basic types of solution:

1 Impose restrictions on the size of individual donations to parties. This is broadly the system used in the USA (though donors can grant funds to thousands of individual candidates). To be effective, the cap would have to be relatively low.

2 Impose tight restrictions on how much parties are allowed to spend. This would make large-scale fundraising futile.

3 Restrict donations to individuals, i.e. outlaw donations from businesses, pressure groups and trade unions.

4 Replace all funding with state grants for parties, paid for out of general taxation.

As we have seen, there already is some state funding of parties in the UK. All main parties receive funds from the Electoral Commission. These are called Policy Development Grants and can be used to hire advisers on policy. Over £2 million is available for this purpose. In addition there is **Short money**, which is distributed to all opposition parties to fund their parliamentary work.

Short money is heavily biased towards large parties because it depends upon how many seats parties have won at previous elections. Thus, since 2015 the Labour Party receives £6.7 million in Short money per annum, while the next biggest grant goes to the SNP with £1.2 million. Interestingly, UKIP refused over half a million pounds in Short money after winning one seat in 2015. The party suggested it was

Key term

Short money Named after Ted Short, the politician who introduced it, Short money refers to funds given to opposition parties to facilitate their parliamentary work (research facilities etc.). The amount is based on how many seats and votes each party won at the previous election.

corrupt and designed to favour established parties. Funds are also available to parties in the House of Lords. This is known as 'Cranborne money'. So, state funding of parties already exists. The real question, though, is whether state funding should *replace* private donations altogether.

Much of the debate about party funding relates to state financing. However, although several political parties favour this, there is little public appetite for it. Taxpayers are naturally reluctant to see their taxes being used to finance parties at a time when attitudes to parties are at a low ebb. However, state funding remains the only solution that could create more equality in the system. As long as funding is determined by 'market forces', it is likely that the large parties will be placed at a significant advantage.

The other popular policy idea is to eliminate the abuses in the system. This involves full transparency, limits on how much business and union donors can give and a breaking of any link between donations and the granting of honours.

Should the state fund political parties?

The idea of somehow replacing private donations with state funding of parties has a good deal of support within the political community of the UK. Certainly both the Labour and Liberal Democrat parties have flirted with the idea without actually making firm proposals. The problem has been a lack of political will and a fear that public opinion will not accept it. The main arguments on both sides of this debate are set out below.

Debate

Should UK parties receive state funding?

Arguments for

- It will end the opportunities for the corrupt use of donations.
- It will end the possibilities of 'hidden' forms of influence through funding.
- It will reduce the huge financial advantage that large parties enjoy and give smaller parties the opportunity to make progress.
- It will improve democracy by ensuring wider participation from groups that have no ready source of funds.

Arguments against

- Taxpayers may object to funding what can be considered to be 'private' organisations.
- It will be difficult to know how to distribute funding. Should it be on the basis of past performance (in which case large parties will retain their advantage) or on the basis of future aspirations (which is vague)?
- Parties may lose some of their independence and will see themselves as organs of the state.
- State funding may lead to excessive state regulation of parties.

Activity

Find two countries that have state funding of parties. On what basis is funding granted in the two countries?

It seems unlikely that state funding will arrive in the UK in the near future. Far more likely is the idea that individual donations should be limited. Greater transparency has largely been achieved, but the problem of 'cash for honours' or the suspicion that large organisations can gain a political advantage through donations persists. Action may well centre on a 'deal' between Labour and the Conservatives. Labour might sacrifice some of its trade union funding in return for caps on business donations. The Liberal Democrats, with their unwavering support for state funding, will have to remain on the sidelines for the time being.

Established political parties

The origins and development of the Conservative Party

Conservatism in the UK has its origins in the conflict that raged during the seventeenth century over the role and authority of the monarchy. Those who supported royal authority (as opposed to Parliament) were known as royalists, but eventually came to be known as 'Tories'. During the seventeenth century, it became clear that the supporters of Parliament and democracy in general (mostly known as 'Whigs') were gaining the upper hand over royalists. However, a new conflict began to emerge as the Industrial Revolution gathered pace in the middle of the nineteenth century.

With industrialisation and the growth of international markets, the capitalist middle classes began to grow in size and influence. Their rise challenged the traditional authority of the aristocracy and the landed gentry, the owners of the great estates whose income was based on rents and the products of agriculture. The middle classes were represented largely by the Whigs and the landed gentry by the Tories, who were beginning to be described as 'conservatives'. They were described as conservatives because they resisted the new political structures that were growing up and wished to 'conserve' the dominant position of the upper classes whom they represented.

As the nineteenth century progressed, conservatism began to develop into something closer to the movement we can recognise today. Sir Robert Peel (prime minister 1834–35 and 1841–46) is generally acknowledged as the first Conservative Party prime minister. He and Benjamin Disraeli (prime minister 1868 and 1874–80) formed the party, basing it on traditional conservative ideas. The party's main objectives were to prevent the country falling too far into inequality, to preserve the unity of the kingdom and to preserve order in society. It was a pragmatic party, which adopted any policies it believed would benefit the whole nation.

The political background to the Conservative Party is best understood by considering two traditions. The first is often known as 'traditional conservatism' and it dates from the origins of the party in the nineteenth century. It is also sometimes described as **'one-nation conservatism'**. The other tradition emerged in the 1980s. It is usually given one of two names — 'New Right conservatism', or 'Thatcherism', after its main protagonist, Margaret Thatcher (prime minister 1979–90).

Traditional conservatism (one nationism)

Originating in the late part of the eighteenth century, traditional conservatism emerged as a reaction against the newly emerging liberal ideas that were the inspiration behind the revolutions in North America (1776) and France (1789). Conservative thinkers such as Edmund Burke (1729–97) became alarmed at the rise of ideas such as freedom of the individual, tolerance of different political and religious beliefs, representative government and a laissez-faire attitude towards economic activity (that is, the state avoiding significant interference in the way in which wealth is distributed in society). Conservatives believed that such a free society, with so little control by government, would lead to major social disorder.

Thereafter conservatives have consistently opposed the rise of any new ideology, so, later in the nineteenth century, the rise of socialism was opposed. This anti-socialist

Key term

One-nation conservatism
A term often used to describe the collection of traditional values held by many conservatives. It refers to the idea that conservative policies should promote social cohesion and reduce social conflict between the classes. The term was notably used by the nineteenth-century prime minister Benjamin Disraeli.

Study tip

It is important to distinguish between conservatism as a political tradition and the Conservative Party. While most members of the Conservative Party subscribe to one or other of the traditions, they may also support important variations from them. The Conservative Party is the movement that has always sought to gain power to promote these values. The best way to distinguish between the two is to put a capital letter in front of members of the party (**C**onservatives), but to use a lower case 'c' for people who simply tend to support conservative ideas (**c**onservatives).

position remained in place until the 1970s when it reached its height under Margaret Thatcher.

But conservatism is not merely a reaction to any dominant ideology, and it is not simply a political philosophy opposed to change. There are some enduring principles, which are described below.

Human nature

Conservatives have tended to adopt a rather pessimistic view of human nature. While liberals see humans as naturally sympathetic to each other, caring of each other's needs and freedom, and while socialists see humankind as naturally sociable and cooperative, conservatives stress the competitive nature of people. They also see humankind as liable to fall into disorder, that we can be easily led to follow false ideas. Despite this, conservatives believe we crave order and security. In fact, they argue, we prefer such security to individual freedom. Far from seeing humankind as naturally sociable, they also see us as individuals who wish to pursue our own individual goals.

Order

Sometimes known as the 'father' of conservatism, Edmund Burke, an MP and political commentator living at the end of the eighteenth century, said: 'Good order is the foundation of all good things.' He was writing in response to the new liberal ideas coming out of France and America at the time. He suggested that the new ideas of liberty, equality and democracy were creating a disordered society and that this flew in the face of humankind's most basic desire for order and security. However 'right' such ideas might be, they were to be opposed because they disturbed society so seriously. Since Burke, conservatives have always been suspicious of new ideas that threaten the existing order.

Tradition and preservation

The conservative preference for the preservation of tradition is related closely to a desire for public order. When we refer to tradition in this context we mean both traditional *institutions*, such as monarchy, established Church (of England) and political constitutions, and *values*, such as the preservation of marriage, the importance of the nuclear family, religion and established morality.

The greatest crime of the French revolutionaries, said Burke, was to abandon traditional forms of authority that, according to him anyway, had stood the test of time. This is summarised in his ringing criticism: 'No generation should ever be so rash as to consider itself superior to its predecessors.'

The very fact that values and institutions have survived, argue conservatives in general, is a testament to their quality. Furthermore, they carry the 'accumulated wisdom of the past' and should therefore be respected. In a similar way, traditions bring to an existing society some of the best aspects of past societies. How people thought and behaved in the past can inform current generations. Thus, the nineteenth-century poet and philosopher G. K. Chesterton called tradition the 'democracy of the dead', allowing the wisdom of previous generations to be involved in the activities of current society.

Burke also praised traditions for their ability to provide continuity between the past and the present, claiming that they give a sense of security and help to prevent violent transformations in society. In his great work, *Reflections on the Revolution in France* (1790), he referred to 'a partnership between those who are living, those who are dead and those who are to be born'.

The early conservative, Edmund Burke, criticised the excesses of the French Revolution

It is these ideas that have led conservatives to support such institutions as the monarchy, the Church of England, the Union of Britain and the great traditions of the political system in general. It also leads to a belief in the enduring quality of what are known as 'British values' — such as tolerance, respect for individual liberty, love of democracy and equality.

One nation and the organic society

Benjamin Disraeli (prime minister 1868 and 1874–80) developed the idea of 'one nationism' during his political campaigning. At that time there was general concern that, as a result of the Industrial Revolution and the growth of capitalism, a great divide was emerging between the middle classes, who were becoming increasingly prosperous, and the working class, who were falling further behind. These 'two nations', as Disraeli put it, would inevitably come into conflict unless steps were taken to bring them together. In other words, conservatives should support policies that would reduce such conflict and oppose measures that would create too much inequality. So, one-nation conservatives are those who oppose excessive inequality.

Associated with the idea of 'one nation' is the concept of the organic society. This idea suggests that society is not just made up of individuals fending for themselves, but is organic, meaning that people are tied together by a common sense of being members of an interdependent society. This implies that those who are well off and own substantial property do have a responsibility to care for the interests of the poorer sections of society. Furthermore, the theory of the organic society leads to a belief that politics should not seek to change society *artificially* (as socialists and liberals believe), but should allow it to develop naturally.

Pragmatism

It would be wrong to suggest that conservatism is a doctrine of 'no change' or that it treats its own principles as eternal and fixed. Conservatives are, above all, pragmatists. Michael Oakeshott (1901–90), a leading conservative philosopher of modern times, particularly advocated this kind of political action. He asserted that politics should be 'a conversation, not an argument' (*On History and Other Essays*, 1983). What he meant was that political action should never be the result of conflict over political dogma and theory. Instead it should be the result of a more gentle relationship between government and the governed. The good conservative politician should engage in a relationship with the people that would allow them to reach decisions based on the 'intimations and traditions' of the community.

Pragmatism implies a flexible approach to politics, incorporating an understanding of what is best for people, what is acceptable to them and what will preserve a stable society. It is also a rejection of the politics of strongly held ideology, a dogmatic approach to decision making. Perhaps the most striking example of this approach has occurred since the financial and economic crisis of 2008. Though most conservatives wanted to see reductions in taxation, they have pragmatically remained determined to resist this idea in the interests of reducing the government's budget deficit.

Property

In the distant past conservatives were seen as the defenders of the property-owning classes, at a time when most people owned no property at all. With widespread property ownership in the modern era, however, it is a less significant conservative trait.

In the modern context, conservatives have always attempted to defend the interests of home owners and of the owners of land and businesses. For them the right to own and enjoy one's own property in security is a fundamental aspect of a civilised existence. Furthermore, property owners are seen to have a greater vested interest in order and so will ensure that there is stability in society. Property ownership for conservatives is a fundamental aspect of individualism and is a desirable aspiration to be shared by all.

Opposition to ideology

We have seen above that traditional conservatives are pragmatists. They see government as an exercise in maintaining continuity, order and security, and avoiding disorder. Government should not, they argue, seek to change society in radical ways. Socialists and liberals may have fixed views of how to change society, but conservatives reject this kind of ideological outlook. They also see ideological politicians as liable to become dictators. Leaders who try to impose their political views on society are by nature undemocratic, they argue.

New Right conservatism (Thatcherism)

The term '**New Right**' was used to describe a group of political values and ideas, largely emerging in the USA in the 1970s and 1980s, which were adopted by many conservatives throughout the developed world. It was a reaction both against the socialist ideas gaining some ground in Europe, Asia and South America, and against traditional conservative values that were seen as too weak to deal with contemporary economic and social policies. It was associated in the USA with Ronald Reagan (president 1983–91) and in the UK with Margaret Thatcher (prime minister 1979–90). Two of the main thinkers behind the movement were Friedrich Hayek (Austrian, 1899–92) and Irving Kristol (American, 1920–2009).

The movement can be divided into two different aspects. These are neo-liberalism and neo-conservatism. Most, but not all, conservatives of the New Right subscribed to both sets of ideas, though often they leant towards one more than the other.

Activity

Research the following conservative thinkers and politicians. In each case outline their main contributions to the conservative movement:

- Sir Robert Peel
- Benjamin Disraeli
- Michael Oakeshott

Key term

New Right A term used for a conservative movement that arose in the 1980s which combined an authoritarian form of neo-conservatism with an economically liberal form of neo-liberalism.

Neo-liberalism

Neo-liberalism is associated with the economic and social philosophers Friedrich Hayek (Austrian, 1899–1992) and Milton Friedman (American, 1912–2006). The main beliefs of neo-liberalism are these:

- Interference in the economy by the state is almost always counterproductive, causing inflation and a lack of dynamism. The state should therefore 'disengage' from economic management. In particular, the state should not run any major industries.
- It follows, therefore, that free markets — for goods, finance and labour — are virtually always seen to be more effective in creating wealth than economies with too much external interference. Markets should not be regulated by the state.
- Powerful trade unions also interfere excessively with labour markets, driving up wages artificially, reducing corporate profits and so dampening economic activity and investment.
- Excessive welfare benefits reduce the dynamism of the economy. They encourage people to remain unemployed and are a disincentive to work. This is called '**dependency culture**'.
- High taxation is a disincentive to economic activity. Taxes should therefore be kept low as an incentive to hard work and wealth creation by businesses because individuals and firms will keep more of their income as a reward for enterprise.

In practical terms, neo-liberals propose reducing direct taxes, privatising industries that have been taken over by the state, such as transport and energy, reducing welfare benefits so that they are only a 'safety net' for those who have no means of supporting themselves, such as those with disabilities, and curbing the powers of trade unions. In addition they propose allowing the economy to find its own natural level, even during recessions, rather than the state actively trying to control economic activity.

Neo-conservatism

Ironically, while neo-liberalism proposes the *withdrawal* of the state from economic activity, neo-conservatism proposes a strong state, albeit a small one, yet both are considered part of the same New Right movement. There is a link between them in that neo-liberalism proposes a very free society and this opens up the possibility of disorder. Neo-conservatives, therefore, seek to maintain authority and discipline in society. The main beliefs of neo-conservatism include these:

- A loose attitude to morality and lifestyles can lead to a breakdown in social order. The movement is, therefore, socially conservative, believing in the retention and restoration of traditional values.
- Law and order are crucial to maintaining security and promoting individualism. The state should therefore be authoritarian in nature.
- Neo-conservatives are normally nationalistic. They see patriotism and support for the united nation as important means by which social order can be maintained.
- Internationally, neo-conservatives are suspicious of multinational associations such as the EU. They also believe that foreign policy should represent the pursuit of the nation's own interests above all else.

We can see that neo-conservatism has much in common with traditional conservatism in that it promotes traditional 'national' values and sees order as a key value to be maintained by the state. However, while most conservatives accept that different

Key terms

Neo-liberalism
A movement from the 1970s and 1980s which proposes that the state should not interfere excessively in economic management, which promotes free markets, and opposes trade union power, high taxes and excessive welfare benefits for those who are able to work.

Dependency culture
A belief that, if welfare benefits are too generous in a society, people become used to depending on such benefits, which then become a disincentive to work. The culture, many claim, is passed down from one generation to the next.

Study tip

Be careful not to assume that neo-liberalism is a branch of liberalism in general. It is not. Though it may seem contradictory, neo-liberalism is a conservative philosophy as it has mostly been supported by conservatives and looks back to a bygone age before the twentieth century, when markets were kept largely free.

Activity

Research the following people and outline what part they played in the development of the New Right:

- Sir Keith Joseph
- Ayn Rand
- Roger Scruton

lifestyles should be tolerated, neo-conservatives seek to impose a single national culture on society.

Conservative ideas and policies today

The economy

When the Conservative Party returned to power in 2010, it was faced with an economic crisis, the main aspect of which was a huge and growing budget deficit. Successive governments had been spending considerably more than their taxation receipts. The national debt was huge. In March 2010 it stood at £1.13 trillion (in March 2015 it stood at approximately £1.6 trillion). This led to the party adopting a highly responsible approach to economic management. Above all, its economic policy was dominated by the aim of eliminating budget deficits (i.e. having a balanced budget) and reducing the national debt. The belief is that only a balanced budget can promote economic growth.

Under Theresa May, after 2016, the goal of a balanced budget was abandoned as a medium-term goal. It was seen as unattainable and was inhibiting economic growth. However, party policy remains pragmatic and cautious about economic policy. Public expenditure, the party stresses, must be kept under careful control. Irresponsible spending is counterproductive in the long term.

The party retains a neo-liberal position in its attitude to markets. Government policy should always promote free markets and free trade. To this end it is determined to curb the power of trade unions to keep labour markets free.

Its attitude to taxation is partly neo-liberal and partly social democratic (see pages 65–67 for a definition of social democracy). On the one hand, personal and company taxation should never be excessively high as this will inhibit enterprise and wealth creation — a neo-liberal view. The party seeks to reduce corporate taxation as much as is feasible. On the other hand, the party has accepted that taxation on lower incomes is too high — an aim of social democracy. It therefore seeks to take many more people out of taxation altogether. The burden of tax has been shifted towards middle-income groups.

Law and order

The party retains the view that prison and stern punishments are the best deterrent against crime. It therefore believes that sentencing policy should be in the hands of elected government and not unelected judges. The party is opposed to 'liberal' ideas about crime and punishment, and opposes such proposals as the legalisation of drugs and the excessive use of 'community' sentences where offenders do not go to prison but make amends in their community.

Conservatives stress the need for security and see it as the first duty of government to protect its citizens. In the fight against terrorism, therefore, they accept that civil liberties (privacy, freedom of movement and expression) may have to be sacrificed in the interests of security.

Welfare

Modern Conservative policy concentrates on the need to ensure that welfare benefits are no longer a disincentive to work. The government is therefore introducing a stricter system of means testing to prevent making unemployment a preferable option. Two other policies seek to restore the balance between work and benefits.

One is the introduction of a generous 'living wage' (or minimum wage) as a greater reward for work at lower levels of pay. The second is an overall cap on total welfare benefits for families, so that unemployment is less attractive.

Party policy is committed to maintaining the welfare state and safeguarding the NHS and the education system. However, the party believes that these two services should be subject to competition and market forces, and that private-sector enterprises should become involved in the provision of services. This, it believes, can increase efficiency so that services can improve without increasing expenditure on them.

Foreign policy

Conservatives support NATO and the close alliance with the USA. However, they also believe that the UK's best national interests lie in retaining an independent foreign policy. If it is in the UK's interest, they believe that the country should intervene in foreign conflicts. The party is committed to retaining the UK's independent nuclear deterrent in the form of Trident submarine-based weapons. After considerable internal conflict, the party has decided to retain the UK's generous contributions to international aid.

Social justice

The Conservative Party has come late to the cause of social justice. However, just as Disraeli came to believe 150 years ago, the party has come to understand that too much inequality breeds social conflict. It has, therefore, sought to reduce excessive inequality by introducing the idea of a living wage and by reducing income tax for those on low incomes, but it has resisted imposing excessively high rates of tax on the wealthy.

The environment

Perhaps surprisingly, the Conservative Party has very much led the way towards more effective emissions control. It is also committed to promoting renewable energy sources, though it prefers nuclear to wind.

The constitution

The Conservative Party lives up to its name when it comes to constitutional change. Conservatives are reluctant to reform the constitution and have effectively blocked reform of both the House of Lords and the electoral system. The party is also strongly unionist in that it opposes policies that might promote independence movements in the nation's regions.

Conservative Party factions

The Conservative Party is possibly more internally divided than any of the other major parties. It has a number of different **factions**, or groupings which hold significantly different ideas than the main body of the party. This is partly because, as we have seen, the party is the product of two different conservative traditions and partly because conservatism has always been a broad organisation which welcomes people with a wide variety of opinions. The ideologies of the party are not especially strong, so it can accommodate many views on the centre and right of UK politics. Here we describe three factions to illustrate the divisions, though there are several other groups.

Theresa May sought to move the Conservative Party to the centre of the political spectrum

Key term

Party faction A faction refers to a distinct group within a political party whose views vary significantly from the main party policies. Often factions are to the left or right of the party's position. Some factions have a formal membership and organisation, while others are loose and represent little more than a policy tendency.

Cornerstone

Cornerstone is a formal group whose motto is 'Faith, Flag and Family'. The motto gives a strong clue to its members' beliefs. The faction wishes to restore very traditional values to the conservative movement. It supports the idea of the UK being a Christian country, it is intensely nationalist in its outlook and it wishes to retain 'family values'. Family values imply a reactionary attitude to social reforms such as gay marriage and legal abortion. Leading members include Edward Leigh and Jacob Rees-Mogg.

Conservative Way Forward

Despite its name, Conservative Way Forward looks back to the age of Margaret Thatcher. It is a largely neo-liberal movement. Members believe the legacy of Thatcher has been diluted. They support the retention of free markets and support free enterprise through low taxation and deregulation of industry. Like other neo-liberals the group is strongly opposed to trade union power and to excessive welfare provision. Leading members include Gerald Howarth and Liam Fox.

Tory Reform Group

This is a group which stands in the centre of politics and is often seen as 'left-leaning'. The faction promotes social cohesion and therefore opposes policies that might divide the nation. Members are sometimes described as 'one-nation Tories'. In particular, they believe that too much economic equality is divisive and so they support policies to reduce inequality in society. They are also concerned to establish and retain equal rights. Former chancellor Kenneth Clarke is a key member.

Under Theresa May none of these factions dominates the party. The Conservatives have traditionally been able to accommodate several groupings under one political roof. Representatives of all of them can be found within the party leadership.

Activity

Research the three Conservative factions listed here. In each case identify as many past or present ministers who are members as you can.

Discussion point

To what extent do current Conservative Party policies conform to the two main conservative traditions — one nationism and New Right? Consider the following issues in relation to each:

- The role of the state in economic management
- The role of the state in regulating finance and industry
- Taxation
- Welfare benefits
- The NHS
- Education
- Foreign policy
- Law and order

The origins and development of the Labour Party

Until the twentieth century the working classes (many of whom did not gain the right to vote until 1884) were largely represented by a collection of MPs and peers from both the Liberal and Conservative parties. When trade unions became legalised towards the end of the nineteenth century, however, the working class at last had organisations which could represent their interests. It was therefore logical that the unions should begin to put up candidates for election to the UK Parliament. But the unions were not a political party and did not seek power. A new party was needed. In fact two parties of the left emerged.

Creation of the Labour Party

The main Labour Party was created in 1900 and was very much an offshoot of the trade union movement. It was funded by the unions and many of its members were union leaders and members. Before that, in 1893, a socialist party had already been founded, known as the Independent Labour Party (ILP). In 1906 the ILP formed an agreement with the new Labour Party. They agreed not to put up parliamentary candidates against each other in the same constituencies. However, this agreement was short lived and the two parties began to go their separate ways.

The ILP was a genuinely socialist party, committed to the overthrow of capitalism and its replacement by a workers' state, albeit by peaceful, democratic means. The Labour Party, by contrast, was a more moderate socialist party which did not propose a workers' state but simply wished to improve the conditions of the working class and to control the excesses of capitalism. The state, as envisaged by Labour, would seek to reconcile the conflicting interests of the working class with those of their employers. Both parties still contained extreme socialists, some of them Marxists (who are perhaps better described as communists), but the distinction was essentially that the ILP was purely socialist while Labour was a more moderate form of socialist party, generally known for **democratic socialism**.

Many of the characteristics of the development of the Labour Party can still be seen today. The party continues to be financed largely by trade unions, and union leaders play a major role in the party organisation. Although the ILP no longer exists, its traditions can still be found among a persistent group of left-wingers who form a faction within the party. Many of this faction were responsible for the election of Jeremy Corbyn, a prominent left-winger, as party leader in 2015. Some of them still promote the ideas that formed the basis of the ideology of the old ILP.

Labour since the Second World War

Labour first came to full power after its crushing victory in the 1945 general election. From then on Labour became the UK's second major party and regularly competed with the Conservative Party for power. However, in the 1980s the party suffered two huge defeats at the hands of Margaret Thatcher's Conservative Party. This ultimately resulted in a split in the party. Some left to form a new party — the Social Democratic Party (SDP); some, led by Michael Foot and Tony Benn, wished to return to Old Labour values and move even further to the left; others, led by Neil Kinnock and John Smith, however, saw the future of the party lying in more moderate policies, towards the centre of politics. This branch of the party became known as 'New Labour', and its policies were characterised as 'third way'. After John Smith's sudden death in 1992, Tony Blair became leader, closely supported by Gordon Brown, Robin Cook and Peter Mandelson. Blair led the party to three election victories in 1997, 2001 and 2005.

Core values and ideas of the Labour Party

As we have seen, Labour's story can be divided into two parts. The first, the Old Labour period, runs from the early days until the 1990s. The second, the 'New Labour' period, runs from the early 1990s until the present, when the party may well be splitting once again.

'Old' Labour

Critics loosely describe the traditions of the Labour Party as 'socialism'. This is an illusion. Labour was never a socialist party. It did not propose a workers' state and has never attempted to abolish capitalism. As mentioned above, it is better thought of as a democratic socialist party. The best way to understand the Old Labour tradition is to look at its general values and then at its actual policies.

> ## Key term
>
> **Democratic socialism**
> A moderate form of socialism that proposes to achieve its aims by democratic means. Its main objectives are to mix state control over production with market capitalism, so that the interests of the working class are advanced within a combination of state-run welfare and major industries, and smaller-scale free enterprise.

Old Labour values

- The key value is *equality*. Unlike Marxists, who pursue complete equality in living standards, Labour used to support redistribution of income to reduce the worst inequalities. A better characterisation of equality for Labour is 'social justice'. Labour has also always supported formal equality, i.e. equal treatment under the law.
- Old Labour supporters tend to see society in terms of *class conflict*, arguing that the interests of the two great classes — working and middle class — cannot be reconciled, so governments must favour the interests of the disadvantaged working class.
- Recognising that total equality was not feasible, Labour championed *equality of opportunity*, the idea that all should have equal life chances no matter what their family background.
- *Collectivism* is a general idea shared by socialists of all kinds. It is the concept that many of our goals are best achieved collectively rather than individually. It includes such practical applications as the welfare state, trade unionism and the cooperative movement.
- While radical left-wing socialists support *common ownership* in general, Old Labour saw common ownership mainly in terms of public ownership of major, strategic industries, run by the state on behalf of the people.
- *Trade unionism* is a key value. Old Labour recognised that workers were weak compared to employers. Support for powerful trade unions was, therefore, vital in restoring the balance of power between employers and workers.
- Old Labour believed that the central state could play a key role in controlling economic activity and in securing social goals. This may be described as *statism*. By placing such responsibilities in the hands of the central state it ensured equality of treatment for all.
- Finally, *welfarism* is important. This is the idea, associated with collectivism, that every member of society should be protected by a welfare system to which all should contribute.

Old Labour policies and actions

Old Labour had two main periods of power during which it could convert some of its values into practical reforms. These were 1945–51 and 1964–79. In those periods, at various times, Labour converted values into political action in the following main ways:

- The welfare state, including the National Health Service (NHS), was created in the 1940s.
- Trade unions were granted wide powers to take industrial action in the interests of their members.
- Major industries were brought into public ownership (nationalisation) and state control in the interests of the community and the workers in those industries. Among the industries were coal, steel, shipbuilding, rail and energy.
- Taxes on those with higher incomes were raised in order to pay for welfare and to redistribute income to the poor.
- Comprehensive education was introduced in the 1960s to improve equality of opportunity.
- Discrimination against women and ethnic minorities was outlawed in the 1960s and 1970s. Equal pay for women was introduced.

'New' Labour

Tony Blair and his cohort of leaders, supported by the economic philosopher Anthony Giddens, creator of the '**third way**', developed a new set of moderate policies, often described as 'social democracy'.

> **Study tip**
>
> Be careful not to call Labour a 'socialist' party. It is more accurate to describe Old Labour as 'democratic socialism' and New Labour as 'social democracy'.

> **Key term**
>
> **Third way** A new political philosophy, developed by Anthony Giddens and Peter Mandelson, which proposed policies which lay somewhere between leftist socialism and rightist neo-liberalism.

New Labour values

New Labour was opposed to the ideas of the 'hard left' in Labour and sought instead to find a middle way (the 'third way') between socialism and the free-market, neo-liberal ideas of the Conservative Party under Margaret Thatcher. Its main values were as follows:

- New Labour thinkers rejected the socialist idea of *class conflict*, arguing that all members of society have an equal right to be supported by the state.
- The party accepted that *capitalism* was the best way of creating wealth, so it should remain largely free of state control.
- Nevertheless it was recognised that capitalism could operate against the interests of consumers, so it should be regulated, though not controlled. The state should be an *enabling state*. Allowing the economy to create wealth and giving it support were needed, but the state should not, on the whole, engage in production itself.
- New Labour de-emphasised collectivism, recognising that people prefer to achieve their goals individually. *Individualism* was seen as a fundamental aspect of human nature.
- *Equality of opportunity* was stressed. Education and welfare would create opportunities for people to better themselves.
- *Communitarianism* is the concept that, although people are individuals with individual goals, we are also part of an organic community and have obligations and duties in return for our individual life chances. This is a weaker form of collectivism.
- The party recognised that the UK was deeply undemocratic and that rights were inadequately protected. It therefore was committed to *political and constitutional reform*.

Key term

New Labour A term applied to the Labour Party under Tony Blair, which moved towards a more centrist position in politics after the mid-1990s.

New Labour policies and actions

New Labour was known as much for what it did *not* do as for what it *did* do. Despite calls from trade unions to have their powers, largely removed in the 1980s, restored, Labour governments refused. Similarly, pressure to bring privatised industries back under state control was resisted. Blair and Brown also resisted the temptation to restore high taxes on the wealthy and on successful businesses to pay for higher welfare, preferring to use public borrowing to facilitate their policies. At first, when the UK experienced an economic boom in the late 1990s and early 2000s, the extra spending could be sustained, but when the economy slowed down after 2007 the debts mounted up.

New Labour's political programme included the following policies:

- Huge increases in expenditure on the NHS
- Similarly large investment in education, especially early years education
- Reductions in corporate taxation to encourage enterprise

Tony Blair and Gordon Brown, two of the architects of New Labour

Activity

Which of the two main Labour Party tendencies, shown in Table 2.5, is in the ascendancy at the time you are reading this? Identify key pieces of evidence for your conclusion.

- An extensive programme of constitutional reform including the Human Rights Act, devolution, freedom of information and electoral reform in devolved administrations
- Through the tax and welfare system, various policies to reduce poverty, especially child and pensioner poverty
- Encouraging employment by introducing 'welfare to work' systems

Labour ideas and policies today

Labour policy is still evolving following the dramatic split in the party in 2015–16. It is therefore advisable to view party policy from the point of view of the two wings of the party — the left and the centre-left. Table 2.5 explains the main tendencies in a number of key policy areas.

Table 2.5 Current Labour policies

Policy area	Centre-left tendency	Left tendency
Economic management	A pragmatic view including targets to reduce public-sector debt	Expansionist: high public expenditure should be used to promote investment, improve public services and create jobs
Social justice	Some adjustments to taxation to promote mild redistribution of income from high to low-income groups	Radical tax reforms to promote significant redistribution of income from rich to poor
Industry	Industry to remain in private hands and be regulated by the state	Large infrastructure industries to be brought into public ownership (nationalised) Strong regulation of private-sector industries and finance
Welfare	Supports a strong welfare state and well-funded health service and education However, welfare benefits to be capped to ensure work pays and prevent abuse of the system	Strong support for the NHS and state education Abolition of university tuition fees More generous welfare benefits to help redistribute real income
Law and order	A mixture of authoritarian measures and 'social' remedies to crime	Emphasis on social remedies to crime
Foreign policy	Retention of a UK independent nuclear deterrent Strong support for NATO and the alliance with the USA	Largely 'isolationist', favouring non-intervention in world conflicts Abolition of the independent nuclear deterrent
Environment	Strong support for environmental protection and emissions control	The same as the centre-left
Constitutional reform	Some reforms are supported, including an elected second chamber and a proportional electoral system	More radical reforms, possibly including abolition of the second chamber altogether and more independence for local government

Labour Party factions

The far left and Momentum

In 2015, Labour suffered a traumatic defeat in the general election. Supported by a large influx of new, mainly young members of the Labour Party, Jeremy Corbyn, the most prominent left-winger in the party in the House of Commons, won the leadership election that was precipitated by the resignation of former leader, Ed Miliband. Along with his close colleague, John McDonnell, Corbyn sought to shift the party sharply to a left-wing, more 'socialist' position.

The movement formed to support and sustain Corbyn's leadership is known as 'Momentum'. Momentum contains members who range from being 'Old Labour' democratic socialists, to Marxist-inspired socialists. They campaign for such policies as:

- large shifts in the distribution of wealth and income through tax reforms
- the public ownership of many major industries
- firm state regulation of the finance industry
- large increases in the creation of subsidised public-sector housing and control of private rents
- a significant increase in the living (minimum) wage
- abandonment of the UK's independent nuclear deterrent

'Blairism' and social democracy

The so-called 'Blairites' in the Labour Party can be described as social democrats (as opposed to the more left-wing democratic socialists). They believe that the policies of 'New Labour', as described above, were popular and successful and should be retained. Their position can, therefore, also be described as 'centrist'. Among the prominent members of this faction are Stephen Kinnock, Hilary Benn and Yvette Cooper. They oppose the party's shift to the left after 2015 and have fought against the leadership of Jeremy Corbyn.

Blue Labour

Blue Labour was founded by an important Labour Party policy adviser, Maurice Glasman. Glasman and his supporters believe that the UK working class do not, on the whole, favour left-wing policies but prefer many ideas associated with conservatism (hence the adjective 'blue'). The loss of former Labour votes to UKIP in the 2015 general election was, claimed Glasman, proof of his theory.

This tendency is socially conservative, believing in traditional British values, is anti large-scale immigration, campaigned for the UK to leave the EU, but also opposes the excesses of big business. It supports free markets but proposes protection for UK industry from foreign competition in order to protect 'British jobs for British workers'. It exists in the Labour Party because it strongly supports the interests of the working class.

The origins and development of the Liberal Democratic Party

The Liberal Democratic Party is the product of an amalgamation of two parties in 1988. These were the Social Democratic Party (SDP), which had split off from the Labour Party and contained a group of moderate social democrats who felt that Labour had moved too far to the left, and the Liberal Party, which was a century old at that time.

- The Liberal Party had formerly existed since 1877. It emerged as a coalition between Whigs and radicals. Its first leaders were Lord Palmerston and William

To what extent do current Labour Party policies conform to 'Old Labour' and 'New Labour'? In your discussion consider both left and centre-left tendencies in the party. Pay special attention to these topics:

- The role of the state in economic management
- The role of the state in public ownership of industry and finance
- Taxation and the redistribution of income
- Welfare benefits
- The NHS
- Education
- Foreign policy
- Equality of opportunity

Nick Clegg and David Cameron in the rose garden of 10 Downing Street following the coalition agreement of May 2010

Gladstone. The party was as important as the Conservatives until the 1920s, when it began to decline. By the end of the Second World War it had been eclipsed by the Labour Party. Until the 1990s it then played a very minor part in UK politics and returned only a handful of MPs to the UK Parliament. Despite its period in the political wilderness, the Liberal Party was always the home of radical political ideas, many of which were ultimately adopted by the two main parties.

- In 1981, the SDP was formed. It soon began talks with the Liberal Party. The problem for the two parties was that they were competing for the same voters. At the 1983 general election the Liberals and SDP made an electoral pact whereby they would not put up candidates against each other. The pact was known as the Alliance. However, the plan failed and the two parties won fewer than 30 seats between them at that election and again in 1987. The decision was taken, therefore, to merge completely and the Liberal Democratic Party was born in 1988.

The Liberal Democrats reached the height of their electoral success in 2005 when the party won 62 seats. It was in 2010, however, that the real opportunity came. With no party winning an overall majority, the Liberal Democrats had a choice of whether to join with Labour or the Conservatives in a coalition. In a fateful decision, their leader, Nick Clegg, chose the Conservatives and they found themselves in government for the next 5 years. But what might have proved to be a resounding breakthrough turned into a disaster. The electorate decided to punish the Liberal Democrats for broken promises (mainly over a commitment not to raise university tuition fees, a commitment they dropped straight away) as well as for the poor performance of the UK economy. As a result the party won only eight seats at the 2015 election. Nick Clegg resigned as leader and was replaced by Tim Farron, but it was now clear that the Liberal Democrats were once again a minor party as they had been for 60 years between the 1930s and the 1990s. Even the 2017 general election brought only a modest revival.

Key terms

Classical liberalism A way of describing nineteenth-century liberalism that proposed a limited state that would be confined to protecting the freedom of individuals and maintaining the security of the state.

Modern Liberals This term is used to describe liberals who came to prominence after classical liberalism began to decline at the end of the nineteenth century. Modern Liberals would tolerate an expanded role for the state into the areas of social justice, welfare and equality of opportunity.

Knowledge check

Look at the detailed regional results of the 2015 general election. The Liberal Democrats lost all their 15 seats in one region. What was that region?

Core values of liberalism

The Liberal Democrats are not just a liberal party. As their title suggests they also espouse social democratic values and ideas. Their values come, therefore, from a mixture of the two traditions. The social democratic values are largely those described above in the section on New Labour. Here we look at the liberal side of their position. The main liberal values adopted by the party include the following:

- *Liberty* is the core liberal value. Of course, complete freedom is not feasible in a modern society, so liberals confine themselves to believing that the state should interfere as little as possible in people's private lives. Privacy, freedom and individual rights must, they insist, be protected. The stress on liberty was a feature of nineteenth-century fundamentalist liberalism, often described as **classical liberalism**. In the latter part of the nineteenth century and the twentieth century, liberals expanded their ideas outside the protection of liberty and began to accept a wider role for the state in promoting welfare and social justice. These were known as New or **Modern Liberals**.

- Liberals also pursue *social justice*. This means three things. First it means the removal of unjustifiable inequalities in incomes in society, second it means equality of opportunity and third it means the removal of all artificial privileges to which people might be born.
- *Welfare* is now a key liberal value. The liberal view is that people cannot be genuinely free if they are enslaved by poverty, unemployment or sickness, or the deprivation of old age. State welfare, therefore, sets people free.
- Liberals are highly suspicious of the power of government. They therefore believe that the power of government should be firmly controlled. The main way in which this can be achieved is by limiting the power of government via a strong constitution. This is known as *constitutionalism*.
- Liberal Democrats are *social reformers*. They strongly support the rights of women, the disabled, ethnic minorities and the LGBT community. They have also been strong supporters of gay marriage.
- The party has always been concerned with the cause of *human rights* and *democracy*, so it has supported constitutional reform. This aspiration is often described as **liberal democracy**.
- *Multiculturalism* is a key theme among liberal values. Different cultures and lifestyles should be tolerated and granted special rights. This links to the liberals' *pluralist* outlook on society.
- A modern value concerns the *environment*. Liberals believe that human life will be enriched by a healthy physical environment and by biodiversity.

It should be stressed that many of these so-called liberal values are also held by many members of other political parties, notable those on the centre-left. Indeed, many of them have become core British values. What distinguishes liberalism from other political traditions is that liberals place these values higher than all others. For example, the rights and liberties of individuals are so precious that they should only be sacrificed in exceptional circumstances.

Liberal Democrat ideas and policies today

The party is still trying to recover from its poor performances in the general elections of 2015 and 2017 and the resignation of its leader Tim Farron after the second election.

The economy

Liberal Democrat economic policy is not especially distinctive. However, it does propose the rebalancing of the UK economy so that wealth and economic activity are spread more widely round the country. On the whole, Liberal Democrats are pragmatic about economic management. For example, government budget planning should not operate in such a way as to favour one section of society over another. Thus, in times of economic recession, the poor in society should be protected and the wealthy should bear the brunt of tighter economic policies. Taxation should always be fair, based on ability to pay, and should redistribute real income from rich to poor.

Law and order

Two principles characterise Liberal Democrat policy:

- Wherever possible, the law enforcement system, including prisons, should seek to rehabilitate offenders as much as punishing them. Liberal Democrats believe that most crime has social causes and these causes should be attacked.

Key term

Liberal democracy
Liberal democracy is both a description of some political systems and a political movement. In politics it implies a democracy in which rights and equality are guaranteed and promoted. As a movement it describes a party or political stance that stresses the importance of democracy and rights. There is a belief among its adherents that other 'good things' will flow from the political system if it is genuinely democratic and respects rights.

- The system of law and order must not become so over-authoritarian that human rights are threatened. There must be a balance between civil liberties and the need for peace and security.

The European Union

The Liberal Democrats would have preferred the UK to stay inside the EU. However, as the UK is leaving it campaigns for a second referendum on the negotiated terms of the UK's exit. The party insists that the UK should remain in the European single market and should allow free movement of people and labour.

Welfare

Education and health are Liberal Democrat priorities. Spending on both should be protected and increased whenever the quality of services is threatened. The benefits system should be designed to encourage work and should be fair, favouring those who cannot support themselves. Poorer pensioners and single parents should be especially supported.

Foreign policy

Though Liberal Democrats support NATO and its aims, they are suspicious of excessive interference by the UK in conflicts abroad. They would abandon the renewal of the Trident nuclear submarine missile system. They strongly support the use of international aid. Wherever possible, international conflicts should be settled through the United Nations (UN) rather than through direct military intervention.

Constitutional reform

In particular Liberal Democrats wish to introduce an elected second chamber to replace the House of Lords, and to see reform of the electoral system for general elections to some form of proportional representation. They also propose the creation of a codified constitution and support further devolution of power to Scotland, Wales and Northern Ireland. Some Liberal Democrats go further in proposing a full federal system for the UK along American lines.

Environmentalism

The party supports strict harmful emissions reduction targets, the conversion of the UK's energy industry to clean renewables as soon as possible, and various other measures to improve the environment.

Along with the Green Party, Liberal Democrats support a stress on renewable energy generation such as wind farms

Social justice

This is a key policy. It mainly consists of proposals to reduce taxation on low-income families and raise taxes on wealthy individuals and businesses. It also implies a welfare system that rewards work and takes children out of poverty.

Liberal Democrat factions
Orange Book liberals

In 2004 *The Orange Book* was published by leading members of the Liberal Democratic Party. Among other proposals, the book suggested that members of the party should reconnect with their liberal roots, even going back to some nineteenth-century values. In particular it suggested that the party should join neo-liberals in supporting the restoration of free markets and the withdrawal of the state from excessive interference. The ideas expressed also urged the party to promote policies that enhance individual liberties. Mark Oaten and Chris Huhne were principal members of this faction, though neither established a significant foothold in the party.

Social liberals

Many of the **social liberals** were formerly members of the Labour Party. Vince Cable, business secretary in the coalition government, is a key example. This group stresses policies concerning social justice, proposing the redistribution of income from rich to poor through taxation and welfare. To some extent the social democrat wing of the party is at odds with the Orange Book group as social justice implies greater state activity to promote social change.

Discussion point

In respect to their current policies, to what extent are the three main UK parties — Labour, Conservative and Liberal Democrat — inspired by the ideas of liberalism? In your discussion pay special attention to these issues:

- The protection of human rights
- Constitutional reform
- Social justice
- Welfare
- Formal equality
- Equality of opportunity
- Law and order
- Foreign policy

Emerging and minor political parties

The growth of other parties in the UK

Up until the mid-1990s the UK political system was dominated by two parties — Labour and the Conservatives. It was a **two-party system**. There was no prospect of any other party gaining a hold on power. The electoral system of first-past-the-post (FPTP) underpinned this dominance. It was difficult for a third party to break through because the electoral system discriminated against parties with dispersed support.

The Scottish National Party (SNP)

As the fortunes of the UK's traditional third party, the Liberal Democrats, have declined, those of the Scottish National Party have blossomed. The SNP won enough seats in the 2007 Scottish parliamentary election to form a government. The party has formed the government of Scotland ever since. At Westminster, by contrast, it made little headway in this period. Then, in 2015, the SNP won 56 of the 59 Westminster seats

Key terms

Social liberals A name often used for liberals, especially members of the Liberal Democratic Party, who share many of the centrist social democratic values of the Labour Party. Vince Cable (business secretary, 2010–15) is a key example; he lost his parliamentary seat in 2015.

Two-party system
A political system in which two parties invariably dominate at elections and in government. Smaller parties consistently fail to make any impact in such a system.

on offer in Scotland. It was an extraordinary result. Scottish voters were disillusioned with the main British parties, while many were interested in greater autonomy or even independence for Scotland. They believed the SNP could deliver this. When the party lost 21 of its Scottish seats in the 2017 general election, however, the issue of independence was placed much lower in their list of priorities.

The UK Independence Party (UKIP)

The UK Independence Party (UKIP) also made a breakthrough in the 2015 general election. The party had already made progress in local elections and elections to the European Parliament, but this was the first time it had made a major effort in a general election. However, the outcome of its success was rather different to that of the SNP. UKIP won 12.6% of the popular vote. However, because its support was so dispersed, this was converted into only one parliamentary seat. Thus UKIP made an impact and took many votes away from the other main parties, but it remains on the fringes of the political system. In the 2017 general election the party's vote slumped, it lost its only parliamentary seat and its leader, Paul Nuttall, resigned. The party seemed to be on the verge of extinction.

The Green Party

The Green Party had a similar experience to UKIP, though on a smaller scale. The Greens' share of the vote rose from 1% in 2010 to 3.8% in 2015. The party won just one seat, in Brighton, where Caroline Lucas, co-leader of the party, remains popular.

Caroline Lucas MP at a march in Westminster in support of refugees, September 2016

Key term

Party system A party system describes how many parties flourish within a political system and have influence. Party systems in the UK have varied from two-party to three-party to multi-party systems at different times, in different circumstances and in different regions.

So the UK has moved from being very definitely a two-party system to being a multi-party system. It is still dominated by two parties, but several other parties are now making an impact, in terms either of parliamentary seats, or of votes or of policy making. It is especially true that in the national regions voters are offered a greater choice of party. In Scotland, for example, five parties have significance and offer a realistic choice. These are the SNP, Labour, Conservative, Liberal Democrat and Green. In Wales four parties compete for significant influence, while in Northern Ireland the electoral system guarantees that at least five parties will have a share in government.

Synoptic links

There is a fuller discussion of **party systems** in Chapter 3.

Policies of other parties

The SNP

The Scottish National Party is a centre-left party. Its main policies are as follows:

- The overall objective is complete independence as a sovereign state within the European Union.
- For as long as Scotland remains within the UK, the party supports constitutional reforms such as an elected second chamber, the introduction of proportional representation for general elections and votes for 16-year-olds.
- The party is social democratic and supports social justice. When Scotland has control over its own direct taxes it intends to redistribute real income from rich to poor. The party also supports the idea of the living wage.
- The party is opposed to the UK retaining independent nuclear weapons and favours the cancellation of Trident.
- The SNP has abolished university tuition fees paid by students. It sees education at all levels as a key component of equality of opportunity. It has reintroduced the Educational Maintenance Allowance (EMA) for students above the age of 16. This has been abolished in England.
- Environmental protection is a key policy. SNP policies are almost as strong as those of the Green Party.
- The party supports the welfare state and would protect generous state provision of health, education and social security benefits.

Activity

Research the performance of the following parties in elections to local government, the European Parliament and the Scottish Parliament since 2000:

- SNP
- UKIP
- Green Party

UKIP

UKIP is a party of the right. Once its main objective — to bring the UK out of the European Union — had been achieved, the party had to reinvent itself. It has been doing so by presenting itself as a populist party, positioned to the right of the Conservative Party. Its policies are still being developed but in 2017 its main policy positions included the following:

- The UK should achieve the best possible trade terms with the EU without accepting the principle of the free movement of people and labour.
- Immigration into the UK should be strictly regulated. Only immigrants with specific skills needed in the country should be allowed in.
- The party is opposed to the excesses of big business and finance and would introduce strong measures to reduce tax evasion and avoidance.
- The party is economically (though not socially) **libertarian**. This is an extreme form of neo-liberalism. It believes that government should interfere as little as possible with economic activity, save to regulate the activities of big businesses which operate against the interests of consumers.
- On social issues the party is conservative and disapproves of the tolerance of lifestyles which are not traditional.
- The party is opposed to the giving of international aid.
- It is protectionist and would ensure that British industries are not subject to unfair competition from abroad, so as to protect jobs for British workers.
- UKIP is strongly unionist and opposes the granting of additional powers to governments in Scotland, Wales and Northern Ireland.

Key term

Libertarianism An extreme form of neo-liberalism. Libertarians propose that the government should interfere as little as possible with economic and social activity. They also support the maximisation of personal liberty.

Activity

Research the following parties and outline three of their main policies:

- Plaid Cymru
- The Democratic Unionist Party (Northern Ireland)
- Sinn Fein (Northern Ireland)

The Green Party

The Green Party obviously has environmental concerns at the centre of its policies. In other areas it has a left-wing stance. Among its radical policies are the following:

- Large numbers of new homes should be financed or built by government to solve the housing crisis.
- There should be massive new investment in public transport.
- University tuition fees for students should be abolished.
- The party proposes an extensive programme of constitutional reform to make the UK more genuinely democratic.
- It proposes a wealth tax on the top 1% of the income ladder, a living wage of £10 per hour and a special tax on large banks making excessive profits.
- The party is opposed to the maintenance of Trident.

Impact of other parties on the policies of the major parties

There can be no doubt that the improvement in the fortunes of smaller parties has impacted on the main parties. Although there is little prospect of one of the emerging parties winning enough seats to share in government power, they are taking votes away from the large parties. In 2015, the rise of UKIP caused Labour to lose the election as millions of its supporters in the north of England defected. The rise of the SNP eclipsed the main parties in Scotland in 2015. Labour, the Conservatives and the Liberal Democrats won only one seat each.

Table 2.6 The political stance of small parties in the UK

Party	Principal policy	General political stance
Scottish National Party	Scottish independence	Centre-left
UKIP	UK to leave the EU	Right
Green Party	Environmental protection	Left
Plaid Cymru	More self-government for Wales	Centre-left
Democratic Unionist Party	Close links between Northern Ireland and the UK	Right
Sinn Fein	Reunification of Ireland	Centre-left

But it was on policy that the impact of smaller parties is most felt. Faced with the prospect of losing votes to small parties, the larger parties have had to modify their proposals in a number of ways. Here are some examples of the impact on policy:

- The rise of the SNP has forced all the main parties to support further devolution to Scotland. To some extent this was a response to the relatively close result in the Scottish independence referendum in 2014, but the shock of the main parties in losing virtually all their Scottish seats was the tipping point.
- UKIP was a key factor in all the parties offering the prospect of a referendum on UK membership of the EU. The party also forced the Conservative Party to announce extravagant targets for the reduction of immigration.
- The slow rise of the Green Party has been a factor in all the main parties adopting more radical policies on environmental protection, notably emissions control.

Study tip

Note that the impact of small parties is not just felt in terms of parliamentary seats won, but in terms of how many votes they may take away from more established parties. This forces those parties to react by modifying their policies to stop their support leaking away.

Knowledge check

From what you have read and researched, which UK party do you think is (a) the most left wing and (b) the most right wing?

Consensus and adversary politics

The terms 'consensus' and 'adversary' politics refer to those periods in UK political history in which there has either been a great deal of general agreement (consensus) over policies among the main parties, or considerable conflict over basic principles and ideologies. Here we can identify two periods in recent UK political history when consensus politics was dominant, and one period when politics was extremely adversarial.

Consensus politics

With consensus politics there are no fundamental, ideological differences between the parties. They may disagree on the details of policy, but there is a general agreement over the goals of policy.

1950s to 1970s

In the 1940s the Labour government under Clement Attlee had undertaken a major programme of reform in the UK. The welfare state was created, including the creation of the NHS. Major industries such as coal, rail and steel were nationalised, a comprehensive system of old-age pensions was initiated, the provision of subsidised housing was expanded and a wide range of new local authority services was introduced. This presented a problem for the Conservative Party when it came to power in 1951 and remained there until 1964 under four prime ministers.

The Conservatives had to decide whether to reverse these developments, especially as they had opposed them when they were being introduced. The measures were popular and no one wanted to return to the days of economic depression that had existed before the Second World War. The issue was further complicated when, in 1955, the Labour Party elected a new leader, Hugh Gaitskell, who was much more moderate than his predecessors. The Conservative leadership therefore decided that it should accept the Labour reforms and build on them. This heralded in a period of consensus which was to last until the 1970s.

There were still to be party conflicts, for example over economic management and social reform, but there was consensus that the new world created after the war should remain. The two main parties also agreed that the days of British imperial power were numbered and there should be an ordered dismantling of the empire. It was often described as 'Butskellism', after the Labour leader Gaitskell and the Conservative chancellor of the exchequer, R.A. Butler, whose political stances were very similar.

1997–2015

This period was more fragile than the earlier consensus era. It is often described as the post-Thatcher **consensus**. Tony Blair and his leadership group became so dominant after 1997 that the Conservative and Liberal Democrat parties had to accept that the core values of 'New Labour' were extremely popular. There was, therefore, general political agreement over key political issues. Among these issues were:

- the maintenance of a strong, well-funded welfare state
- constitutional reforms to make the UK more democratic and less centralised
- improved protection for human rights and social equality among different groups
- the reduction of poverty, especially among families with children and pensioners

> ### Key term
>
> **Consensus** This refers to a situation where two or more significant parties in a political system agree on fundamental ideas and aims. Consensus can also mean 'general agreement'. When there is a consensus, parties only disagree on details of policy and how to implement their aims.

- public investment in services and infrastructure to promote economic growth and so generate public funds for such measures
- a stress on improved education to promote equality of opportunity
- the general promotion of individualism by encouraging home ownership and keeping personal taxes as low as possible

Not all these aims were fully realised but all three main parties shared similar aspirations for the UK. The consensus, at least remnants of it, persisted through the coalition government from 2010 to 2015. Indeed, Prime Minister David Cameron, a Conservative, admitted that Tony Blair, a Labour Party leader, was a role model for him. Theresa May, on coming to power in 2016, declared her own personal manifesto which echoed that of New Labour back in 1997, so perhaps the post-Thatcher consensus is still alive and well. The Labour left wing and Conservative right wing have very different ideologies, but there is still a large group of politicians in all parties who stand around the centre of politics and who hold similar, consensual views.

Adversary politics

In contrast to consensus, adversary politics exists when there are deep divisions between (and sometimes within) the parties. The UK is a generally highly stable political system and has been for generations. This means that adversary politics is rare.

1979–90

In modern times there has been just one significant period of adversary politics in the UK. This occurred in the 1980s. The Conservative Party, under Margaret Thatcher's premiership, moved to a position known as 'New Right' politics (see pages 58–60). Meanwhile the Labour Party, under the leadership of Michael Foot, moved to the left. Political conflict became deep and intense. The two parties had very different visions of which direction the UK should be moving in.

Table 2.7 shows the some of the main areas of contention in that period. We can see from Table 2.7 how fundamental these conflicts were. If the current Labour Party continues to move to the left, as it is threatening to do, we might be witnessing the beginning of a new era of adversary politics.

Table 2.7 Adversary politics during the 1980s

'New Right' Conservative policies	'Left-wing' Labour policies
Publicly owned industries were privatised by being sold to private investors. These included gas, electricity, telecommunications, coal, steel and water.	Labour opposed the privatisations and sought to nationalise more industries including, possibly, the banks.
A number of legal restrictions were placed on the activities of trade unions.	Labour opposed these and proposed additional worker protection measures.
Tenants in council homes were encouraged to buy their properties at discounted prices and on low mortgage rates. This became a legal right.	Labour opposed the 'right to buy' policy and proposed increased local authority house building and controls on private rents.
Legal regulations on the financial system were removed.	Labour opposed this and even suggested big banks might be nationalised.
Rates of income tax for high-income groups and tax on businesses were significantly reduced.	Labour proposed a steeply progressive tax system to redistribute real income from rich to poor. A wealth tax was also proposed.

Study tip

Learn how to spell consensus. It contains three s's. This is because the root of the word is 'consent', not 'census'!

Study tip

Do not confuse the terms 'adversary' or 'adversarial' politics with the term 'adversarial style'. Adversary or adversarial politics refers to periods when there is deep ideological conflict between parties. Adversarial 'style' refers to the way politics is being conducted, usually in Parliament. This style is one where politicians give the impression that they are violently opposed to each other whether or not they disagree fundamentally. Adversarial style is most often seen at Prime Minister's Question Time.

UK political parties in context

Party systems

A party system describes the features of a political system in relation to the parties that operate within it. The term 'system' describes both how many parties there are and how many of those parties make a significant impact. The party system can help us understand how a political system works. It can also help us to explain change. This has been especially true in relation to the UK in recent times. Descriptions of different kinds of party system are provided below.

One-party system

This is where only one party is allowed to operate. This is normally associated with highly authoritarian regimes and we would not consider them to be democratic in the generally accepted sense of the word.

Dominant-party system

Here we are referring to democratic systems which do allow parties to operate freely, but where only one party has a realistic chance of taking governmental power. Such systems are highly stable, though there is a lack of accountability and competition.

Two-party system

These systems are less common than they used to be. As the name suggests, only two parties have a realistic chance of forming a government. It also implies that two parties win the vast majority of the votes at elections and most of the seats in the representative assemblies of the state.

Three-party system

These used to be very common but are less so today. It is unusual to find systems where three parties compete on equal terms. Much more normal is a situation where two parties dominate, but not sufficiently to govern alone. The third, smaller party, therefore, is in a pivotal position. One of the larger parties must always make a coalition or some kind of agreement with the smallest party in order to govern. This gives the small party a potentially disproportionate amount of power.

Multi-party system

These are common in Europe and growing more so. As the name suggests, there are several or many parties competing for votes and power. There is no set number to define a multi-party system, so we will suggest here that more than three significant parties constitute such a system. Four-party systems are particularly common. They tend to be much less stable than systems with fewer parties.

Synoptic links

Party systems should not be looked at in isolation from the electoral systems used in various countries, as there are strong links between electoral and party systems. This section should therefore be read in conjunction with the material in Chapter 3, which describes various electoral systems and their impacts.

Activity

Look at Table 2.8, showing party systems in different countries. Apart from the one-party states of China, Cuba and North Korea, where true elections do not take place, research elections in the countries listed and identify which electoral system each country uses.

Activity

Research the most recent general elections in the following countries. In each case, decide what kind of party system the country seems to have.

- The Netherlands
- Japan
- Canada

Knowledge check

What kind of party systems flourish in Wales and Northern Ireland?

Table 2.8 illustrates where the various party systems can be found and some of their features.

Table 2.8 Examples of party systems

Party system	Countries	Features
One-party system	China, Cuba, North Korea	All three describe themselves as communist states. The communist party is the only legal party.
Dominant-party system	Scotland (SNP)	The SNP holds nearly all the UK parliamentary seats and has governed Scotland since 2007.
Two-party system	USA, Australia	Democrats and Republicans hold virtually all elected positions at all levels of government in the USA. In Australia the dominant parties are Labour and the Liberals (who are, despite the name, conservatives).
Three-party system	Ireland	Three parties dominate — Fine Gael, Fianna Fail and Sinn Fein. Sinn Fein recently replaced Labour as the significant third party.
Multi-party systems	Italy, Germany	Italy has so many parties it is remarkably unstable. Governments tend to fall regularly. Germany has a four-party system with the Christian Democrats and Social Democrats dominating, but they have to form coalitions with either the Greens or the Free Democrats.

The effect of the electoral system

A question worth asking is what effect the electoral system has on the party system. This is particularly interesting in the context of the UK, where there are several different electoral systems operating in different parts of the country and different party systems resulting.

The normal analysis suggests that systems using FPTP return two-party systems. This is borne out in the USA and Canada, where two parties dominate completely. In 2010 and 2015 in the UK, however, the two-party dominance broke down. Even so, if we remove Scotland, Wales and Northern Ireland from the equation in UK general elections, we can say that England remains dominated by two parties.

Conversely, systems that use proportional representation (PR) tend to produce multi-party systems. This is clearly to be seen in such countries as Sweden, Norway and Italy, although there is no guarantee. In the past, for example, Sweden was dominated by one party — the Social Democrats — which regularly won nearly 50% of the popular vote.

The most unpredictable link seems to occur when some kind of hybrid system is used, notably the additional member system (AMS), which is partly FPTP and partly by proportional representation. Germany has a kind of 'two plus two' system, Scotland has one dominant party and Wales is essentially multi-party.

What this all means is that although the electoral system can give us a clue as to what kind of party system it will produce, the evidence is still not conclusive.

The party system in Westminster and beyond

The dominance of two parties in the UK has varied over the long term. Table 2.9 illustrates the dominance of two parties in terms of *seats* in the period 1979–2017. However, Figure 2.2 demonstrates that two-party dominance in terms of *votes* remained less pronounced until such dominance was restored in June 2017.

Table 2.9 Two-party dominance in the UK, 1979–2017

Election year	Conservative seats	Labour seats	Third party seats	% of seats won by two main parties
1979	339	269	11	95.8
1983	397	209	23	93.3
1987	376	229	22	93.0
1992	336	271	20	93.2
1997	165	418	46	88.4
2001	166	413	52	87.8
2005	198	356	62	85.6
2010	307	258	57	86.9
2015	331	232	56	86.7
2017	318	262	35	89.2

However, the decline in domination in terms of seats was still modest. The third party made little impact. But when we look beyond seats and review the proportion of votes won in general elections by the two parties, we have a different picture. Figure 2.2 demonstrates this decline in two-party dominance over the same period.

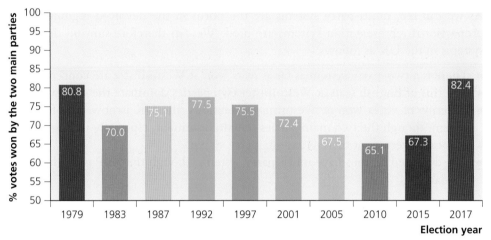

Figure 2.2 The decline in two-party dominance, 1979–2017

That other parties have been unable to convert their increasing proportion of votes won into significant numbers of seats is almost wholly due to the electoral system, which discriminates against them. It is therefore accurate to say that the UK remains a two-party system in terms of *seats* but is a multi-party system in terms of *votes*. As Figure 2.2 shows, however, two-party dominance showed signs of returning in 2017. The impact of the FPTP system is discussed in detail in Chapter 3.

When we consider party support at local and devolved elections, the position is very different. There is no doubt that the UK is a multi-party system outside Westminster. Figure 2.3 shows the seats won in English local councils in the 2016 elections. It can be seen that, though the two main parties dominate, other parties did win a significant proportion of the seats. Turning to the devolved national regions, we can see that they are definitely multi-party systems. The two main 'English' parties certainly do not

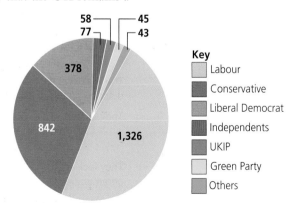

Figure 2.3 Party strengths (number of seats won) in English local government elections, 2016

Key
- Labour
- Conservative
- Liberal Democrat
- Independents
- UKIP
- Green Party
- Others

dominate in Wales and Scotland; they do not contest seats in Northern Ireland. Figures 2.4, 2.5 and 2.6 show the results of devolved elections in 2016.

Knowledge check

What kind of electoral system is used (a) in Northern Ireland and (b) in Wales and Scotland?

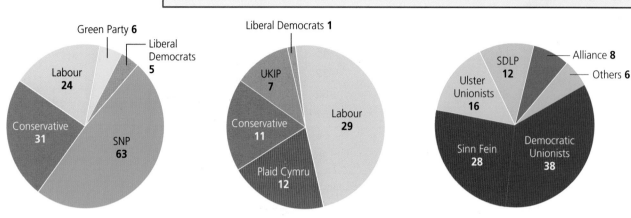

Figure 2.4 Elections to the Scottish Parliament, 2016 (number of seats won)

Figure 2.5 Elections to the Welsh Assembly, 2016 (number of seats won)

Figure 2.6 Elections to the Northern Ireland Assembly, 2016 (number of seats won)

As we can see, multi-party systems are the norm in the devolved regions where proportional representation systems are used. We can therefore sum up the party systems in the UK as follows:

- There is a two-party system as far as seats won at Westminster are concerned.
- In terms of English seats at Westminster two parties dominate the seats won.
- In terms of votes won at Westminster elections, the UK is now a multi-party system, though the two main parties remain dominant, especially in England.
- In local government there is a multi-party system.
- The devolved regions have multi-party systems, though the SNP is dominant in Scotland.

Factors that affect party success

Synoptic links

This section should be read in conjunction with Chapter 4, which deals with electoral behaviour and what determines the outcome of elections.

Here we briefly examine three aspects of parties that go some way to determining why they should succeed or fail. We should first, however, consider why small parties have so much difficulty in achieving a breakthrough. This is shown in Table 2.10.

Table 2.10 Why small parties find it difficult to make an impact and how they can nevertheless succeed

Why small parties fail	How small parties can succeed
They lack funding.	They may find wealthy benefactors to support them, as occurred with UKIP after 2010.
The electoral system may discriminate against them.	In devolved regions, proportional representation helps small parties.
They lack media exposure.	A strong charismatic leader may help to gain public support, as occurred with the SNP, led by the popular Nicola Sturgeon.
They lack organisation in communities.	They may gain widespread popular support with populist ideas, as UKIP achieved.
People consider voting for them is a wasted vote.	In proportional systems, fewer votes are wasted.

Leadership

This is crucial. Voters do respond to the quality of the individual who leads a party and who therefore, in the case at least of the two main parties, is a potential prime minister. The qualities that voters prefer, disregarding for the moment their political beliefs, include:

- experience
- decisiveness
- ability to lead
- media image
- intelligence
- apparent honesty

The importance of these qualities was thrown into clear focus in 2016 when Theresa May became Conservative leader and prime minister in 2016. Her poll ratings rose immediately after she took office and remained high. As a former home secretary for 6 years, she had experience of government at the highest level. She was elected unopposed by her party, demonstrating leadership qualities. She had a good media image as being tough and having integrity, and had a reputation for being clever and able to handle complex questions. In other words, she enjoyed all the qualities voters like.

By contrast, Jeremy Corbyn, the Labour leader when May took over, had no ministerial experience, was not seen as especially intelligent and had a poor media image. While most accepted his honesty, few trusted his ability to lead, especially as most Labour MPs passed a vote of no confidence in him in July 2016. Nevertheless, he was elected leader of the party (twice — in 2015 and again in 2016). In the 2017 general election, however, a remarkable change took place. Theresa May's standing with the public fell steadily and Jeremy Corbyn's stock rose dramatically. This demonstrated that election campaigns can make a difference. Corbyn campaigned more effectively than May. The result was an unexpectedly close result.

In the past we have seen leaders who damaged the prospects of their party — Gordon Brown, Ed Miliband and Nick Clegg are examples — and others who enhanced their party's fortunes, such as Margaret Thatcher and Tony Blair (at least until they both fell from grace). However, it was among smaller parties that leadership became important in 2015. Nicola Sturgeon, SNP leader, made a hugely favourable

Nicola Sturgeon, leader of the SNP, during a televised debate for the 2015 general election

impression in TV debates, as did Nigel Farage of UKIP. Farage was a master at manipulating the media, ensuring that his party was constantly in the news, while Sturgeon enjoyed very positive public approval ratings in the opinion polls.

Leaders do not win or lose elections, but in 2010 and 2015, and in elections to devolved assemblies, there is no doubt that the parties' fortunes were influenced by the performance and image of their leaders.

Unity

It is often said by political commentators that a disunited party has no hope of being elected. The facts appear to bear this out. Some examples in both directions can illustrate this.

- In the 1980s the Conservative Party united around the leadership of Margaret Thatcher while Labour was split between its left and right wings. In fact the party did literally split in 1981. This resulted in two huge victories for the Conservatives at the 1983 and 1987 general elections.
- In 1997 Labour was a virtually totally united party around the banner of New Labour under Blair. The Conservatives under John Major had been wracked by internal division, mainly over the UK's position in Europe. The result was a crushing victory for Labour.
- In 2016 the united Conservative Party dominated the disunited Labour Party. However, in the 2017 general election campaign, Labour succeeded in uniting around a radical manifesto, which resulted in a dramatic improvement in its fortunes.

The evidence is therefore compelling that the commentators are right. United parties will always have a huge advantage over disunited parties.

The media

Synoptic link

The influence of the media is also explored in Chapter 4.

Whatever the true policies of a party are, the electorate will often be influenced by the image of the party as portrayed in the media, notably the press. The newspapers tend to line up predictably at election time. Research suggests that newspapers only reinforce existing political affiliations, and do not change minds, but there remains the probability that their campaigns may well persuade people to vote for the party they support. Some wavering voters may also be swayed.

Table 2.11 shows which party each major newspaper supported and gives the proportion of their readership who voted for that party.

Table 2.11 Newspaper affiliations and voting, 2017 general election

Newspaper	Party supported	% of its readers who voted for the paper's favoured party
Sun	Conservative	39
Daily Mirror	Labour	62
Daily Mail	Conservative	57
Daily Telegraph	Conservative	72
Times	Conservative	60
Guardian	Labour	50
Independent	Uncommitted	n/a

Source: Ipsos MORI

We can see from Table 2.11 that there is a close correlation between the political views of the readership of the newspapers and the political stance of the papers themselves. However, this may be because readers tend to buy newspapers with whose views they agree. There is scant evidence that newspapers significantly influence voting. Indeed, in the 2017 general election the vast majority of newspapers backed the Conservatives, but to little avail, as the party lost its Commons majority following a Labour resurgence.

Broadcasters have to be neutral and balanced by law. Nevertheless, TV in particular does give exposure to party leaders. The TV debates have had an impact on the fortunes of the parties. In 2010, for example, Liberal Democrat leader Nick Clegg's performance in the TV debates was widely praised. Partly as a result, the Liberal Democrats did well enough to enter a coalition with the Conservatives. In 2015, by contrast, Labour leader Ed Miliband performed poorly and this was a factor in Labour's failure to win the election.

The media are not decisive, nor is leadership and nor is a party's level of unity, but, put together, they *are* influential. However, it is still the performance of the outgoing government and the policies of the opposition parties that determine the outcome of elections.

Discussion point

Look back at the introduction to this chapter. Which of the two views of parties held by Adams and Disraeli do you think is more appropriate in a modern democracy?

A summary of the role of parties in the UK

How well do parties enhance representative democracy?

Political parties play a number of key roles in the UK's representative form of democracy. These are, in particular, the following:

- By producing manifestos and political programmes, they ensure that government is accountable.
- They are vital in the selection of candidates for office. Without parties, candidates would campaign as individuals, which would make it difficult for voters to make rational choices.
- They mobilise support for political *programmes*, not just individual policies. This is known as aggregation. Without such aggregation, politics would become incoherent.
- Parliament itself relies on party organisations to operate in an effective way. The parties organise debates and ensure that ministers are called to account. They also organise the staffing of parliamentary committees.

On the other hand, parties can also distort representation. The governing party is always elected without an overall majority of the national vote and yet it claims to have the mandate of the people. The 'winner takes all' nature of party politics may result in governing which is too partisan and does not seek a consensus of support for policies. Coalition government between 2010 and 2015 was a rare example of parties cooperating with each other.

Parties also tend to reduce issues to 'binary' decision making. That is, they tend to claim that one type of decision is either wholly wrong or wholly right. In reality this is rarely the case, but adversarial party politics tends to create these kinds of false choices.

How inclusive are parties?

Parties are open organisations. Anyone can join a party provided they do not hold beliefs that are significantly at odds with the party's main ideas and policies. Indeed, in 2015 the Labour Party made itself even more inclusive by allowing people to become registered supporters for a mere £3 (later increased to £25). Parties also make few demands on their members. It is possible to be a passive member, paying one's subscription but playing no active role, or perhaps only becoming involved at election time.

This does not tell the whole story. The other question is, how 'elitist' are the parties internally? Do ordinary members have any realistic influence on the making of policies? The Labour, Liberal Democrat and Scottish National parties do claim the virtue of being internally democratic, as do Plaid Cymru and the Greens, and it is certainly true that the broad sentiments of the membership are taken into account by the leaderships. However, there is no doubt that, in the main parties at least, the party elites have a dominant role.

A secondary, but equally important, question is how possible is it for ordinary members to rise up through the party ranks? The UK has a good record in this regard. Many of the country's political leaders have come from backgrounds which might be described as 'modest' and not part of a social elite. Individuals such as James Callaghan (prime minister 1976–79), John Major (prime minister 1990–97), Gordon Brown (prime minister 2007–10), Jeremy Corbyn (Labour leader 2015–) and Theresa May (prime minister 2016–) are all examples of individuals who have risen through their party ranks to the top without any privileged background.

Activity

Research the characteristics of MPs in the Conservative, Labour and Scottish National Parties. What proportion of MPs are women in each party?

Could UK democracy operate without parties?

All modern democracies have parties as a central feature of their representative systems. This suggests that they are fundamental elements in representation. Parties in the USA are very loose coalitions with little formal organisation and no mass memberships, making that country the closest thing to a partyless democracy in the West.

The answer to this question is, therefore, probably no. Elections would be incoherent, Parliament would have difficulty operating effectively, the opportunities for people to participate in politics would be severely reduced, government would not be made properly accountable and it would be difficult to identify future political leaders.

The main positive aspect of a democracy without parties is that there would be a greater possibility for consensus building. Without the support of parties, policies would have to be developed on a consensual basis rather than on an adversarial basis.

Table 2.12 summarises the role of parties in a representative democracy.

Table 2.12 The role of parties in the UK's representative democracy

Positive aspects	Negative aspects
They provide open opportunities for people to become active in politics. They are inclusive and make few demands on members.	Adversarial party politics is negative in that it denies the creation of consensus and reduces issues to false, simplistic choices.
They make political issues coherent and help to make government accountable.	Parties claim legitimacy through their electoral mandate even when they are elected to power with a minority of the popular vote.
They help to make elections and the operation of Parliament effective and understandable to the public.	Parties sometimes become over-elitist so that small leadership groups can dominate policy making to the detriment of internal democracy.
They identify, recruit and 'train' people for political office and leadership.	

Key concepts in this chapter

Aggregation A process, undertaken by political parties, of converting policies, demands and ideas into practical policy programmes for government. This involves eliminating contradictions and making some compromises.

Cash for honours A phrase used by the media to describe the suspicion that some donations to parties are made in the hope and expectation that the giver will receive an honour such as a peerage or knighthood. The practice is considered to be unlawful but is difficult to prove.

Classical liberalism A way of describing nineteenth-century liberalism that proposed a limited state that would be confined to protecting the freedom of individuals and maintaining the security of the state.

Consensus This refers to a situation where two or more significant parties in a political system agree on fundamental ideas and aims. Consensus can also mean 'general agreement'. When there is a consensus, parties only disagree on details of policy and how to implement their aims.

Democratic socialism A moderate form of socialism that proposes to achieve its aims by democratic means. Its main objectives are to mix state control over production with market capitalism, so that the interests of the working class are advanced within a combination of state-run welfare and major industries, and smaller-scale free enterprise.

Dependency culture A belief that, if welfare benefits are too generous in a society, people become used to depending on such benefits, which then become a disincentive to work. The culture, many claim, is passed down from one generation to the next.

Left wing A general description of policies that conform to 'socialist' principles. Typical left-wing ideas include the redistribution of income from rich to poor through both taxation and welfare, public ownership and state control of key enterprises, the elimination of privilege and its replacement by equal rights and the promotion of equality of opportunity.

Liberal democracy Liberal democracy is both a description of some political systems and a political movement. In politics it implies a democracy in which rights and equality are guaranteed and promoted. As a movement it describes a party or political stance that stresses the importance of democracy and rights. There is a belief among its adherents that other 'good things' will flow from the political system if it is genuinely democratic and respects rights.

Libertarianism An extreme form of neo-liberalism. Libertarians propose that the government should interfere as little as possible with economic and social activity. They also support the maximisation of personal liberty.

Mandate A term referring to the consent granted to a political party at election time by the electorate. The mandate gives legitimacy to all the winning party's manifesto commitments.

Modern Liberals This term is used to describe liberals who came to prominence after classical liberalism began to decline at the end of the nineteenth century. Modern Liberals would tolerate an expanded role for the state into the areas of social justice, welfare and equality of opportunity.

Neo-liberalism A movement from the 1970s and 1980s which proposes that the state should not interfere excessively in economic management, which promotes free markets, and opposes trade union power, high taxes and excessive welfare benefits for those who are able to work.

New Labour A term applied to the Labour Party under Tony Blair, which moved towards a more centrist position in politics after the mid-1990s.

New Right A term used for a conservative movement that arose in the 1980s which combined an authoritarian form of neo-conservatism with an economically liberal form of neo-liberalism.

One-nation conservatism A term often used to describe the collection of traditional values held by many conservatives. It refers to the idea that conservative policies should promote social cohesion and reduce social conflict between the classes. The term was notably used by the nineteenth-century prime minister Benjamin Disraeli.

Party faction A faction refers to a distinct group within a political party whose views vary significantly from the main party policies. Often factions are to the left or right of the party's position. Some factions have a formal membership and organisation, while others are loose and represent little more than a policy tendency.

Party manifesto A collection of beliefs, aspirations, commitments and promises presented to the electorate by parties at election time. The manifesto forms the basis of the winning party's electoral mandate and allows parliaments or regional assemblies and the public to hold government to account.

Party system A party system describes how many parties flourish within a political system and have influence. Party systems in the UK have varied from two-party to three-party to multi-party systems at different times, in different circumstances and in different regions.

Policy A set of intentions or a political programme developed by parties or by governments. Policies reflect the political stance of parties and governments.

Political party An association of people who share common values and political beliefs and who seek political power in order to convert those beliefs and values into practice.

Populism A political movement, often represented by a political party, that appeals to people's emotions and which tends to find supporters among sections of the community who feel they have not been represented by conventional politics and politicians.

Right wing Policies often associated with conservatism. Typically they may include the promotion of individualism in contrast to left-wing ideas of collectivism, the withdrawal of the state from economic and social control, low personal and company taxation, a strong, authoritarian position on law and order and a stress on patriotism and nationalism.

Short money Named after Ted Short, the politician who introduced it, Short money refers to funds given to opposition parties to facilitate their parliamentary work (research facilities etc.). The amount is based on how many seats and votes each party won at the previous election.

Social liberals A name often used for liberals, especially members of the Liberal Democratic Party, who share many of the centrist social democratic values of the Labour Party. Vince Cable (business secretary 2010–15) is a key example; he lost his parliamentary seat in 2015.

Third way A new political philosophy, developed by Anthony Giddens and Peter Mandelson, which proposed policies which lay somewhere between leftist socialism and rightist neo-liberalism.

Two-party system A political system in which two parties invariably dominate at elections and in government. Smaller parties consistently fail to make any impact in such a system.

Summary

Having read this chapter, you should have knowledge and understanding of the following:
→ What political parties are and do, and why they are so central to an understanding of how government and politics works in the UK
→ How parties are funded, the main issues concerning party funding and what proposals for reform have been offered
→ How political parties and their leaders fit into the left–right spectrum in UK politics
→ Why the doctrine of mandate and manifesto is so important in UK politics
→ How the main political parties developed historically and what are the main ideological principles behind them
→ What different traditions and factions exist within UK political parties
→ The nature and impact of smaller parties in various parts of the UK
→ The nature and significance of consensus and adversary politics
→ The nature of the different party systems that exist within the UK, why they differ and the significance of those differences
→ In what ways and to what extent small parties make an impact on UK politics
→ The main reasons why some parties are successful and others are less successful

Further information and web guide

Websites

Information about all political parties can be found on their websites. This is also true of important party factions:

www.conwayfor.org (Conservative Way Forward)

cornerstonegroup.wordpress.com (Cornerstone Group)

www.trg.org.uk (Tory Reform Group)

www.peoplesmomentum.com (Momentum)

Information about party regulation and funding can be found on the Electoral Commission site: **www.electoralcommission.org.uk**.

More information is on the UK Parliament site: **www.parliament.uk**.

Books

Two books published in 2012 are very useful, although the information needs a little updating. They are:

Cole, M. and Deigham, H. (2012) *Political Parties in Britain*, Edinburgh University Press.

Cook, A. (2012) *Political Parties in the UK*, Palgrave Macmillan.

Perhaps the best book on the theory of party politics is Driver, S. (2011) *Understanding British Party Politics*, Polity.

Bale, T. (2011) *The Conservative Party from Thatcher to Cameron*, Polity, is excellent but stops in 2010.

Thorpe, A. (2016) *The History of the British Labour Party*, Palgrave, is up to date but goes back to the origins of Labour.

AS

1 Using examples, describe the nature of party factions. (10)

2 Describe the nature of 'left-wing politics'. (10)

3 Using the source, explain party factionalism. *In your response you must use knowledge and understanding to analyse points that are only in the source. You will not be rewarded for introducing any additional points that are not in the source.* (10)

> **The Conservative Party today**
>
> Although we think of the Conservative Party as a united body, it is, in fact, seriously internally divided. For example, there has long been a wing of the party known as the 'eurosceptics'. They have consistently caused trouble for the leadership. Even when the UK voted to leave the EU, they exerted pressure on the cabinet to withdraw from the European single market and to curb immigration.
>
> There are also many conservatives who look back favourably to the age of Margaret Thatcher in the 1980s when strong controls over unions were introduced, but regulation of industry was relaxed. Thatcherism, also known as the 'New Right', has been abandoned, say such conservatives, in favour of progressive liberal ideas. They wish to see a return to those policies. In addition, of course there are some members of the party who are moderate, centre ground politicians and who have remained loyal to the leadership of David Cameron and Theresa May.
>
> The real question is, however, not whether there are minority views within the party, but how much they have affected policy making in the party.

4 'Small political parties are having an increasingly important impact on UK politics.' How far do you agree? (30)

5 'Modern Conservative policies do not conform to the traditional ideas of the party.' To what extent do you agree? (30)

A-level

1 Using the source, evaluate the view that the Labour Party has returned to its original ideological position. *In your response you must compare the different opinions in the source and use a balance of knowledge and understanding both arising from the source and beyond it to help you to analyse and evaluate.* (30)

> There are two ways of viewing the 'Corbyn revolution' which emerged within the Labour Party in 2015. Some argue that this a return to the roots of the Labour Party. Many of Corbyn's ideas were forged in the 1970s and 1980s when he was a young party member and when such ideological figures as Tony Benn, Ken Livingstone and Michael Foot were prominent in the party. His proposals for the state ownership of the railways and state control over utility industries come straight from that era. He also believes in the power of the state to create greater economic equality and to curb the excesses of capitalism.
>
> Others see it as a temporary insurgency. Many new supporters who voted for Corbyn in the leadership elections are seen as Marxist 'entryists'. For such critics the legacy of Tony Blair and New Labour is where the modern Labour Party is and should position itself. They point out that most Labour voters are actually moderate and that the majority of Labour MPs and peers do not support Corbyn. They support more centrist policies on taxation, welfare and the role of the state.
>
> It remains to be seen whether Labour can survive this split and, indeed, which ideological position will prevail.

2 Using the source, evaluate the extent to which two-party dominance has declined in the UK. *In your response you must compare the different opinions in the source and use a balance of knowledge and understanding both arising from the source and beyond it to help you to analyse and evaluate.* (30)

Two-party dominance in the UK			
Election year	Conservative seats	Labour seats	Third-party seats	% of seats won by two main parties
1979	339	269	11	95.8
1983	397	209	23	93.3
1987	376	229	22	93.0
1992	336	271	20	93.2
1997	165	418	46	88.4
2001	166	413	52	87.8
2005	198	356	62	85.6
2010	307	258	57	86.9
2015	331	232	56	86.7

3 Evaluate the view that all the main UK parties support liberal ideas. (30)

4 Evaluate the case for introducing the state funding of parties. (30)

3 Electoral systems

In 1832 William Marcy, following the victory of the Democrats in the US presidential election, stated 'to the victor belong the spoils'. He was referring to the right of the new president, Andrew Jackson, to make hundreds of appointments to government office and to dismiss the existing office holders. Victory in the election, Marcy added, gave him such wide powers. Victors in war enjoy the 'spoils' of their victory — territory, wealth, social honour etc. Elections are similar, he commented, in that the winners gain considerable rewards. To this day the idea of the 'spoils system' persists in the USA. Winning parties and candidates gain the right to award jobs and possibly even government contracts to their supporters.

In this chapter we examine how elections work and their importance in the political system, as well as the controversies that persist about how they operate. We also look at the rewards and obligations that come with victory. There is a 'spoils system' in UK politics, but it is far less pronounced than in other democracies. Then we examine the impact of the growing use of referendums in the UK. Even if it is true, as some critics have claimed, that voting in elections changes little, referendums do change things, as the EU vote of 2016 proved so dramatically.

David Cameron launching the Conservative Party manifesto, April 2015

Objectives

This chapter will inform you about the following:

→ How the UK national electoral system works
→ The principal impacts of the first-past-the-post (FPTP) system, the controversies surrounding it and the case for and against reform
→ The various other electoral systems in use in different parts of the UK
→ Comparisons between FPTP and other systems
→ The way in which referendums work, including how and why they are called, and the main impacts of those held in the UK since 1975
→ The arguments for and against the use of referendums
→ The general importance of elections in a democracy
→ The relationship between electoral systems and party systems
→ The relationships between electoral outcomes and government formation
→ The effects of electoral systems on voters

Different electoral systems

The working of first past the post

The main electoral system used for general elections in the UK is commonly known as **first past the post** (or **FPTP**). This is a misleading title. Its true description should be 'plurality in single-member constituencies'. The country is divided into 650 constituencies of roughly equal size. The average adult population of constituencies is 75,000, though there may be some variation and, of course, the *geographical* size of constituencies varies considerably. Tightly populated London constituencies are clearly much smaller than sparsely populated constituencies in the highlands of Scotland. To win a seat in a constituency it is only necessary to win more votes than any of one's rivals. This is known as a **plurality**. A plurality should be seen in contrast to an *absolute* majority. An **absolute majority** is when a candidate wins at least 50% of the votes available.

To illustrate this, Tables 3.1 and 3.2 show the results in two constituencies in 2017. Table 3.1 shows a candidate winning an absolute majority in the Arundel constituency (62.4%), while Table 3.2 shows a candidate winning merely a plurality (32.6%) in the Lanark and Hamilton East constituency.

Table 3.1 Arundel and South Downs constituency 2017 election result

Candidate	Votes won	% of total votes
Herbert (Conservative)	37,573	62.4
Fife (Labour)	13,690	22.7
Kapadia (Lib Dem)	4,783	7.9
Prior (Green)	2,542	4.2
Wallace (UKIP)	1,668	2.8

Table 3.2 Lanark and Hamilton East constituency 2017 election result

Candidate	Votes won	% of total votes
Crawley (SNP)	16,444	32.6
Corbett (Conservative)	16,178	32.1
Hillard (Labour)	16,084	31.9
Robb (Lib Dem)	1,214	2.4
Mackay (UKIP)	550	1.1

Key terms

First past the post (FPTP) The name commonly used to describe the UK's electoral system for general elections, although its more formal title is 'plurality in single-member constituencies'.

Plurality This term refers to the result of an election where the winner only has to obtain more votes than any of their opponents. It does not mean the winner has an absolute majority.

Absolute majority This refers to the result of a vote where the winner receives more votes than all the other candidates put together. In other words, the winner receives at least 50% of the total votes.

Constituency A constituency is a geographical area used to determine which people each elected representative represents. UK parliamentary constituencies are roughly 75,000 voters in size. Constituencies in devolved systems and local government are much smaller but also roughly equal in size. Elected representatives are expected to look after the interests of their constituency.

These results illustrate the character of the FPTP system. Furthermore, if we look back at the 2015 general election, more characteristics emerge. Only 319 out of 650 MPs won an absolute (50%+) majority of the votes in their constituency. Fifty MPs even secured a seat with less than 40% of the popular vote in their constituency. So, most elected MPs had to admit in 2015 that more people voted *against* them than *for* them.

The importance of concentrated support

There is no doubt that the FPTP electoral system has the effect of favouring those parties that have their support concentrated in certain areas. This can be shown if we consider the overall general election result in 2017. This is shown in Table 3.3.

Table 3.3 The result of the UK general election, June 2017

Party	% votes won	% seats won	No. of seats won	Notes
Conservative	42.4	48.9	318	Conservative support is concentrated in south and central England.
Labour	40.0	40.3	262	Labour support is concentrated in northern England and Wales.
Scottish National Party	3.0	5.4	35	The SNP suffered significant losses in 2017.
Liberal Democrats	7.4	1.8	12	The party's support is widely dispersed.
Democratic Unionist Party (DUP)	0.9	1.5	10	The DUP only contests seats in Northern Ireland.
Sinn Fein	0.7	1.1	7	Northern Ireland only.
Plaid Cymru	0.5	0.6	4	Contests seats in Wales.
UKIP	1.8	0	0	UKIP support is dispersed and collapsed in 2017.
Green Party	1.6	0.2	1	Support is dispersed.
Others	1.7	0	0	Very dispersed.

Knowledge check

Which was the single seat won by the Green Party in 2017, who was the elected MP and what was the size of her majority? Can you account for her rare victory?

The reason why this occurs is that parties with dispersed support, such as UKIP, the Green Party and the Liberal Democrats (as well as Labour and the Conservatives in Scotland), win few individual constituency contests and hence gain few seats in Parliament. This can be seen in the result of the Lanark and Hamilton East election in Table 3.2. Labour and the Conservatives, whose support in Scotland is widely dispersed (unlike in England), came a strong second and third, both just behind the winning SNP candidate. This kind of result was replicated all over the country, though few were as close as this one.

In England, Conservative support is heavily concentrated so that results like that shown for Arundel and South Downs (Table 3.1) are quite common. The winning candidate achieved an overall majority of the votes in the constituency. In Scotland, the SNP does well because its support is also concentrated in specific areas of the country.

It was the other parties — Conservative, Labour and Liberal Democrats — who suffered from dispersed support in Scotland.

Votes per successful candidate

Another way of considering the impact of FPTP is to look at how many votes, on average, it took for each party to secure the election of a candidate. This can be calculated by dividing the total number of votes won by each party nationally by the number of seats the party won. Table 3.4 shows these calculations for the parties in 2017.

Study tip

It is important to review the result of the general election of June 2017 and add any statistics which further illustrate or amend the information in this section.

Table 3.4 Average votes needed to elect one member in the 2017 general election

Party	Total votes won nationally (a)	Seats won nationally (b)	Average votes per winning candidate (a) ÷ (b)
Green Party	525,371	1	525,371
Liberal Democrat	2,371,772	12	197,583
Labour	12,874,985	262	49,141
Conservative	13,667,213	318	42,978
Plaid Cymru	164,466	4	41,116
Sinn Fein	238,915	7	34,130
SNP	997,569	35	28,501
DUP	292,316	10	29,232

Table 3.4 shows great disparities between how efficiently the parties turned votes cast for them into seats won by them. The Northern Ireland parties (Democratic Unionist and Sinn Fein) have low averages largely because they are evenly matched and because of low turnouts. However, it is striking how big a disparity there is between the Green Party and the Liberal Democrats with very high averages, and the SNP with its very low average. We can also see that the Conservative Party has an advantage over Labour, though perhaps not a decisive one.

Clearly and predictably the 'losers' in this system complain the loudest while the main 'winners' (Conservatives and Labour) have the least interest in reforming the system to remove such discrepancies.

Summary

We can now summarise the main features of first past the post:

- Each constituency returns a single Member of Parliament, who can represent the whole of the constituency.
- It is a simple system and voters can understand exactly what they are voting for.
- It gives an advantage to parties that have concentrated support in certain regions.
- It is disadvantageous to parties whose support is dispersed widely.
- It favours the large parties and prevents serious challenges from small parties.

Synoptic links

Consideration of the first-past-the-post system must be linked with the section on the two-party system in the UK in Chapter 2. The persistence of two dominant parties in UK general elections is partly the result of the electoral system.

Majority government
A government whose
members and supporters
constitute a majority of the
members of the legislature
(e.g. House of Commons
or Scottish Parliament).
This means they find it
relatively easy to pass
legislation and tends to
make them stable and
long lasting.

Minority government
A government whose
members and supporters
do not constitute a
majority of the members.
In other words, there
are more opposition-
supporting members than
government-supporting
members. Such a minority
government finds it
difficult to pass legislation
and is likely to be unstable
and short lived.

Safe seat A constituency
where it is highly unlikely
that the seat will change
hands from one party to
another at an election.

Marginal seat
A constituency where the
results of past elections
suggest that the result of
an election will be close.
The BBC definition is where
the winner of the seat at
the previous election won
by less than 10% from their
nearest rival.

- There is a 'winner's bonus' where the biggest party tends to win more than its proportionate share of the vote. In 2017 the Conservatives won 42.4% of the votes, which was converted into 48.9% of the seats.
- Because it favours the large parties it tends to produce an outright winner — that is, a party that has an overall majority in the House of Commons. However, in recent general elections — 2010, 2015 and 2017 — the system has failed to produce a decisive government majority, suggesting this characteristic may be changing.
- FPTP is therefore associated with single-party or **majority government**, even though in 2017 there was a **minority** single-party **government**. It is not yet clear whether the UK is ready to accept the more common experience of coalitions and minority governments — as often found in the rest of Europe — in the future.

Activity

Research the last *three* elections to the Westminster Parliament, the Scottish Parliament and the Welsh Assembly. Identify those occasions when there was a *minority* government as a result of the election and the occasions when there was a *majority* government.

Safe and marginal seats
The FPTP system produces two phenomena that are virtually unique to this system. These are so-called 'safe' and 'marginal' seats.

Safe seats
A **safe seat** is a constituency where it is almost certain that the same party will win the seat at every general election. The Electoral Reform Society (**www.electoral-reform.org.uk**) estimates that 368 seats out of 650 were safe seats in 2015. Furthermore, the society calculates that as many as 25.7 million voters live in safe seats. The implications of there being so many safe seats include the following:

- The parties will pay little attention to safe seats in the election campaigns, so voters will receive less information.
- MPs sitting for such safe constituencies are less accountable for their actions because they have virtually no chance of losing their seat at the next election.
- Voters in safe seats may feel their votes are 'wasted' because they have no realistic chance of influencing the outcome. This may be the case whether they support the winning party or one of the losing parties.
- It means that votes are, effectively, not of equal value. Votes in safe seats are worth less than votes in seats that are closely contested where the voters may have an impact.
- The Electoral Reform Society estimated that, in the 2015 general election, three-quarters of the voters, numbering 22 million, were effectively casting 'wasted' votes because they had no chance of influencing the outcome in their constituencies as the seats were safe.

Marginal seats
There is no precise definition of a **marginal seat**. However, in general, marginal seats are those where the outcome of the election is in great doubt. Such seats are very likely to change hands from one party to another at each election. It is, therefore,

often said that elections are won and lost in the marginal constituencies. In the 2015 general election the BBC estimated that there were 194 marginal seats in the UK. They defined a marginal seat as one where the last winning candidate led by 10% or less from the nearest challenger.

The implications of the existence of marginal seats include these:

- The parties concentrate their efforts on marginal seats, so voters there receive much more attention and information.
- Votes in marginal seats are clearly more valuable than votes in safe seats as the voters in marginal seats will feel they may influence the result.
- The character and policies of the candidates become more important in marginal seats. In safe seats the qualities of individual candidates matter little, but in marginals they can be crucial.
- Marginal seats may result in 'tactical voting'. A tactical vote is when a voter who supports a party that is unlikely to win a constituency switches allegiance to one of the other parties in the hope of influencing the outcome. A typical example is when Liberal Democrat supporters in marginal seats vote either Labour or Conservative, in other words their second choice.

Activity

Research the parliamentary constituency in which you live. Look at the results in the constituency for the past three general elections. Decide whether it is a safe seat or a marginal seat.

By-elections

A by-election takes place when a sitting MP (or member of any other representative assembly, including local councils) dies or resigns their seat. This creates a vacancy. In order to fill it, a by-election takes place only in that constituency. The same electoral system is used as for regular elections. By-elections can produce strange results and no such seats are 'safe'. The voters may use a by-election to 'punish' the party in government and so defeat a representative from the governing party unexpectedly. The policies and personality of the candidates are also placed under greater focus, so unpredictable results can happen. Nevertheless, by-elections do provide an additional means by which voters can call government to account by punishing them with a defeat or rewarding them with a victory.

The case for and against FPTP

The first-past-the-post system is highly controversial. It has its supporters and its detractors. Among the supporters are established members of the two main parties. This is not surprising as the Conservative and Labour parties are the main beneficiaries of the system, although the Labour Party has considered changing its policy position towards reform of the system. It is also not surprising that it is small parties that support a change to the system. Even the Scottish National Party, which now benefits so strongly from FPTP, supports reform. Pressure groups such as the Electoral Reform Society and Unlock Democracy are also prominent campaigners for change.

It is one of the most important debates in contemporary UK politics whether first past the post is desirable and should be retained, or whether it is undemocratic and should be replaced. The arguments on both sides are summarised below.

These arguments about the retention of FPTP are balanced. However, the debate should also be considered in the light of the main alternative voting systems. These are assessed in the following sections.

Should FPTP be retained?

The case for retention

- It is easy to understand and produces a clear result in each constituency. The result is also known very quickly.
- It produces one single representative for each constituency and so creates a close constituency-MP bond.
- Accountability of the individual MP is clear to the electors.
- The system tends to produce a clear winner in the general election, i.e. a single party with a parliamentary majority. This helps to promote strong, stable, decisive government.
- It helps to prevent small parties breaking into the system. This is useful if the small parties are undesirable 'extremists'.
- Arguably FPTP has stood the test of time. Abandoning the system would be a dangerous step into the unknown.
- A switch to a different system might have all sorts of unintended consequences.
- In 2011, a referendum decisively rejected a proposal for change.
- In elections with complex concerns – as occurred in 2017 when the Brexit issue was combined with other social and economic matters – FPTP gives voters the opportunity to choose a candidate based on their individual attitude to such issues, rather than merely according to their party allegiance.

The case against retention

- The overall outcome is not proportional or fair. Some parties win more seats than their support warrants, while others win less than they deserve.
- It means that many votes are effectively wasted because they can have no impact on the outcome in safe seats. Many seats become part of party 'heartlands', where there is no possibility of a realistic challenge from other parties. It also produces 'electoral deserts', where there is effectively no party competition.
- Votes are of unequal value in that votes in safe seats are less valuable than votes in marginal seats (see Table 3.4). UKIP votes were of hugely less value than Conservative votes in 2015.
- It encourages some voters to vote tactically and so abandon the party they really want to support.
- It prevents new parties breaking into the system and so produces political 'inertia'.
- It has, since 1945, always resulted in the winning party securing much less than half the popular vote. In 2015 the winning Conservative Party was elected with just 36.9% of the popular vote; 63.1% of the voters voted against the governing party. In 2005 Labour won the election with a majority of 66 from only 35.2% of the popular vote. This calls into question the legitimacy of the government.
- FPTP always used to deliver governments with a majority of the seats in the House of Commons. However, in 2015 and 2017 the system failed to do this, returning governments without such an overall majority. If it is failing to achieve its main objective in modern times, this suggests it should be replaced with a fairer system.

Other electoral systems in the UK

The first-past-the-post system is described as a plurality system. Alternative systems used both in different parts of the UK and around the world have different descriptions. The main examples are as follows.

Proportional systems

These are systems that produce an outcome whereby the competing parties are awarded seats in the legislature in proportion to the votes cast for them, either exactly or approximately. So, a directly proportional system would award 40% of the available seats to a party that won 40% of the popular vote.

Majority systems

These are used to elect a single candidate, for example a president or a mayor. They are designed to ensure that the winner can claim the support of an overall majority of voters.

These are a mixture of two systems. The main example is the additional member system, which is a mixture of FPTP and a proportional system.

The systems described below fall into one of these categories.

The additional member system (AMS)

The additional member system is a hybrid system that combines FPTP with a **proportional representation** system. It is used in Scotland and Wales and for the Greater London Assembly. A version is also used in Germany. A proportion (which varies from country to country) of the seats is awarded through FPTP. The rest are awarded on a regional list system. This means that every voter has two votes. One is for a constituency candidate in the normal way, the other is from a choice of party lists.

So, some of the elected representatives have a constituency to look after, while others do not. The latter have been elected from the lists and are free of constituency responsibilities. No real distinction is made between the two, though the senior party members tend to be elected from lists rather than in constituencies.

AMS is something of a compromise. It is designed to make a system *partly* proportional, but also preserves the idea of parliamentary constituencies with an MP to represent them. It helps smaller parties, but also favours the larger ones. It achieves two objectives at the same time — preserving the idea of constituencies and a constituency representative, but producing a much more proportional result than FPTP.

How AMS works in Scotland and Wales

- Two-thirds of the seats are elected using FPTP, as for UK general elections.
- The other third of the seats are elected on a proportional system based on several regions of the country. This is known as the regional list part of the system.
- There is an important variation in the regional list part of the vote. The variable top-up system adjusts the proportions of votes cast on the list system. This is a complex calculation, but, in essence, what happens is that the seats awarded from the list system are adjusted to give a more proportional result. It is known as the D'Hondt method.
- Parties that do less well in the constituencies (typically Conservatives or Greens) have their proportion of list votes adjusted upwards. Those that do proportionally well under first past the post (typically Labour) have their list votes adjusted downwards.
- The overall effect of variable top-up is to make the total result in seats close to proportional to the total votes cast in both systems.

Table 3.5 An assessment of the additional member system (AMS)

Its advantages	Its drawbacks
It produces a broadly proportional outcome and so is fair to all parties.	It produces two classes of representative — those with a constituency and those elected through the lists. The latter tend to be senior.
It gives voters two votes and so more choice.	It is more complex than first past the post. Having two votes can confuse some voters.
It combines preserving constituency representation with a proportional outcome.	It can result in the election of extremist candidates.
It helps small parties which cannot win constituency contests.	

Key term

Proportional representation (PR) This refers to any electoral system that tends to produce a proportional outcome. In other words, the seats in a representative body are awarded in an election broadly in the same proportion as the votes cast for each party. So, for example, if a party wins 40% of the votes it will be awarded approximately 40% of the seats available. The regional list system and single transferable vote system are good examples of PR.

Study tip

A common error made by students is to believe that proportional representation is an electoral system. It is not. It is a *description* of *various* electoral systems that tend to produce a proportional outcome between the parties. (See the key term description above.)

The Holyrood Parliament building in Edinburgh

When we look at the results of elections under AMS we can see that a party wins some of its seats through constituency contests and the rest from the regional list elections in which voters choose a party rather than an individual. Table 3.6 shows the results of the elections to the Scottish Parliament in 2016. It shows how well each party performed in both the constituency elections and the list elections. Bear in mind that the seats on the regional list system are manipulated to produce a more proportional result.

Table 3.6 Results of the elections to the Scottish Parliament, 2016

Party	Constituency seats won	Regional list system seats awarded	Total seats won	% seats won	% votes won in the regional lists
SNP	59	4	63	48.8	41.7
Conservative	7	24	31	24.0	22.9
Labour	3	21	24	18.6	19.1
Green Party	0	6	6	4.7	6.6
Liberal Democrat	4	1	5	3.9	5.2
Others	0	0	0	0	4.5

We can see that the proportion of seats won by each party is quite close to the proportion of votes each of them won in the party list contest, so the result is broadly proportional. We can also see that all the smaller parties won very few constituency seats. Conversely, the SNP won 59 out of the 73 constituency seats available. Had this election been conducted under first past the post, the SNP would have dominated by winning 104 (81%) out of 129 seats! Under AMS, the SNP won 48.8% of the seats on 41.7% of the popular vote — a much more proportional outcome.

The single transferable vote (STV)

STV is the system used in Northern Ireland for all its elections. It is also used for local government elections in Scotland and for general elections in the Republic of Ireland. It is commonly described as a proportional system.

It is a complex system, especially when it comes to the counting and the establishment of the result. This is how it works. Some detail has been omitted for the sake of brevity, but the following features are what you need to know:

- There are six seats available in each constituency.
- Each party is permitted to put up as many candidates as there are seats, i.e. up to six. In practice, parties do not adopt six candidates as they have no chance of winning all six seats available. Four is the normal maximum number from each party.
- Voters place the candidates in their order of preference by placing a number 1, 2, 3 etc. beside their names.
- Voters can vote for candidates from different parties or even all the parties, though few do.
- At the count, an *electoral quota* is calculated. This is established by taking the total number of votes cast and dividing it by the number of seats available plus 1. So, if 50,000 votes were cast and six seats are available, the quota is $50,000 \div (6 + 1 = 7)$. This works out as 7,143. One is then added, giving a final figure of 7,144.
- At first all the first preferences are counted for each candidate. Any candidates who achieve the quota are elected automatically.
- After this stage the counting is complex. Essentially, the second and subsequent preferences from the ballot papers of the elected candidates are added to the other candidates. If this results in an individual achieving the quota, he or she is elected.
- This process continues until six candidates have achieved the quota and are elected.

The complex counting system is designed to ensure that voters' preferences are aggregated up to make sure that the six most popular candidates *overall* will be elected. The overall outcome tends to be highly proportional, with each party achieving its fair share of the votes and seats.

An example of a single-constituency contest from the Northern Ireland Assembly election in 2016 illustrates how this works. This is Fermanagh and South Tyrone, with results shown in Table 3.7.

Table 3.7 Results of Fermanagh and South Tyrone constituency, 2016

Party	Number of candidates offered	Candidates elected
DUP	2	2
Sinn Fein	4	2
Ulster Unionists	2	1
SDLP	1	1
Others	6	0

The quota was 6,740. Only one candidate (Arlene Foster of the DUP) achieved the quota on first preference votes.

Activity

Research the result of the election to the Welsh Assembly in 2016. Which parties seemed to benefit most from the AMS system and which party or parties did not? Explain your answers with the use of statistical evidence from the results.

Activity

Research the *full* result of the Northern Ireland Assembly election of 2016. How many parties won at least one seat? How many independent candidates won a seat?

Table 3.8 Results of the Northern Ireland Assembly election, 2016

Party	Seats won	% seats won	% first preference votes won
Democratic Unionists	38	35.2	29.2
Sinn Fein	28	25.9	24.0
Ulster Unionists	16	14.8	12.6
SDLP	12	11.1	12.0
Alliance	8	7.4	7.0
Others	6	5.6	15.2

Table 3.8 shows the overall results in Northern Ireland in 2016. Here we can clearly see how proportional the outcome is. Every party won approximately the same proportion of seats as the proportion of first preference votes gained. It is also interesting to see how many parties won some representation.

Table 3.9 An assessment of the single transferable vote (STV) system

Its advantages	Its drawbacks
It produces a broadly proportional outcome.	It is quite a complex system that some voters do not understand.
It gives voters a very wide choice of candidates to choose from. The second and subsequent choices of the voters are taken into consideration in the counting.	The vote counting is complicated and can take a long time.
Voters can vote for candidates from different parties and show a preference between candidates of the same party.	It can help candidates with extremist views to be elected.
As there are six representatives per constituency, each voter has a choice of those to represent them and usually can be represented by someone from the party they support.	With six representatives per constituency, the lines of accountability are not clear.
It helps small parties and independent candidates to be elected.	

The supplementary vote

This system is used where a single candidate is to be elected. It is designed to produce a winner who can claim to be supported overall by a majority of the voters. In the UK its main use is to elect city mayors. It could be used to elect MPs but there is no appetite for this kind of reform. Most reformers prefer the idea of proportional representation rather than the supplementary vote.

Voters have two choices, a first and second choice. If any candidate achieves an overall majority, i.e. 50%+, of the first choice or round, he or she is automatically elected. If this does not happen, the top two candidates go into a second round of counting. All the others drop out. The second choice votes are added to the first choices to give two final totals. As there are only two candidates left, one of them must achieve an absolute majority. So the winner has an overall majority of a combination of first- and second-choice votes. Table 3.10 illustrates how this worked in the election of the London mayor in 2016. Sadiq Khan, the eventual winner, could only achieve 44.2% of

Sadiq Khan, mayor of London since 2016

the first-choice votes, but 161,427 voters put him as their second choice and this was enough to give him a comfortable overall majority.

Table 3.10 Elections for Mayor of London, 2016

Candidate	Party	1st round votes	% votes	2nd round votes	% total
Sadiq Khan	Labour	1,148,716	44.2	1,310,143	56.8
Zac Goldsmith	Conservative	909,755	35.0	994,614	43.2
Sian Berry	Green	150,673	5.8	–	
Caroline Pidgeon	Lib Dem	120,005	4.6	–	
Peter Whittle	UKIP	94,373	3.6	–	
Seven other candidates	Various	173,439	6.6	–	

Table 3.11 assesses the effectiveness and desirability of the supplementary vote system. In reality, however, it has few serious rivals when it comes to electing a single official. It is used in the vast majority of democracies for this kind of election. The USA is an exception where the presidential election is concerned. A more complex 'electoral college' system is used there to reflect the federal nature of the political system.

Table 3.11 An assessment of the supplementary vote system

Its advantages	Its drawbacks
The winning candidate can claim to have an overall majority of support.	A winning candidate may not enjoy the first-choice support of an overall majority.
It is relatively simple for voters to understand.	The winning candidate may win on second choices.
Voters' first and second choices are relevant.	

Electoral systems in context

Table 3.12 summarises the use of electoral systems in different parts of the UK. What is immediately striking is the fact that so many different systems are being used. The main reason for this is that decision makers hoped to produce a party system that was most desirable in each of the different contexts. For example, STV was adopted in Northern Ireland in order to reflect the fact that it is a very divided community and that all the different communities should be represented in a multi-party system. So, five different parties achieved significant representation in the Northern Ireland Assembly.

Table 3.12 Summary of electoral systems used in the UK

System	Type of system	Where used
First past the post	Plurality	UK general elections English and Welsh local government elections
Additional member system	Hybrid	Scottish parliamentary elections Welsh Assembly elections Greater London Assembly elections
STV	Proportional	All Northern Ireland elections Local elections in Scotland
Supplementary vote	Majority	To elect city mayors

Similarly, in Scotland, after devolution in 1997 the danger was perceived to be that the Labour Party would dominate the country in elections if FPTP were retained. The change to AMS ensured that the main English parties could not dominate. Ironically, the change worked too well! The political system in Scotland is now dominated by the SNP and the English parties have been placed at a disadvantage. In Wales, however, AMS has done its work well and there is a very balanced party system there.

Returning to FPTP, it seems destined to remain as the system used for general elections for some time to come. This is largely because the political establishment (in both main parties) takes a broadly conservative view of the issue. Most senior politicians prefer the status quo and fear the unknown, as represented by proportional representation.

Comparing FPTP with other systems

Here we are asking the question: Should the UK abandon the first-past-the-post electoral system for general elections and replace it with an alternative? Before considering the answer we should remember that the British people did reject an alternative system in a referendum in 2011. The system concerned was the *alternative vote (AV)*, a system used, for example, in Australia.

We have not described AV here because it is seldom used (being reserved to by-elections in STV systems) and is unlikely to be considered in the future. Nevertheless, the result of the 2011 referendum (which decisively rejected AV) should not be taken to indicate that public opinion is opposed to reform. There were a number of reasons why the voters rejected AV which are unrelated to their desire for some kind of change:

- The proposal was promoted by the Liberal Democrats (in coalition government with the Conservatives) and the party was very unpopular at that time. It is therefore estimated that many voters used the referendum to show dissatisfaction with the Liberal Democrats rather than to reject AV.
- AV is quite a complex system, so many voters rejected it because they did not understand it.
- The pro-reform campaign was poorly run while the anti-reform campaign was well organised and funded.

So we must start our discussion with a clean slate. The issue is whether to replace FPTP with another proportional system, but not AV. It is also advisable to consider the issue from three different points of view:

1 What effect would change have on the party system and would the change be desirable?

2 What effect would change have on government formation and would such change be desirable?

3 What effect would change have on the UK's democracy and on the experience of voters, and would such change be desirable?

The issues are examined in this format below.

Effects on the party system

Introducing proportional representation for UK general elections would produce a multi-party system. Parties such as UKIP, the Green Party, the Liberal Democrats and Plaid Cymru would win significant numbers of seats. The larger parties — Labour, the Conservatives and the SNP — would win considerably fewer seats than currently. For some, this is a desirable outcome as it would provide a pluralist, more representative result and mean that voters were better represented. On the other hand, some argue it might give an opening for extremist parties and possibly create a chaotic political system with too many competing parties.

Effects on government formation

The kind of multi-party system described above would prevent any party from winning an overall majority in Parliament. This can be seen as a desirable outcome as it would prevent governments being excessively powerful. In order to govern as a minority government or coalition, a government would have to seek a consensus

Activity

Research the 2011 national referendum on the possible introduction of AV. What was the majority rejecting the proposal and what was the overall turnout?

on every issue and democracy would be better served. Critics, however, point to the instability this would produce, with governments frequently falling and having to be re-formed, as occurs in some European states. Without a parliamentary majority, governments would lose decisiveness and be unable to deliver their electoral mandate.

Effects on voters

Supporters of the introduction of a proportional system insist that voters' interests would be better served. Every vote would count and be of equal value, and there would be more voter choice. Proportional systems favour the selection of women and members of ethnic minorities as candidates. Above all, voters would no longer need to vote tactically and would be able to support their first-choice party. Critics point out that proportional systems are more difficult to understand. They also say that the loss of the close relationship between MPs and constituencies would be a blow to democracy.

Ultimately the supporters of proportional representation see the debate as democracy versus over-powerful government, equality versus discrimination. Those who favour the retention of FPTP see the issue in terms of order versus chaos, strong versus weak government.

Referendums

How referendums operate

Before 1975 **referendums** were almost unknown in the UK political system. (An attempt to hold a referendum in Northern Ireland in 1973 had failed as half the community boycotted it.) In 1975, however, there was a national referendum on whether the UK should remain a member of the European Community (the forerunner of the European Union), which the country had joined just 2 years earlier. It was seen as a once in a generation event and so it proved. The next *national* referendum was not held until 2011, when the question was whether the UK should adopt a new electoral system for general elections. In between those two national referendums there were some regional and local referendums, but it seemed that the device of holding a referendum to determine key issues was seen as something of a 'last resort'.

However, since 2011, two ground-breaking referendums have been held, so that it seems that they are now established as a part of the UK Constitution. Those two referendums were the 2014 vote on whether Scotland should become an independent state and the 2016 referendum, whose outcome meant that the UK had to leave the EU.

A referendum can be simply defined. It is a vote, conducted at local, regional or national level, in response to a question which has a simple 'yes' or 'no' answer. (In the case of the 2016 referendum voters were asked to choose between 'leave' and 'remain'.) The key reason why a referendum might be held is that, for some reason, it is felt preferable that the people themselves should resolve an issue rather than the elected representatives of the people. Why should a people's vote be preferable to a vote in an elected assembly? After all, it can be argued, in a representative democracy we elect people to make decisions on our behalf, to use their judgement and to mediate between competing demands. Why should we make the decisions ourselves? This question has several possible answers:

- The issue may be so crucial that it is felt that only a popular vote can resolve it. This was the case with the proposal to reform the electoral system in 2011.
- It may be that the issue causes so much conflict *within* the political system and among its elected representatives that the only way to resolve it without excessive

Activity

Research the 2017 general election result. Note down the proportion of the national vote won by all the parties that won seats. Calculate what proportion of the 650 seats each party *would have won* had the seats been awarded in the same proportion as the votes cast.

Key term

Referendum A vote, which may be national, regional or local, in which qualified voters are asked a single question about a proposal where the answer is either 'yes' or 'no'. National referendums are not legally binding on Parliament or government, but it is unthinkable that their outcome would be ignored.

Key term

Government by consent
The idea, developed by liberal theorists, that government must enjoy the consent of the people who are to be governed. This also implies that the people must show consent to *how* they are governed and what the system of government should be.

political conflict is to let the people decide directly. Both sides in a political conflict have to accept the outcome. This was the case with both referendums on UK membership of the EC in 1975 and the EU in 2016.

- A referendum may be the only way to solve conflict within the wider community. In 1998, for example, the people of Northern Ireland were invited to vote on whether to accept the Good Friday Agreement (also known as the Belfast Agreement), which was to end many years of conflict between the nationalist and loyalist communities in the province and establish a power-sharing system of government.
- The liberal doctrine of '**government by consent**' demands that the system of government to which people submit can only exist with the consent of the people themselves. This implies that any fundamental change to the way we are governed must achieve direct consent through a referendum. Thus, when increased powers were proposed to be given to devolved administrations in Scotland and Wales in 1997 (so-called devolution), it had to be put to the people of those nations.

Referendums in the UK

Table 3.13 details most of the important referendums that have been held in the UK since 1975. There have been a number of other regional and local referendums held over the period which are not shown in the table. These have involved such issues as the introduction of congestion charges in city centres, whether a city should have an elected mayor and whether the powers of the Welsh Assembly should be extended. These referendums had variable outcomes.

Table 3.13 Referendums in the UK

Year	Issue	Level	Why held	% yes	% no	% turnout
1975	Should the UK remain a member of the European Community?	National	The Labour government was divided on the issue.	67.2	32.8	64.5
1997	Should additional powers be devolved to Scotland and a Scottish Parliament established?	Scotland	A fundamental change in the system of government needed popular consent.	74.3	25.7	60.4
1997	Should additional powers be devolved to Wales and a Welsh assembly established?	Wales	A fundamental change in the system of government needed popular consent.	50.3	49.7	50.1
1998	Should the Belfast Agreement be implemented?	Northern Ireland	This required support across the whole divided community.	71.7	28.9	81.0
2004	Should additional powers be devolved to northeast England and a regional assembly established?	Northeast England	A fundamental change in the system of government needed popular consent.	22.1	77.9	47.7
2005	Should a 'congestion charge' zone be introduced in Edinburgh?	Edinburgh	It was a highly controversial proposal.	25.6	74.4	61.7
2011	Should the UK adopt the alternative vote system for general elections?	National	The coalition government was divided on the issue of electoral reform.	32.1	67.9	42.2
2014	Should Scotland become a completely independent country?	Scotland	A fundamental question about who governs Scotland	44.7	55.3	84.6
2016	Should the UK remain a member of the EU?	National	A fundamental constitutional question. The governing Conservative Party was split on the issue. Also to meet the challenge of UKIP	48.1	51.9	72.2

The process of holding a referendum

Holding a referendum is no simple task. It requires a great deal of preparation and planning. In general, the stages leading to a referendum are these:

- The governing party adopts a policy that a referendum should be held on an issue.
- The precise wording of the referendum question is established.
- Legislation is passed in Parliament, setting up the arrangements for a referendum including the date it is to be held.
- The referendum is held and the result announced.
- Referendums are never legally binding, but it is virtually unthinkable that a representative body should not obey the outcome. If the result requires a change, legal and political arrangements for the change are made.

A number of regulations tend to govern the conduct of referendum campaigns. In national and regional referendums there is official recognition of the bodies that campaign on each side of the question. Expenditure on referendum campaigns is regulated to ensure that each side spends approximately equal funds. This is done by the Electoral Commission. The Electoral Commission also ensures that both sides in the campaign do not issue false information and organises the counting of votes.

Referendums and initiatives

A variation of the referendum system is the **initiative**. An initiative occurs when the people themselves decide that a referendum should be held. In the UK it is government and the legislature that decide when a referendum should be held. Initiatives are widely used in some states of the USA. The way initiatives normally work is that citizens must create a petition asking for a popular vote. When an agreed number of names are on the petition, a referendum (sometimes also known as a 'proposition' in the USA) is triggered. In California, for example, the petition number required equals 5% of voters at the last election for governor.

Some interesting propositions in the USA have been these:

- **2008, Arizona State** To amend the state constitution to prohibit same-sex marriage. Passed
- **2012, California State** To temporarily increase sales tax in the state to pay for improved education and other services. Passed
- **2012, Massachusetts State** To make assisted suicide legal. Failed
- **2014, Oregon State** To legalise recreational use of marijuana. Passed

Switzerland operates a similar system to the USA. There, 100,000 signatures are needed to trigger a referendum. Some Swiss examples include:

- **1971** To grant voting rights to women. Passed
- **2014** To order the government to prevent 'mass immigration'. Passed
- **2016** To authorise the building of a new road tunnel under the Alps. Passed
- **2016** To expel all foreign-born criminals from the country. Failed

In the UK, however, it remains firmly in the hands of government and Parliament which issues should be put to the electorate in a referendum.

Referendums and elections

Referendums are very different to elections. The key differences between the two devices include the following:

- Referendums are always on a single issue whereas elections are fought on a wide range of issues across all the business of government.

Activity

Consider the referendums shown in Table 3.13.

- Why was the turnout so high in any two referendums and so low in two others?
- Outline two reasons why Scotland voted against independence.
- Outline two reasons why the UK voted against a change to AV.

The imposition of congestion charges in city centres usually requires the consent of the residents.

Key term

Initiative A device used in some countries, including Switzerland and parts of the USA, whereby a petition signed by large numbers of voters can trigger a referendum. The voters, rather than government, decide what issues should be put to a referendum.

- Referendums demand a single yes/no answer whereas elections result in a more nuanced, varied outcome, with different levels of representation awarded to different parties.
- As we have seen, the government and Parliament decide when referendums should be held. Elections, by contrast, normally occur at regular intervals determined by law.

Yet, despite the differences there is one crucial similarity. Both referendums and elections grant legitimacy to decisions. In the case of an election, the winners claim a mandate for their policies; with referendums, the electorate are directly granting authority to government to implement a specific decision.

The impact of referendums

There is a maxim in politics that governments should never call for a referendum unless they are very confident about what the answer will be. There are two reasons why this is a sensible principle. The first is that, normally, governments use referendums as a way of securing direct consent for policies they might have introduced themselves. A good example was devolution of power to Scotland, Wales and Northern Ireland in the late 1990s. Devolution was, effectively, a policy of the Labour government of the day, but it needed to be reinforced by confirmation in a referendum. The government was also confident it would win the three votes. So it proved.

The second reason is that, if a government supports one side of a referendum debate, it will be placed in a difficult position if it loses the debate. It is a severe blow to its authority. This occurred, of course, in 2016 when the UK voted to leave the EU. The result was traumatic. Above all, the prime minister, David Cameron, felt his position was untenable and he resigned. The wider result was a complete change in the government's stance on Europe and many ministers lost their positions. The referendum also shook the Labour Party. Its leader, Jeremy Corbyn, lost the support of most of the party's MPs largely on the grounds that he had campaigned so poorly in favour of remaining in the EU.

It goes without saying that the 2014 vote on Scottish independence was what the government of the UK hoped for. However, it did have a major impact on the politics of devolution. The closeness of the outcome was a huge boost to the Scottish National Party. Before that, during the campaign, as the outcome was thrown increasingly into doubt, all three main English parties were forced to promise the Scots greater powers for their parliament and government. The government won the vote but it was too close for comfort. The Scottish referendum did not result in independence but it did result in a major shift in power towards Edinburgh. Then, 2 years later, when the UK voted to leave the EU a fresh Scottish crisis ensued. The problem was that 62% of Scottish voters voted to *stay* in the EU. This meant that the Scots were being dragged out of the EU against their expressed will. The result has been renewed calls for a second referendum on Scottish independence so that people in Scotland can choose to stay in the EU.

So referendums can change things whatever the outcome. They can promote political change and they can also remove policies from the immediate political agenda, as occurred when electoral reform was soundly rejected in 2011. Whether such impacts are desirable is considered in the next section.

Knowledge check

Which public body organises and regulates the conduct of referendums?

Activity

Research David Cameron's resignation speech in June 2016 following the EU referendum. Why did Cameron feel he needed to resign?

Campaigners for leaving the EU

The case for and against the use of referendums

Until recently the tide of public opinion seemed to be turning in favour of the use of referendums, especially after the vote on Scottish independence in 2014. That referendum was deemed a success in that it involved the vast majority of the people of Scotland and its result was emphatic enough to settle the issue for some time to come. Then the referendum on the UK's membership of the EU changed attitudes again. The result, which shocked the political establishment and was totally unexpected in the light of the opinion polls, demonstrated how divided a society the UK had become.

In this sense it settled the issue — the UK had to leave the EU — but also led to fears that the narrow minority which voted to remain in the EU was being tyrannised by the majority. Furthermore, many commentators suspected that many of those who voted to leave were not voting on the issue of the EU itself, but on their broader concern that their voices were not being heard by the political system based in London. The EU poll revealed many of the concerns that people have expressed about referendums. Of course, the winning side had a different perspective. For them it was a hugely successful exercise in popular democracy. Conventional politics had been defeated by the will of the majority. For this one exciting moment the people had made history for themselves.

So we have two perspectives on referendums thrown up by the 2016 EU poll.

Referendums are a controversial democratic device. It is a matter for debate, whether they are a positive or negative method of settling major issues. The arguments are set out below.

Synoptic links

Any assessment of referendums should be considered in the light of the discussion on direct and representative democracy laid out in Chapter 1.

Knowledge check

Which political thinker coined the term 'tyranny of the majority' and what was the context of his remark?

Debate

Should referendums be used to settle political issues?

Arguments for

- Referendums are the purest form of democracy, uncorrupted by the filter of representative democracy. They demonstrate the pure will of the people, as occurred in the EU vote.
- Referendums can mend rifts in society, as occurred with the decisive result of the 1998 vote on the Belfast Agreement.
- Referendums can solve conflicts *within* the political system and so stave off a crisis. This was especially the case with the EU referendums in both 1975 and 2016.
- Referendums are particularly useful when the *expressed* (as opposed to *implied*) consent of the people is important, so that the decision will be respected. This was very true of the votes on devolution in 1997.
- Arguably the people are much more informed than they have ever been in the past. The internet and social media in particular have facilitated this. This makes them more capable of making decisions for themselves rather than relying on elected representatives.

Arguments against

- The people may not be able to understand the complexities of an issue such as the consequences of leaving the EU or adopting a new electoral system.
- Referendums can also cause social rifts. This arguably occurred in both 2014 in Scotland and 2016 in the EU referendum.
- There is a danger that the excessive use of referendums may undermine the authority of representative democracy. This has been a particular danger in some states in the USA.
- A referendum can represent the 'tyranny of the majority'. This means that the majority that wins the vote can use their victory to force the minority to accept a change which is against their interests. The Scots, who voted strongly to stay in the EU in 2016, claimed they were being tyrannised by the English majority.
- Voters may be swayed by emotional rather than rational appeals. It may also be that they are influenced by false information.
- Some questions should not be reduced to a simple yes/no answer; they are more complicated. The 2011 question on electoral reform is an example of this. Perhaps several *different* options should have been considered, not just one.

The 2016 referendum on the EU was like no other and was more controversial than anything before. This was for two main reasons.

- First, the decision was so incredibly significant, determining the whole future of the UK.
- Second, it caused so much fragmentation within the political system. Both the Labour and Conservative parties were convulsed by the result and a major schism developed between Scotland and the rest of the UK. Furthermore the losing side especially argued that the campaign had been distorted by false information and by negative campaigning, playing on people's irrational fears.

Future governments are likely to be very wary before sanctioning a future referendum.

Study tip

When answering questions on referendums and direct democracy it is essential to use the context and impact of at least three relevant referendums to illustrate your discussion.

Discussion point

Was the 2016 referendum on UK membership of the EU a successful exercise in popular democracy or an example of everything that is wrong with referendums?

Referendums and representative democracy

When we consider the use of referendums as a democratic device we should be comparing them with the way in which decisions are reached by elected representatives. The advantages of representative democracy when it comes to making key decisions are outlined below.

- Representatives are more likely to adopt a rational approach and resist emotional reactions to questions. For example, many voters were concerned about immigration in the EU referendum and were responding to appeals to their patriotism and the perceived dangers to 'British values' posed by too many migrants entering communities. Elected representatives, on the other hand, could weigh up the benefits as well as the problems of high numbers of migrants.
- Elected politicians have an army of well-informed advisers to help them make decisions. They can ensure that the information on which they base their judgements is accurate. Most people have to rely on the media — print, broadcast and social — for their information, which is at best conflicting and at worst dubious. This certainly was a problem thrown up in the EU referendum campaign.
- Elected representatives have to concern themselves with the competing interests of both the majority and minorities. Voters, on the other hand, and for understandable reasons, usually only have to think of their own interests. The people of Edinburgh and Manchester, for example, have voted in local referendums against the imposition of congestion charges on motorists entering the city centre. It seemed that a disgruntled majority did not consider the minority of public transport users. In contrast, congestion charges were introduced in London by the elected mayor (Ken Livingstone) in 2003. He could take into account the interests of public transport users and the wider population (in terms of air pollution) as well as motorists.
- We also hope, of course, that our elected representatives have better judgement even than ourselves. Judgement and good sense are qualities we consider when electing them.

Set against these considerations, we can see the disadvantages of referendums more clearly. All of the advantages listed above are lost when a referendum is used. Those who opposed the use of a referendum in 2016 on whether the UK should leave the UK were adamant that such a key decision should have been made by Parliament — perhaps the subject of a free vote in the House of Commons — and not by the people, who were poorly placed to exercise a rational judgement.

Electoral outcomes

The role and importance of elections

Elections are not as simple as they first appear. Indeed they have a number of functions which complement each other. Here we consider the various functions of elections when electing a representative body. Elections *within* organisations, including political parties, have a specialised function and these are not included here. However, this description applies to elections held at local, regional and national levels.

The main functions and importance of elections include the following:

- Elections are used to choose representatives. In a democracy, legislators and decision makers have to be elected.
- Elections are the most important way in which citizens become involved in politics. For many it is their *only* form of political participation. It is vital that citizens do participate to ensure the public accountability of government and the legislature.
- Elections are a time when government and elected representatives can be called to account. During the campaign the candidates must justify what they and their party have done. All their past record and their current policies are put under close scrutiny during the run-up to an election.
- Democracy demands that the people have choice over who represents their interests. Elections provide that choice, thoroughly explained.
- Elections have an educative function. An informed citizenry is essential if democracy is to remain healthy. During election campaigns the public can become better informed over the key political issues that face their locality, region or nation.
- Finally, but certainly not least significantly, elections provide a *mandate*. The winners in an election are granted democratic legitimacy, the political authority to carry out the political programme that they are proposing. Without such a mandate and the accountability that goes with it, democracy will fail.

How fair are elections?

There is an ongoing debate in UK politics as to how fair elections are. Views tend to be polarised on the issue, with supporters and detractors taking entrenched positions. Here we examine both sides of the argument.

Positive aspects of UK elections

UK elections enjoy the following positive features:

- There is relatively little corruption. Some electoral fraud takes place in some areas but it is rare and usually detected. The secrecy of the ballot is virtually guaranteed. The counting of votes is carefully and thoroughly regulated. The conduct of elections is safeguarded by the Electoral Commission, which is independent of government.
- The constituency system ensures clear representation for citizens.
- Elections usually produce a clear, decisive result — 2010 was a rare exception.

Activity

Consider the 2017 general election. Identify features which further illustrate the role and importance of elections.

Synoptic links

When considering the importance of elections you should also consider the wider principle of mandate and manifesto, covered in Chapter 2.

Research the Fixed Term
Parliaments Act. Establish
what circumstances could
result in an 'early' election.

- Elections are held on a regular basis and since 2011, when the **Fixed Term Parliaments Act** was passed, all elections take place on set dates in the future.
- UK elections are free in that it is relatively easy and cheap for any citizen to stand for election and virtually all adults are permitted to vote.
- Elections in Scotland, Wales and Northern Ireland are based on broadly proportional lines so the outcome could be said to be fair to the parties.
- There is freedom of information and of the media so that the voters have free access to independent information upon which they can base their choice.

Vote counting in a general election starts soon after the close of the polls at 10 p.m.

Negative aspects of UK elections

UK elections suffer from the following negative features:

- The first-past-the-post system used for general elections and local elections in England and Wales is widely acknowledged to be unfair and certainly unrepresentative. This means that many votes are wasted and votes are of unequal value.
- Small parties find it difficult to gain a foothold because of the electoral system in England.
- UK general elections produce governments that do not enjoy the support of a majority of the electorate. In recent elections the winning party has failed to achieve 40% of the popular vote.

There are more positive than negative features of UK elections, suggesting they are highly democratic — and, in comparison with many parts of the world, they are. However, hanging over any discussion of their effectiveness lies the problem of the FPTP electoral system. Its virtual guarantee of a clear winner can be seen as both a positive and a negative feature.

Discussion point

With reference to Table 3.14 and what you have read on these pages, consider the merits of elections in a democracy.

Table 3.14 Do elections enhance democracy?

Positive arguments	Negative arguments
Elections allow the electorate to hold the outgoing government to account. There is a clear choice between the government and other parties.	Voters may feel that a vote for smaller parties is wasted, so the choice is not as wide as may appear to be the case.
Elections create representative assemblies in an organised way and at regular intervals.	Referendums can also cause social rifts. This arguably occurred in both 2014 in Scotland and in 2016 in the EU referendum.
There is widespread public confidence that elections in the UK are well regulated and that the outcomes are genuine expressions of the will of voters.	There is a danger that the excessive use of referendums may undermine the authority of representative democracy. This has been a particular danger in some states in the USA.
Under FPTP, elections usually produce strong and stable governments, with majorities in the House of Commons.	Under FPTP, elections produce majority governments that are, nevertheless, supported by a *minority* of the electorate.
UK elections provide strong constituency representation so that voters are confident that there will be representation of their interests.	While elections to devolved assemblies are generally proportional, elections to the Westminster Parliament are not proportional, exaggerating the popularity of large parties and discriminating against small parties.

The electoral system and government

We must not separate the nature of elections from the nature of government. The voters, although they are choosing from a selection of candidates, are actually deciding which party they prefer and who will form the government. Indeed, that is what is probably uppermost in their minds when they enter the polling station. The problem is, as we have seen, the majority of voters — up to 60% of them — will not get the government they voted for.

On the other hand, elections in the UK have proved to be effective in producing strong and stable governments at all levels. This is, though, beginning to change. In Scotland and Wales, for example, no majority government emerged in the 2016 elections. In the UK as a whole, three consecutive elections — 2010, 2015 and 2017 — failed to produce a government with a decisive majority, and twice with no majority at all. This may lead us to the conclusion that the traditional link between FPTP and single-party government has been broken.

If the UK were to adopt proportional representation for local and national elections, the country would have to get used to the idea of multi-party government. We might also have to get used to the idea of unstable government. The experience of coalition government in the UK in 2010–15 is mixed. It was stable and lasted for 5 years with few major defeats in Parliament. However, there was also widespread concern that the junior coalition partner, the Liberal Democrats, did not have sufficient influence, so government was still dominated by one party. The evidence that voters were unhappy with the experience of coalition, two-party government is that they turned decisively against the Liberal Democrats by defeating all but eight of their candidates. Even so, it is difficult to judge the *real* level of support for small parties because so many voters do not support them as they fear it will be a wasted vote.

Electoral systems and party systems

The interesting questions to be asked about the UK party system are these:

- Does the UK have a two-party system *because of* the nature of the FPTP electoral system or does it have a two-party system because that is how people prefer it — a simple choice between two main parties?
- Does the UK now have a multi-party system in terms of voter support, but *not* in terms of parliamentary seats, because of the electoral system? In other words, if we changed the electoral system, would a multi-party system immediately take over?
- The fact that we have a two-party system at Westminster does not mean that we don't have a multi-party system at local and regional government levels.

Activity

Identify any changes in the party system that may have taken place as a result of the 2017 general election.

Certainly there has been a decline in support for the two largest parties over the past few decades and certainly there has been a rise in support for smaller parties such as UKIP, the SNP and the Green Party. Another way of considering this is to ask whether the UK political system is now *pluralistic*, with voters seeking parties that are more focused on their particular concerns. If this is the case, the two-party system must be doomed, irrespective of the electoral system. On the other hand, voters may ultimately shrink from a multi-party system and return to a preference for a two-party choice.

Electoral systems and voter choice

How much choice do voters really want? If the UK adopted proportional representation (PR) for general elections, would more voters opt for smaller parties? As things stand, voters tend to be *forced* into voting either Labour or Conservative because any other vote would automatically be wasted. They are also sometimes forced to **vote tactically**, opting for their second choice in order to influence the outcome.

Under PR every vote counts and every vote is of equal value. With some systems, such as STV, voters are even able to discriminate between candidates of the *same* party. The lack of choice under FPTP is quite stark but we do need to ask whether voters want more choice, especially if greater choice leads to less stable government.

Key term

Tactical voting When voters in UK general elections feel that their first-choice vote will be wasted because it is for a party that has no chance of winning the constituency, they may change their vote to a second choice. By doing this they may have an influence on the outcome. Typically, supporters of the Liberal Democrats or Green Party vote either Labour or Conservative because their first-choice party cannot win the constituency. This is known as tactical voting.

> **Discussion point**
>
> Do elections accurately reflect the will of the people in terms of representation and make accurate judgements about the performance of government and other parties?

When voters were asked whether they wanted a change to the electoral system in the 2011 referendum, they rejected it decisively. This may suggest they prefer the status quo — i.e. a two-party system underpinned by a plurality voting system. However, this may be an illusion. The alternative proposed was the alternative vote (AV), which did offer more choice, but was far from proportional. If the electorate were asked to choose between FPTP and a proportional system today, the answer might be different.

Absolute majority This refers to the result of a vote where the winner receives more votes than all the other candidates put together. In other words, the winner receives at least 50% of the total votes.

Constituency A constituency is a geographical area used to determine which people each elected representative represents. UK parliamentary constituencies are roughly 75,000 voters in size. Constituencies in devolved systems and local government are much smaller but also roughly equal in size. Elected representatives are expected to look after the interests of their constituency.

First past the post (FPTP) The name commonly used to describe the UK's electoral system for general elections, although its more formal title is 'plurality in single-member constituencies'.

Government by consent The idea, developed by liberal theorists, that government must enjoy the consent of the people who are to be governed. This also implies that the people must show consent to how they are governed and what the system of government should be.

Initiative A device used in some countries, including Switzerland and parts of the USA, whereby a petition signed by large numbers of voters can trigger a referendum. The voters, rather than government, decide what issues should be put to a referendum.

Majority government A government whose members and supporters constitute a majority of the members of the legislature (e.g. House of Commons or Scottish Parliament). This means they find it relatively easy to pass legislation and tends to make them stable and long lasting.

Minority government A government whose members and supporters do not constitute a majority of the members. In other words, there are more opposition-supporting members than government-supporting members. Such a minority government finds it difficult to pass legislation and is likely to be unstable and short lived.

Plurality This term refers to the result of an election where the winner only has to obtain more votes than any of their opponents. It does not mean the winner has an absolute majority.

Proportional representation (PR) This refers to any electoral system that tends to produce a proportional outcome. In other words, the seats in a representative body are awarded in an election broadly in the same proportion as the votes cast for each party. So, for example, if a party wins 40% of the votes it will be awarded approximately 40% of the seats available. The regional list system and single transferable vote system are good examples of PR.

Referendum A vote, which may be national, regional or local, in which qualified voters are asked a single question about a proposal where the answer is either 'yes' or 'no'. National referendums are not legally binding on Parliament or government, but it is unthinkable that their outcome would be ignored.

Safe seat A constituency where it is highly unlikely that the seat will change hands from one party to another at an election.

Tactical voting When voters in UK general elections feel that their first-choice vote will be wasted because it is for a party that has no chance of winning the constituency, they may change their vote to a second choice. By doing this they may have an influence on the outcome. Typically, supporters of the Liberal Democrats or Green Party vote either Labour or Conservative because their first-choice party cannot win the constituency. This is known as tactical voting.

Summary

Having read this chapter, you should have knowledge and understanding of the following:

→ How the first-past-the-post system works in the UK
→ The main outcomes and impacts of FPTP
→ What are the main alternatives to FPTP
→ The relative merits of FPTP and alternative electoral systems
→ The arguments and debates about reform of the UK electoral system
→ How referendums work in the UK
→ The impact of referendums in the UK
→ Distinctions between elections, initiatives and referendums
→ The case for and against the use of referendums
→ Why elections are important
→ The positive and negative aspects of elections in the UK
→ The impact of different electoral systems on party systems, government formation and voter choice

Further information and web guide

Websites

The best sites for information about electoral systems are these:

www.electoral-reform.org.uk. This is the Electoral Reform Society. As this is a campaign group, the website may not be objective, but there is also a great deal of accurate factual information there.

www.electoralcommission.org.uk. The body that regulates elections and referendums — this is an objective site.

Another campaign group that discusses electoral systems is Unlock Democracy:
www.unlockdemocracy.org.

The official parliamentary website also has information: **www.parliament.uk**.

Books

Up-to-date and accessible books on electoral systems and electoral reform are thin on the ground. A few are:

Farrell, D. (2011) *Electoral Systems*, Palgrave Macmillan. This is excellent, though it contains information about systems used throughout the world, so the UK experience is only one part.

Renwick, A. (2011) *A Citizen's Guide to Electoral Reform*, Biteback. This deals well with all the arguments about various systems.

Geddes, A. and Tonge, I. (eds) (2015) *Britain Votes*, Hansard Society. This deals with the performance of the parties and voting behaviour, and also analyses the effects of the first-past-the-post electoral system.

Look too at the Electoral Reform Society's Annual Reports. They contain analyses of recent elections and how the various UK electoral systems worked.

AS

1 Describe the main features of the first-past-the-post electoral system. (10)

2 Describe the workings of any two electoral systems in use in the UK other than first-past-the-post. (10)

3 Using the source, assess the impact of the additional member electoral system (AMS) in Scotland. *In your response you must use knowledge and understanding to analyse points that are only in the source. You will not be rewarded for introducing any additional points that are not in the source.* (10)

Results of the elections to the Scottish Parliament, 2016				
Party	Constituency seats won	Regional list system seats awarded	Total seats won	% seats won	% votes won in the regional lists
SNP	59	4	63	48.8	41.7
Conservative	7	24	31	24.0	22.9
Labour	3	21	24	18.6	19.1
Green Party	0	6	6	4.7	6.6
Liberal Democrat	4	1	5	3.9	5.2
Others	0	0	0	0	4.5

4 'Referendums are the best way of determining important political and constitutional questions.' How far do you agree with this statement? (30)

5 'First-past-the-post guarantees strong and stable government.' How far do you agree? (30)

A-level

1 Using the source, evaluate the impact of first-past-the-post in terms of representative democracy. *In your response you must compare the different opinions in the source and use a balance of knowledge and understanding both arising from the source and beyond it to help you to analyse and evaluate.*

(30)

The result of the UK general election, May 2015				
Party	% votes won	% seats won	No. of seats won	Notes
Conservative	36.9	50.9	331	Conservative support is concentrated in southern England.
Labour	30.4	35.7	232	Labour support is concentrated in northern England.
Scottish National Party	4.7	8.6	56	In Scotland the SNP won 95% of the available seats on 50% of the Scottish vote.
Liberal Democrats	7.9	1.2	8	The party's support is widely dispersed.
Democratic Unionist Party	0.6	1.2	8	The DUP only contests seats in Northern Ireland.
Sinn Fein	0.6	0.6	4	Northern Ireland only
Plaid Cymru	0.6	0.5	3	Contests seats in Wales
UKIP	12.6	0.2	1	UKIP support is very widely dispersed.
Green Party	3.8	0.2	1	Support for the Greens is very dispersed.
Others	2.5	1.0	6	Mostly in Northern Ireland

2 Using the source, evaluate the use of referendums to determine important political and constitutional issues. *In your response you must compare the different opinions in the source and use a balance of knowledge and understanding both arising from the source and beyond it to help you to analyse and evaluate.* (30)

> ### The EU referendum, 2016
>
> The 2016 referendum on the UK's membership of the European Union was perhaps the most important democratic exercise in the history of the country. The question was important, of course, but the fact that many millions of voters took part in making such a momentous decision was most impressive. It certainly settled the issue after many years of political conflict and people who felt they did not have a voice were now listened to. The vote created both legitimacy and public consent for the decision.
>
> But behind the euphoria there were also serious concerns. The referendum campaign was dogged with controversy about misinformation and lack of clarity. The press were also accused of bias, with most popular tabloids campaigning relentlessly for a 'Leave' vote. Perhaps more importantly, some sections of the community felt they had been steamrollered into a decision against their will. Younger voters, the Scots and Londoners were all groups who voted strongly to remain within the EU, but they were overwhelmed by the national majority. The result was also very close — hardly a decisive outcome.
>
> But, however much we may analyse the result, in the end the people had spoken and democracy had been served.

3 Evaluate the criticisms that have been levelled against the use of referendums in the UK. (30)

4 Evaluate the case for introducing proportional representation for UK general elections. (30)

4 Voting behaviour and the media

If we were to ask what the typical Labour voter looks like, what his or her characteristics are, we might draw this picture:

- She is probably slightly more likely to be a woman.
- She will be under 40 years old.
- She works in the public sector, perhaps in the NHS or as a teacher or social worker.
- Her income is average, perhaps just above average or much lower than average.
- She is from an ethnic minority.
- Her parents probably also voted Labour.
- She lives in the north of England.

Not surprisingly, the typical Conservative voter has the opposite of this profile.

If explaining the results of elections were that simple, we could predict the outcome by just counting up the number of people who fit into such typical profiles. Unfortunately this is too simplistic. There may be discernible *tendencies* among various sections of the population, but there are so many other factors at play that such social factors need to be treated with great caution. They do, however, explain voting patterns, and members of the parties who campaign during elections are well aware of these tendencies.

This chapter will examine the many other factors that determine the outcome of elections. These include the image of the parties, the past performance of parties, the changing perceptions of parties and their leaders, as well, of course, as how the public judge the performance of the incumbent government. The media may also have an impact, as we shall see, although this is difficult to judge. All these factors help to determine what is known as voting behaviour in UK elections.

Objectives

This chapter will inform you about the following:

→ How various demographic factors affect the way people vote and why some voters do not conform to the expected pattern — in other words, who are 'deviant voters'

→ Why the impact of social class on voting has declined

→ How and why turnout at elections varies and why there has been a long-term decline in turnout at elections

→ How and why turnout varies between different social groups

→ What factors, other than demographics, influence the way people vote

→ What tactical voting is and how much it occurs

→ How much the image of party leaders influences voting behaviour

→ The impact of the media on voting behaviour

→ The role played by opinion polls and the extent to which they may affect actual voting

→ How to construct a 'template' for the study of three general elections, which may be used as case studies to illustrate voting behaviour

Social class and other social factors

Social class

Before we look at the influence of **social class** on voting, we need to explain the normal classifications used by researchers in this field. Table 4.1 shows the meaning of four different classifications. The table also shows what proportion of the total population is in each class, according to the last national census in 2011.

> **Key term**
>
> **Social class** The way in which social researchers classify people on the basis of their occupations and, to some extent, their income. Class can explain various forms of typical behaviour, including political attitudes and voting trends.

Table 4.1 How people are classified in the UK

Classification	Description	Typical occupations	% of population in each classification
AB	Higher and intermediate managerial, administrative, professional occupations	• Banker • Doctor • Company director • Senior executive	22.17
C1	Supervisory, clerical and junior managerial, administrative, professional occupations	• Teacher • Office manager • IT manager • Social worker	30.84
C2	Skilled manual occupations	• Plumber • Hairdresser • Mechanic • Train driver	20.94
DE	Semi-skilled and unskilled manual occupations, unemployed and lowest grade occupations	• Labourer • Bar staff • Call centre staff • Unemployed	26.05

Source: 2011 census

Key terms

Deviant voting This occurs when a person does not vote the way we would expect, given their social characteristics, especially their class. Examples are working-class Conservatives and wealthy entrepreneurial Labour supporters.

Floating (or swing) voter A voter who tends to vote unpredictably in different elections and who is liable to change the way they vote fairly often.

If we had asked the question 'How much does a person's class influence the way they vote?' back in the 1960s and before, the answer would have been something like 'We can predict with great accuracy how a person will vote if we know to which social class they belong.' Possibly as many as 80% of people voted the way their social class indicated. The vast majority of AB voters favoured the Conservatives while the DE classes mostly voted for Labour. The C1 class was typically, though not overwhelmingly, Conservative, and C2 was mostly for Labour. This meant, of course, that the political battle was largely fought among two types of voter: those whose class identity was not clear and those who did not vote the way their class indicated that they might. The latter group were known as '**deviant voters**'. They were also known as '**floating voters**' because it was difficult to predict how they would vote.

The reasons why class used to be closely associated with voting trends are fairly straightforward. Three links stand out:

- The way one voted was a part of one's class identity. To be middle or upper class was to be conservative, to be working class meant you would support the party of the working class. Voting Labour expressed your class solidarity. Voting Conservative added to your status (even though it was a secret ballot).
- Both major parties developed strong, deep roots within communities, so there was a culture of voting for one party or another. The wealthy commuter belt around London, for example, was steeped in Conservative values while the poorer east of London had a strong sense of being a Labour-led community. Such roots were strengthened by Labour's associations with strong trade unions.
- There was a selfish reason. The Conservative Party was perceived to govern more in the interests of the middle class and the better off while Labour developed policies to help the working class and the poor. It was therefore rational to choose the party associated with your class.

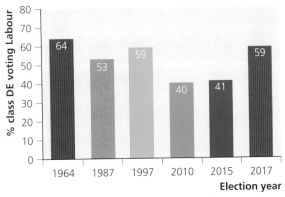

Figure 4.1 Class DE voting for Labour
Source: Ipsos MORI/Earlham Sociology/Ashcroft polling

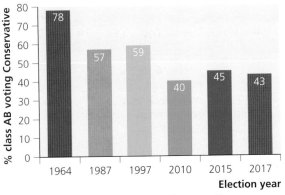

Figure 4.2 Class AB voting for the Conservatives
Source: Ipsos MORI/Earlham Sociology/Ashcroft polling

In recent years, class voting has declined noticeably. This is not to say it has disappeared, but it is certainly less pronounced. Figure 4.1 shows patterns of voting for Labour by those in class DE, while Figure 4.2 shows the link between class AB and Conservative voting. A close link between class and party support is often described as 'voting attachment'.

We can see from Figures 4.1 and 4.2 that voting on the basis of class has declined. The main features shown by these statistics include the following:

- In 1964, 64% of class DE voted for Labour, as we would expect.
- There was still a tendency for some, up to a third, of the old working class to vote Conservative, but the correlation between class and voting remained strong.
- 'Deviant' Conservative support among the working class was understood to be the result of a factor known as 'deference'. This was a tendency for some members of this class to 'defer' to or respect those whom they considered to be their superiors — i.e. members of the upper and middle classes who were perceived to be Conservatives.
- Some lower-middle- and working-class voters *aspired* to be middle class and so voted Conservative as evidence of their aspiration.
- The correlation between class AB and Conservative voting has always been stronger. There have been fewer deviant voters in this class.

Nevertheless the decline has been marked, falling from 78% voting Conservative in 1964 to only 40% in 2010, with a small recovery in 2015 and 2017. To some extent this was a reflection of 'New' Labour's achievement in attracting middle-class support away from the Conservatives, but the decline in class-based voting habits has deeper roots. Among the causes of the decline are these:

- A trend known as **class dealignment** has been important. This is a tendency for fewer and fewer people to define themselves in terms of class. In other words, social class has declined in importance within UK culture.
- The main parties, including the Liberal Democrats, have tended, especially after the 1980s, to adopt policies which are 'centrist' and consensual, and can therefore appeal to a wider class base, largely in the centre of society.
- There has been a rise in the influence of other factors, notably valence. This has tended to replace social class as a key factor in voting behaviour.

Table 4.2 demonstrates the influence of class on voting for smaller parties. It uses the 2015 election mainly because it was then that UKIP made its breakthrough.

> **Key term**
>
> **Class dealignment**
> A trend whereby progressively fewer people consider themselves to be a member of a particular social class and so class has a decreasing impact on their voting behaviour.

Table 4.2 Class and voting for smaller parties, 2015 general election

Party	Class AB (%)	Class C1 (%)	Class C2 (%)	Class DE (%)
Liberal Democrat	12	8	6	5
UKIP	8	11	19	17
Green	4	4	4	3

Source: Ipsos MORI

> **Knowledge check**
>
> Study Table 4.2. What are the distinctions in support for small parties between better-off individuals and poorer individuals?

Before leaving class, we should observe the impact of class on voting in the 2016 EU referendum. This is shown in Figure 4.3.

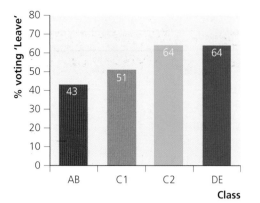

Figure 4.3 Class and voting in the EU referendum of 2016

Source: Ashcroft polling

Key term

Instrumental voting

A term referring to voting behaviour which is motivated by self-interest. In other words, voters favour a party that they believe will do most good for themselves through its policies.

As we can see, it was the working class, made up of manual workers, skilled and semi-skilled, and lower income groups who were more likely to vote Leave. This accords with the tendency of these groups to support UKIP, which was not a surprising conclusion. We do, however, need to treat this with caution. It may well be that these voting trends were not due to class but were issue based. In other words, those in social class groups C2, D and E believe that they have been most disadvantaged by EU membership, in particular the perceived adverse effect on employment and wages created by free movement of labour within the EU. Thus support for UKIP and the Leave campaign may be less a case of class voting and more a case of self-interested or **instrumental voting**.

It is, of course, possible (and no doubt future academic research projects will investigate this) that members of what we can describe loosely as the 'working class' *did* see this as a class issue, 'us against them', so to speak. Many of the 'leave' voters may well have felt that their voices are ignored because they are working class, and this was a chance to have some influence at last *because* every vote would count.

Gender and age

Gender

We can dispense with gender as a factor in voting behaviour very quickly. The statistics reveal that there is virtually no difference between the way men and women typically vote. Table 4.3 illustrates this.

Table 4.3 Gender and voting in general elections

Year	% voting Conservative		% voting Labour		% voting Liberal Democrat	
	Men	Women	Men	Women	Men	Women
1992	41	44	37	34	18	18
2001	32	33	42	42	18	19
2010	38	36	28	31	22	24
2015	38	37	30	33	8	8
2017	43	40	35	42	10	9

Source: Ipsos MORI

We can see from the figures that there is no significant difference between the way men and women vote. What's more, there is no noticeable trend in the comparative figures over the 23 years shown. Over a long period, there is a *slight* tendency for more women to vote Labour than men, but it is highly variable and not statistically very significant. It will be interesting in future to observe how gender voting may be affected by the arrival of a second female prime minister. In the 1983 and 1987 general elections, when Margaret Thatcher was prime minister, there is conflicting evidence (see Table 4.4).

Age

When we consider age, however, it is a different story. There is a strong correlation between party support and age. Table 4.5 illustrates this well.

Table 4.4 Proportion of men and women voting Conservative when Margaret Thatcher was prime minister

	Men (%)	Women (%)
1983	42	46
1987	43	43

Table 4.5 Age and voting in four general elections

Age range	1979			1997			2015			2017		
	% Con	% Lab	% All*	% Con	% Lab	% LD*	% Con	% Lab	% LD*	% Con	% Lab	% LD*
18–24	42	41	12	27	49	16	27	43	5	18	67	7
25–34	43	38	15	28	49	16	33	36	7	22	58	9
35–44**	46	35	16	28	48	17	35	35	10	30	50	9
45–54				31	41	20	36	33	8	40	39	9
55–64***	47	38	13	36	39	17	37	31	9	47	33	9
65+				36	41	17	47	23	8	59	23	10
Total, all ages	45	38	14	31	43	17	37	30	8	42	40	7

* The third party was the SDP/Liberal Alliance in 1979, the Liberal Democrats thereafter.
** In 1979 the figures are for age 35–54.
*** In 1979 the figures are for age 55+

Source: Ipsos MORI/Ashcroft polling

Knowledge check

Study Table 4.5. What has been the trend in voting behaviour by the over-65 age group?

There are clear patterns in Table 4.5. Two stand out:

1 The younger a voter is, the more likely they are to vote Labour and the less likely to vote Conservative. This can be seen in all the four elections analysed in the table.

2 Younger age groups are more likely to vote for the third party, normally the Liberal Democrats.

Table 4.6 shows voting by age group for the Green Party and the Scottish National Party in 2015. It indicates a similar pattern to third-party voting.

We can now identify a numbers of clear tendencies among young people in terms of voting:

- Younger people do not wish to be seen as 'conservative' in the more general sense of the word and voting Conservative might be a symptom of that emotion.
- There is a tendency for the young to hold more left-wing views — this may be the result of a heightened interest in such ideas as quality, justice and freedom, more associated with Labour than with the Conservatives.
- It is alleged that Winston Churchill once commented, 'If a man is not a socialist by the time he is 20, he has

Older people vote in much greater numbers than the young

Table 4.6 Voting by age for the Green Party and the SNP, 2015 general election

Age range	% Green Party	% Scottish National Party*
18–24	8	5.5
25–34	7	5.5
35–44	4	5.0
45–54	4	5.0
55–64	2	4.8
65+	2	3.1
Total, all ages	4	4.7

Source: Ipsos MORI. YouGov
* Percentage relates to proportion of votes in Scotland only.

A young person is more likely to hold left-wing views

no heart. If he is not a conservative by the time he is 40, he has no brain.' Churchill's remark suggests that young voters are emotional whereas older voters are rational.

- Perhaps it is more compelling to suggest that younger people have fewer responsibilities, and can therefore indulge in more outward-looking ideas, whereas later in life the responsibilities of a career, a family and property ownership may lead to more cautious views. The older generation may see the Conservatives as the party that is more family friendly, more security conscious and more sympathetic to property owners.

- Voting by the young for what may be described as 'radical' parties is more understandable. The young tend to adopt more radical ideas, for example, about environmental protection, social justice and democratic reform. Table 4.5 shows a small bias among younger groups to the Liberal Democrats, but the more dramatic illustration can be found in Table 4.6. It can be seen that voting for the Green Party increases markedly as we look at younger age categories. In 2015, 8% of voters aged 18–24 voted Green, but only 2% of the 65+ range — a 400% difference. The Greens are a radical left party on many issues, not just environmental.

- To reinforce the link between radicalism and the young, it has been noted that a large proportion of new members of the Labour Party in 2015–16, most of whom joined to support Jeremy Corbyn, were young voters.

- The SNP is radical in one respect — its support for Scottish independence — but generally it can be seen as a moderate left-wing party. In the 2015 general election we see from Table 4.6 that there was some age effect, though less dramatic than that for Green voting. It should be noted also that voting for independence for Scotland in the 2014 referendum on that issue was more prevalent among the young. Figure 4.4 shows a remarkable age bias in voting for independence, with 71% of the new 16- to 17-year-old voters voting in favour and only 27% of the 65+ category.

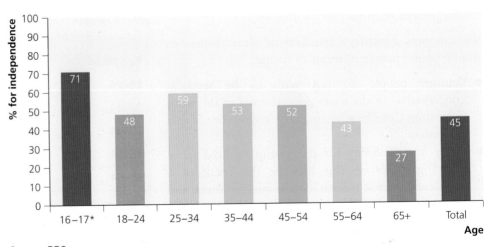

Figure 4.4 Percentage of the voting population voting for independence in the 2014 Scottish referendum, by age

Source: BBC

* This age group can only vote in Scotland.

Ethnicity

On the face of it there seems to be no reason why members of various ethnic groups, including black voters, should favour one party more than others. All parties declare themselves to be 'colour blind' and to accept that all ethnic groups should have the same rights in the UK and that discrimination against black people or members of ethnic minorities should be outlawed. Yet there is a very strong bias against the Conservatives and towards Labour among such groups. Table 4.7 shows BME (black and minority ethnic) voting in three recent elections.

Activity

Look at Tables 4.3, 4.5 and 4.6. Identify two statistics from each table which illustrate the impact of *gender* and *age* on voting behaviour most effectively.

Table 4.7 Ethnicity and voting

Election	% BME voting Conservative	% BME voting Labour	% BME voting Liberal Democrat
1997	18	70	9
2010	16	60	20
2015	23	65	4
2017	21	65	6

Source: Ipsos MORI/Ashcroft polling

The bias towards Labour is both clear and consistent. There was a reduction in the gap in 2015–17 and this has been confirmed by British Future, a think tank that studies attitudes towards migration and ethnicity. British Future suggests that the ethnic bias towards the Conservatives may be waning. Indeed research suggests that a majority of the Hindu and Sikh community now support the Conservative Party. Black people and Muslims, meanwhile, continue to support Labour in large numbers. British Future also reports that the black population is the most likely group to favour Labour.

The answer to why the BME community favour Labour in general is probably related to economic factors. This community is, on the whole, poorer than the white community, more will be in classes C2, D and E, and so they will be more likely to hold left-wing preferences. In other words, the factor at work is not race, but class and income. This would also explain why the Hindu and Sikh communities have moved towards Conservative voting. These well-established groups have prospered more than the black and Muslim populations and so are becoming increasingly middle class; with middle-class status comes Conservative Party voting.

Discussion point

Why is that that the black population, the young and low-income groups should favour Labour so strongly and why should elderly voters favour the Conservative Party?

Region

Here we are looking at voting bias in various regions of the UK. However, we need to be cautious. Wealth, income and prosperity are not evenly distributed in the UK. We know that the southeast corner of England is much wealthier than the rest of England. We also know that there are regions of great deprivation, including the far southwest and northeast of England and South Wales as well as several decayed city centres and areas where traditional industries have declined. It would be surprising, therefore, if such areas did not favour left-wing policies, as proposed by Labour. The same is true of Scotland, though it is not Labour that is the beneficiary of voting in depressed areas, but the Scottish National Party. In other words, regional variations may in fact be class variations rather than geographical ones.

Tables 4.8 and 4.9 demonstrate the variability of regional voting in the UK.

Table 4.8 Voting by region, 2015 general election

Region	% Conservative	% Labour	% Liberal Democrat	% Green	% SNP or Plaid Cymru	% UKIP
North of England	30.7	43.1	6.7	3.4	n/a	15.0
South of England	45.7	25.5	9.9	5.0	n/a	13.1
Midlands of England	42.5	32.3	5.5	3.1	n/a	15.7
London	34.9	43.7	7.7	4.9	n/a	8.1
Scotland	14.9	24.3	7.5	1.3	50.0	1.6
Wales	27.2	36.9	6.5	2.6	12.1	13.6

Knowledge check

Study Table 4.9. Answer these questions:

1 Which region is most dominated by the Conservatives?

2 In which two regions does Labour do best?

3 Where is Conservative support weakest?

4 Where do Liberal Democrats do best?

Table 4.9 Voting by region, 2017 general election

Region	% Conservative	% Labour	% Liberal Democrat	% SNP or Plaid Cymru
North of England	37	53	5	n/a
South of England	54	29	11	n/a
Midlands of England	50	42	4	n/a
London	33	55	9	n/a
Scotland	29	27	7	37
Wales	34	49	5	10

We can draw a number of conclusions about regional voting in recent general elections, based on the statistics in Tables 4.8 and 4.9:

- The south of England is very solidly Conservative.
- The Conservatives are also dominant in the English Midlands, though slightly less so than in the south.
- Labour leads in the north of England but this is not a decisive lead.
- Scotland has moved from being a Labour stronghold before 2010, to being dominated by the SNP and then returning to a three-party contest in 2017.
- Until 2015 Wales was not dominated by any one party, but there was genuine competition between four parties there. However, Labour still dominates after 2017.
- Liberal Democrats have little support outside London and the south of England.

There is a sense that Labour does have deep roots and strong local party organisations in the north of England and in Wales, so it is inevitable that the party will poll well in those regions. Similarly, voting for the Conservative Party in the south of England is understandable because, in rural and suburban areas, the Conservatives have long dominated the political culture. These regional variations are, therefore, real factors. However, as we saw above, much of the variation can be traced to economic rather than regional influences. There are many more depressed and declining areas in the north of England, Wales and Scotland (though in 2015 it was the SNP that took advantage of the Scottish situation, taking over from Labour as the entrenched party).

Leanne Wood, leader of Plaid Cymru, on the campaign trail with a party candidate before the 2015 general election

Northern Ireland has its own, unique political culture and the major English parties do not compete there. We do not, therefore, consider voting behaviour in Northern Ireland as this is a highly specialised field.

A summary of social and demographic factors

At the beginning of this section we drew an idealised view of a 'typical' Labour voter and her opposite number as a Conservative supporter. Of course this was a huge generalisation as we have seen above. This is because everyone is an individual. Many voters will make up their own minds about which party to support, whatever their class, age or ethnic background and no matter where they live. They are influenced by many other factors than their personal circumstances. Nevertheless, social and demographic factors tell us a great deal about voting behaviour.

Table 4.10 summarises these factors and offers an estimation of how significant they are in predicting voting tendencies.

Table 4.10 The influence of social and democratic factors

Factor	Estimated influence
Gender	There is virtually no difference in voting habits between men and women. There is a slight tendency for women to favour Labour.
Age	This is a key factor. Older voters favour the Conservatives (and UKIP) very significantly. Young voters have a Labour bias and also tend to support the Green Party.
Ethnicity	Ethnicity is significant, although there are signs that it is weakening as a factor. A further trend is for more established immigrant groups to move towards favouring the Conservative Party.
Class	Class used to be the most important determinant of voting behaviour but is becoming much less influential. It does, however, remain significant.
Region	There are wide regional variations in voting patterns. Scotland is the most remarkable, with the SNP currently in complete dominance. The south of England is solidly Conservative, leaving Labour with a mountain to climb in that region. UKIP has made inroads into Labour's former dominance of northern England. This leads to what are known as electoral heartlands, where only one party wins any seats.

Study tip

When discussing demographic factors in voting behaviour, make sure you have one or two key statistics as evidence for your assertions. Have key statistics for each of the factors you are describing.

Activity

If you were a policy maker, what policies might you adopt to attract the votes of the following demographics?

- The 18–24 age group
- Women
- Members of first generation ethnic minorities
- Migrants from the EU
- The 45–64 age group
- The over 65s

Activity

Access **https://yougov.co.uk/news/2015/06/08/general-election-2015-how-britain-really-voted/.** What trends in party support can you find using the following demographic factors?

● Home ownership versus renting
● Education level
● Working in the private or public sector
● Income level

The influence of social and demographic factors is complicated by the effects of **turnout**. Turnout, the proportion of those qualified to vote who do actually cast their vote, can have a further impact, but that impact is variable. This is because turnout varies among different groups. The next section examines the importance of such differential turnout rates.

Turnout

Before considering the impact of turnout in detail, we should consider the turnout statistics over a considerable period of time. Figure 4.5 shows national turnout figures since 1974.

Key term

Turnout Turnout is the proportion of those eligible to vote who do actually turn up to vote. It is expressed as a percentage of the electorate.

Synoptic link

The issue of voter turnout is part of a wider issue of political engagement and participation. These are examined fully in Chapter 1.

Activity

Look into the turnout at the 2017 general election. Identify what effect, if any, it had on long-term voting trends.

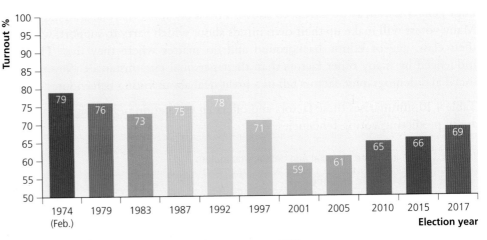

Figure 4.5 Turnout figures in UK general elections since 1974

We can see from Figure 4.5 that there was a sudden dip in turnout at the turn of the century. Before that the statistics were relatively healthy and very much in line with historical levels of turnout. Since then low turnouts have been a matter of growing concern. Apart from the fact that low numbers turning up at the polls suggests a worrying level of disillusionment with politics, when small numbers actually vote it can erode the legitimacy of the elected government.

Two questions have to be asked about turnout at elections, especially general elections.

1 Why does turnout vary from one election to another?

2 Is there a long-term trend in turnout figures?

Knowledge check

In which election since 1945 was turnout at its highest level? (You will need to do some research.)

Variable turnout

The first question may be answered in a number of ways, but possibly the most important consideration is how close the election appears to be — how much in doubt is the outcome? There is a correlation to be seen in Figure 4.5, which seems very clear. Turnout was relatively high in February 1974 (the election was so close it resulted in a hung parliament) at 79%, in 1992 which was a narrow win for the Conservatives, and in 2010 and 2015. The turnout figures for those last two elections were still historically low, but represented a significant recovery from the previous two elections. Both elections were very close results. By contrast, 2001 and 2005 were foregone conclusions — Labour was going to win against a disunited Conservative Party — so turnout slumped. Even the landmark election of 1997, which swept Labour into power after 18 years in the wilderness, saw a fall-off in turnout. Again the outcome was predicted months before the actual poll. So, we can say that the main factors in variable turnouts are how important the election might be and how close the outcome is.

Long-term downward trend

There is also, however, a long-term downward trend in turnout figures at general elections, especially from 1997 onwards. Virtually all of this trend can be explained by an alarming and rapid fall in voting figures for the age group 18–34. Figure 4.6 demonstrates this trend very clearly.

Study tip

Consider this point: Perhaps the outcome of elections is determined as much by who does not vote as by those who do.

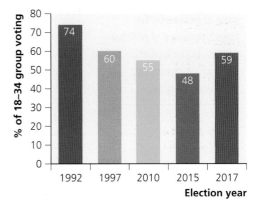

Figure 4.6 Voting trends at general elections, age group 18-34

Source: Warwick University Policy Lab/Ipsos MORI

Between 1992 and 2015 voting among young people fell by approximately 50%. By contrast turnout among other groups, especially those aged 55+ held up well. There are a number of possible explanations for this.

- There is widespread **disillusionment** with conventional politics among the young. This may be caused by the fact that politicians have introduced policies which discriminate against this age group, notably rising university tuition fees and the abolition of educational maintenance allowances (EMAs). However, it is also ascribed to general **apathy**, to a belief that politics has nothing to do with the things that concern the young and that voting will not make a difference.
- The young are increasingly finding alternative ways of participating in political activities, such as e-petitions, direct action and social media campaigns, thus moving away from conventional political activities.
- Younger people tend to be interested more in single issues than in broad political ideologies. This is reflected in low election voting figures, less interest in political parties, but increased participation in pressure group activity and online campaigning.
- Many young people feel the need to abstain. **Abstention** is when someone does not vote because they do not feel that any of the parties is worthy of their support; no party represents their own views and aspirations adequately. Abstention may also have a deeper meaning. Some non-voters may be protesting at the nature of the *whole* political system, believing it to be insensitive at best, corrupt at worst. Some voters spoil their ballot paper as a form of protest.

Then from 2014 there was a dramatic change in these trends:

- The Labour Party, Liberal Democrats and Green Party all report growing memberships, largely among the young, after the 2015 general election and the EU referendum.

Synoptic link

Reasons why young people participate less in voting, and discussion of proposed remedies to this situation, can be found in Chapter 1.

Key term

Apathy and disillusionment A phenomenon that particularly affects the attitudes of the young and the very poor. It is a belief that politics and politicians do not take into account the interests of the young and the very poor, that politics cannot change anything for them. It is a significant factor in non-voting.

Key term

Abstention This is when people, especially the young, refuse to vote (i.e. they abstain), not on the basis of ignorance or apathy but because they wish to protest about the state of politics or the collective failure of political parties, or the lack of a party which represents them effectively.

- Voting turnout among the young at two recent referendums was relatively high. In the Scottish independence referendum, polling organisation ICM estimates that 75% of 16- to 17-year-olds, 54% of the 18–24 group and 72% of those aged 25–34 turned up to vote. In the EU referendum, polling by Opinium suggests that 64% of those aged 18–34 voted.
- In the June 2017 election voting among the young increased dramatically. Around 54% of the 18–24 age group voted, largely the result of a drive to persuade them to register to vote. As a result, Labour enjoyed a resurgence of support, most pronounced in university towns.

Age, class and turnout

Age

The impact of age on voting patterns is distorted by the fact that there is a great difference between turnout among different age groups. As we have seen, in general, younger voters are more reluctant to turn out and vote than older generations. This has the effect of exaggerating the impact of age on the outcome of elections and referendums.

Table 4.11 shows the turnout figures for three recent elections, broken down by age categories.

Table 4.11 Percentage voting turnout in UK general elections by age range

Age range	2017	2015	2010
18–24	54	43	44
25–34	55	54	55
35–44	56	64	66
45–54	66	72	69
55–64	71	77	73
65+	71	78	76
Overall	69	66	65

Source: Ipsos MORI

The statistics shown in Table 4.11 are remarkable. In 2005, a year of a very low national turnout, only 37% of the youngest group of voters (18–24) actually turned up to vote. This compared with over 70% in each of the two oldest age categories. In 2015 the turnout figure of the 18–24 age group, at 43%, was well below the very high figures of 77% and 78% in the two oldest groups. All the statistics in the table show that the older a person is, the more likely they are to vote.

If we combine these findings with the observation that the older age groups are much more likely to vote Conservative than the young (see Table 4.5), we can see that the age demographic advantage that the Conservative Party enjoys is magnified by turnout trends.

However, in June 2017 there was a significant change, as Table 4.11 shows. There was a surge in voting by younger age groups, most of whom support the Labour Party. As a result, Labour's share of the national vote rose by about 10% compared to 2015. This was enough to prevent the Conservative Party winning an overall majority in parliament.

Class

Turning to turnout figures broken down by class, we can see a further significant effect. Table 4.12 reveals that members of class AB are much more likely to vote than members of class DE. So, combining voting preferences and turnout figures, we can see a further disadvantage suffered by the Labour Party. The class that favours Labour turns up to vote in much smaller numbers than their Conservative counterparts in class AB. When we add the class turnout effect to the age effect on turnout it is apparent that the Labour Party has a bigger problem trying to persuade its natural supporters to vote than it does to persuade people to support the party in the first place!

Table 4.12 Percentage *voting turnout* in UK general elections by social class

Social class	2017	2015	2010
AB	69	75	76
C1	68	68	66
C2	60	62	58
DE	53	57	57
Overall	69	66	65

Source: Ipsos MORI

Why those in social classes C2, D and E are more reluctant to vote than those in classes A, B and C1 is a complex issue. However, if we accept that the main reason why people do not vote in general is that they do not feel the outcome will make any difference, we can find some clues. The other factor is that people will vote if they understand the issues, but not if they don't.

Table 4.13 summarises the important points that arise from Tables 4.11 and 4.12.

Table 4.13 The links between turnout and demographics

Feature	Significance
In 2005 and 2015, the 18–44 age group in particular had especially low turnout figures.	It is difficult for more radical parties such as the Greens to make an impact. It discriminates slightly against the Labour Party.
The 65+ age group shows high turnout figures in all elections.	This gives a large advantage to the Conservative Party and UKIP, which are most supported by the elderly.
In all three elections, turnout among the AB classes was much higher than among the DE classes.	This gave a large advantage to the Conservatives, who are more supported by classes AB, and discriminates against Labour, whose support is concentrated in classes DE.
Overall turnout in the three elections shows an upward trend across all age groups and social classes.	This suggests that the 'participation crisis' may be gradually coming to an end, though this may be due to the fact that all these elections were relatively 'close'.

Discussion point

Does it matter how many people vote? Do low turnouts mean that the results of general elections are not democratically valid?

We cannot leave the issue of voter turnout without remarking that turnout at local elections, elections to devolved assemblies and for city mayors remains much lower than the numbers at general elections. In searching for a reason we should recall the basic reason for voter apathy. This is that people will not vote if they do not believe their vote will make a difference. At local and regional government levels

Activity

Study the result of the 2015 general election in the constituency where you live. What was the turnout figure? Was it higher or lower than the national figure for that year? If it was particularly high or low, can you offer a reason for that?

Key terms

Core voters These are voters who will invariably support one or other of the main parties. Core voters mostly, though not always, fall into patterns based on social class and region, as described in the first section of this chapter. It is believed the core Conservative and Labour votes have been eroded in recent decades.

Partisan dealignment A process which began in the 1970s whereby voters who used to be strongly attached to one party, identified with that party and always voted for it, detached themselves from that relationship in ever greater numbers. It is closely associated with class dealignment.

there is a general perception that power is concentrated at the centre so that the representatives they are being asked to vote for have relatively little power of their own. This is further borne out by the fact that voting behaviour at local level is largely determined by *national* issues rather than local ones. This may change as devolved administrations in Scotland, Wales and Northern Ireland gain even more powers and as city mayors become more established, but, for the time being, voting turnout at below central government level remains low.

Voting trends and theories

Core voters and partisan dealignment

The previous section described and measured what can be termed the **core vote** enjoyed by the main parties. In this section we concentrate just on Labour and the Conservatives, as, in 2015, the Liberal Democrat vote collapsed so dramatically that it is doubtful whether it has a significant core group of voters who will always support the party. Similarly, UKIP, the Green Party and the SNP have only recently emerged as major forces in UK politics, so talk of these parties having a 'core vote' may be premature.

Figure 4.7 shows an interesting story as far as support for the two major parties is concerned. Between 1970 and 2001 we could say that the UK was still dominated by two parties, though their dominance was in gradual decline. In the early years of the twenty-first century, this dominance was reduced significantly, falling to a low point in 2010, when less than two-thirds of the votes were cast for Labour or the Conservatives. It seemed that the two-party system was coming to an end.

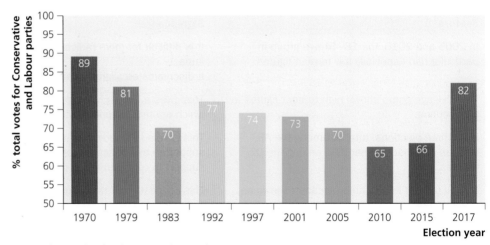

Figure 4.7 Voting for the two major parties

There were a number of reasons for the decline of two-party dominance up to 2017:

- Voters often reported that they could see relatively little difference between the main parties as they both sought to capture the majority of votes in the 'centre ground' of political opinion. This loosened people's attachment to one party.
- The emergence of several alternative, smaller parties attracted the support of former core voters. These included the Liberal Democrats (between 1992 and 2010), UKIP, the Green Party and, in Scotland, the SNP.
- There was been a long-term process of what is known as **partisan dealignment**. This is closely associated with class dealignment as described above.

Partisan dealignment meant that the core vote for the major parties was shrinking. It also meant that voters were less likely to support the party that we would expect them to vote for. It meant that fewer voters would express their preference with statements such as: 'I am Labour through and through and always will be; they represent the oppressed working class, don't they?' or 'I am a Tory and proud of it; it represents all that is good about being British.' So, increasing numbers of classes DE and AB were not voting Labour or Conservative, respectively, as we would have predicted.

In the 2017 general election, however, there was a dramatic increase in voting for the two major parties. It leapt up to the levels seen before the 1980s. There were a number of possible reason for this:

- Support for UKIP collapsed after the 2016 EU referendum result.
- There were very clear ideological differences between the main parties.
- Younger people began to vote again in large numbers. Most voted for Labour.
- Voting for the SNP in Scotland fell significantly, with these votes mostly picked up by the two main parties.

So, there has been a return to two-party dominance in 2017. It remains to be seen whether this is permanent or temporary.

Valence, rational choice, issue voting and economic issues

Valence

Most political commentators today will argue that **valence** is the most important predictor of voting behaviour, especially with the emergence of partisan dealignment, as described above. Leading political analyst, Peter Kellner, summed up valence like this:

> [M]illions of swing voters don't [take a strong view on individual issues], they take a valence view of politics. They judge parties and politicians not on their manifestos but on their character. Are they competent? Honest? Strong in a crisis? Likely to keep their promises?
>
> YouGov, 29 July 2012

Valence voting is sometimes contrasted with 'positional voting'. Positional voting is where voters choose a party based on its position on one or a group of issues. For example, which party will cut personal taxes most? Which party will spend most on the NHS or education, or which party will reduce university tuition fees?

As well as general competence, voters pay special attention to economic competence. This includes how well they believe a party will manage the UK economy and how well they believe it has done so when in power in the past. This may be described as judgements about **governing competence**. Who will be most responsible with the taxpayers' money? Who will do most to spread wealth or promote growth? This is also sometimes described as **economic voting**. It is a powerful influence on voting behaviour, as one might expect.

Voters will look at the performance of the UK economy and decide which of the parties has done most to improve it, and which party has damaged the economy in the past. A prime example was the problem the Labour Party had after the economic crisis from 2008 onwards. Labour was blamed by many voters for contributing to the crisis and for allowing government debt to rise by an alarming amount. The Conservative Party, in contrast, has an image of fiscal (financial) responsibility and good management. Labour defeats in the 2010 and 2015 elections were based partly

Key terms

Valence issues Where most of the electorate hold similar views on an issue, they may decide to vote for one party or another based on how well they think the party and/ or its leader will manage that issue, as well as on a judgement of how well the party managed it in the past. These are known as valence issues. Valence can also refer to the general 'image' of a party and its leader which may affect voting behaviour. Valence voting is sometimes also called 'competence' voting.

Governing competence A key valence issue. Voters often base their decision in voting on how competent they feel the outgoing government has been and the potential competence of other parties.

Economic voting As the name suggests, this occurs when voters decide that the economy and its management is a key factor and make a decision about which party is most likely to manage the economy well.

on such economic voting. In 2016 the new chancellor of the exchequer, Philip Hammond, stated he would manage the economy on a 'pragmatic' basis so people could feel confident about his competence.

How united a party is can also be an important factor. It is often said that a disunited party has no chance of winning a general election. Voters dislike uncertainty and a disunited party creates such uncertainty. Disunity became the major problem faced by Jeremy Corbyn when he became Labour leader in 2015. Indeed, Corbyn as a party leader has suffered one of the most negative images in recent political history. However, by the time of the June 2017 election, Corbyn's image had vastly improved and, as a result, most of the Labour Party rallied behind him, creating at least the illusion of a united party.

Leadership (discussed in more detail below) is a key valence issue. Voters like strong leaders with desirable personal characteristics. They will look at the leaders' past record as politicians, just as if they were applying for any job. Weak leaders are rarely supported. Labour's Ed Miliband and Liberal Democrat leader Nick Clegg suffered from being perceived as weak in the 2015 general election. Gordon Brown, who was defeated in the 2010 general election, was punished by the electorate for being seen as indecisive.

There are other valence issues to consider, but those described above are most commonly cited by those who seek to analyse election results.

Valence issues can be summed up as follows:

- How generally competent was the previous government and how competent do voters think other parties would be if in government?
- How economically competent was the government and are other parties likely to be?
- How united are the parties?
- Are they led by a dominant, decisive leader with a good record as a politician?

Activity

Consider the 2017 general election outcomes. Identify any factors that might have affected the result – consider valence, leadership and the role of the media.

Key terms

Rational choice model Many voters, who are not committed to any particular party or ideology, make a rational choice between the parties when voting, weighing up the strengths and weaknesses of each. These are of particular importance to parties during election campaigning.

Salience The general meaning of salience is 'importance' or how crucial something is. In politics, an issue is 'salient' if it is especially important to some voters when they are making up their minds which party to support.

Discussion point

Four valence issues are described above. What other valence issues can be identified? What valence issues apply to the main parties at the time you are having this discussion?

Rational choice and issue voting

The **rational choice model** of voting behaviour suggests that some voters, who are not especially committed to one party or another and who do not hold firm and extreme political views, make a rational decision at each election and base their vote on that. This is also sometimes described as 'issue voting'. Among those who are rational choice or issue voters, some political issues are more **salient** than others. In other words, there are policy areas which do affect the way people vote and others that do not. A great deal of research is undertaken by parties to determine what are the salient issues at each election, as this will inform them about how to adjust policies and frame their campaign.

Discussion point

Discuss and try to identify four issues which you think were salient at the most recent general election.

Opinion polls spend a good deal of time researching the salient issues before each election and 2015 was no exception. In 2014 Ipsos MORI asked voters what were their most important issues. The result was as shown in Figure 4.8, the percentages indicating what proportion placed the issue top of their list of priorities.

The next most important issue was only favoured by 13% of respondents, so there were four dominant issues. A year later, YouGov polling carried out a similar survey and found similar results and the same three top salient issues. The Conservatives were trusted more on the top two issues, which goes some way to explaining their victory over Labour.

Two variations of rational choice voting are 'expressive' and 'instrumental' voting. If we assume that voters rationally seek to derive some benefit from their choice of candidate and party when voting, we can identify two types of benefit.

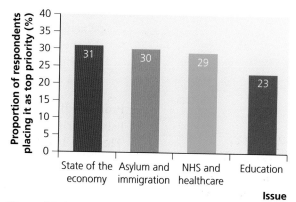

Figure 4.8 Issue of greatest importance to voters, 2015

- A voter will derive satisfaction if he or she votes for a party that will benefit *society as a whole*. This is also sometimes called 'altruistic' or 'expressive' voting.
- The other kind of benefit is to choose a party whose policies are likely to favour the voter him- or herself. This is self-interested voting, usually described as 'instrumental' voting. For example, a business person may choose a party which promises to reduce business taxes, while a benefit claimant will support a party that promises to make benefits more generous.

Both kinds of voting behaviour are 'rational' because they are based on a calculation of good outcomes versus bad outcomes.

Party leaders

Here we are examining the impact of party leaders, and particularly *public perceptions* of the leaders, on voting behaviour. It has to be remembered that, at a general election, the voters are choosing a future prime minister as well as a ruling party and a local MP. The image and qualities of party leaders are crucial. Are they trustworthy? Are they decisive? Do they promote a strong image of the UK abroad? Can they keep the government united? Certainly in the 2015 general election, David Cameron enjoyed a much more positive image than Ed Miliband, his Labour opponent. Tony Blair began in 1997 with an extremely positive image, and won two more elections, but by 2007 his image was so tarnished that the Labour Party replaced him with Gordon Brown in 2007. Brown himself suffered a poor image, based on negative media portrayals and his reputation for indecisiveness. This contributed to Labour's election defeat in 2010.

The kind of qualities that the public normally cite as important in a leader include:

- record in office (if they have been in office)
- compassion
- decisiveness
- apparent honesty and sincerity
- strong leadership
- clear vision
- communication skills

The press and broadcasters would certainly have us believe that the character and image of the party leaders are vital factors in the outcome of elections. The evidence, however, suggests otherwise.

Writing on the BBC website before the 2015 general election, emeritus professor of politics at Oxford University, Archie Brown, made this assertion:

> It [the idea that party leaders can win or lose elections] is very rarely true. It is only in an extremely close-run race that the personality of the leader and the gulf between that leader's standing and the popularity of his or her principal opponent can make the difference between victory and defeat. It is not even particularly uncommon for the political party of the less popular leader of the two main parties to be the one that wins the election.

BBC news/politics, 7 January 2015

Professor Brown went on to quote the example of the 1979 general election, when Labour prime minister James Callaghan led his Conservative opponent, Margaret Thatcher, by 20% in popularity polls but lost the election. Similarly, in 2010, Liberal Democrat leader Nick Clegg was the most popular of the party leaders, following impressive showings in televised leadership debates, but his party's share of the vote fell by 1% and the party lost five of its parliamentary seats.

Despite Professor Brown's assertion, however, there appears to be some evidence that party leaders and their popularity (usually described as 'satisfaction' and 'dissatisfaction' ratings by opinion polls) *do* swing elections. Table 4.14 seems to demonstrate this.

Table 4.14 Satisfaction ratings of government and party leaders, April 2015

Leader	% satisfied	% dissatisfied	Net satisfaction
David Cameron (Con)	46	48	−2
Ed Miliband (Lab)	35	54	−19
Nick Clegg (Lib Dem)	34	55	−21
Nigel Farage (UKIP)	31	56	−25
Nicola Sturgeon (SNP)*	51	18	+33
The government	41	52	−11

Source: Ipsos MORI/TNS Scotland

* Rating among Scots only

Ed Miliband, whose poor public image contributed to Labour's 2015 defeat at the polls

At first sight Table 4.14 seems to confirm that party leadership ratings do make a difference. David Cameron had the best poll rating of all the leaders shown (though he was well behind Nicola Sturgeon in Scotland and his net rating was still negative) and his Conservative Party did win the election. However, if we investigate more closely, a different conclusion emerges. Labour's vote rose *more* than the Conservative vote, 1.5% to 0.8% between 2010 and 2015, while UKIP's share of the vote shot up by 9.5%. Yet the Labour leader was far less popular than Cameron, and UKIP's Nigel Farage was the least popular of all the party leaders. Nicola Sturgeon is an exception, but we must remember that her popularity was largely the popularity of her *party*. In other words, there does not seem to be a correlation between leaders' popularity and election outcomes, as Professor Brown suggests.

The Corbyn effect, 2017

During the 2017 general election a remarkable phenomenon occurred. Starting the campaign as an underdog, reviled by much of the press, opposed by many MPs in his own party and unpopular among voters, Jeremy Corbyn created a bandwagon effect, mostly among the young. There is little doubt that his resurgence was a major influence on the outcome of that election and the Labour revival. Leadership can, it seems, make a difference.

Tactical voting

Tactical voting is undertaken in special circumstances and in specific constituencies. In elections many votes are considered 'wasted' votes. This is because they will have no influence on the outcome. A common form of wasted vote is a vote for a small party, such as the Liberal Democrats or the Green Party. Those who support such parties may be frustrated by their inability to affect the result. Some, therefore, may abandon their first-party preference and vote instead for one of the parties that *does* have a chance of winning in a constituency. Typical of this is a Liberal Democrat supporter living in a constituency where the Liberal Democrats have no chance of winning, but where the contest may be close between the Conservatives and Labour. Such a tactical voter may vote for one of the main parties as their second choice so as to influence the final outcome.

Typical examples of tactical voting have been as follows:

- Labour supporters voting Conservative to keep out a UKIP candidate in a close UKIP–Conservative contest.
- Green Party supporters voting Labour to keep out a Conservative in a close Labour–Conservative contest.
- Labour supporters in Scotland voting for the SNP to keep out a Conservative candidate in a close SNP–Conservative contest.
- Conservative Party supporters in Scotland doing likewise to keep out a Labour candidate in a close SNP–Labour contest.
- Plaid Cymru supporters in Wales voting Liberal Democrat to keep out a Conservative in a close Conservative–Liberal Democrat contest.

It is difficult to estimate how much tactical voting occurs and even harder to establish whether it has any effect on electoral outcomes. John Curtice, a leading election expert at Strathclyde University, estimated that, in the 2015 general election, tactical voting *could have* affected the result in as many as 77 constituencies, but this does not mean that many actually *were* affected in the event. Ipsos MORI's research into voting at the 2010 general election suggested that as many as 10% of voters chose their second preference and the figure was especially high among Liberal Democrat supporters at 16%. But this still does not answer the question of how much influence tactical voting has on final results.

Circumstantially, the evidence from Scotland in 2015 suggests that tactical voting had no effect. Most attempts to persuade people to vote tactically involved keeping

Key term

Tactical voting When voters in UK general elections feel that their first-choice vote will be wasted because it is for a party that has no chance of winning the constituency, they may change their vote to a second choice. By doing this they may have an influence on the outcome. Typically, supporters of the Liberal Democrats or Green Party vote either Labour or Conservative because their first-choice party cannot win the constituency. This is known as tactical voting.

out SNP candidates, but the SNP won handsomely, suggesting there was no great impact. On the other hand, the slump in Liberal Democrat voting in the 2015 general election might in some way be explained by tactical voting. None of the parties has ever issued formal instructions for its supporters to vote tactically and until this happens it may remain impossible to estimate its impact.

The media and opinion polls in politics

Before looking at the media's influence on politics, we should consider the fact that the nature of the media is changing. Increasingly, people are accessing news online. Furthermore, social media are being increasingly used to disseminate information, opinion and even propaganda. The main issue concerning this change is that it has become more difficult to distinguish between fact and fiction. Some have called this the 'post-truth' era. The spreading of unsubstantiated facts and sometimes deception is thought to have been an influence in both the EU referendum campaign in the UK and the 2016 US presidential elections. There has been an assumption that the truth will ultimately emerge, but there is no guarantee that this will happen.

Broadcasting

All broadcasters in the UK are bound by law to remain neutral and to offer balanced reporting of election and referendum campaigns. This means they have no intentional influence on voting behaviour. Although the BBC has sometimes been accused of a liberal or left-wing bias, nothing has been proved or substantiated. This is in contrast to the USA, where networks are allowed to be politically biased, and Fox News in particular is well known for its conservative, pro-Republican bias. It is just as well that there is a legal neutrality requirement as research indicates that television and radio are the main sources of information for voters in UK election campaigns.

We should not leave this subject, however, without referring to the televised debates that have now become a common feature of elections. The BBC, ITV and Channel 4 have all held leadership debates in recent elections and do so under scrupulous conditions, overseen by the Electoral Commission. However, it is not at all clear that leadership debates have any significant impact on the voters. We have already seen that Nick Clegg's spectacularly good performance in the 2010 debates still led to a decline in his party's share of the popular vote. Similarly, in a BBC Challengers' debate held in April 2015, just before that year's election, and in which David Cameron did not take part, the opinion polls suggested that Ed Miliband narrowly won, even over the enormously respected Nicola Sturgeon, but Miliband's poor standing in leadership polling did not change and his party lost an election it was expected to win.

All we can really assert about broadcasting is that the parties use television and radio as a key way of getting their messages across, but they do not expect to gain any special advantage from it.

The press

Following the 1992 general election, when the Conservatives won a surprise victory after most predicted a Labour win, the *Sun* newspaper famously proclaimed, 'It's the Sun Wot Won It.' Certainly the *Sun* had run a relentless campaign against the Labour Party and especially its leader, Neil Kinnock, and the opinion polls, at first

Study tip

When we say the press in the UK is independent, we only mean that it is free of government control and influence. Independence does *not* mean that newspapers are neutral. Most newspapers have a strong political bias. The broadcasters, though, do have a legal duty to be neutral.

The front pages of British newspapers on the day of the EU referendum vote

predicting a comfortable Labour victory, turned round near the election date and John Major's Conservatives secured a majority. Whether or not it was indeed the press that had changed voters' minds, however, is open to contention.

Unlike television and radio, there is no press regulation in terms of political bias and the UK newspapers are highly politicised. Table 4.15 lists the main UK daily newspapers (outside Scotland and Northern Ireland), their circulation figures in 2017 and the party they supported in that year.

Activity

Identify which party each of the main newspapers supported during the 2017 general election campaign.

Table 4.15 The political affiliations of the main UK newspapers at the 2017 election

Newspaper	Political preference	Circulation (000s)	% of its readers who support the paper's preferred party
Sun	Very strongly Conservative	1,667	59
Daily Mail	Very strongly Conservative	1,514	74
Daily Mirror	Very strongly Labour	725	68
Daily Telegraph	Very strongly Conservative	472	79
Daily Express	Very strongly UKIP	393	77
The Times	Moderate Conservative	451	58
Daily Star	No preference	443	n/a
Financial Times	Conservative/Liberal Democrat	189	40/14
Guardian	Moderate Labour	157	73

Source: Press Gazette/YouGov

Activity

Table 4.15 shows that the Sun, which is mostly read by working-class people, and the Daily Mail, which is a largely middle-class newspaper, both have a Conservative bias. Can you explain this?

We can see two clear features in Table 4.15. The first is that more of the newspapers support the Conservative Party than other parties, and that the two largest circulation tabloids, the *Sun* and the *Daily Mail*, both support the Tories. The second is that there is a fairly close, though not exact, correlation between the newspapers' preferences and the way most of their readers vote. At first sight, therefore, we may conclude that newspapers *do* influence the way people vote. However, this may be an illusion.

While large sections of the public do believe the press influences them, research suggests it does not. Instead the newspapers tend to *reflect* the typical political views of their readers rather than leading them. The papers may also reinforce *existing* political attitudes, but there is no strong evidence that they can change them. Indeed, giving evidence to the Leveson Inquiry into press behaviour in 2012, the *Sun*'s owner, Rupert Murdoch, admitted that newspapers do not swing votes, they do merely reflect readers' opinion. However, the fact that the *Sun* has backed the winning party at every election between 1979 and 2015 does raise some questions about its influence.

Newspaper expert Roy Greenslade believes that the press can and does influence voters, though he accepts that the effect is small and cannot really be proven. Tom Felle of City University's newspaper journalism department disagrees, suggesting that it might have been the case in the past but is decreasingly so. Felle also points out that younger voters increasingly rely on social media for their information, so the influence of the press is waning.

Social media

Although parties and government increasingly use social media as a way of communicating with the public and of 'listening in' to public opinion, it is too early to assess its influence. Certainly, as it is an open medium, unlike the printed media, it is more difficult for any one party or political group to gain any special advantage.

Unlike the broadcasters, the web is unregulated so there are opportunities for any group to gain some political traction. It is especially useful to small parties such as the Greens and UKIP, which do not have the resources to be able to compete with the large parties in conventional campaigning. Yet social media still remain a modest aspect of how people gain political knowledge.

The only bias that can be detected is the fact that, as we would expect, social media are mostly used by the young. It is the young who are more likely to support radical parties and candidates. This does, therefore, give opportunities for such political aspirants to gain a foothold. A key example has been the growth in membership of the Labour Party after 2015 and the use that Momentum, the radical left-wing movement in the Labour Party, has made of social media. In 2017 radical social media platforms such as Canary began to galvanise youth opinion, as was indicated by voting statistics described above. It seems likely they will begin to take over from the traditional media in forming opinions in the future.

Public opinion polls

Opinion polls have been a feature of British political life since the 1940s when the first poll was carried out by the Gallup organisation. Gallup (an American company that had started polling in the USA before the Second World War) predicted that

Synoptic link

There is a fuller discussion of the role of digital democracy in Chapter 1.

Discussion point

Are people, especially the young, more likely to be politically influenced by social media than by traditional broadcast and print forms?

Key term

Political opinion poll
These are carried out by research organisations using a sample of typical voters. They are mainly used to establish voting intentions, but can also be used to gauge leaders' popularity and the importance of specific issues in voters' minds.

Labour would win the 1945 general election, much to the surprise of most commentators of the day. Gallup was right and from then on polls became increasingly used to gauge political opinion. Since their early days, however, opinion polls have become both more influential and increasingly controversial.

Two questions need to be asked about opinion polls. The first is: do they have any effect on voting behaviour? The second is: if they do, how much does it matter that they have often proved to be inaccurate, in which case the electorate are being influenced by false information?

Question 1 Do they affect voting behaviour?

There is some evidence that polling figures could affect voting. The most striking piece of evidence concerns the 2015 general election. In that election, most opinion polls were predicting close to a dead heat between the two main parties, resulting in a second hung parliament. In that event, it was widely suggested, the Scottish National Party, which was heading for a huge victory in Scotland, would hold the 'balance of power'. In other words, there would probably be a Labour–SNP coalition with the Scots calling the shots. Indeed, the Conservative Party began to campaign on that basis, hoping to gain votes and win an outright victory. Table 4.16 shows the opinion poll results in the last few days before the 2015 election.

Table 4.16 Final opinion polls before the 2015 general election*

Polling company	Date	Con (%)	Lab (%)	Lib Dem (%)	UKIP (%)	Green (%)
Populus	7 May	33	33	10	14	5
ICM	7 May	34	35	9	11	4
Panelbase	6 May	31	33	8	16	5
YouGov	6 May	34	34	10	12	4
Ashcroft	6 May	33	33	10	11	6
Ipsos MORI	6 May	36	35	8	11	5
Survation	5 May	33	34	9	16	4
ComRes	5 May	35	32	9	14	4
Result	**7 May**	**37**	**30**	**8**	**13**	**4**

Source: BBC

* Rounded to nearest whole number

Question 2 Does it matter if they are inaccurate?

We can see from Table 4.16 that the polls over-estimated the Labour vote and under-estimated support for the Conservatives. The question is: was there a late surge for the Conservatives, fuelled by voters wishing to avoid a hung parliament with the Scots in control? Certainly the Conservative Party campaigned on that basis. Similarly, the polls were showing the Liberal Democrats doing poorly in the campaign. Did this lead to further defections from the party as increasing numbers of voters decided to vote tactically and so depressed the Liberal Democrat vote even further?

The opinion polls were also inaccurate in the June 2017 general election. Most showed a Conservative lead varying between 5% and 12%, outcomes which would have won the party a comfortable parliamentary majority. In the event, however, the Conservatives came in barely 2% ahead of Labour and there was a hung parliament. Survation and YouGov were the only polls among many that predicted such an result.

> **Activity**
>
> Write an assessment, with statistical evidence, of how accurate or inaccurate the opinion polls were during the 2017 general election.

That opinion polling is inaccurate is in little doubt. The polls on the whole were significantly wrong in the 2014 Scottish independence referendum, the 2015 and 2017 general elections and the 2016 EU referendum. They may also have affected voting behaviour, though we cannot be sure as there is scant research data available. In any event there has been so much concern about their impact that the British Polling Council conducted an investigation into their performance. It concluded that inaccurate sampling and statistical methods were to blame. The polls, said the report, will inevitably over-estimate Labour support as they are currently conducted. The report did, however, stop short of recommending banning the publication of polls in the run-up to elections in case they influence voting. What is more likely to happen is that politicians, the media and the public will increasingly ignore their findings.

Debate

Should the publication of opinion polls be banned in the run-up to elections?

For banning

- Opinion polls may influence the way people vote.
- Opinion polls have proved to be inaccurate so they mislead the public.
- Arguably politicians should not be slaves to changing public opinion as expressed in the polls.

Against banning

- It would infringe the principle of freedom of expression.
- If publication of opinion polls is banned, they will become available privately for organisations that can afford to pay for them.
- Opinion polls give valuable information about people's attitudes which can guide politicians usefully.
- The polls would still be published abroad and people could access them through the internet.

A summary of factors affecting voting behaviour

The study of electoral behaviour is a complex one. Many different factors are at play in any election campaign. However, we can identify two key sets of influences. The first determines the size of each party's core voter base and explains why this may be increasing or reducing. The second concerns those voters who are not part of this core, so that their votes are 'up for grabs' — they are known as swing or floating voters.

Tables 4.17 and 4.18 summarise these factors and offer an evaluation of how important they are in explaining voting behaviour.

Table 4.17 Factors that determine the size of the parties' core vote

Factor	Explanation	Estimate of impact
Social class	Classes AB mostly support the Conservative Party while DE voters are usually Labour supporters.	Strong but in decline as a factor
Age	The older a voter is, the more likely they are to vote Conservative or UKIP. Young voters favour the Liberal Democrats and the Greens.	Strong and consistent
Region	The south of England is solidly Conservative, the Midlands is mixed and the North is mostly but not exclusively Labour country.	Strong
Ethnicity	Black and Muslim voters strongly prefer Labour, but other ethnic groups are more mixed in their support.	Significant but variable
Gender	No significant difference in party support	Insignificant
Class dealignment	Progressively fewer people are attached to a particular social class.	This reduces the impact of class on party choice.
Partisan dealignment	Progressively fewer people identify strongly with the aims of a particular party and more are becoming floating voters.	The size of the main parties' core vote is shrinking gradually but not dramatically.

Study tip

The information in Table 4.17 shows *long-term* factors in voting behaviour. Table 4.18 shows *short-term* factors. Be careful to make a distinction between the two.

Table 4.18 Factors that affect how floating voters will vote

Factor	Explanation	Estimate of impact
Valence	The image of the parties and their leaders and general beliefs about the competence of the parties	Very strong
Economic voting	Choice on the basis of the performance of the economy and how voters believe parties will manage the economy	Strong
Rational choice	Rational voters deciding which party will most benefit the community as a whole or themselves	Moderate
Issue voting	Voters deciding which issues are most important and which parties have the best policies relating to those issues	Moderate
Tactical voting	Voters opting for their second choice party if they think their first choice is a wasted vote.	Uncertain, probably moderate
Party leaders	People deciding who would make the best prime minister	Some significance but weak
The press	People being influenced by newspaper campaigns and preferences	Probably weak
Opinion polls	Voters may decide to change their mind because they do not want the outcome predicted in the polls	Probably weak

Study tip

When considering election results, it is important to look at changes since the previous election. These can be more revealing than the current statistics.

Three election case studies

You are required to study any three general elections since 1945, including 1997. We recommend you study 1979, 1997 and 2015. These are reviewed below.

Case study

The 1979 general election

Table 4.19 Results of the 1979 general election

Party	Seats won	Change since 1974	% votes won	Change since 1974
Conservative	339	+63	43.9	+8.1
Labour	269	−50	36.9	−2.3
Liberal	11	+1	13.8	−4.5
Others	16	+5	5.4	−1.4

Turnout: 76%

Demographic issues

A key factor which emerged at around the time of this election was the sharp decline in the number of people describing themselves as 'working class'. This may have eroded Labour's vote. Conversely, the size of the middle class was growing, helping the Conservatives.

Valence and other issues

The image of the Labour Party had suffered in the lead-up to this election. It was seen as the party of the trade unions and trade unions were unpopular at the time. The government of James Callaghan was seen as weak in the face of challenges by the unions.

Party leaders

Ironically, James Callaghan, Labour prime minister before the election, had a more favourable image than his opponent, Margaret Thatcher. He was seen as reliable and likeable whereas she was seen as distant and too 'posh'. Thatcher had also been an unpopular education secretary in the early 1970s. Some members of the electorate may also have been reluctant to vote for a female prime minister. Nevertheless, the Conservatives won, perhaps in spite of, rather than because of, their leader.

Turnout and its significance

Turnout was a little down on past trends, largely due to abstentions by the working class and union members, Labour's core voters. However, it held up well and was not a significant factor in the result.

The political issues

Perhaps *the* key issue in this election was the power of trade unions. In the winter of 1978–79 there was a wave of strikes by public-sector workers, leading to bins being left unemptied, shortages of power and dislocation of public transport. It became known as the 'Winter of Discontent'. Therefore, a key issue was: which party was best placed to control union power? The answer for many floating voters was the Conservative Party.

Other factors affecting the result

The UK economy was not in a good state. There was high inflation, growing unemployment and falling growth. The Conservative response was to plan a return to free markets and to curb union power. Prices would come down, they argued, if unemployment continued to rise so that wages would fall. The middle classes were especially attracted to such policies. Much of the change in voting preference was economic in nature.

Events

The key event was the Winter of Discontent, which was the main reason for the Labour defeat.

Outcome

The Conservatives were to be in power for the next 18 years.

The 1997 general election

Table 4.20 Results of the 1997 general election

Party	Seats won	Change since 1992	% votes won	Change since 1992
Labour	418	+145	43.2	+8.8
Conservative	165	−165	30.7	−11.2
Lib Dem	46	+30	16.8	−1.0
Others	30	+6	9.3	+3.4

Turnout: 71%

Demographic issues

Tony Blair and the Labour leadership recognised that the traditional working class, Labour's natural core vote, was diminishing in size and that the party could not rely on it to put it into power; it simply did not have enough votes. They therefore decided to woo the middle classes, part of the Conservatives' core vote, by adopting centrist ('third way') policies. This was achieved to great effect. The young were also persuaded to vote Labour as it represented a break from traditional, out-of-date politics.

Valence and other issues

The image of the Conservative Party, which had been in power for 18 years, was a tired one, but above all the party was disunited, largely over Europe. It had also presided over a deep economic recession in the early 1990s, so competence was an issue. By contrast, Labour had no economic record to defend and appeared to be a younger, fresher party, united around a definable set of policies — the so-called third way.

Party leaders

There could hardly be a greater contrast between the two main party leaders. Conservative prime minister John Major appeared to be grey, unexciting and weak, whereas Tony Blair was clearly in command, was young and attractive and had a clear vision. The Liberal Democrat leader, Paddy Ashdown, also enjoyed a positive image, reflected in a good election for his party.

Turnout and its significance

In this election we saw the first signs of a long-term decline in turnout. The figure of 71% seems healthy by modern standards, but was much lower than typical levels in the past. There does not seem to have been any impact on the result, but this was a watershed in political participation.

The political issues

There were two main salient issues — the NHS and the state of education. Both services had been in decline. Labour promised to make huge investments in both to raise standards. Chancellor Gordon Brown promised to be financially responsible, which was a strong message, especially as Labour had a bad reputation as a 'tax and spend' party. Labour was fortunate that an economic recovery was under way when it took office, so it could pay for the improvements in public services.

Other factors affecting the result

The main problem for the Conservatives was that the electorate remembered the recession of the late 1980s and early 1990s and blamed them for it. There was also a general sense that the Conservatives had mismanaged the economy.

Events

In the years 1992–94 John Major had presided over a Conservative Party hopelessly divided over the Maastricht Treaty, which transferred large amounts of power to the European Union. The hangover from this was still present in 1997.

Outcome

This was massive defeat for the Conservatives, one from which it took over 10 years for the party to recover. Labour was to stay in power for the next 13 years. It was, though, the last general election to be totally dominated by the two main parties.

The 2015 general election

Table 4.21 Results of the 2015 general election

Party	Seats won	Change since 2010	% votes won	Change since 2010
Conservative	330	+28	36.9	+0.8
Labour	232	−24	30.4	+1.5
SNP	56	+50	4.7	+3.1
Lib Dem	8	−48	7.9	−15.1
UKIP	1	+1	12.6	+9.5
Others	23	−5	7.5	+1.0

Turnout: 66%

Demographic issues

A significant feature of this election was the fact that a good deal of Labour's core working-class vote was captured by UKIP, especially in depressed areas of the country. It was also notable that the Liberal Democrats lost all 15 of their seats in southwest England. This dispelled the idea of the Liberal Democrat core vote in that region. The Conservatives, by contrast, dominated the south of England as a whole. In Scotland the SNP nearly swept the board. Again, Labour's regional heartland was taken away.

Valence and other issues

With the exception of the Scottish National Party, all the parties suffered from a negative image. The Conservatives were still divided over European and immigration. The Liberal Democrats were blamed for many of the shortcomings of the coalition government of 2010–15, while Labour was not trusted with the economy. Labour's competence was constantly called into question. The media may have had an impact by warning about the dangers of a likely Labour-SNP coalition, as indicated by opinion polls. Some voters turned away from this prospect by switching to the Conservatives.

Party leaders

None of the party leaders, apart from SNP leader Nicola Sturgeon, suffered a negative image with the public. David Cameron's image was, however, the least negative. Nick Clegg of the Liberal Democrats and Ed Miliband for Labour were both short of public respect. It seems probable that images of party leaders played little part in the outcome.

Turnout and its significance

Turnout recovered a little in this election, though it was still well down on historic levels. Perhaps as many as 2 million former non-voters turned up at the polls, many supporting UKIP. If this is the case, the turnout of supporters for the other main parties must have been very low.

The political issues

A key issue was economic management. The Conservatives were still more trusted with the economy than Labour. The election was dominated, however, by the prospect of a referendum on UK membership of the EU. The Conservatives were rewarded (as was UKIP) for their support of such a referendum.

Other factors affecting the result

It seems that UKIP took more votes from Labour than from the Conservatives. The Conservatives also benefited most from the collapse of voting for the Liberal Democrats. In Scotland the SNP won 56 out of 59 seats and so decimated the other parties there. This ensured that Labour could not win an overall majority or even lead a coalition government. It has been argued that the Conservatives picked up support from voters who were determined to prevent a Labour-SNP coalition.

Events

In many ways the Scottish referendum of 2014 was a key event. The campaign in that referendum put the SNP in a powerful position in Scotland. As we have seen above, fear of a possible Labour-SNP coalition may have brought many votes to the Conservatives. The future EU referendum also dominated proceedings.

The outcome

The shock of defeat completely destabilised the Labour Party. There was a huge left-wing backlash against the failed policies of the leadership, so the party elected extreme left-winger Jeremy Corbyn in place of Ed Miliband. This precipitated divisions within Labour and a split in the parliamentary party.

Key concepts in this chapter

Abstention This is when people, especially the young, refuse to vote (i.e. they abstain), not on the basis of ignorance or apathy but because they wish to protest about the state of politics or the collective failure of political parties, or the lack of a party which represents them effectively.

Apathy and disillusionment A phenomenon that particularly affects the attitudes of the young and the very poor. It is a belief that politics and politicians do not take into account the interests of the young and the very poor, that politics cannot change anything for them. It is a significant factor in non-voting.

Class dealignment A trend whereby progressively fewer people consider themselves to be a member of a particular social class and so class has a decreasing impact on their voting behaviour.

Core voters These are voters who will invariably support one or other of the main parties. Core voters mostly, though not always, fall into patterns based on social class and region, as described in the first section of this chapter. It is believed the core Conservative and Labour votes have been eroded in recent decades.

Deviant voting This occurs when a person does not vote the way we would expect, given their social characteristics, especially their class. Examples are working-class Conservatives and wealthy entrepreneurial Labour supporters.

Economic voting As the name suggests, this occurs when voters decide that the economy and its management is a key factor and make a decision about which party is most likely to manage the economy well.

Floating (or swing) voter A voter who tends to vote unpredictably in different elections and who is liable to change the way they vote fairly often.

Governing competence A key valence issue. Voters often base their decision in voting on how competent they feel the outgoing government has been and the potential competence of other parties.

Instrumental voting A term referring to voting behaviour which is motivated by self-interest. In other words, voters favour a party that they believe will do most good for themselves through its policies.

Partisan dealignment A process which began in the 1970s whereby voters who used to be strongly attached to one party, identified with that party and always voted for it, detached themselves from that relationship in ever greater numbers. It is closely associated with class dealignment.

Political opinion poll These are carried out by research organisations using a sample of typical voters. They are mainly used to establish voting intentions, but can also be used to gauge leaders' popularity and the importance of specific issues in voters' minds.

Rational choice model Many voters, who are not committed to any particular party or ideology, make a rational choice between the parties when voting, weighing up the strengths and weaknesses of each. These are of particular importance to parties during election campaigning.

Salience The general meaning of salience is 'importance' or how crucial something is. In politics, an issue is 'salient' if it is especially important to some voters when they are making up their minds which party to support.

Social class The way in which social researchers classify people on the basis of their occupations and, to some extent, their income. Class can explain various forms of typical behaviour, including political attitudes and voting trends.

Tactical voting When voters in UK general elections feel that their first-choice vote will be wasted because it is for a party that has no chance of winning the constituency, they may change their vote to a second choice. By doing this they may have an influence on the outcome. Typically, supporters of the Liberal Democrats or Green Party vote either Labour or Conservative because their first-choice party cannot win the constituency. This is known as tactical voting.

Turnout Turnout is the proportion of those eligible to vote who do actually turn up to vote. It is expressed as a percentage of the electorate.

Valence issues Where most of the electorate hold similar views on an issue, they may decide to vote for one party or another based on how well they think the party and/or its leader will manage that issue, as well as on a judgement of how well the party managed it in the past. These are known as valence issues. Valence can also refer to the general 'image' of a party and its leader which may affect voting behaviour. Valence voting is sometimes also called 'competence' voting.

Summary

Having read this chapter, you should have knowledge and understanding of the following:
→ The meaning of party core votes and the factors that affect the size of the core vote for each party
→ Changes in people's attachment to social class and to parties
→ What factors affect the way floating voters behave
→ The influence of party leadership on election outcomes
→ The influence of the media — broadcast, print and social
→ The part played by opinion polls in elections and their significance
→ Summaries of the outcome of three key elections
→ A template guiding you on how to study electoral outcomes

Further information and web guide

Websites

The best information about voting behaviour can be found on the websites of opinion poll organisations. Among the best are:
https://today.yougov.com
www.ipsos-mori.com
www.lordashcroftpolls.com
www.pollingdigest.com
Information about voting and elections can also be found at the Electoral Commission site:
www.electoralcommission.org.uk.

Books

A quirky, but entertaining and informative work on the 2015 general elections is Cowley, P. and Ford, R. (2015) *Sex, Lies and the Ballot Box*, Biteback.
Macmillan/Palgrave publishes a book about every general election by various authors. Each one is packed with facts, figures and analysis. These are titled *The British General Election of 1979*, *The British General Election of 1983* etc.
An authoritative work is Norris, P. (2010) *Electoral Engineering: Voting Rules and Political Behaviour*, Cambridge University Press.
The classic work, a little out of date, but the very best book on the subject by the ultimate expert is Denver, D. (2nd edn 2006) *Elections and Voters in Britain*, Palgrave.

AS

1 Describe the nature of partisan dealignment. (10)

2 Describe the significance of age in voting behaviour in the UK. (10)

3 Using the source, assess the importance of leadership in the outcome of elections. *In your response you must use knowledge and understanding to analyse points that are only in the source. You will not be rewarded for introducing any additional points that are not in the source.* (10)

> ### Leadership
>
> Leadership is said to be one of the key factors in the success or failure of parties at elections. Indeed, some have claimed that the voters are as interested in the image and character of the party leaders as they are in their parties' policies. There is certainly evidence to support this contention.
>
> In 1997 there was a gulf between the image of Tony Blair, a young, decisive leader leading a united, dynamic party, and the grey image of his Conservative opponent, John Major, who had failed to unite his party. Similarly, in 2015 David Cameron enjoyed a much more positive image than Ed Miliband, Labour's leader. Miliband was seen as weak generally and, in addition, he ran a poor election campaign.
>
> On the other hand, many theorists suggest that it is the image of the party as a whole that is decisive. The way in which voters view the qualities of the parties is commonly known as valence. They prefer parties that have a good economic record, are united and have shown they can be trusted.

4 'Class is no longer the key factor in predicting voting behaviour.' How far do you agree? (30)

5 'The press can influence the outcome of elections in the UK.' How far do you agree with this statement? (30)

A-level

1 Using the source, evaluate the importance of class in voting behaviour. *In your response you must compare the different opinions in the source and use a balance of knowledge and understanding both arising from the source and beyond it to help you to analyse and evaluate.* (30)

Class DE voting for Labour	
Election year	**% class DE voting Labour**
1964	64
1987	53
1997	59
2010	40
2015	41

Source: Ipsos MORI/Earlham Sociology

Class AB voting for the Conservatives	
Election year	**% class AB voting Conservative**
1964	78
1987	57
1997	59
2010	40
2015	45

Source: Ipsos MORI/Earlham Sociology

2 Using the source, evaluate the influence of the press in general elections in the UK. *In your response you must compare the different opinions in the source and use a balance of knowledge and understanding both arising from the source and beyond it to help you to analyse and evaluate.* (30)

The political affiliations of the main UK newspapers at the 2015 election			
Newspaper	**Political preference**	**Circulation (000s)**	**% of its readers who support the paper's preferred party**
Sun	Very strongly Conservative	1,858	39
Daily Mail	Very strongly Conservative	1,631	57
Daily Mirror	Very strongly Labour	882	62
Daily Telegraph	Very strongly Conservative	486	72
Daily Express	Very strongly UKIP	438	44
Daily Star	No preference	420	n/a
The Times	Moderate Conservative	394	60
Financial Times	Conservative/ Liberal Democrat	212	62/10
Guardian	Moderate Labour	176	50
Independent	Conservative/ Liberal Democrat	59	17/16

Source: Cowley, P. and Kavanagh, D., *The British General Election of 2015*, Palgrave, 2015

3 Evaluate the relative importance of different demographic factors in voting behaviour. (30)

4 Evaluate the impact of turnout in determining the outcome of elections. (30)

COMPONENT 2

UK GOVERNMENT

5 The constitution

On most days in Washington DC a queue of Americans can be seen waiting to enter the National Archives Building. What they are anxious to see is the original version of the constitution of the USA. It is revered in America with almost religious fervour, so it is not surprising that so many want to visit. Written in the hot summer of 1787 in Philadelphia, the US Constitution appears on a single document, signed by the men who created it and who are known in the USA as the 'founding fathers'. By 1805 the US Supreme Court had further ruled that this constitution should be supreme and would be enforced against everyone in the land, from the president downwards. That constitution was unique in its day — the whole system of government written in one single place, supreme above all other laws and safeguarded against change by temporary governments. It was the first time such a thing had been seen. It is still enforced, largely in its original form, in the USA.

This is in direct contrast to the situation of the UK. In short, there is no 'constitution of the United Kingdom', in the sense that there is no single document that people can queue to look at. More precisely, there *is* a UK Constitution, but it is not to be found in one document, it was never created at one moment in time and there are no laws that are supreme. Instead, what is supreme in the UK is the parliament of the day, and constitutional rules are contained in a variety of forms that have emerged over centuries of constitutional development. Furthermore, the constitution can be easily changed if the people, Parliament and government wish to do so.

The National Archives Building in Washington DC

Objectives

This chapter will inform you about the following:

→ How the UK Constitution has developed through history
→ What a political constitution is, why countries have constitutions and what constitutions are for
→ The unusual way in which the UK Constitution has come into existence and what forms it takes
→ The key principles and concepts that lie behind constitutions in general
→ The different kinds of constitution that exist in different countries
→ Why and how the UK Constitution has been reformed since 1997
→ An assessment of what aspects of the UK Constitution are strong, democratic and effective as against aspects that are weak and less democratic and effective
→ Debates about how effectively the UK Constitution has been reformed
→ The debate about whether the UK Constitution should now be codified

What is a constitution?

Before we examine the nature of the UK's unusual and elusive constitution, we need to establish what a constitution — any constitution — actually *is*.

Virtually every country in the world operates its political system within the constraints of a constitution. In most cases, too, the constitution of the state is a written document that has been agreed on some particular occasion. Such constitutions are usually described as **codified**.

There are, however, a few countries, including the UK, that operate without such a specifically written constitution. Even so, these countries have a general 'sense' that a set of constitutional rules exists.

The functions of a constitution

So, constitutions, whether codified or not, are a vital aspect of most stable political systems. All constitutions, no matter where they exist, perform the same set of functions. These are as follows:

- They determine how political power should be distributed within the state. This includes federal states where power is divided between the central government and regional institutions, as in the USA, or unitary states where ultimate power lies firmly in one place, as with the UK's parliamentary system. Similarly, constitutions determine the balance of power between government and parliament, between president and prime minister and between two chambers in systems that are bicameral (two houses of Parliament).
- Linked to this first function, constitutions also establish the political processes that make the system work. This includes the relationships between institutions and the rules that govern how they operate.
- A constitution normally states what the limits of governmental power should be — in other words, what is the competence of government. The UK Constitution is unusual in this sense as it places no limits at all on the competence of Parliament. Being sovereign, Parliament is able to do what it likes. The Swiss political theorist, Jean-Louis de Lolme, wrote in his *Constitution de l'Angleterre* in 1784 that 'Parliament can do everything but make a woman a man and a man a woman.' This may be a strange statement but it remains true today. Of course, we would not expect the UK Parliament to act in a dictatorial way, but it has the legal power to do what it likes. By contrast, US government is circumscribed by that country's constitution.

> **Key term**
>
> **Codified constitution**
> A constitution that is contained in a single document that was created at a particular time. The term also implies that a codified constitution contains a set of laws that are superior to all other laws and that cannot be amended except by a special procedure that safeguards them.

- Just as constitutions limit governmental power, so do they assert the rights of the citizens against the state. Most countries that at least claim to be democratic have some kind of 'bill of rights', a statement that prevents the government from trampling on the civil liberties of its citizens.
- Constitutions establish the rules by which nationality is established — in other words, who is entitled to be a citizen and how outsiders may become citizens. This also implies that a constitution defines the territory that makes up the state.
- Finally, we must remember that constitutions have to be amended from time to time. It is therefore essential that a constitution contains within itself the rules for its own amendment. The UK is, once again, unusual in this respect as its constitution changes in two ways. One is through a simple parliamentary statute; the other is by the slow evolution of unwritten rules, known as **conventions**. Normally, states have special arrangements for amending their constitution. In France and Ireland, for example, a referendum is needed to approve a change. In the USA it is necessary to secure a two-thirds majority of both houses of Congress and the approval of three-quarters of the 50 states that make up the Union. The UK has no such methods of amendment; its constitution has evolved naturally over the course of history.

So we have established six main functions of a constitution. Issues that concern any of these matters are therefore described as 'constitutional' in nature. Now we must examine the UK Constitution and the country's constitutional arrangements specifically.

Key term

Constitutional convention
A convention is an unwritten rule which is considered binding even though it is not a law. Large parts of the UK Constitution are governed by such conventions. They tend to develop gradually over long periods of time.

The development, nature and theory of the UK Constitution

Stages in the development of the UK Constitution

As we have seen, the UK Constitution has gradually developed over time. To some extent this is an unseen process, so slow and subtle that we hardly notice it. Constitutional change is something that concerns lawyers and politicians but few members of the public. From time to time, however, an event takes place that everyone notices. These events form the main landmarks in the development of the UK Constitution. Among them are these:

- **Magna Carta, 1215** Little in Magna Carta has survived, save for a few common law traditions and some principles which have been turned into statute law. However, it was a key moment in history. It established that the rule of law should apply and the

Visitors to an exhibition at the British Library in 2015, marking 800 years of Magna Carta

monarch should operate within the framework of law. It was to be centuries before this principle became normal practice, but Magna Carta was an important staging post in the development of constitutional rule.

- **Bill of Rights, 1689** This Act of Parliament resulted from the replacement of King James II by the joint monarchy of William III and Mary. Parliament was anxious that the new monarchs would not exceed their powers, so the Bill of Rights effectively stated that Parliament was sovereign and would have the final word on legislation and the government's finances.
- **The Act of Settlement 1701** The Act finally established the rules governing the succession to the throne. It also stated that the monarch should be a member of the Church of England. However, its main significance was that it established the monarch's position as the ruler of the whole of the United Kingdom of Scotland, Wales and Ireland (Northern Ireland after 1921).
- **The Acts of Union 1707** Abolished the separate Scottish Parliament and so established the modern United Kingdom. Of course the devolution of power to Scotland in 1998 brought back the Scottish Parliament, although it was still not the sovereign body in that country.
- **The Parliament Acts 1911 and 1949** These two Acts settled the relationship between the House of Commons and the House of Lords. Before 1911 the two houses were, in theory at least, of equal status. In 1911, however, the House of Lords lost its powers to regulate the public finances and could only delay legislation for 2 years. It could no longer veto proposed legislation for good. The 1949 Act reduced the delaying period to 1 year. As a result, the House of Commons is very much the senior house.
- **The European Communities Act 1972** This was the Act that brought the UK into the European Community, which later became the European Union. The UK joined in 1973. This Act is now consigned to history, as the UK voted to leave the EU in 2016. It was, however, for nearly 50 years, a key feature of the UK Constitution.
- **The European (Notification of Withdrawal) Act 2017** This gave parliamentary consent to the UK's exit from the European Union.

Activity

Research the 1689 Bill of Rights. In what ways did it establish parliamentary sovereignty?

There have been many other key moments in constitutional development and many of them are described in this chapter. Those described above have been perhaps the most prominent in the history books. They trace the changing role of the monarchy and the growth in the authority of Parliament and the improved protection of citizens' rights.

The nature and theory of the Constitution

Here we consider some key principles concerning constitutions and their status, and compare different types of constitution.

Codification

As we saw in Chapter 1, the UK Constitution is not codified. It is not contained in a single document. This is not the same as saying that it is unwritten — in fact much of the UK Constitution *is* now written. For example, the European Convention on Human Rights is a well-known document. Constitutional statutes are also written. To be codified, a constitution has to have three features:

- It is contained in a single document.
- It has a single source and was therefore created at one moment in history, even if it has since been amended.
- The constitutional laws contained in it must be clearly distinguished from other, non-constitutional laws.

Key terms

Entrenchment

A constitutional principle whereby constitutional rules are safeguarded against change by a future government or legislature. It means in practice that constitutional change requires special arrangements which are more difficult to make than the passage of normal laws. The UK Constitution is not entrenched as Parliament can change it by a simple Act. However, most democratic constitutions are entrenched in some way.

Parliamentary sovereignty

This principle, established after 1689, means that the UK Parliament (not the Scottish Parliament) in Westminster is supreme within the political system. Only Parliament can grant power to other bodies and it can legislate on any matter it wishes. Its laws cannot be overridden by any other body, even the government or the monarch. It also means that the current parliament cannot bind any future parliaments. Each newly elected parliament is sovereign and cannot be bound by what has gone before.

Virtually all modern countries have a codified constitution. The famous US Constitution, which millions of proud Americans have travelled to Washington to see in its original form, is perhaps the earliest example of a modern codified constitution. The UK is very unusual in not having one. The main advantage of a codified constitution is that it is a clear document with which all citizens can identify and which can be examined when there is any doubt over its meaning. However, the key principle is not whether a constitution is codified; rather it is whether it is **entrenched**.

Entrenchment

This is a rather more important principle than codification. Entrenchment is the device that protects a constitution from short-term amendment. It is important because constitutional change makes a fundamental and important difference to the political system of a country. The constitution is too important to be placed in the hands of a *temporary* government. A country must be sure that any proposed constitutional change meets two tests:

- that there is widespread popular support for it
- that it is in the long-term interests of the country

An example of this principle concerns the guarantees of human rights that exist in most states. It may be in the interests of a particular government to set aside some of these rights by amending that part of the constitution that deals with civil rights. But this would clearly damage the long-term interests of the people. Similarly, a dictatorial government might seek to grant itself additional powers to protect its own position. If this occurred, democracy in general would be under threat.

To ensure that the two tests are met, therefore, special arrangements need to be established. Thus a referendum, for example, ensures popular support for change, while special parliamentary procedures can ensure that constitutional amendment is in the long-term interests of the state.

But the situation in the UK is unusual. It is not possible to entrench constitutional principles. This is because the UK Parliament is sovereign. The **sovereignty** of Parliament asserts that each individual parliament cannot be bound by its predecessors, nor can it bind its successors. This means, in effect, that every new parliament is able to amend the constitution as it wishes. All Parliament has to do is to pass a new parliamentary statute, using the same procedure as for any other statute. It can be done in as little as two days. Furthermore, of course, government in the UK is normally able to dominate Parliament, using its majority in the House of Commons and the mandate of the people that is granted at elections. So a dominant government can effectively control the constitution.

An example of executive power was demonstrated when the UK Parliament passed the Human Rights Act in 1998. This incorporated the European Convention on Human Rights into UK law. It became binding on all political bodies other than Parliament itself. No special procedures were needed. A fundamental change to the British Constitution was made through a simple Act of Parliament. It occurred in this way because the UK Constitution is not entrenched.

The problem of the UK's failure to adopt any system of entrenchment was illustrated by the curious case of the **Fixed Term Parliaments Act 2011** described below.

Fixed-term parliaments

After 2010 the new coalition government wished to change the constitution to introduce fixed-term parliaments. It proposed a law stating that each new parliament should sit for a fixed term of 5 years before the next general election. The Fixed Term Parliaments Act would take away the unwritten convention that the prime minister could name the date of the next general election. It was intended that this law should be entrenched — in other words, every new parliament would have a life of 5 years. However, it is not possible to entrench laws in the UK. In practice, this means that a future parliament (after the 2015 election, for example) could simply repeal or amend the Fixed Term Parliaments Act 2011 and either shorten or lengthen its life, or perhaps give back to the prime minister the right to choose the date of the next general election.

This means we cannot say that the idea of fixed-term parliaments is a permanent feature of the UK Constitution. What *may* happen, however, is that it will become a convention (an unwritten long-term arrangement which is binding) that each new parliament will set the date of the next general election at 5 years into the future. It will, in other words, become part of the constitution without entrenchment.

Referendums

Despite the inability to entrench constitutional laws in the UK, it is becoming common practice to hold a **referendum** when constitutional change is proposed. This was done for the devolution of power to Scotland and Wales in 1997, the introduction of elected mayors in London and a number of other locations, and to approve the Good Friday Agreement in Northern Ireland in 1998.

Where a referendum has produced a 'no' result, as was the case with the vote on a change to the electoral system in 2011 or on Scottish independence in 2014, a constitutional change cannot realistically take place. The effect of such referendums is to entrench constitutional developments. It is inconceivable that the changes would be reversed without another referendum to approve such a reversal. Thus, the UK is moving gradually towards a system of entrenchment through referendum.

The referendum on EU membership in June 2016 was the most dramatic example of all. Despite calls for Parliament to reverse the decision of the electorate to leave the EU or for a second referendum, general opinion was that the people's voice was binding and that the decision was irrevocable.

Table 5.1 shows a selection of methods by which various other countries have entrenched their constitutions.

> ## Key term
>
> **Referendum** A vote held among the electorate at national, regional or local level to resolve an important issue. Referendums in the UK are usually held to approve a change in the system of government or to a country's constitutional arrangements.

Table 5.1 Comparison of how countries amend their constitutions

Country	Year constitution was introduced	Method of amendment	Number of amendments since its establishment
France	1958	Referendum or three-fifths majority of Parliament	18
Germany (constitution known as Basic Law)	1949	Two-thirds majority in Parliament. Some sections cannot be amended at all	4
USA	1787	Two-thirds majority of Congress plus approval of three-quarters (38) of the 50 states	27
Irish Republic	1937	Referendum	23
Iraq	2005	Constitutional Review Committee recommends change, but this must be ratified by a referendum	0
UK	Not applicable	Various methods including parliamentary statutes, emergence of new conventions and judicial rulings	Innumerable

Activity

Research the constitutions of the following states and outline the way a constitutional amendment can be made:

- Spain
- Italy
- Russia

Study tip

You must be careful to distinguish between *power* and *sovereignty*. Sovereignty is ultimate power, normally safeguarded by a constitution. Power is temporary and the distribution of power is constantly shifting. Power can often be extended or removed without constitutional change.

Key term

Federalism A constitutional principle that divides sovereignty, or ultimate power, between central government and regional governments. Federalism normally occurs when a number of separate states come together to form one single state. A federal arrangement preserves *some* of the original states' autonomy. The USA, Germany and India are good examples.

We can see from Table 5.1 that the constitutional arrangements of the UK are very different from other democracies.

Sovereignty

The concept of sovereignty is vital to an understanding of how constitutions work. This is because a large part of any constitution is concerned with the distribution of sovereignty. A working definition of legal sovereignty would be: *Ultimate power and the source of all political power, as enforced by the legal system and the state.* This means that any body that is granted legal sovereignty within a constitution holds power that cannot be overruled by any other body. In many ways, too, an entrenched, codified constitution is also legally sovereign. If any individual or body challenges or abuses constitutional power, they must expect to be limited and sanctioned by the legal system.

Power should not be confused with legal sovereignty. Power is a more flexible concept and it can be added to or reduced or removed by bodies that hold sovereignty. The distribution of power within a political system is constantly changing, while the distribution of sovereignty is usually fixed by the constitution.

Some states place legal sovereignty in one place, while others divide it between different bodies. This distinction is discussed below. A word of caution is needed here. In the UK we often refer to the monarch as 'The Sovereign'. This is potentially confusing as it implies that ultimate political power lies with the monarch. This may have been true before the seventeenth century but it no longer represents anything like reality. It is, in other words, a historical curiosity, a throwback to a former age. The sovereign is not *actually* sovereign.

Unitary and federal constitutions

In a unitary constitution, sovereignty lies in one single place. The sovereign body in such a constitution is the ultimate source of all political power. A **federal** constitution, by contrast, divides sovereignty between a central body and regional, sub-central bodies. The only way to change the distribution of ultimate power in an entrenched, codified federal constitution is by amending the constitution. The UK is a unitary system (though without an entrenched constitution), while many other countries are federal, with the USA as possibly the best-known example of a federal constitution.

Unitary states	Federal states
United Kingdom	USA (50 states)
France	Germany (16 Länder)
Spain	Russia (37 Oblasts and republics)
Italy	Australia (8 states)
China	Canada (13 provinces and territories)

The UK, however, is distinctive in another way. It is certainly unitary, but sovereignty is also not located in an entrenched constitution. Instead it resides in the UK Parliament — in other words, in a constantly changing body rather than in a fixed, codified constitution. This means that it is very easy in the UK to change the distribution of power among individuals and bodies. It simply requires an Act or resolution of Parliament. This was done, for example, in 2016 when the government decided to grant extensive additional financial powers to the city of Manchester and its elected mayor. In states with entrenched constitutions, on the other hand, a change in the distribution of sovereignty requires a more complex constitutional amendment.

Discussion point

Is there a case for making the United Kingdom a federal system? How would you divide it up if it were federal?

Codified and uncodified constitutions

It is rare for a modern state not to have a codified constitution. The UK is unusual in not having a codified constitution. It is important to say that the few countries that do not have a codified constitution have highly flexible political systems, while countries whose constitution is codified have far more rigid political systems that are difficult to amend. Israel and New Zealand, for example, currently join the UK in the uncodified 'camp'.

Study tip

Do not confuse the words 'written' and 'codified' in relation to constitutions. All constitutional principles are written in some form or other. The key issue is whether they are written in one single place and whether they are superior to other laws.

The sources of the UK Constitution

The UK Constitution is not codified. This means it is not contained in a single document. If it were in one single document, as the US Constitution is, we would say it had one, single source. But it is not codified. It has a whole range of different sources. These are described below.

Parliamentary (constitutional) statutes

These are Acts of Parliament that have the effect of establishing constitutional principles. The **Human Rights Act 1998**, described above, is an example, but we can add the **Parliament Act 1949**, which established limitations to the power of the House of Lords, and the **Scotland and Wales Acts**, which devolved power to those countries. Further examples of constitutional statutes are shown in Table 5.2.

One of the distinctive features of the UK's constitutional arrangements is that a constitutional statute looks no different from any other statute. Because Parliament is sovereign and can amend or repeal any statute, all statutes look alike and have the same status. The wording of a constitutional statute does not contain the words, 'This is a Constitutional Statute.' In most other countries a constitutional statute is clearly differentiated from other laws and is superior to them.

Constitutional conventions

A convention is an unwritten rule that is considered binding on all members of the political community. Such conventions could be challenged in law but have so much moral force that they are rarely, if ever, disputed.

Many of the powers of the prime minister are governed by such conventions. It is, for example, merely a convention that the prime minister exercises the Queen's power to appoint and dismiss ministers, to conduct foreign policy and to grant various honours, such as peerages and knighthoods, to individuals. It is also a convention (known as the Salisbury Convention) that the House of Lords should not block any legislation that appeared in the governing party's most recent election manifesto.

Table 5.2 The main sources of the UK Constitution

Type of source	Examples
Statutes	**Equal Franchise Act 1928** established full and equal voting rights to women **Life Peerages Act 1958** introduced the appointment of life peers to add to the hereditary peerage **Human Rights Act 1998** incorporated the codified European Convention of Human Rights into UK law **Scotland Act 1998** established a Scottish Parliament with legislative powers **House of Lords Act 1999** abolished all but 92 of the hereditary peers in the House of Lords **Freedom of Information Act 2000** introduced the right of citizens to see all official documents not excluded on grounds of national security **Fixed Term Parliaments Act 2011** replaced the prime minister's power to call an election at any time with the rule that elections should take place every 5 years, unless Parliament passes a vote of no confidence in the government
Conventions	The Salisbury Convention states that the House of Lords should not block any legislation that appeared in the governing party's most recent election manifesto. Collective responsibility means that all members of the government must support official policy in public or resign or face dismissal (though occasionally suspended for national debates such as the referendum on UK membership of the EU in 2016). Government formation is based on the rule that, following an election, the Queen must invite the leader of the largest party in the Commons to form a government.
Historical principles and authoritative writing	The sovereignty of Parliament establishes the supremacy of Parliament in legislation. The rule of law states that all, including government itself, are equal under the law. Constitutional monarchy is a principle that the monarch is limited in its role and can play no active role in politics. The 'O'Donnell Rules' of 2010 establish how a coalition government may be formed.
Common law	Most common law concerns principles of rights and justice. These have mostly been replaced by the European Convention on Human Rights. However, some of Parliament's powers and procedures are contained in common law. Interestingly, the definition of homicide still resides in common law. The prerogative powers of the prime minister, exercised on behalf of the monarch, are essentially common law powers, which have never been codified.
Tradition	The practices and traditions of Parliament

A new convention that seems to be emerging is that the prime minister must consult Parliament before committing British armed forces to serious action. This was not the case before David Cameron appeared to accept it when seeking approval for air action in Syria in 2013. Parliament, on that occasion, refused to sanction the action.

Historical principles and authoritative writings

Similar to conventions, these principles have become effectively binding because they have been established over a long period of time. The most important is the sovereignty of Parliament. We could add a similar concept, which is *parliamentary government*, the principle that the authority of the government is drawn from Parliament and not directly from the people. The *rule of law* is a more recent development, originating in the second part of the nineteenth century. The rule of law establishes, among other things, the principles of equal rights for citizens and that government is itself limited by legal limitations. On the whole, historical principles are attributed to important constitutional theorists such as Blackstone (parliamentary sovereignty) and A. V. Dicey (rule of law). The rules on how to form a coalition are now an authoritative constitutional work, having been drawn up by the then cabinet secretary, Gus O'Donnell, in 2010.

The Queen's Speech sets out the government's programme for the coming year

Common law

'Common law' is a largely Anglo-Saxon principle. It refers to the development of laws through historical usage and tradition. Judges, who occasionally must declare and enforce common law, treat it as any rule of conduct that is both well established and generally acknowledged by most people.

The most important application of common law has concerned the protection of basic rights and freedoms from encroachment by government and/or Parliament. The right of people to free movement and to gather for public demonstrations, for example, are ancient freedoms, jealously guarded by the courts. So, too, was the principle that the Crown could not detain citizens without trial.

For the most part, common law principles have been replaced by statutes and by the European Convention on Human Rights, which became UK law in 2000. But from time to time, when there is no relevant statute, the common law is invoked in courts by citizens with a grievance against government.

The prerogative powers of the prime minister are considered common law powers. They have never been codified or put into formal legislation. These powers are exercised by the prime minister on behalf of the monarch and include commanding the armed forces, negotiating foreign treaties, calling general elections and making appointments to government. More information on prerogative powers can be seen below.

Customs and traditions

Similar to common law, constitutional traditions and customs govern many of the rituals of parliamentary government. The procedures of both houses of Parliament are traditional in nature, as are some of their rituals. The practice of allowing the Queen to announce the legislative programme for the coming year (the so-called Queen's Speech) is such a tradition, as are many of the rules of debate.

Constitutional reform in the UK

Study tip

When answering questions where you are evaluating the effectiveness of constitutional reforms, you should compare the outcomes with the original intentions, as described on this page.

The principles of constitutional reform

Before examining constitutional reform in detail, we should consider *why* such reforms have taken place. Constitutional reform has not occurred simply because politicians have believed it would be a good idea or that it would be popular with public opinion. Indeed, reforming the constitution is not a great vote winner! So why do they do it? The answer lies in deep beliefs they hold that the UK political system can be improved; constitutional reform is normally designed to achieve improvement.

There are a number of ways in which reform since 1997 hoped to achieve such improvements. The main motivations are as follows.

Democratisation

Too much of the British political system has been seen as undemocratic. The prime targets have been the unelected House of Lords and the unrepresentative electoral system. Neither of these two aims have, however, been achieved. It is true that the devolved administrations in Scotland, Wales and Northern Ireland use proportional electoral systems, but the main measure — reforming the system for general elections — failed following an unsuccessful referendum in 2011. A small reform of the House of Lords, namely the removal of most of its hereditary peers, has been made, but the main measure, to elect the second chamber, remains in doubt.

Under the coalition government of 2010–15 some democratisation of the House of Commons took place, but this aspect of reform remains incomplete.

Decentralisation

Here a great deal of progress has been made. Devolution dispersed power away from central government considerably in 1998. Since then all the administrations of Scotland, Wales and Northern Ireland have received additional powers. The introduction of elected mayors in London and other cities has helped to move power to local centres. The introduction of elected police commissioners after 2012 will also help to decentralise control over the police. In 2016 devolved powers over health and social care were also granted to Manchester.

Stronger protection of rights

During the 1980s there had been fears that the rights of citizens in the UK had been consistently eroded. In fact, the process could be traced back to earlier periods, but the Labour Party concentrated on what had occurred under the Conservatives. In addition, Labour wished to bring the UK more into line with European practice in constitutional matters. The party therefore proposed the incorporation of the European Convention on Human Rights into UK law. In addition, a Freedom of Information Act was seen as essential in a drive to create more open and accountable government. These two developments are now having a major impact on the safeguarding of rights in the UK.

Modernisation

Governments since 1997 have all sought to bring the British Constitution into line with other modern arrangements which exist in Western democracies. Certainly the stronger protection of rights and the right to obtain official information for citizens bring the UK into line with most other democracies. The idea of fixed-term parliaments is also in line with most other democracies. Referendum use has grown in the UK, bringing the UK into line with a common European practice. Nevertheless, the failure to reform the second chamber or to codify the constitution means that the British system remains 'traditional' rather than 'modern'.

Reform, 1997–2010

When the Labour Party was elected to power in 1997 it had grand plans for reform of the constitution. Furthermore, it was committed to completing most of the changes within 5 years. This was indeed ambitious. One of the reasons for the rush was that the party had a huge 179-seat majority in the House of Commons and so felt it could push through the reforms with minimal opposition. It was almost inevitable that such a large project could not be completed, but the government did implement a high proportion of its proposals by the time it lost office in 2010.

Devolution

Devolution was a key element of Lahore's post-1997 reform programme. It is described in detail on pages 175–82.

Parliamentary reform
House of Lords

The government of 1997 wanted to reform the House of Lords quite radically, but had to move in two stages.

1 The first stage was the removal of the **hereditary peers** and their voting rights. In other words, there would be an all-appointed chamber of life peers and Church of England bishops. There was some obstruction to this and the government had to compromise with the peers by allowing 92 hereditary peers to retain their seats.

2 Stage two was to be an elected, or partly elected, chamber. However, this ran into more obstruction and a lack of political consensus. The measure was, therefore, taken off the agenda.

Although the **House of Lords Act 1999** did reduce the number of hereditary peers to 92, the House of Lords threatened to use its powers to obstruct and delay reform. It was in return for the Lords' compliance that the government left a number of hereditary peers in place.

It should be emphasised that, although the 1999 Act was a limited reform, it did have the effect of making the Lords a largely appointed chamber. The much higher proportion of peers who held their position *on merit* rather than by birth meant that the Lords became a more professional and efficient body.

House of Commons

Reform of the Commons, meanwhile, has been piecemeal and superficial. The main reform concerned the departmental select committees of the House of Commons. These committees of backbench MPs which scrutinise the work of government departments are becoming more important and have enjoyed some enhancement in status. In 2004, the chairs of the committees were awarded additional salaries to raise their status. In 2010, one of the last acts of the outgoing Labour government was to introduce a system for electing members of the select committees. Before the reform they had been largely selected by party leaders. Election of members (by other MPs) has increased their independence of mind and action.

Study tip

When discussing constitutional reforms, you must always quote at least one example of each type of reform.

Key term

Hereditary peers
Members of the aristocracy who owe their title to their birth, in other words they inherit their titles from their father. Some titles go back deep into history. Ninety-two such peers have a right to sit in the House of Lords.

Synoptic link

To fully understand the principles and detail behind the reform of both houses of Parliament, you need to read Chapter 6.

Also in 2010, a Backbench Business Committee was established. This gave MPs control of over 20 parliamentary days to debate issues of their choosing. This represented a small increase in backbench influence and control.

Human rights reform

In 1998, the UK Parliament passed the Human Rights Act, possibly the most significant development in the protection of human rights in the UK since Magna Carta was drafted nearly 800 years before. Its provisions came into force in 2000. What the Act did was to incorporate the European Convention on Human Rights (ECHR) into UK law. The convention was made binding on all public bodies, including the government. All UK courts have an obligation to enforce the convention whenever it becomes relevant in any case coming before them.

In order to preserve the principle of parliamentary sovereignty, the convention is not strictly binding on the UK Parliament, though any laws passed that contravene the convention can only be passed if the government declares an overwhelming reason why it is necessary to do so. In practice, therefore, the terms of the ECHR are now binding in all parts of the UK.

The ECHR contains 18 articles that establish the following freedoms:

- To life
- From torture
- From servitude (slavery)
- To liberty and security
- To a fair trial
- From being accused of crimes retrospectively
- To privacy
- Of conscience and religion
- Of expression
- Of association
- To marry
- Of redress against the state when rights are abused
- From discrimination
- From unreasonable emergency powers
- To equal treatment for all citizens of the European Union

In addition, the convention required all signatory states to do the following:

- Abolish the death penalty
- Grant foreigners the same legal rights as citizens of the state
- Preserve family life
- Hold free and fair elections
- Not deny anybody an education
- Not threaten the right to own property

A number of factors led the Labour government that came to office in 1997 to incorporate the European Convention on Human Rights into British law:

- There was a general desire to bring the UK Constitution into line with the rest of Europe, all of whose states have special arrangements to protect individual rights.
- The increase in the powers of the police and the courts that had occurred in the 1980s and 1990s was now seen as a major threat to our rights.

Study tip

The Human Rights Act 1998 (HRA) was the legislation that brought the European Convention on Human Rights (ECHR) into UK law. Therefore the HRA is not a 'bill of rights'; the ECHR, however, is effectively a 'bill of rights'. Be careful to differentiate between them.

- The UK government had been brought before the European Court of Human Rights (which seeks to enforce the convention) more than 50 times since 1966 and had lost most of the cases. Although the decisions of the court are not legally binding, these cases had been an embarrassment to the government.
- The government stressed the idea of active citizenship. This concept included the principle that citizens have responsibilities to their communities and to the country as a whole. In return for these responsibilities it was believed that rights should be better understood and safeguarded.
- It was part of the devolution settlements that the Welsh and Northern Ireland assemblies and the Scottish Parliament should be bound by the convention. This was designed to reassure the citizens of these nations that devolution would not threaten their rights.

So it was that the **Human Rights Act** (passed in 1998) made the European Convention on Human Rights part of UK law in 2000.

The Human Rights Act marked a change not just in human rights in the UK but also in constitutional development. For the first time there was a genuinely codified element of the constitution and, furthermore, it was safeguarded by the fact that its terms were not set by Parliament. Instead, the ECHR was set by an *external* body — the Council of Europe. Moreover, it was to be enforced and interpreted by a group of European judges — the European Court of Human Rights.

The UK did not actually lose sovereignty by passing the Human Rights Act. Parliament can repeal it at any time and so the ECHR would no longer be enforced. Indeed, the Conservative government that came to power in 2015 was committed to replacing the Act with a new *British* Bill of Rights.

Synoptic link

Further discussion on the nature and status of rights in the UK, as well as the ways in which they are protected, can be found in Chapter 1.

Electoral reform

Since the 1960s the issue of electoral reform has been a persistent political issue. Reform takes three forms:

- The *franchise* — that is, the right to vote — might be changed. In practice the only issue here is whether the voting age should be reduced to 16.
- The *way* in which people vote and the rules concerning voting might be reformed.
- The electoral *system* might be changed. The system refers to the way in which votes are converted into seats won. The system used for general elections in the UK is known as first past the post (FPTP).

Votes at 16

The age at which citizens are entitled to vote in the UK was last changed in 1969 when it was reduced from 21 to 18. In the referendum on Scottish independence in 2014, for the first time in British history, 16- and 17-year-olds were entitled to vote. It was a great success and led to renewed calls to extend the lower age to all elections. An attempt to include the measure in the referendum on

In 2014 16- and 17-year-olds were allowed to vote in the Scottish independence referendum

European Union membership in 2016 failed, and the issue was taken off the agenda. However, it continues to be a future possibility. This issue is further explored in Chapter 3 above.

Voting reform

Low turnout at all elections has been a concern for policy makers. Various proposed reforms have been suggested, the most persistent of which is the idea of making voting compulsory. Voting is compulsory in Australia and has led to turnouts of over 90%. However, like votes at 16, compulsory voting does not yet enjoy sufficient support to progress.

Measures have been taken to make postal voting easier and it is possible that online voting will be introduced in the future. This is problematic, given the possibilities of fraud on the internet, but it is the main idea that might have a positive effect.

Changing the voting (electoral) system

The UK came close to introducing a new voting system in 1974 when the Liberal Party (the forerunner of the Liberal Democrats) won enough seats in Parliament to promote the issue. However, neither Labour nor the Conservative Party would support the proposal and it was abandoned. The issue re-emerged in 1997 when devolution was being considered.

There were to be new elected assemblies introduced in Wales and Northern Ireland and a parliament in Scotland. The question was: what **electoral system** should be used? It was decided at an early stage that the system used should reflect the party systems in those countries and should avoid domination by one or two parties, as was the case in England. It was therefore agreed that forms of proportional representation should be used. If FPTP had been adopted, Wales and Scotland would have been dominated by Labour and the Unionists would have controlled Northern Ireland. In the event the additional member system (AMS) was adopted for Scotland and Wales, while the single transferable vote (STV) was used in Northern Ireland.

When a coalition government was formed in 2010, the junior coalition partner, the Liberal Democrats, insisted that electoral reform should be considered as a price of their cooperation. They wanted proportional representation introduced, but the Conservatives were opposed. A compromise was reached, which involved a referendum being held in 2011, not on proportional representation but on a less radical reform, the introduction of the alternative vote (AV). However, the referendum rejected the proposal decisively. Once again, the issue of electoral reform for general elections was set back a generation.

The unsuccessful attempt in 2011 to reform the electoral system for general elections is perhaps the greatest failure for reformers since 1997. However, proportional representation is now commonly used for sub-central elections in the UK and for elections to the European Parliament, so it is not true to say that no reform has taken place.

Key term

Electoral system
An electoral system is the mechanism by which votes at elections are converted into seats awarded to candidates and parties. Many different electoral systems are used in the democratic world.

Synoptic links

There is further discussion and detail about elections and electoral systems in Chapter 3.

Freedom of information

The lack of any citizen's right to obtain publicly held information was one of the features of the British Constitution that lagged behind the European and US experience in the 1990s. The Labour Party, supported by the Liberal Democrats, made a firm commitment to introduce such a measure. However, the legislation, when it appeared in 1997, proved to be a disappointment to civil rights campaigners. There are two strands to **freedom of information**.

- The first gives the right to citizens to see information that is held about them by public bodies. These include government, schools, medical bodies and other institutions of the welfare state. This has been relatively uncontroversial. Indeed, the right to view records held on computer files had already been established under the **Data Protection Act 1998**. The main disappointment here was that this right would not come into existence until 2005.
- The second strand has caused more problems. This concerns the right to see documents and reports that are held by government and its agencies. In other words, there was to be a public right to see inside the very workings of government. The ability to suppress information would be limited, while the media and Parliament would have much greater access to information. In theory, this represents a major move towards more open government. If implemented in full, freedom of information would have virtually ended the British culture of secrecy in government.

The Freedom of Information Act 2000

As with electoral reform, the new Labour government of 1997 proved to be less enthusiastic about reform once it was in office than when it had been in opposition. The **Freedom of Information Act 2000** was a watered-down version of similar measures in operation elsewhere in Europe. The security services were exempt, while the rest of government was given a key concession. The 'normal' situation is that governments have to justify any reason for suppressing information.

The UK version, however, gives the government the right to conceal information if it feels it might prejudice the activities of government. In other words, the onus is on the 'outsider' to prove that a document or other information should be released. Nevertheless, an Information Tribunal was also set up. The tribunal can rule on what information can and should be released. In the event, this tribunal has proved to be more sympathetic to freedom of information than was envisaged.

When the Freedom of Information Act was passed, human rights campaigners thought it was too weak. Experience tells us otherwise, however. One major development illustrates its power. In 2008 a request was made to the Information Tribunal to release details of expenses claims made by MPs. Parliament attempted to block the request through the High Court, but failed. The information was released and immediately leaked to the *Daily Telegraph*. When the revelations were made in the newspaper, it became clear that there had been widespread abuse of the generous expenses system. As a result, a kind of witch-hunt was undertaken, in which hundreds of MPs were accused of 'milking' the system for their own benefit (though most claimed successfully that they had operated within the rules). The results of the revelations were far reaching. Many MPs were forced to give up their seats, Parliament was subjected to widespread ridicule and public condemnation, and the expenses system had to be radically reformed.

Key term

Freedom of information
This is a principle of legislation, since 2000 in the UK, which states that all citizens have a right to see certain kinds of information held by public bodies, including NHS bodies, schools and universities, as well as all levels of government. The main kinds of information available are: information about the citizen him- or herself (but not other citizens); factual information, statistics and reports held by government bodies; information held by parliamentary bodies and the minutes of meetings by non-confidential bodies. Information can be withheld if it may jeopardise national security or the efficient running of government.

Activity

Research the so-called 'MPs' expenses scandal' of 2009–10. Describe the issue and explain why the Freedom of Information Act was important in it.

The Freedom of Information Act also proved to be significant in such areas as health care provision, defence procurement and local authority procedures. It is, therefore, one of the most important constitutional reforms of recent times.

City government in London

In 1985 the Greater London Council (GLC), a powerful local government body with wide powers and responsibilities, was abolished by the Conservative government. Prime Minister Thatcher was determined to remove from power what she saw as a socialist enclave in the centre of Conservative Britain.

Labour, when it returned to power in 1997, was determined to restore government to London, a measure that has been seen as an extension of local government rather than devolution. In addition, a new innovation was to be introduced. This was the election of a mayor with a considerable degree of executive power. Elected mayors were unheard of in British history. In the past, mayors had been holders of ceremonial offices, appointed by councils and with no executive power at all.

In 2000, following a decisive referendum in which the people of London approved the introduction of an elected mayor and assembly, elections were held for the two new institutions. However, the legislation seemed to ensure that neither would enjoy a hugely significant amount of *political* power.

The mayor controls the allocation of funds to different uses in London, funds that are distributed and administered by the elected assembly of 25 members. But at the same time, the assembly has the power to veto the mayor's budgetary and other proposals, provided there is a two-thirds majority for such a veto. Similarly, while the mayor has powers of patronage, controlling a variety of appointments, the assembly again has rights of veto. This was a classic example of the introduction of a system of 'checks and balances', on the American model. Furthermore, the electoral system used for the assembly — AMS (additional member system), as in Scotland and Wales — meant that there was no possibility of a single party enjoying an overall majority. This ensured that the mayor would always face obstruction for controversial measures.

Key term

City government and city devolution The transfer of wide powers to cities and city regions, led by an elected mayor with extensive control over the budget and some tax-raising powers.

Knowledge check

Identify the two new electoral systems introduced for devolved assemblies in 1998.

The office of London mayor was granted relatively limited power under the legislation. The holder of this office cannot be said to enjoy a similar position to powerful mayors in New York and Paris, for instance. However, within the limitations, it could be said that Ken Livingstone and his successors Boris Johnson and Sadiq Khan have been involved in several significant developments in London. Accepting that the mayor possesses *influence* rather than power, Livingstone and Johnson were wholly or partially instrumental in the following initiatives:

- Improved community policing
- The growth in the arts scene in the capital
- Vastly improved public transport

Reform of the judiciary

At the start of the twenty-first century, there was growing concern that the judiciary — that is, the senior levels of the court system — was in need of reform. The **Constitutional Reform Act 2005** was passed to address these issues.

Effects of judicial reform

The Constitutional Reform Act had three main effects.

1 **Separation of judiciary and government** Most importantly, it was seen as crucial that there be a clearer separation between the senior members of the judiciary and the government. In the past, the position of the Lord Chancellor had been ambiguous. He (or she) was a cabinet minister and senior member of the governing party. At the same time, the holder of the office was head of the judiciary and presided over the proceedings of the House of Lords. This placed the Lord Chancellor in all three branches of government. Although the occupant of the post might protest that they understood the difference between their neutral *judicial* role and their *political* role as a cabinet minister, suspicions persisted that one role would interfere with another. This perception of lack of **independence of the judiciary** had to be addressed in a modern system. The judicial role of the Lord Chancellor was therefore largely removed. The post was combined with that of justice secretary, a cabinet post, but the holder ceased to have a judicial role; he or she was in charge of justice *policy*, but not *practice*.

2 **Supreme Court** The highest court of appeal had been the House of Lords, meeting as a court rather than as part of Parliament. The senior 'Law Lords' — usually in groups of five — would hear important appeal cases, often with great political consequences. There was disquiet over recent years that it was not appropriate that members of the legislature (i.e. the Law Lords) should also be the highest level of the judiciary. In other words, it was seen as vital that law and politics should be completely separated to safeguard the rule of law. It was therefore decided to take the senior judges out of the Lords and to create a separate Supreme Court.

   The Supreme Court was opened in the autumn of 2009 and began work immediately to establish its new independence. In reality, the change to a Supreme Court is partly a cosmetic exercise. The new court has the same powers as the old House of Lords. However, it is symbolically important and the early signs have indicated that it will indeed prove to be a genuinely independent body.

3 **Appointment of senior judges** Finally, there was opposition to the continued practice of senior appointments to the judiciary being in the hands of politicians — mainly the Lord Chancellor and the prime minister. There was a constant danger that such appointments might be made on the basis of the political views of prospective judges rather than on their legal qualifications. A Judicial Appointments Commission (JAC) was therefore set up to ensure that all candidates should be suitable, using purely legal considerations. The government has the final say on who shall become a senior judge, but this must be after approval by the JAC. The most senior appointments — to the Supreme Court — have been placed in the hands of a non-political committee of senior judicial figures.

Key term

The independence of the judiciary The constitutional principle that the judges should be independent from pressure by politicians so that they do not only deliver judgements favourable to government.

Synoptic link

The work and importance of the Supreme Court and the judiciary in general are discussed in more detail in Chapter 8.

Key term

Separation of powers The constitutional arrangement whereby the three branches of government — legislature, executive and judiciary — have separate powers and can control each other's power.

Principles of judicial reform

The principles of judicial reform have been fourfold.

1 To increase the **separation of powers** between government, legislature and judiciary

2 To improve the independence of the judiciary

3 To eliminate the ambiguity of the role of the Lord Chancellor

4 To bring Britain into line with modern constitutional practice

Constitutional reform since 2010

Fixed-term parliaments

When a coalition government had to be formed in 2010 there was an overwhelming fear that it would be unstable and possibly not last very long. If the two parties — Conservative and Liberal Democratic — came into conflict with each other, it would be easy for Parliament to defeat the divided government and so force a general election. In addition, because the power to dissolve Parliament and call an election lay in the hands of the prime minister (by constitutional convention), this power could be used to 'bully' the Liberal Democrats into agreement. To avoid this undesirable possibility, the **Fixed Term Parliaments Act** was passed in 2011. It meant that there could be disagreement within government without the danger of it falling apart.

The Act was also designed to take away the prime minister's power to call a general election whenever he or she wishes, thus giving their own party an advantage by surprising the opposition with a 'snap election'. An early election would only occur if a vote of no confidence in the government were to be passed or if a two-thirds majority in the House of Commons passed a motion for an early election.

However, in April 2017 Theresa May announced such a snap election, to take place on 8 June, and avoided the restrictions of the Act by introducing such a motion and achieving a two-thirds majority in the Commons. The opposition could not oppose the motion because they would have appeared weak in avoiding an election. Thus, it seems the prime minister still has considerable power over when general elections are held.

Elected mayors

The 1997–2010 Labour government's enthusiasm for reform of local government in general withered quickly after it was elected to office in 1997. Cities, towns and districts were given the opportunity to elect mayors following a local referendum. However, few held referendums and fewer still voted in favour of an elected mayor (originally only 11 cities voted for an elected mayor).

Similarly, local authorities were given the option of changing to a 'cabinet' system of government. This involves the creation of a central cabinet of leading councillors from the dominant party or from a coalition, who may take over central control of the council's work, making key decisions and setting general policy. This replaces the former system where the work of the council was divided between a number of functional committees. But, as with elected mayors, the take-up for the new cabinet system has been patchy. Moreover, it is generally acknowledged that this kind of

Activity

Research the most recent elections for mayor of Manchester, Liverpool and Birmingham. If the turnouts are low, can you explain why there was so little interest in them? If they are high, can you explain why?

internal change does not tackle the real problems of local government. These are seen as threefold:

1 Lack of autonomy from central government

2 Lack of accountability to local electorates

3 Largely as a result of the first two problems, low levels of public interest in local government and politics

Elected police commissioners

The most important development under the coalition government in 2010–15 was the introduction of elected mayors in more English cities, together with provision for the election of new police commissioners, who are accountable for the quality of policing in all English and Welsh areas. It was hoped that police commissioners would improve accountability for policing in local areas, but this has not been the case. Turnout at commissioner elections has been low and few people are even aware of who their local police commissioner is.

City devolution outside London

The Conservative government that took office in 2015 — its chancellor, George Osborne, in particular — was committed to granting more autonomous powers to large cities. In October 2015 Osborne announced that local authorities would be allowed to keep all the revenue from business rates (local tax levied on commercial businesses) rather than giving it to the central exchequer. This gave them considerable financial independence, allowing them to finance important projects and policies. Furthermore, any city which adopted an elected mayor system would have the power to increase the level of business rates and so finance major projects. This represented a first step towards more independent local government.

Manchester's Metrolink tram system — better public transport is where elected city mayors can make a difference

The next step was to allow one city — Manchester — to control its own budgets for health and social care from March 2016. This represented a budget of £6 billion per annum, previously controlled by central authorities but now in the hands of the Manchester mayor and his or her own government. If this proves successful, it may be extended to other cities, provided they have an elected mayor.

City devolution, both in and beyond London, if it is extended, will begin to look like the US model, where city mayors have considerable control over how local taxes are spent. American mayors are all elected and so are accountable to their local community. Liverpool, Manchester and Birmingham are expected to become semi-autonomous and to introduce elected mayors in 2017.

Debate

Should cities be given more independent powers?

Arguments for

- Local democracy is closer to the people and will therefore reflect their demands more accurately.
- Local needs vary a great deal, so the 'one size fits all' suggested by central government control is not realistic.
- The UK as a whole is too 'London-centred', so autonomous local government may boost local economies and spread wealth and economic development more evenly.
- Demonstrating that local councils and mayors have significant powers will give a boost to local democracy.

Arguments against

- Central control means that all parts of the UK should receive the same range and quality of services.
- Central control of finance will prevent irresponsible local government overspending.
- Turnouts at local council and mayoral elections tend to be very low, so local government is not accountable enough.
- There is a danger that the traditional unity of the UK might be jeopardised.

Recall of MPs

The **Recall of MPs Act 2015** provided for constituencies to 'recall' an MP who had been involved in some kind of misbehaviour. It requires a petition supported by at least 10% of the MPs' constituents to set the process in motion. It is a limited measure in that MPs cannot be recalled on the basis of their voting record or their policy statements. If an MP is imprisoned or suspended from the House of Commons, they may be subjected to a by-election, which they would be likely to lose and so lose their seat.

Extension of Scottish and Welsh devolution

In 2016 the new Conservative government was forced to grant further powers to the Scottish government. This was in response to the surge in nationalist feeling following a close result in the 2014 Scottish independence referendum. The new powers included the ability to vary the rate of income tax and some other taxes and to control welfare. This gave a great deal of financial autonomy to Scotland and was known as 'devo-max'.

In Wales, the way has now been paved for future increases in the powers of the assembly. Provided the Welsh Assembly requests legislative powers, it is clear these will be granted.

Table 5.3 summarises constitutional reform since 1997.

Table 5.3 A general summary of constitutional reform in the UK since 1997

Reform	Detail
House of Lords	Abolition of voting rights of most hereditary peers
House of Commons	Limited changes to the select committee system
	Fixed-term parliaments (though not entrenched)
	New control for backbenchers over the Commons agenda
Human Rights Act	Inclusion of the European Convention on Human Rights into British law, effective from 2000
Electoral reform	The introduction of new electoral systems for the Scottish Parliament, Welsh and Northern Ireland assemblies, elections to the European Parliament, for the Greater London Assembly and for elected mayors
Freedom of information	Introduction of freedom of information, effective from 2005
	Public right to see official documents
City government	Introduction of an elected mayor and assembly for Greater London and devolution of powers over health and social care to the Manchester mayor and government
Local government	Introduction of a cabinet system in local government and the opportunity for local people to introduce elected mayors by referendum
Devolution	Transfer of large amounts of power from Westminster and Whitehall to elected bodies and governments in Scotland, Wales and Northern Ireland
Party registration and the electoral commission	A new electoral commission was set up to regulate elections and referendums, including the funding of parties.
	This reform also required the first ever registration of political parties.
Reform of the judiciary	The 'political' office of Lord Chancellor was abolished. The holder was no longer head of the judiciary or Speaker of the House of Lords. This function was replaced by an office known as justice minister.
	The House of Lords Appeal Court was replaced by a separate Supreme Court in 2009.
	Senior judicial appointments are controlled by an independent committee of senior judges.
Fixed-term parliaments	The 2010 Act removed the prime minister's power to determine the date of general elections. Each parliament should, except under exceptional circumstances, last for 5 years.
English votes for English laws (EVEL)	A change in parliamentary procedure that means that MPs from Scottish constituencies will not be allowed to vote on issues that affect only England, or England and Wales.
Recall of MPs	If an MP is imprisoned or suspended from the House of Commons for misbehaviour, a petition signed by 10% of the voters in a constituency can trigger a by-election.
The UK and the EU	In 2016 a referendum determined that the UK will leave the EU in the years that follow. This will have wide-ranging constitutional impacts.

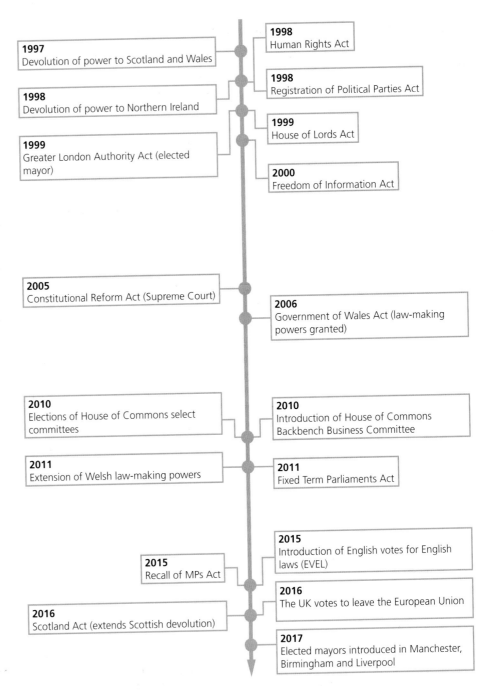

Figure 5.1 Timeline on constitutional reform

1997
Devolution of power to Scotland and Wales

1998
Human Rights Act

1998
Devolution of power to Northern Ireland

1998
Registration of Political Parties Act

1999
Greater London Authority Act (elected mayor)

1999
House of Lords Act

2000
Freedom of Information Act

2005
Constitutional Reform Act (Supreme Court)

2006
Government of Wales Act (law-making powers granted)

2010
Elections of House of Commons select committees

2010
Introduction of House of Commons Backbench Business Committee

2011
Extension of Welsh law-making powers

2011
Fixed Term Parliaments Act

2015
Recall of MPs Act

2015
Introduction of English votes for English laws (EVEL)

2016
The UK votes to leave the European Union

2016
Scotland Act (extends Scottish devolution)

2017
Elected mayors introduced in Manchester, Birmingham and Liverpool

A note on referendums

There has not been a piece of legislation establishing the practice of holding referendums to provide popular consent for constitutional changes. Nevertheless, it has become firmly established that a referendum will be held if any power is to be transferred away from central government in the UK. This transfer could be upwards to the European Union or downwards to regional or local bodies.

In other parts of the democratic world, referendums are often used as a special arrangement for constitutional reform. In the past, Britain has not had special arrangements for constitutional amendments — they have been created either by Act of Parliament or by the emergence of new unwritten conventions. But the referendum is now a regular feature in the UK, so much so that we can describe its use as an important constitutional reform.

Three recent referendums demonstrate how important they have become:

- **2011** Should the UK adopt the alternative vote system for general elections?
- **2014** Should Scotland become an independent state? (In Scotland only)
- **2016** Should the UK remain a member of the European Union?

Devolution

The nature of devolution

Devolution is an important constitutional development in the context of the UK. It is vital to understand precisely what the term means. A good definition, applied to the UK, looks like this:

> *Devolution is a process of delegating power, but not sovereignty, from the UK Parliament to specific regions of the country. This is power which can be returned to Parliament through a constitutional statute. Therefore it is a transfer of power without eroding the sovereignty of Parliament.*

Although we do not expect any devolved powers to return to Westminster in the foreseeable future, the arrangement is not the same as a federal settlement. With a federal settlement, such as that which operates in the USA, the powers are divided by a constitutional provision and they cannot be changed without a full amendment to the constitution. In other words, the division of power is *entrenched*. Having said that, some have argued that, because the devolution arrangements of the UK were approved by referendums (1997 in Scotland and Wales, 1998 in Northern Ireland), they are to all intents and purposes entrenched. In other words, it is unthinkable that devolved power would return permanently to Westminster without another referendum to approve the measure. This kind of semi-entrenchment has led to some calling devolution in the UK **quasi-federalism**.

One other difference between devolution and federalism in the context of the UK is what is known as asymmetry. In a federal system, each regional government is granted equal powers. In the UK's system, this is not the case. The UK has what is known as **asymmetric devolution**. The Scottish government, in particular, has been granted more power than Wales and Northern Ireland, so powers were devolved asymmetrically.

The differences between devolution and federalism are summarised in Table 5.4.

Table 5.4 Distinctions between federalism and devolution

Federalism	Devolution
Legal sovereignty is divided between central government and regional governments.	Power but not sovereignty is delegated from central government to regional governments.
Federalism is entrenched in a constitution.	Devolution is not entrenched and is therefore flexible.
The powers granted to regional governments are equal and symmetrical.	Powers may be delegated in unequal amounts to various regional governments.
Any powers not specified in the constitution are normally granted to regional governments.	Any powers not specified in devolution legislation are reserved to central government.

Three types of devolution

Devolved powers fall into three general categories:

- **Legislative powers** This means that the devolved assemblies or parliaments can make laws that will be enforced within their territories.

Synoptic link

The issues surrounding the use of referendums in the UK are discussed at length in Chapter 3.

Knowledge check

What were the results of the three referendums listed here? Find the proportion who voted 'yes', the proportion who voted 'no', and the percentage turnout.

Key terms

Devolution A term referring to the division of powers among regions of the country, while actual sovereignty, or ultimate legal power, remains with the Westminster Parliament.

Quasi-federalism A system of devolution where it is so unlikely or difficult for power to be returned to central government, that it is, to all intents and purposes, a federal system even though it is not in strict constitutional terms.

Asymmetric devolution A type of devolution where the various regions have been granted unequal amounts of power.

- **Administrative powers** These are powers that have been devolved to regional governments. It refers to their power (and responsibility) to implement and administer the laws and to organise state services.
- **Financial powers** Devolved governments have funds made available to them by the central government so that they can provide services. However, financial devolution takes this further. It allows devolved governments to raise their own funds from taxation or other means, so that they become financially independent.

As we have seen, devolution is not symmetrical in the UK. For example, Scotland does have independent financial powers whereas Northern Ireland does not. Furthermore, the legislative powers delegated to each of the three countries vary.

The road to devolution

The first calls for devolution emerged in the 1970s. The Labour government of 1974–79 considered the measure, largely under the influence of the Liberal Party (the forerunner of the Liberal Democrats). Labour had only a small parliamentary majority, so it relied on Liberal support for much of its time in government. One of the prices of that support was the idea of devolution. The Liberal Party believed that devolution would enhance democracy in the UK and bring government closer to the people. It was also in response to some early signs of nationalist sentiment in Scotland.

Labour was unenthusiastic but went ahead with referendums in Scotland and Wales. The proposal, however, was doomed from the start. Parliament insisted on a safeguard. It insisted that, for devolution to take place, it would be necessary not only that the majority of Scots or Welsh voted in favour, but also that at least 40% of the adult population approved — taking into account non-voters. Wales rejected the proposal anyway, while a majority of Scots voted in favour, but the number fell short of the 40% threshold.

Devolution was forgotten for nearly two decades. In the late nineties, however, circumstances changed. First there were renewed signs of growing nationalism in Scotland and Wales. Second, and coincidentally, Labour was elected to power with a huge mandate to reform the UK Constitution. Devolution was a key aspect of those reforms. Meanwhile, in Northern Ireland, a peace settlement had been reached between the warring Republican and Loyalist communities. In order to cement the peace, a devolution settlement with Northern Ireland was also negotiated. This would allow power sharing to be introduced so that a political settlement could underpin the military peace. Thus, by 1997, the stage was set for a full set of devolution proposals and referendums to approve them.

Devolution in England

At the time when devolution to the UK's three national regions was being implemented, the deputy prime minister, John Prescott, was also floating the idea of devolution to the English regions. His plan was to devolve a similar amount of power to the regions as that being transferred to Wales, in other words administrative but not legislative or financial devolution. In order to test public opinion, a referendum was held in the North East region in 2004. The voters rejected the idea by a majority of 78% to 22%. This was so clear a verdict that the idea was promptly abandoned.

The more recent version of devolution to the regions is city devolution. This is not *strictly* devolution, but rather the decentralisation of some powers to city government. It is described and explored on pages 171–72. English devolution can also refer to the creation of an English parliament. This is discussed below.

Activity

Research the taxation powers of the Scottish government. How much can it allow tax in Scotland to vary from the rest of the UK?

English votes for English laws (EVEL)

EVEL was introduced in 2015. It addressed the problem, sometimes known as the West Lothian Question, whereby MPs representing Scottish constituencies in the House of Commons were allowed to vote on issues which *only* affected England, or England and Wales. These included such matters as health, education and criminal law.

The system means that the Speaker of the House of Commons may declare that a debate and a parliamentary vote concerns England, or England and Wales, only and that MPs from Scottish constituencies shall therefore not take part. It will be some time before the meaning and significance of the measure becomes apparent, but it does appear to create equality among MPs from all over the UK.

A more radical version of this has been proposed — the creation of a completely separate English parliament. This would meet separately from the Westminster parliament and could even be separately elected. It would resolve all 'England-only' issues. For the time being, this solution is not well supported but it would represent a complete version of English devolution if it were implemented and would place England on the same constitutional status as Scotland, Wales and Northern Ireland.

Scottish devolution

Scotland was a special case. There had been administrative devolution in Scotland since the nineteenth century. What this meant was that a non-elected Scottish Executive administered various services in Scotland on behalf of the UK government. Matters such as education, health, local authority services and policing were managed separately in Scotland. The country also had its own laws. However, there had been no Scottish Parliament to pass these laws since 1707. Rather strangely, it was the UK Parliament in Westminster that made the laws for Scotland. So Scotland was partly on the road to devolution before 1997. In addition, it should be noted that nationalist sentiment was much stronger in Scotland than it was in Wales or Northern Ireland, so devolution was all the more urgent a matter.

Scotland Act 1998

In 1997 a referendum was held in Scotland to gauge support for devolution. The Scots voted overwhelmingly in favour, by 74% to 26% on a 60% turnout. The following year the **Scotland Act** was passed, granting devolution. It was implemented in 1999 and the first Scottish Parliament was elected. The main powers that were devolved to this parliament, and the executive which was drawn from it, were as follows:

- Power over the health service
- Power over education
- Power over roads and public transport
- Power to make criminal and civil law
- Power over policing
- Power over local authority services
- Power to vary the rate of income tax up or down by 3%
- Other miscellaneous powers

At the same time, a new electoral system was introduced for the Scottish Parliament. This was the additional member system. The government of Scotland would be formed by the largest party in the parliament or by a coalition. The first minister, leader of the largest party, would head the government.

Activity

Study the following elections and trace the rise in the fortunes of the Scottish National Party:

- The 2007 Scottish parliamentary election
- The 2010 UK general election
- The 2011 Scottish parliamentary election
- The 2015 UK general election
- The 2016 Scottish parliamentary election

Scotland Act 2016

After the start of the twenty-first century, Scottish nationalism continued to grow in popularity, so much so that a referendum on full independence was held in 2014. Though the Scots voted against independence, it was clear there was an appetite for greater devolution. This was reflected in a second devolution stage. This was the **Scotland Act 2016**. This Act included the following measures:

- Widening of the areas in which the Scottish Parliament may pass laws
- Power over the regulation of the energy industry transferred to Scotland
- Control over a range of welfare services including housing and disability
- Control of half the receipts from VAT collected in Scotland
- Control over income tax rates and control over all receipts from income tax
- Control over air passenger duty and control over its revenue
- Control over some business taxes

The Act represented a large transfer of powers and independence of action. It means that the Scottish government now has an enormous amount of administrative, legislative and financial autonomy. It still stops well short of independence, but it does go a long way to making Scotland feel like a separate country, in charge of its own future.

The UK's decision to leave the EU in 2016, however, has once again destabilised the Scottish situation. The problem is that the Scots voted by a large majority to remain inside the EU. For many Scots, the only way to stay in the EU was once again to demand full independence.

Welsh devolution

Study tip

When discussing devolution, pay special attention to the differences between the powers granted to the Scottish, Welsh and Northern Irish governments.

The referendum on Welsh devolution in 1997 was a close-run thing. The majority was only 50.5–49.5 on a low turnout of around 50%, so only a quarter of the Welsh electorate actually voted in favour of devolution. It was therefore no surprise that considerably fewer powers were devolved to Wales than to Scotland.

Government of Wales Act 1998

The **Government of Wales Act 1998** set up an elected Welsh National Assembly, and a Welsh Executive to be drawn from the largest party in the assembly and headed by a first minister. The assembly had no powers to make or pass laws and the country was given no financial control. In other words, devolution to Wales in 1998 was purely administrative. The Welsh government now runs a number of services, but cannot pass laws relating to those services. It does, however, have the power to decide how to allocate the funds it receives from central government between various services.

The main areas of government devolved to Wales included these:

- Health
- Education
- Local authority services
- Public transport
- Agriculture

Without its own means of raising finance, the Welsh government relies on an annual grant from the UK government.

Government of Wales Act 2014

Nationalist sentiment did not grow in Wales after the first stage of devolution. Nevertheless, demands for further devolution did begin to grow after 2010. The fact that the Liberal Democratic Party was part of the coalition government after 2010 helped the process as the Lib Dems supported further decentralisation of power.

There were also fears that, if considerable new powers were devolved to Scotland, the difference between the powers of the Welsh and Scottish governments would be too wide. There had been a small increase in devolved powers through the **Government of Wales Act 2006**, but it was in 2014 that a significant change came about. The **Government of Wales Act 2014** included these provisions:

- There would be referendum in Wales to decide whether the government of Wales should have partial control over income tax.
- The Welsh government was granted control over various taxes including business taxes, stamp duty charged on property sales and landfill tax.
- The government of Wales would have limited powers to borrow money on open markets to enable it to invest in major projects and housing.

The following year, in 2015, the UK government announced that the Welsh government could take control of some income tax, up to £3 billion per annum, without the approval of a referendum. It appears that Welsh governments in the future will enjoy a good deal of financial as well as administrative devolution.

Northern Ireland devolution

Northern Ireland is very different to Wales and Scotland and the devolution process reflected this. This is because the devolution settlement was part of the wider resolution of 30 years of conflict between the Republican (largely Catholic) and Loyalist (largely Protestant) communities. There had been devolved government in the province between 1921 and 1972, with a Northern Ireland Parliament (often known as Stormont, where it met) and government in control of such issues as education, welfare, health, policing, much criminal and civil law, housing and local government. With increasing sectarian violence breaking out in the 1970s, the Parliament was dissolved in 1972.

The Belfast Agreement, 1998

The Belfast Agreement — also known as the Good Friday Agreement — of 1998 restored the province's devolved powers. In place of the Parliament, an assembly was to be elected using proportional representation (PR) instead of first past the post. The reason PR was introduced was to ensure that all sections of a divided society would gain representation. Meanwhile the Northern Ireland Executive was based on power sharing. This meant that all major parties were *guaranteed* ministerial places. This was part of a device to try to head off any possibility of future armed conflict.

Powers devolved to Northern Ireland include the following:

- The passage of laws not reserved to Westminster
- Education administration
- Healthcare
- Transport
- Policing
- Agriculture
- Sponsorship of the arts

To emphasise the fact that devolution in the UK is not a federal system, the UK government dissolved the Northern Ireland Assembly in 2002 in the face of increased tension between the two communities and the failure of ministers from the two communities to cooperate with each other. The suspension lasted until 2007.

Devolution in Northern Ireland remains fragile, although the nationalists in the government continue to campaign for more powers to be devolved. However, progress is likely to be slow, as the Loyalist, unionist community is not particularly enthusiastic about home rule.

A summary of devolution throughout the UK is shown in Table 5.5.

Table 5.5 Devolution in the UK, 1979–2016

Year	Scotland	Wales	Northern Ireland
1979	Referendum on Scottish devolution. It fails to reach the threshold of 40% of the electorate approving.	Referendum on devolution held in Wales. Only 20% vote in favour.	
1997	A referendum on devolution passes with a comfortable majority.	A referendum on devolution passes with a narrow majority.	The Belfast Agreement is successfully negotiated and agreed by leaders of the two communities.
1998	The Scotland Act establishes further devolution, a Scottish Parliament and a Scottish Executive.	Government of Wales Act grants considerable administrative devolution to Wales. It also promises a referendum on income tax raising powers.	The Belfast Agreement is approved in a referendum. The Northern Ireland Act is passed, granting devolution. First elections to the Northern Ireland Assembly
1999	The first Scottish Parliament since 1707 meets and the Scottish government starts to operate.	The Welsh Assembly is elected and holds its first meetings. A Welsh Executive is also formed.	Northern Ireland power-sharing government takes power.
2002			The Northern Ireland Assembly is suspended. Central government takes over in the province.
2007			Northern Ireland devolved government is restored.
2014	A referendum on full independence is defeated by 55% to 45%.	Wales Act gives the Welsh government powers over several taxes and promises a referendum on income tax raising powers.	
2015		The UK government announces the government of Wales may be given future powers over a proportion of income tax raised in the country without the approval of a referendum.	
2016	The Scotland Act grants wide-ranging financial powers to the Scottish government, including control over income tax rates.		

The Senate Chamber of the Northern Ireland Assembly

Has devolution made a difference?

Devolution is pointless unless it reflects some kind of difference in how the countries of the United Kingdom wish to be governed. In the early days there did not seem to be a great deal of impact. This may have been because Wales and Scotland were both effectively governed by the Labour Party, the same party that was governing the whole of the UK. It was hardly surprising, therefore, that differences were not immediately apparent. Later, however, as the Scottish National Party grew in strength in the Scottish Parliament and Plaid Cymru gained a foothold in power in Wales, differences did begin to emerge. Meanwhile, in Northern Ireland, devolution was hugely significant, not least because the minority Republican community now enjoyed a share in political power.

A selection of the key impacts of devolution is shown in Table 5.6.

Table 5.6 Differences made by devolution: examples of how the countries differ from England (2016)

Country	Differences
Scotland	The dominant party is the Scottish National Party.
	Personal care for the elderly is free.
	Prescriptions are free (this is under threat).
	There are no university tuition fees for Scottish students.
	There are greater restrictions on fox hunting.
Wales	No school league tables are published.
	There are free prescriptions for everyone under 25.
	There is free school milk for under 7s.
	Greater help is provided for the homeless.
	More free home care is provided for the elderly.
Northern Ireland	The Republicans and Loyalists have to cooperate in government under permanent power sharing.
	Gay marriage is not recognised.
	There are greater restrictions on abortion.
	Prescriptions are free (likely to change).
	A large proportion of schools are based on either Catholicism or Protestantism.

Activity

Look at the varying levels of devolution granted to Scotland, Wales and Northern Ireland. Identify the following:

- A power enjoyed by all three
- A power enjoyed by Scotland but not the other two
- A power enjoyed by Northern Ireland but not Wales

These are important differences, but the more significant distinctions will come once financial powers are devolved. With the ability to levy their own taxes and the freedom to spend the revenue as they wish, the devolved authorities will have the power to introduce more fundamentally distinct policies.

Has devolution been successful?

Assessment of devolution is possibly too early to be conclusive. We can attempt some sort of assessment and we can rehearse the arguments in favour of and against devolution, but it will take at least a generation before we can make a definitive judgement. One question has, in a sense, been answered, however. It was assumed that devolution would reduce nationalist sentiment and prevent the break-up of the United Kingdom. In Scotland this has certainly not happened. In fact nationalism has grown, not declined in Scotland. In Wales there has never been great enthusiasm for independence and this remains true. Whether devolution is responsible for the continued indifference to nationalism is difficult to assess.

Key term

The Barnett formula
A way of adjusting the finance made available to devolved governments from UK tax revenues to take account of the fact that needs, in terms of health and welfare, for example, vary from one country to another. In effect, English tax revenues subsidise expenditure in Scotland, Wales and Northern Ireland to adjust for their greater needs.

Table 5.7 summarises some early arguments about whether devolution has been a success.

Table 5.7 An early assessment of devolution

Positive indications	Negative indications
The United Kingdom has not broken up.	Scottish nationalism is endangering the United Kingdom.
The peace has largely held in Northern Ireland.	Turnouts in elections to devolved assemblies have been low, suggesting political apathy.
There remains widespread public support in all three countries for devolution (not reflected in voting turnouts). No serious proposals have been made to reverse it.	The introduction of proportional representation systems has inhibited decisive government in the three countries.
It has made some decisive differences (see Table 5.6).	The three countries still have to receive a subsidy from the Treasury to maintain their services (**the Barnett formula**), in other words they are not yet fully self-supporting.

Current debates on further constitutional reform

The UK leaving the European Union

Before we consider the future of constitutional reform it has to be emphasised that the decision to leave the European Union was by far the most significant, far-reaching reform of all. Not only is it changing the status of Parliament and the UK courts (restoring all their national sovereignty), but it also affects the way in which the UK is governed. It has also affected the politics of devolution. At the time of writing, the process of leaving the EU is only beginning. It will probably be complete some time in 2019. Before the UK formally leaves, the treaties of the EU will still be in force. We have to say, therefore, that, until this happens, the UK is in a state of constitutional transition. Leaving the EU will also create a great deal of constitutional change, especially in terms of the status of the UK courts.

Synoptic link

The UK's relationship with the EU, which is currently in a state of change, is discussed more fully in Chapter 8. In that chapter the full effects of the UK's exit from the EU are explained, as well as the political fallout from the decision.

An assessment of constitutional reform since 1997

The position with regard to constitutional reform in Britain at the start of the twenty-first century is certainly paradoxical. On the one hand, the years after 1997 have seen the greatest constitutional changes in the UK probably since 1832 — and, some have suggested, even since Parliament became effectively sovereign in 1688. The list of reforms shown in Table 5.3 is impressive. Yet the record of reform has disappointed progressive politicians in all the main parties.

Here we divide constitutional reform into three sections — successes, partial successes and failures.

The successes

- **Reform of the judiciary** Possibly the greatest success has been the reform of the judiciary, created by the **Constitutional Reform Act 2005**. The Supreme Court has been established and the senior judiciary is now seen as genuinely independent of government. This is regarded as a key element in the improved protection of human rights and brings the UK closer to modern conceptions of democracy.

- **Devolution** has proved popular, especially in Scotland. Support for greater autonomy has also grown in Wales where the original referendum on whether to introduce devolution was only passed with a very narrow majority on a low turnout in 1997. There have been problems with the government of Northern Ireland, but at the very least devolution has helped to retain the fragile peace since the 1990s after 30 years of armed conflict.
- **The Freedom of Information Act**, though disliked by successive governments, has proved invaluable in extending the media's ability to investigate effectively the work of government and other public bodies. It has also allowed citizens to prevent injustices by accessing the formerly secret information held about them.

The partial successes

The Liberal Democrats and constitutional pressure groups such as Unlock Democracy and Liberty see reform as only half completed. They point to the following gaps in the programme needed to make Britain a truly modern democracy:

- **The House of Lords** The new, largely appointed House of Lords falls short of being properly accountable, authoritative and representative. Only a fully elected second chamber, it is argued, is acceptable. However, there has been some benefit in terms of making the Lords more professional and effective in checking government power and improving legislation.
- **The House of Commons** as a whole remains ineffective and inefficient. Lack of government accountability is seen as a fundamental problem and only a reformed, revitalised House of Commons can provide this. However, the select committees are considerably more effective since their reform.
- **The Human Rights Act**, though a vital development, has not been given the political status it needs. The fact that the European Convention cannot overrule Acts of Parliament means that rights can still be trampled on by powerful governments. The anti-terrorism measures that were enacted after the September 11 terrorist attacks on the USA were seen as a case in point, as were the measures to increase police and intelligence services powers of surveillance over private communications in 2015–16.

Study tip

Although you should be familiar with the main constitutional developments in the history of the UK, it is especially important to know the details of at least four constitutional reforms (other than exit from the EU) that have occurred since 1997.

Protest outside the Houses of Parliament in July 2015, demanding electoral reform

- **Devolution** is widely seen as a success, though many reformers in Scotland and Wales still argue that it did not go far enough. The problem, however, is being addressed, with further powers having been transferred after 2016. It is only a partial success because the long-term relationship between the UK as a whole and its national regions has never been permanently established. It remains fluid and controversial with the constant threat of a break-up of the UK hanging over it.

The failures

- **Electoral reform** Perhaps most importantly, governments have failed to deliver electoral reform for parliamentary or local elections. It is this measure that is most often seen as the way in which the political system can be fundamentally changed for the better.
- **Reform of the second chamber** The failure to introduce a democratic, elected second chamber remains a negative record for all the major parties. There is a widespread consensus that the second chamber should be fully or partly elected, but no government has been able to implement meaningful reform.

Debate

To what extent has constitutional reform since 1997 improved the state of UK democracy?

Democratic improvements

- The judiciary can now be said to be genuinely independent.
- Through regional and city devolution, power has been decentralised.
- Proportional representation for elections to devolved regional assemblies has improved representation.
- Elected mayors improve local democracy.
- Citizens' rights are now better protected.
- Freedom of information has been established.
- The increased use of referendums has extended popular democracy.
- The introduction of fixed-term parliaments has weakened executive power.

Democratic failures

- The electoral system of FPTP for general elections remains grossly unrepresentative in its outcomes.
- The House of Lords remains an unelected, undemocratic part of the legislature.
- The prerogative powers of the prime minister remain indistinct and largely unconfined.
- The largely unreformed House of Commons remains weak and unrepresentative.
- The UK Constitution remains uncodified, creating uncertainty and lack of public understanding, and retaining the danger of excessively powerful government.

Activity

Identify three possible constitutional reforms that would make the UK more democratic. Establish why they would improve democracy in each case.

Discussion point

What further constitutional reform needs to be made in order to make the UK more democratic?

The debate over further devolution in England

There remains a question of whether devolution should be extended to English regions. It appears that regional devolution will be confined to only a few definable areas. Most, though not all of these, are based on cities. The debate about granting devolved powers to the English regions is summarised in Table 5.8.

Table 5.8 Should devolution be extended to the English regions?

Arguments for	Arguments against
It would extend democracy and improve democratic accountability by bringing government closer to communities.	It would create a new layer of government which would be expensive.
Devolved government could better reflect the problems specific to regions.	It would create a need for too many elections, promoting voter apathy.
It would help to prevent excessive differences between living standards and the quality of life in different parts of the UK.	There are few signs of any great demand for such devolution.
It might improve local participation in politics.	Regional devolution might create greater divisions in society, promoting disunity rather than unity.

The codification debate

Should the UK introduce a codified constitution? In the main, it is conservatives who oppose such a proposal. However, Labour governments have also avoided the issue. Labour, on the whole, has preferred to make *incremental* changes to the constitution, gradually introducing new legislation such as the Human Rights Act, the Freedom of Information Act, the Devolution Acts and House of Lords reform, to create a clearer set of arrangements. But, like the Conservatives, Labour does not believe the time is right for a fully codified constitution.

Ranged against these conservative forces are the Liberal Democrats, small progressive parties and pressure groups such as Unlock Democracy and Liberty. They present a number of powerful arguments in favour of coming into line with nearly all other modern democracies by writing a new UK Constitution. In particular, they are concerned with the need for robust human rights and controls on the power of government.

Knowledge check

Excluding the UK, identify two countries in each of these categories:

- With a federal constitution
- With a unitary constitution
- With an uncodified constitution
- With a codified constitution

The arguments for retaining an uncodified constitution

Flexibility

Supporters of the current arrangements say that the flexibility of the constitution is a positive quality. The constitution can, they say, adapt to a changing world without major upheavals. It is said that the UK's constitution is 'organic'. This means that it is rooted in society, not separate from society. Thus, when society and its needs and values change, the constitution can do so automatically without undue delay or confusion. Parliament can pass a new Act relatively quickly and new unwritten conventions can develop to take account of social and political change.

Some examples of such 'organic' and natural development can help to illustrate this quality:

- As the authority of the British monarchy gradually declined from the eighteenth century, to be replaced by elected bodies — government and Parliament — no specific amendments needed to be made. Power and authority simply moved naturally away from the Crown towards government and the Parliament. In particular, many of the so-called 'prerogative' powers of the monarch have been taken over by the prime minister — to declare war, to negotiate foreign treaties and to appoint ministers, for example. The power of the monarchy to make law had already largely been lost in a peaceful process known as the Glorious Revolution in 1688–89. In countries where such powers are codified and entrenched, changes have tended to cause major upheaval and even violent revolutions. We can think of nineteenth-century France or Germany between the two world wars in this context.

- Since the 1960s the position of the prime minister has become more significant, largely as a result of media concentration on the importance of that office. Here again the growth in prime ministerial power, largely at the expense of the cabinet, has been a gradual and natural process.

The threat of international terrorism has become more acute since the attack on the Twin Towers in 2001

- After the 9/11 attack on New York in 2001, the threat of international terrorism became more acute. Had the UK had an entrenched and codified constitution, it would have been extremely difficult for Parliament to pass a wide range of anti-terrorist measures because of too many constitutional constraints. The lack of a codified constitution meant that Parliament could do as it wished. The USA and many European countries have had greater problems dealing with terrorism because of a fixed constitution. (The same applies to the stubborn refusal in the USA to introduce stricter gun laws in case such a measure falls foul of the constitutional right of citizens to bear arms.)

- When the 2010 general election failed to produce an outright parliamentary majority for any one party, there was some confusion about what should be done in the absence of any codified rules. Such an event had not occurred for over 70 years. Nevertheless, the system was flexible enough to adapt. A new set of principles was quickly drawn up and a coalition government was formed relatively smoothly.

Executive power

Because constitutional safeguards in the UK are weak or absent, government can be more powerful. This can be viewed positively or negatively. Supporters of the current uncodified constitution argue that, on balance, it is better to have a government that can deal with problems or crises without too much inhibition. They point to the USA where government and Congress are frequently prevented from acting decisively by the fear that the constitution will prevent them doing so. The constant battle against crime in the USA, for instance, has been compromised by such constraints. Conversely, the constitutional weakness of the Congress in controlling the military powers of the president has also created much tension. In the UK, the relationship between government and Parliament is flexible; in countries with codified constitutions it tends to be fixed and can inhibit effective governance.

Conservative pragmatism

The typical conservative attitude to the UK Constitution suggests that it has served the country well for centuries. There have been no violent revolutions and no major political unrest. Change has occurred naturally and when it has been necessary rather than when reformers have campaigned for it. Furthermore, say conservatives, codifying the constitution would be an extremely difficult exercise and the meagre benefits would not be worth the problems incurred. Conservatives often say of the UK uncodified constitution, 'If it ain't broke, don't fix it.'

The dangers of politicising the judiciary

A codified constitution would involve the courts, the Supreme Court in particular, in disputes over its precise meaning and application. As seen in the USA, many of these issues would be intensely political. For example, there would be conflicts over the exact powers of government, the nature of rights, relations with the EU or relations between England, Scotland, Wales and Northern Ireland. Bringing judges into political conflict puts the independence of judges into jeopardy, it is argued. Of course, disputes like these can arise with an uncodified constitution, but they could become more common following codification. In other words, the constitution would become *judiciable*. The problem with such a development is that judges are not elected and therefore not accountable. Critics point out that such political issues should not be resolved by judges — it is for elected representatives, they say, to make final decisions on constitutional meanings.

Knowledge check

In order to be classified as 'codified', a constitution must have at least three features. What are these features?

The arguments for introducing a codified constitution

Human rights

Perhaps at the top of the reformers' shopping list is the need for stronger safeguards for individual and minority rights. The UK has adopted the European Convention on Human Rights (by passing the Human Rights Act in 1998), but this remains weak in that it can be overridden by Parliament. Parliament remains sovereign and no constitutional legislation can remove that sovereignty. With a codified constitution, Parliament could not pass any legislation that offended human rights protection.

Executive power

We have seen that conservatives and others have wished to retain the powerful position of government in the UK. Liberals and other reformers, however, argue that executive, governmental power is excessive in the UK. They say over-powerful governmental power threatens individual rights, the position of minorities and the influence of public opinion. A clear, codified constitution would, they assert, inhibit the apparently irreversible drift towards greater executive power. In particular, supporters of a codified constitution suggest that there are no real 'checks and balances' — a principle upon which the US Constitution is based. It is argued that Parliament needs to have more codified powers to enable it to control government on behalf of the people.

Clarity

Most citizens of the UK do not understand the concept of a constitution. This is hardly surprising as there is no such thing as the 'UK Constitution' in any concrete form. There is, therefore, an argument for creating a real constitution so that public awareness and support can grow. If people know their rights and understand better how government works, it is suggested, this might cure the problem of political ignorance and apathy that prevails.

The case study below shows what a part of the UK Constitution would look like if it were codified. This gives an idea of how much clearer it would be than the current imprecise organisation.

Case study

An imagined codified UK Constitution

What would a UK Constitution look like if it were codified? Certainly it would be many pages long. Presented here is just a very condensed extract from a codified constitution. It contains some *real* features of the UK's constitutional arrangements as they exist in 2017, plus some theoretical arrangements that might be adopted in the future, but it does not include the many details that would have to be included in a genuine, working constitution.

The head of state

The head of state shall be the reigning monarch. On the death of the monarch the position of head of state shall pass to his or her eldest child. Should he or she have no surviving children, the monarchy shall pass to the nearest living relative.

The monarch shall have no political role and shall delegate all his or her powers to the prime minister. Only in an emergency and following a resolution of the UK Parliament shall the monarch recover his or her delegated powers from the prime minister.

The legislature

The legislature of the United Kingdom shall be vested in the UK Parliament. The UK Parliament shall contain 600 members in the House of Commons and there shall be 750 members in the House of Lords. Members of the House of Commons shall be elected in free and fair elections, using a system to be determined by the UK Parliament. Ninety-two members of the House of Lords either shall be holders of hereditary titles, elected by all hereditary peers, or shall be senior bishops of the Church of England or shall be appointed. Appointments to the House of Lords shall be made by an Appointments Commission, selecting from nominations made by members of the public, by the monarch, by the prime minister or by party leaders in general.

In order to be binding on society, all laws and regulations must be passed by both houses of the UK Parliament, using procedures to be determined by each house. As well as legislating, the UK Parliament shall have power to amend legislation, to call members of the government to account, and to raise matters of national and local concern. The House of Commons shall have the power to dismiss a government by passing a vote of no confidence with a simple majority.

The executive

The chief executive of the United Kingdom shall be the prime minister. The prime minister shall be the leader of a party, or combination of parties, that can command the support, temporary or permanent, of the majority of members of the House of Commons. The prime minister shall enjoy all powers delegated to him or her by the reigning monarch. These shall include: conducting foreign policy, commanding the UK armed forces, and appointing and dismissing ministers. The prime minister shall appoint a cabinet of up to 25 members. The cabinet shall determine the policies of the government, propose legislation and organise the implementation of legislation, and organise the discharging of all government business, including the budget of the UK.

The judiciary

The highest court in the United Kingdom shall be the Supreme Court. The Supreme Court shall hear cases on appeal sent from lower courts. The court shall interpret UK laws according to the rule of law. The court may also hear appeals from members of the public and associations of citizens who believe their rights have been abused by public bodies. The Supreme Court shall also rule on cases which require interpretation of this constitution.

Amending the constitution

This constitution may be amended from time to time by resolution of a simple majority of members of the House of Commons together with the approval of a national referendum.

Rights of citizens

The rights and freedoms of UK citizens are contained in the European Convention on Human Rights. No legislation or action by a public body shall infringe the rights of citizens as contained in the convention.

Modernity

As we have seen, the UK is unusual in not having a codified constitution. Many people regard this as an indication that the UK is backward in a political sense and has not entered the modern world. This became more pressing when the UK joined the European Community (an argument that has now receded).

Rationality

As things stand, constitutional changes occur in an unplanned, haphazard, arbitrary way. If the constitution were codified and entrenched, amendments and developments would be made in a measured, rational manner, with considerable democratic debate.

Debate

Should the UK introduce a codified constitution?

Arguments for

- It would clarify the nature of the political system to citizens, especially after changes such as devolution and House of Lords reform.
- The UK would have a two-tier legal system and so constitutional laws would be more clearly identified.
- The process of judicial review would be more precise and transparent.
- Liberals argue that it would have the effect of better safeguarding citizens' rights.
- It might prevent the further drift towards excessive executive power.
- The UK needs to clarify its relationship with the European Union.
- It would bring the UK into line with most other modern democracies.

Arguments against

- The uncodified constitution is flexible and can easily adapt to changing circumstances, such as referendum use and the changing role of the House of Lords. If codified, constitutional changes would be difficult and time-consuming. It can also respond quickly to a changing political climate.
- Conservatives argue that it is simply not necessary — the UK has enjoyed a stable political system without a constitution.
- As the UK operates under a large number of unwritten conventions, especially in relation to the monarchy and prerogative powers, it would be difficult to transfer them into written form.
- The lack of constitutional constraints allows executive government to be strong and decisive.
- A codified constitution would bring unelected judges into the political arena.

Arguably, the UK is in the process, particularly since 1997, of creating a codified constitution, bit by bit. True, it may never be contained in a single document for the foreseeable future, but increasingly large parts of the constitution are now both written and effectively entrenched. The aspects of the constitution that conform to this analysis are as follows:

- The European Convention on Human Rights, brought into law by the **Human Rights Act 1998**, is effectively a bill of rights. Although it could be fully or partly repealed in the future, this seems politically unlikely.
- The **Devolution Acts 1998** codify the powers enjoyed by the Scottish Parliament and the Welsh, Northern Ireland and Greater London assemblies.

- The public's right to see public information is codified in the **Freedom of Information Act 2000**.
- The status and conduct of political parties is now codified in the **Political Parties, Elections and Referendums Act 2000**.
- Important constitutional changes are effectively entrenched by the fact that they have been approved by referendum and can therefore be repealed only by referendum.
- The Electoral Commission has created a codified set of rules for the conduct of elections and referendums.

So the old boast, or perhaps criticism, that the UK Constitution simply evolves and remains in the control of the parliament of the day is out of date. Since 1997, when a new Labour government started the process of constitutional reform, the UK Constitution has gradually become increasingly written and codified. Yet it remains fundamentally an uncodified constitution in the strict sense of the words.

Constitutional reform will have to continue in the UK. Apart from the effects of leaving the EU, the UK has to deal with the continuing pressure for the decentralisation of power to the regions and away from London. If the multi-party system persists, there will be continuing pressure for electoral reform. It is also difficult to imagine how the bloated House of Lords, dominated by people who have merely received the reward of a peerage for political loyalty, can continue in its present form.

More change seems inevitable. Table 5.9 summarises the prospects for future change.

Table 5.9 Prospects for possible future reform of the UK Constitution

Constitutional issue	Possible reform
House of Lords	Proposals to introduce an elected second chamber or reduce the powers of the unelected House of Lords
Electoral system	Another indecisive general election result may renew calls for proportional representation, but it remains a remote possibility.
Devolution	Extensions of devolution to Scotland and Wales are in progress. The main developments involve devolution to city regions, together with more elected mayors.
Human rights	Further protection of rights seems unlikely. The Conservatives would like to replace the European Convention with a British Bill of Rights but this does not have widespread support.

Activity

You should now be in a position to write a full-length essay of 1,000–1,200 words.

Title: To what extent have constitutional reforms in the UK since 1997 removed the weaknesses of the UK Constitution?

Your answer should include the following:

- The weaknesses that existed in the constitution in 1997
- The main reforms that addressed those weaknesses
- An assessment of the degree to which the weaknesses have been removed

Asymmetric devolution A type of devolution where the various regions have been granted unequal amounts of power.

The Barnett formula A way of adjusting the finance made available to devolved governments from UK tax revenues to take account of the fact that needs, in terms of health and welfare, for example, vary from one country to another. In effect, English tax revenues subsidise expenditure in Scotland, Wales and Northern Ireland to adjust for their greater needs.

City government and city devolution The transfer of wide powers to cities and city regions, led by an elected mayor with extensive control over the budget and some tax-raising powers.

Codified constitution A constitution that is contained in a single document that was created at a particular time. The term also implies that a codified constitution contains a set of laws that are superior to all other laws and that cannot be amended except by a special procedure that safeguards them.

Constitutional convention A convention is an unwritten rule which is considered binding even though it is not a law. Large parts of the UK Constitution are governed by such conventions. They tend to develop gradually over long periods of time.

Devolution A term referring to the division of powers among regions of the country, while actual sovereignty, or ultimate legal power, remains with the Westminster Parliament.

Electoral system An electoral system is the mechanism by which votes at elections are converted into seats awarded to candidates and parties. Many different electoral systems are used in the democratic world.

Entrenchment A constitutional principle whereby constitutional rules are safeguarded against change by a future government or legislature. It means in practice that constitutional change requires special arrangements which are more difficult to make than the passage of normal laws. The UK Constitution is not entrenched as Parliament can change it by a simple Act. However, most democratic constitutions are entrenched in some way.

Federalism A constitutional principle that divides sovereignty, or ultimate power, between central government and regional governments. Federalism normally occurs when a number of separate states come together to form one single state. A federal arrangement preserves *some* of the original states' autonomy. The USA, Germany and India are good examples.

Freedom of information This is a principle of legislation, since 2000 in the UK, which states that all citizens have a right to see certain kinds of information held by public bodies, including NHS bodies, schools and universities, as well as all levels of government. The main kinds of information available are: information about the citizen him- or herself (but not other citizens); factual information, statistics and reports held by government bodies; information held by parliamentary bodies and the minutes of meetings by non-confidential bodies. Information can be withheld if it may jeopardise national security or the efficient running of government.

Hereditary peers Members of the aristocracy who owe their title to their birth, in other words they inherit their titles from their father. Some titles go back deep into history. Ninety-two such peers have a right to sit in the House of Lords.

Independence of the judiciary The constitutional principle that the judges should be independent from pressure by politicians so that they do not only deliver judgements favourable to government.

Parliamentary sovereignty This principle, established after 1689, means that the UK Parliament (not the Scottish Parliament) in Westminster is supreme within the political system. Only Parliament can grant power to other bodies and it can legislate on any matter it wishes. Its laws cannot be overridden by any other body, even the government or the monarch. It also means that the current parliament cannot bind any future parliaments. Each newly elected parliament is sovereign and cannot be bound by what has gone before.

Quasi-federalism A system of devolution where it is so unlikely or difficult for power to be returned to central government, that it is, to all intents and purposes, a federal system even though it is not in strict constitutional terms.

Referendum A vote held among the electorate at national, regional or local level to resolve an important issue. Referendums in the UK are usually held to approve a change in the system of government or to a country's constitutional arrangements.

Separation of powers The constitutional arrangement whereby the three branches of government — legislature, executive and judiciary — have separate powers and can control each other's power.

Summary

Having read this chapter, you should have knowledge and understanding of the following:
→ What political constitutions are, what their functions are and what forms they typically take, with examples to illustrate this knowledge
→ Why the UK Constitution is different to most other constitutions in the modern world
→ How the UK Constitution came to evolve into its current form (using both this chapter and the introductory chapter)
→ How the unique nature of the UK Constitution affects the nature of the political system
→ Why considerable reform of the UK Constitution began in 1997
→ What reforms have been successfully accomplished, what reforms remain incomplete and what reforms still need to be considered
→ The nature of devolution and the prospects for its further development
→ The main arguments that suggest the UK Constitution is unsatisfactory contrasted against what are perceived to be its strengths
→ What codification of a constitution is and how codification might affect government and politics
→ The nature of the debate as to whether it is now time to codify the UK Constitution

Further information and web guide

Websites

The best website to use for further information on constitutional issues is the Constitution Unit of University College, London: **www.ucl.ac.uk/constitution-unit**.

On the Constitution Unit site, read a paper by Vernon Bogdanor, in which he discusses, among other matters, the debate on codifying the constitution: **https://constitution-unit.com/the-constitution-unit-and-20-years-of-british-constitutional-reform**.

There is an excellent article published by the British Library. This traces the historical development of the uncodified constitution:

www.bl.uk/magna-carta/articles/britains-unwritten-constitution.

The government's own site looks at constitutional reform proposals:

www.gov.uk/government/policies/constitutional-reform.

For information on reforming the constitution look at the site for Unlock Democracy:

www.unlockdemocracy.org.

The pressure group Liberty campaigns mostly on rights issues in the constitution:

www.liberty-human-rights.org.uk.

Books

Perhaps the best book on this subject, written in 2010, is: King, A. (2010) *The British Constitution*, Oxford University Press.

A recent historical review that also looks at the future of constitutional change is: Blick, A. (2015) *Beyond Magna Carta: A Constitution for the United Kingdom,* Hart Publishing.

A review of the early stages of constitutional reform is: Brazier, R. (2008) *Constitutional Reform: Reshaping the British Political System,* Oxford University Press.

Two good books on devolution are:

Bromley, C. et al. (2006) *Has Devolution Delivered?*, Scottish Centre for Social Research.

Mitchell, J. (2011) *Devolution in the UK,* Manchester University Press.

Practice questions

AS

1 Describe the importance of constitutional conventions. (10)

2 Describe the importance of the Human Rights Act. (10)

3 Using the source, assess the significance of the UK Constitution being uncodified. *In your response you must use knowledge and understanding to analyse points that are only in the source. You will not be rewarded for introducing any additional points that are not in the source.* (10)

The Miller case

The UK constitution is neither codified nor entrenched. This means that disputes are bound to arise from time to time about what the constitution means and how it should operate. The Supreme Court is sometimes called up to interpret the meaning of the constitution.

The Miller case, which was heard in 2016–17 was a case in point. The High Court and the Supreme Court both held that the government did not have the power to trigger Article 50 which would start the process of the UK leaving the EU. Instead, the courts ruled, the decision had to me made by Parliament. This ruling firmly established the principle that Parliament is sovereign. It also declared that prerogative powers did not extend to being able to remove the rights of UK citizens.

At least the ruling settled the dispute and we now know a little more about the UK Constitution. The government of the day did not agree with the judgement, but had to obey it.

---

4 'Constitutional reform since 1997 has significantly improved democracy in the UK.' How far do you agree? (30)

5 'The UK should introduce a codified constitution.' To what extent do you agree? (30)

A-level

1 Using the source, evaluate the effectiveness of constitutional reform since 1997. *In your response you must compare the different opinions in the source and use a balance of knowledge and understanding both arising from the source and beyond it to help you to analyse and evaluate.* (30)

> Constitutional reform since 1997 has had four major objectives. These have been:
> - To improve democratic legitimacy and accountability
> - To decentralise power away from central government
> - To provide better protection for human rights
> - To bring constitutional arrangements up to date
>
> The record of these reforms has been mixed. In some cases, power has been successfully decentralised, with devolution being the key example. Human rights are undoubtedly better protected since the passage of the Human Rights Act and the Freedom of Information Act. The Constitutional Reform Act of 2005 has also guaranteed the independence of the judiciary.
>
> On the other hand, the picture on legitimacy and accountability is less clear. The failure to significantly reform the House of Lords and the electoral system are serious omissions. Furthermore, the nationalists in parts of the UK complain that devolution has not gone far enough.

2 Using the source, evaluate the extent to which the UK is now effectively a federal system. *In your response you must compare the different opinions in the source and use a balance of knowledge and understanding both arising from the source and beyond it to help you to analyse and evaluate.* (30)

Distinctions between federalism and devolution	
Federalism	**Devolution**
Legal sovereignty is divided between central government and regional governments.	Power but not sovereignty is delegated from central government to regional governments.
Federalism is entrenched in a constitution.	Devolution is not entrenched and is therefore flexible.
The powers granted to regional governments are equal and symmetrical.	Powers may be delegated in unequal amounts to various regional governments.
Any powers not specified in the constitution are normally granted to regional governments.	Any powers not specified in devolution legislation are reserved to central government.

3 Evaluate the extent to which rights are effectively protected by the UK's constitutional arrangements. (30)

4 Evaluate the extent to which the UK Parliament remains effectively sovereign. (30)

6 Parliament

About a mile south of Charing Cross, the geographical centre of London, on the north bank of the River Thames, stands the Palace of Westminster, commonly known as the Houses of Parliament. It is an iconic place. Parliament stands at the very centre of the UK political system. The UK Parliament is important both because of its history and because it is the sovereign body of the United Kingdom. All national legislation must pass through Parliament and obtain its approval. All power stems from Parliament — it can grant powers to an individual or a body, and it can take them away. All members of the government of the UK must also be Members of Parliament, in either the Commons or the Lords. And between general elections, the government has to make itself accountable to the UK Parliament. (Note at this stage that we are calling Westminster the *UK* Parliament to distinguish it from the Scottish Parliament. The term 'Westminster' is another way of distinguishing the UK Parliament from any other.)

Government in the UK sits in Parliament and ministers must attend regularly to lead debate, justify policies and accept criticism where it is due. Yet government is also separate from Parliament. The two great institutions have different roles. Government formulates policies whereas Parliament debates those policies and passes its opinion on them; government drafts legislation whereas Parliament scrutinises that legislation, suggests changes and occasionally may veto it; government ministers and their departments run the day-to-day affairs of the country while Parliament seeks to ensure that they do this efficiently, give good value for taxpayers' money and govern fairly. The relationship between government and Parliament is crucial to an understanding of how the political system works.

Objectives

This chapter will inform you about the following:

→ How the importance of Parliament developed historically

→ An introduction to the relationship between government and Parliament

→ The nature and importance of legal and political sovereignty

→ The structure and membership of the House of Commons and the House of Lords

→ The respective roles played by the House of Commons and House of Lords and the key differences between them

→ The work of MPs and peers, including their role in select committees

→ The relationship between Parliament and the executive

→ The changes that are taking place in the role and importance of Parliament

→ The state of representation in Parliament

→ The current state of parliamentary reform

Background

The history and status of Parliament

The **Parliament** of the United Kingdom is often described as the 'mother of parliaments'. This is for two main reasons. One is its great age. Arguably, the first real English Parliament met in 1265. The second reason is that it has become a model for the many other parliaments that have been established in the modern world of democracy. The first claim — Parliament's long history — is certainly true; the second, however, is problematic, mainly because most modern parliaments have very different structures and functions to the Westminster model.

From the time of the Norman conquest of England in 1066, and probably for centuries before, English monarchs had ruled with the help of some kind of 'royal council', made up of the monarch's most trusted advisers who were mainly noblemen and some senior members of the clergy. These royal councils eventually evolved into the modern House of Lords. Of course, the House of Lords has grown vastly since then (now over 800 members and rising) and the monarch no longer presides over its meetings, but remnants of its ancient origins still persist in its strange customs and traditions.

The House of Commons has more complex origins. Meeting in 1265, the body that is widely acknowledged as the first English Parliament assembled in Westminster Hall, a magnificent building that still stands in front of the current Houses of Parliament and can be visited by the public. It was called by a rebellious nobleman, Simon de Montfort. The de Montfort Parliament was made up of knights from the shires and two burgesses (wealthy citizens) from each large town or city. It was not an elected parliament as we would understand it, but de Montfort did claim it was a representative body. Above all, he understood that his authority to govern was weak, so he needed such a body to grant him that authority. This principle is still true of Parliament today.

In the event, de Montfort's rebellion was soon defeated and his parliament met only three times. This first parliament was, however, described as an assembly of 'The Commons', confirming it as the origin of today's House of Commons.

> **Key term**
>
> **Parliament** The most common name for an elected body that forms the legislature. Strong parliaments can control both government and legislation, while weaker parliaments play a minor advisory role and are dominated by government.

King Henry III and the de Montfort Parliament, 1258

After 1272, however, King Edward I began to summon the Commons on a regular basis. From that time onwards the Commons had three main functions:

- to advise the king on his proposed legislation (known then and sometimes still as 'statutes')
- to receive and deliver petitions from people with grievances against the authorities
- to grant permission for the king to levy new taxes

We can recognise all three of these functions in the modern UK Parliament. All legislation must now be approved by both houses of Parliament, the Commons remains a forum where MPs bring to the attention of government and the public the grievances of citizens, and the government can only levy taxes and spend public funds with the permission of the Commons.

Over the centuries since that first meeting in 1265 Parliament has grown in size, complexity and significance. The following developments are key to its modern form and functions.

- From meeting sporadically and at the pleasure of the monarch, it now meets for most of the year on a regular basis.
- In its origins the House of Commons was not elected. Gradually elections evolved and were finally regularised in 1832 (by the **Great Reform Act** — see the introduction to this book), with full adult suffrage (the right to vote) finally established in 1928.

- Its role in law making has evolved from merely an advisory one to an important part of the process of passing laws. It also now has a veto over laws which do not command widespread support.
- In the course of the nineteenth and early twentieth centuries, the House of Commons became the senior house and the Lords lost much of its authority.
- During the nineteenth century, it was established that the government should be drawn *only* from Parliament and mostly from the House of Commons.
- As government is drawn from Parliament, it follows that its ministers are now also accountable to Parliament.

The term 'UK Parliament' dates from 1801 when the **Act of Union** established the union of England, Scotland, Wales and Ireland. While Scotland and England had come together in 1707, the United Kingdom did not come into existence until Ireland was added in 1801.

Parliamentary government

Before we examine Parliament in detail, we must establish the principles that lie behind its position in the government and politics of the United Kingdom. The term 'parliamentary government' is the most appropriate description.

Parliamentary government implies the following features:

- The UK Parliament is the highest source of political authority. This means that political power may be exercised only if it has been authorised by Parliament. The government must be drawn from Parliament — either the Commons or the Lords. In other words, all members of the government must also be members of one of the two houses.
- There is, therefore, no strict separation of powers between the legislature and the executive. Instead, we say that the powers of the government and those of the legislature are fused. In reality, this often means that the government is able to dominate Parliament because a majority of its members are government supporters and so are likely to back the government.
- Government must be accountable to Parliament. This means two things. First it means that the government, including the prime minister and other ministers, must regularly appear in Parliament to explain and justify policies and decisions, and must subject themselves to criticism. Second, in extreme circumstances, Parliament may remove a government through a **vote of no confidence**, in which case a general election will be held to summon a new Parliament.

Parliamentary sovereignty

The principle of parliamentary government is key to an understanding the UK system of government, but the reality of parliamentary sovereignty is of equal importance.

The UK Parliament is said to be *legally sovereign*. This means the following:

- Parliament is the source of all political power. No individual or body may exercise power unless it has been granted by Parliament. In effect, of course, Parliament does delegate most of its powers — to ministers, to devolved governments in Scotland, Wales and Northern Ireland, to local authorities and to the courts of law.
- Parliament may restore to itself any powers that have been delegated to others.
- Parliament may make any laws it wishes and they shall be enforced by the courts and other authorities. There are no restrictions on what laws Parliament may

Activity

Research the following events and explain the reasons why they are important in the development of the UK Parliament:

- The English Civil War of the 1640s
- The Glorious Revolution of 1688
- The Great Reform Act of 1832
- The Parliament Acts of 1911 and 1949

Key term

Parliamentary vote of no confidence This is a vote that may take place in the House of Commons, usually called by opposition parties. It follows a debate during which the government will have been criticised by its opponents and defended by its supporters. Usually such votes fail, though they do call government to account. Occasionally (the last time this happened was in 1979), if opponents outnumber supporters, the government may lose and will normally resign to face a general election.

make. In this sense, Parliament is said to be 'omnicompetent' (literally, capable of any act).

- Parliament is not bound by its predecessors. In other words, laws passed by parliaments in the past are not binding on the current parliament. Existing laws may be amended or repealed at will.

- Parliament cannot bind its successors. This means that the current parliament cannot pass any laws that will prevent future parliaments from amending or repealing them. In effect, therefore, we can say that laws cannot be *entrenched* against future change. For this reason, the UK cannot have a fixed, entrenched constitution as long as the current principle of parliamentary sovereignty endures.

If, however, we consider another type of sovereignty — *political* sovereignty — we can say that Parliament has lost much of its sovereignty. Political sovereignty refers not to strictly *legal* power but to where political power lies *in reality*. It is the *practical* location of power rather than its *theoretical* location.

In reality, most political power lies with government. Normally, though not always, the government of the day enjoys a majority in the House of Commons and can therefore virtually guarantee that its proposals will be passed by Parliament. It is sometimes said, therefore, that 'the sovereignty of Parliament is, in reality, the sovereignty of the majority party'. It is generally understood that the government has an electoral mandate to carry out its manifesto commitments and Parliament should not thwart that authority. We expect Parliament to block government plans only if it is seen to be abusing its mandate or operating beyond it. In addition, of course, at a general election, political sovereignty returns to the people, who are both electing a new parliament and giving a new government a fresh mandate.

But before we dismiss Parliament as the sovereign body in theory only, we must remember that Parliament retains enormous **reserve powers**. In some circumstances it can block legislation (in modern times the House of Lords does this quite frequently) and in really exceptional circumstances Parliament can dismiss a government by passing a vote of no confidence. This was last done in 1979 when James Callaghan's Labour government was removed prematurely from office.

In summary, therefore, we can say that Parliament in the UK is legally sovereign, but that political sovereignty is less clearly located. It lies with the people at elections, with the government between elections, but with the proviso that Parliament can ultimately overrule the government.

Key term

Reserve powers Powers which exist and are very significant, but are only expected to be used in unusual or extreme circumstances. Instead they are held 'in reserve'. The UK Parliament has two key reserve powers — to veto legislation proposed by government and to dismiss a government in which it has lost confidence. The monarch also has such reserve powers but is even less likely than Parliament to use them.

Synoptic link

There is further discussion of aspects of sovereignty elsewhere in this book (see, for example, Chapters 1 and 2). This section on parliamentary sovereignty should be considered in relation to the constitutional principle of sovereignty.

The erosion of parliamentary sovereignty

There are five main senses in which it can be said that parliamentary sovereignty has been eroded. These are as follows:

1 A great deal of legislative power moved to the European Union after 1973. European law is superior to British law, so if there is any conflict, EU law must prevail. At the same time, Parliament may not pass any law that conflicts with EU law. However, with the UK's commitment to leaving the EU some time after 2018, all this sovereignty will be returned to Westminster. There remain large areas of policy that have not passed to Brussels, including criminal law, tax law, social security, health and education, but nevertheless there have also been significant shifts of legislative authority — over trade, environment, employment rights and consumer protection, for example.

2 As we have seen, executive power has grown considerably in recent decades. This involves a transfer of political but not legal sovereignty to government. The Gina Miller Supreme Court case in 2017 helped to clarify this relationship (see page 278).

3 It is increasingly the practice to hold referendums when important constitutional changes are being proposed, such as devolution, EU membership, the electoral system or the election of city mayors. Although the results of such referendums are not technically binding on Parliament, it is almost inconceivable that Parliament would ignore the popular will of the people. So, in effect, sovereignty in such cases returns to the people.

4 There is some room for controversy over the status of the Human Rights Act and the European Convention on Human Rights (ECHR), which it establishes in law. The ECHR is not legally binding on the UK Parliament, so Parliament retains its sovereignty. However, it is also clear that Parliament treats the ECHR largely as if it *were* supreme. In other words, it would only be in extraordinary circumstances that Parliament would assert its sovereignty over the ECHR.

5 Finally, there is devolution, especially to Scotland. As with referendums, Parliament can restore to itself all the powers that it has delegated, but it is difficult to imagine circumstances in which the powers granted to the Scottish Parliament and the Welsh or Northern Ireland assemblies would be removed. Here again sovereignty has been transferred in reality, though not in constitutional law.

So we could say that parliamentary sovereignty is now partly a myth. But before we jump to such a conclusion we must remind ourselves again of Parliament's reserve powers. The UK has now decided to leave the EU and so restore all its sovereignty. Parliament can thwart the will of the government, devolution could be cancelled (bear in mind that the Northern Ireland Assembly has been suspended and direct rule from London restored on several occasions), and Parliament could, under exceptional circumstances, decide not to accept the verdict of a referendum. Furthermore, if there comes a time when the government does not enjoy a secure parliamentary majority, it could be that the balance of power — both legal and political — will return to Parliament, much as it did in the middle part of the nineteenth century.

Study tip

Be careful not to confuse the terms 'parliamentary government' and 'parliamentary sovereignty'. The former describes the *political* reality of the UK, while the latter is a constitutional principle, which describes *legal* reality.

The House of Commons and House of Lords

The structure of the UK Parliament and its office holders

The UK Parliament is divided into two houses, the House of Commons and the House of Lords. A word of caution is needed here. The House of Lords is often referred to as the *upper* house. This is misleading. It is a throwback to a former time when the House of Lords was indeed the upper or senior house. The House of Commons, not surprisingly known as the *lower* house, is now very much the senior house despite its name. As we shall see, the main reason for this reversal is that the Commons is elected and the Lords is not.

Study tip

Do not confuse ministers and MPs. While it is true that frontbench MPs who are members of the governing party are all ministers, this does not mean that MPs in general are ministers. Backbench MPs are *not* ministers, whichever party they belong to.

A parliament with two houses, or chambers, is known as **bicameral**. Most democratic systems in the world are bicameral. The usual reason for this — and this applies to the UK — is that it creates some kind of balance in the political system. Very often the second chamber has a different kind of membership to ensure better representation and to prevent the first chamber having too much power. The UK system evolved naturally, however, so the position of the second chamber, the House of Lords, is somewhat unclear. In systems with codified constitutions it is much more obvious why the second chamber exists.

A brief comparison between the two second houses in the UK and the USA is useful at this stage and is shown in Table 6.1.

Table 6.1 The bicameral (second chamber) systems in the UK and USA

Country	Name of second chamber	Composition	Number	Main roles
UK	House of Lords	Mostly appointed, 92 hereditary peers, some Church of England bishops	Approximately 800	Scrutinising and amending legislation Debating major issues Delaying legislation for further consideration Representing minority interests
USA	Senate	Two senators elected by each state every 6 years Two senators per state, no matter what size the state is	100	Ensuring equal representation for all states, so preventing large states dominating Full legislative powers, including a veto over proposals, scrutiny and amendment of legislation, scrutiny of foreign policy

We can see from the comparison in Table 6.1 that the Senate in the USA is much more powerful than the House of Lords and has the very specific role of ensuring equal representation for all 50 states. Nevertheless, they have in common the role of preventing too much power falling into the hands of the first chamber.

The structure of each legislative chamber in the UK is described separately below.

The structure of the House of Commons

The main features of the House of Commons structure are as follows:

- There are 650 Members of Parliament (MPs), each elected from a constituency. Constituencies are of roughly equal size, normally containing between 60,000 and 80,000 voters. Most constituencies are in England (533). There are 59 constituencies in Scotland, 40 in Wales and 18 in Northern Ireland. There is a proposal to reduce this number to 600 by 2020.
- All MPs in the UK represent a political party. Occasionally, independent (non-party) MPs have been elected, but this is rare.
- MPs are divided into frontbench MPs and backbench MPs.
- Frontbench MPs are more senior. In the governing party, they are ministers and party officials appointed by the prime minister. Normally there are about 90 frontbench MPs on the governing side. The leading members (spokespersons and shadow ministers) of the main opposition party are also described as frontbench MPs. There would normally be about 50 of these. The total number of frontbench MPs is therefore 140–50. Frontbench MPs are expected to be loyal to their party leaderships, though this tendency collapsed when Jeremy Corbyn became Labour Party leader after 2015 and especially after Labour MPs passed a vote of no confidence against him in June 2016.
- **Backbench** MPs are very much the majority. They can be more independent than frontbench MPs but are still expected to show party loyalty.

Key terms

Bicameral An adjective describing a political system with two legislative chambers. If there is only one chamber, it is described as 'unicameral'.

Backbencher A name given to MPs who do not hold any government post or are not senior members of the main opposition party. Backbenchers are typically more independent than frontbench MPs but are still 'whipped' by the whips to try to ensure that they support their party.

- MPs do much of their work in committees. The main two types of committee are select committees and legislative committees. The nature and work of these committees are described below.
- All main parties appoint **whips** who work under a chief whip. The whips are mainly concerned with ensuring that MPs in their parties are informed about parliamentary business. They also try to ensure party loyalty and to persuade reluctant MPs to support their party's line. Whips may also inform their party leadership how MPs are feeling about an issue and may warn of possible rebellions and dissidence.
- The proceedings of the House of Commons are presided over by the Speaker. He or she is an MP who is elected by all other MPs. Though the Speaker comes from one of the parties, he or she is expected to put aside their party allegiance when chairing the Commons. The Speaker (there are also deputies who sit temporarily) is expected to organise the business of Parliament along with the party leaderships, to maintain order and discipline in debates, to decide who gets to speak in debates or question times and to settle disputes about Parliament's work. In the Parliament elected in 2017, John Bercow was the Speaker.
- Figure 6.1 shows the make-up of the House of Commons according to party in 2015.

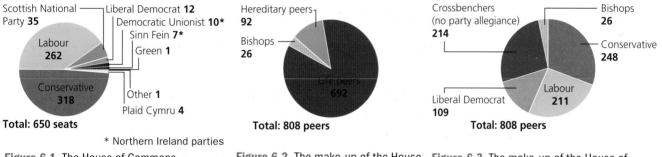

Figure 6.1 The House of Commons elected in June 2017

Total: 650 seats

* Northern Ireland parties

Figure 6.2 The make-up of the House of Lords by type of peer, June 2016

Total: 808 peers

Figure 6.3 The make-up of the House of Lords by party allegiance, April 2016

Total: 808 peers

Key term

Party whip A party official appointed by the party leader whose role is to maintain party discipline and loyalty, to inform MPs about parliamentary business and to act as a communication between backbenchers and party leaderships. The term originates from fox hunting where a rider known as the 'whipper in' tried to keep the hounds in order.

How to become an MP

It is virtually impossible (though there have been rare examples) to be elected to the UK parliament unless a person is adopted by a political party as their 'official' candidate. Therefore, in order to enter the House of Commons they must first be selected as a candidate by a party. Selection is carried out by local party constituency committees who draw up a shortlist of proposed candidates and interview them, much as if they were applying for any job.

All proposed candidates will be party members, and many will have 'cut their teeth' in politics as a local government councillor. However, sometimes prominent national figures may be chosen because of their high profile. Labour frontbencher Keir Starmer MP is an example — he is a former Director of Public Prosecutions. Boris Johnson MP was also an obvious choice as he was still London Mayor at the time of his selection. It helps if the person lives in the constituency they are applying for, but this is not essential. The central party leadership will often try to influence local committees in their choice, but this does not always work. Having been selected as the party candidate, they must then wait for the election and hope that they win.

The structure of the House of Lords

The House of Lords is a curious body, largely because it has evolved gradually over history and because repeated attempts to reform it, in order to make it more

John Bercow, Speaker of the House of Commons since 2009

democratic and rational, have failed. Its size is not regularised by law and the method of appointing its members remains dubious. Its structure looks like this:

- Ninety-two members are hereditary peers, people (nearly all men) who have inherited a title which entitles them to sit in the Lords. The number was determined in the **House of Lords Act 1999**. When a hereditary peer dies, his or her successor must be elected by all the remaining hereditary peers. Although they are not professional politicians, hereditary peers in the Lords are expected to take their position seriously, attend and vote regularly, and take part in committee work.
- Twenty-six members are archbishops and bishops of the Church of England. This reflects the fact that Anglican Christianity is the established religion of the UK. Recently, however, leaders of other religions which flourish in the UK have also been appointed.
- The other members of the Lords, commonly known as life peers, are appointed. Technically, life peers are appointed by the reigning monarch, but this power was given up many years ago. Unlike hereditary peers, they cannot pass their title on to their children; it dies with them. Most life peers are nominated by the prime minister and the leaders of the other main parties. In other words, they are *political appointments* and this means that they are expected to follow their party's line on most issues. There are also non-political peers appointed on the recommendation of non-government organisations and even by members of the public. There is a House of Lords Appointments Commission, which decides which people shall be appointed and which can also veto unsuitable nominees nominated by party leaders.
- There is no firm constitutional principle concerning the balance of party members in the Lords. In general, there is a convention that parties are able to make nominations roughly in proportion to their strength in the House of Commons. Thus, since 2010, the Conservative Party has made more nominations than other parties. Before 2010 the Labour Party made more nominations than the others. But, as life peers are appointed for life, it can take many years to change the balance of party strengths in the House of Lords. Figures 6.2 and 6.3 show the make-up of the House of Lords as it was in May 2016.
- The *political* make-up of the House of Lords is different to that of the Commons. In particular, it is now always the case that the governing party does *not* have an overall majority of members. There are so many non-political members (known as **crossbenchers**) that there cannot be a government majority. In Figure 6.3, for example, it can be seen that the Conservative Party had only 248 out of a total of 808 members.
- There are frontbench spokespersons in the House of Lords, just as there are in the Commons. The government must have representatives in the Lords as virtually all its business goes through both houses. Like their counterparts in the Commons, frontbench peers are expected to be especially loyal to their party leaderships.
- The equivalent of the House of Commons Speaker is the Lord Speaker.
- As in the Commons, much of the work of peers takes place in committees. There are legislative committees (in which all peers are allowed to participate) to consider proposed legislation, and select committees. However, select committees in the House of Lords are much less significant than those in the Commons. The work and nature of legislative committees in the House of Lords are discussed below.

The functions and importance of Parliament

There is no doubt that the UK Parliament stands at the centre of the political system. Nevertheless, we should not fall into the trap of believing that it is a

Key term

Crossbencher A name given to members of the House of Lords who are not formal members of any political party and so are independent minded.

Knowledge check

Identify three key differences between the House of Commons and the House of Lords.

genuinely law-making body, as its name suggests it might be. In fact the UK Parliament makes very little law. While it is true that a law is only legitimate and will only be enforced if it has been passed by the UK Parliament, this does not mean that Parliament *makes* the laws which it passes. This distinction will be explored below. It is also important to distinguish between the roles of the House of Commons and the House of Lords. They both make up what we call 'Parliament', but they have differing functions.

The functions of the House of Commons
We can identify several functions performed by the Commons. These are as follows.

Legitimation
This is the UK Parliament's most important *constitutional* function. It involves the process of passing legislation and approving public finances. As we have seen, the UK Parliament does not develop laws; that is the role of the government. The government is elected with a mandate to carry out its manifesto plans. MPs, by contrast, are elected to represent their constituencies. Nevertheless the government does need a device to make its legislative proposals legitimate. This means that it needs some way of securing the **consent** of the people. The people cannot be continually assembled to approve legislation, or hold a referendum every time a new law is proposed, so Parliament does it for them. That is what it has been elected to do. If Parliament did not exist, the proposals produced by government would be arbitrary and would lack democratic legitimacy. In this sense, therefore, Parliament is supporting government by granting it legitimacy for what it does. It strengthens government, rather than weakens it.

An additional aspect of this function concerns the public finances. As we saw above in the historical development of Parliament, monarchs usually sought the approval of the Commons when contemplating levying new taxes (usually for the purpose of war in medieval times). This was essential to gain the consent of those who were to pay the taxes. Without it, tax collection would at best be difficult and at worst might end in armed revolt. The modern equivalent is that the House of Commons (this has not been a function of the House of Lords since the 1911 Parliament Act) must approve taxation and expenditure by the government every time a change is proposed. This process occurs every spring and summer after the chancellor of the exchequer has announced the annual Budget. It is extremely rare in modern times for the Commons to obstruct such proposals, but formal approval is always required.

Legislating
This is the function of passing laws. While legitimation involves consent, the process of actually passing laws is a formal set of procedures designed to ensure that legislation is acceptable to both houses and gives them an opportunity to suggest amendments. It is described in full on pages 212–13.

There are occasions when backbench MPs develop their own legislation. This is called 'private members' legislation'. An MP can present a bill to Parliament but his or her chances of seeing it through to law are very small. The government has many opportunities to thwart such a procedure if it wants to. There are rare occasions when the government supports a Private Member's Bill, in which case it might pass, but this is unusual. So Parliament and its members do not make law on the whole.

Making government accountable
This is probably the most important *political* function of the UK Parliament, especially the House of Commons. As with consent, the government cannot be continuously **accountable** to the people. That only occurs at general elections. Instead, it is

Key terms

Consent This is the idea that a proposed law or decision by the government is formally consented to by the people. This is vital in a democracy. However, in a parliamentary democracy, the elected Parliament can grant consent on behalf of the people.

Accountability A principle that is key to true democracy. Those who have been elected, including governments and MPs, are accountable to the people for what they do. This means they must explain what they do, face criticisms and perhaps be removed from office if they fail.

the Commons that calls government to account on a regular basis. This role has a number of aspects:

- It can take the form of criticising the government. This can occur on any parliamentary occasion, but usually happens during the sessions devoted to questions to ministers or Prime Minister's Question Time (PMQT) every Wednesday.
- It can simply refer to the idea of forcing the government to justify its policies and decisions. If a minister knows they must face the Commons, they will be careful to prepare a good case for what they propose to do or what they have just done.
- Largely through the departmental select committees and the Public Accounts Committee (see below, pages 219–20), members of the Commons have opportunities to investigate the *quality* of government, in other words how well we are governed, whether taxpayers' money is being well spent, whether government is efficient and rational, and whether policies have been well investigated. These committees are often critical of government and sometimes recommend alternative courses of action.
- Although Parliament is generally considered to be dominated by government, the Commons can refuse to pass a piece of legislation. This occurred, for example, in April 2016, when the Commons voted against a new law extending legal opening hours for large stores on Sundays, much to the consternation of ministers. Voting against government legislation rarely occurs, but the mere threat that it *might* happen is usually enough to force government to think again. This occurred in March 2016 when the government withdrew a proposal to reduce entitlement to disability benefits in the face of widespread opposition from MPs.
- On extremely rare occasions, the Commons can remove a government by passing a vote of no confidence (see page 199). If this occurs twice in a short period, the government must resign and a general election will be triggered. This dramatic action last occurred in 1979 when the Labour government of the day was ousted.

Scrutiny of legislation

This is one of the functions that the Commons shares almost equally with the House of Lords. All backbench MPs are required to serve on legislative committees (also known as Public Bill Committees). These committees examine proposed legislation (i.e. bills), often examining every line, to see whether it can be improved and whether additions or amendments can be made to protect the interests of minorities. It does *not* mean that Commons committees have the power to reject proposed legislation altogether. Only the Commons as a whole can do this.

The legislative committees are a weak aspect of the work of the House of Commons. This is largely because they are dominated by the government and its whips. Legislative committees rarely amend a piece of legislation without the approval of government. This is not to say it is an illusory function. There are occasions when proposals by groups of MPs are accepted by government.

Constituency representation

It is widely acknowledged as a great strength of the UK political system that every MP represents the interests of his or her constituency. This is a neutral, non-partisan role in that an MP is expected to take care of the interests of *all* constituents, no matter for whom they voted. It may involve lobbying a minister whose department might be proposing something that is unpopular in the constituency, it might involve raising the matter on the floor of the House of Commons where it will receive considerable publicity and it might involve joining a local campaign of some kind.

Activity

Find out who your local MP is. Look at his or her website. Identify three local issues they have been concerned with.

Sometimes the interests of a constituency may run counter to government policy. This presents a dilemma for MPs from the governing party. What are they to do if a government policy may cause strong dissent in the constituency? This has occurred, for example, with the fracking debate. The Conservative government supports fracking but many constituencies with a Conservative MP representing them feel threatened by fracking. Usually MPs abandon their party loyalty on such occasions and lobby for their constituency. The party whips do not like this but usually allow an MP to put constituency before party allegiance. Similar problems have arisen for Conservative MPs in the Thames valley over the proposed expansion of Heathrow airport.

It also happens that individual constituents approach their MP for help if they are in dispute with a public body such as the HMRC over tax, or the Benefits Agency over welfare payments. Indeed, constituency work of this kind takes up much of the average MP's time. Most MPs hold regular 'surgeries' when constituents can bring their problems to his or her attention. If MPs feel their constituents have a good case, they will try to put things right on their behalf. This function is often described as the **redress of grievances**.

Key term

Redress of grievances
This is an ancient function of the House of Commons. It involves an MP pursuing a grievance that a constituent may have against a public body, usually claiming that they have been unfairly or unequally treated. MPs may lobby ministers and officials or raise the matter in the House of Commons.

The representation of interests

MPs do not only represent the narrow concerns of their constituents, they often also pursue the interests of a section of society or a particular cause. This is often the result of their background before they became MPs. For example, members of trade unions will tend to support their former fellow workers, while former business leaders will support their former industry. All pressure groups try to recruit MPs to their cause as it gives them exposure in Parliament. Organisations such as the Countryside Alliance, Friends of the Earth and Age UK all enjoy the support of groups of MPs. Furthermore, increasingly, campaign groups encourage supporters to write to MPs in large numbers to try to further their cause. Modern examples of this concern opposition to such issues as fracking, HS2 (the building of a high-speed rail line from London to the Midlands and North), Heathrow expansion and banking regulation.

MPs have also formed themselves into groups to pursue a particular interest or cause. Among these have been all-party parliamentary groups on these subjects:

- ageing and older people
- betting and gaming
- counter-extremism
- Islamophobia
- motor neurone disease
- race and community
- sex equality

These groups transcend party allegiance and seek to exert collective pressure on government over key issues. Needless to say, they have varying degrees of success.

Former MP John Leech during a street surgery in Manchester

National debate

From time to time a great national issue arises which stands above party politics. More often than not it is an issue that concerns foreign policy and the use of the armed forces, but it has also involved the signing of foreign treaties. A word of caution is needed. Increasingly, when an important *constitutional* change is being proposed, a referendum is held. Such referendums are replacing Parliament as the final decision maker. They are, in other words, exercises in *direct* democracy, rather than *representative* democracy. But, when a referendum is not appropriate, as in the case of an armed conflict, it is Parliament (both houses) that is called on to debate the issue and to express the *national* will. Here, Parliament is often seen at its best, when party allegiances are set aside, when powerful speeches are heard, and when the representatives of the people can be heard above the noise of party conflict.

Some examples of such great debates are shown in Figure 6.4.

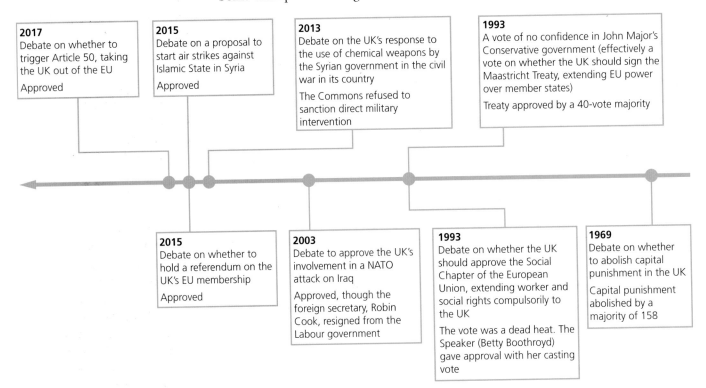

Figure 6.4 Examples of recent great debates in Parliament

The functions of the House of Lords

The fact that the House of Lords is neither elected nor accountable means it lacks democratic legitimacy. This in turn means that its roles are more limited than those of the House of Commons, which is elected and accountable. Before looking at the narrower role of the Lords, we must examine its political and legal constraints. These are as follows:

- Because members of the House of Lords recognise their own lack of legitimacy, they tend to restrain themselves and only challenge government in unusual circumstances.
- The Salisbury Convention, dating from the 1940s, is an unwritten rule of the constitution that establishes that the Lords must not obstruct any proposal that was contained in the current government's last election manifesto. This is because the elected government has an electoral mandate to carry out its legislative programme. The unelected Lords has no authority to defy the people's mandate.
- Amendments to legislation proposed in the Lords must be approved by the House of Commons. Occasionally, the Lords repeatedly passes the same amendment even after it has been rejected each time in the Commons. This game of 'legislative ping pong', as it is known, can go on for some time but the Lords usually back down in the end.

Two Parliament Acts, in 1911 and 1949, have established two principles — first that the House of Lords can have no control over the financial business of the government and, second, that the Lords can only refuse to pass a piece of legislation once. If the legislation is passed in two consecutive years in the Commons, the Lords will be bypassed. This means the Lords can delay legislation, but not veto it.

Yet, despite these limitations, the House of Lords does have some important functions. These are listed below.

Scrutiny and revising of legislation

The Lords does not really legitimise legislation. While it is true that any legislative bill must be passed by the Lords before becoming law, this does not mean the Lords is granting consent as the Commons does. It does, however, give the Lords the opportunity to scrutinise proposed legislation, to give its opinion, possibly to ask the government and Commons to think again, and possibly to amend the proposals in order to improve them.

There are many members of the House of Lords who are experts in their field and who represent important interests and causes in society. When scrutinising legislative proposals, therefore, they have a great deal to offer.

Apart from general debates, the main way in which the Lords carries out **scrutiny** is through what is known as the 'committee stage' of a bill. At this stage, any peers may take part in debating the details of proposed legislation and may table or propose amendments. This is possibly the key role of the House of Lords. The committee stage often improves legislation, adds clauses that protect vulnerable minorities, clarifies meaning and removes sections that will not operate effectively. Occasionally the Lords may amend a bill so severely that the government is forced to drop it altogether.

Delaying

As we have seen, the Lords only has the power to delay a piece of legislation for 1 year. In effect, when it does this, the Lords is saying to government, 'Think again. We know we do not have the power to stop it but we have serious reservations about your proposal and want you to reconsider.'

There are several examples of the Lords trying to defy the government but being bypassed by the Parliament Act rules. These are as follows:

- **The War Powers Act 1991** allowing the UK government to prosecute war criminals even if the offences were committed outside the UK
- **European Parliamentary Elections Act 1999** establishing a new closed list system for elections to the European Parliament
- **Sexual Offences Amendment Act 2000** lowering the age of consent for gay men to 16
- **The Hunting Act 2004** banning fox hunting with packs of hounds

In each case the Lords performed its function of asking the government and House of Commons to reconsider, but in each case it was the Commons and the government which prevailed.

Scrutinising secondary legislation

A great deal (indeed, most) legislation emerging from government is actually **secondary legislation**. Secondary legislation, sometimes called **delegated legislation**, refers

Key terms

Scrutiny A process conducted by both Houses of Parliament. It is the examination of proposed legislation, usually coming from government, to ensure that it is clear and fair, and that it protects minorities. In extreme cases, scrutiny may involve amending legislation to change its character completely. Government tries to control the process of scrutiny but MPs and peers may try to act independently.

Secondary legislation Laws, regulations and orders mostly made by government ministers. They require parliamentary approval but do *not* have to pass through the full procedure. Most secondary legislation is not discussed in Parliament, but passes through automatically or 'on the nod'. Only the occasional controversial piece of secondary legislation provokes debate and a vote in Parliament. The House of Lords pays more attention to secondary legislation than the Commons.

Delegated legislation Laws and regulations made by ministers and other public bodies under powers granted by parliament. On the whole they do not require parliamentary approval, though the UK parliament reserves the right to review them.

to any law making or changes to the law that are being made by any member of government which do not need to pass through normal parliamentary procedures. These are detailed aspects of law and regulations that ministers can make because they have been previously granted the power to do so according to a parliamentary statute. In other words, Parliament has *delegated* powers to ministers.

Another way of looking at this is to say that primary legislation means important laws that need parliamentary approval, while secondary legislation refers to more minor or specialised pieces of law that do not need to follow full parliamentary procedure. For example, primary legislation grants power to the secretary for transport to set speed limits on the roads, while secondary legislation concerns the minister actually setting those limits. Most of such legislation takes the form of *statutory instruments*.

Statutory instruments are increasingly being used to make law. This is a matter of concern as most statutory instruments are not considered by Parliament, so there is little or no scrutiny and few checks on their use or quality. The House of Lords, however, does have more time and expertise to consider such legislation. The House of Lords Secondary Legislation Scrutiny Committee considers all secondary legislation and decides what proposals might cause concern. Where concern is expressed, the matter is brought to the attention of the whole house and from there referred to the Commons. Such referrals are rare, but they do provide an important discipline on government. Members of the Lords also share in the work of the Joint Committee on Statutory Instruments, which checks secondary legislation for errors in wording and meaning. This role is one where the Lords can claim to be more important than the Commons.

A key example of the House of Lords performing this function occurred in October 2015, when the Lords voted against a piece of secondary legislation which would have reduced the level of tax credits paid to low-income families. This action forced the government to amend the legislation until it was acceptable to peers.

National debates

Like the House of Commons, the Lords occasionally holds debates on important national issues. The Lords tends to specialise in issues that have a moral or ethical dimension. In recent years, therefore, the Lords has held debates on such issues as assisted suicide, control of pornography, treatment of asylum seekers and refugees, stem cell research and the use of genetically modified (GM) crops. Such debates do not normally result in decisions but help to inform decision makers, especially as the Lords contains so many experts in these fields.

Comparing the powers of the House of Commons and House of Lords

Comparing formal powers and functions

Here we examine the differing powers and functions of the two houses of Parliament. Table 6.2 shows which powers are shared by both houses, which are exclusively held by the House of Commons and which roles are largely reserved to the House of Lords. The House of Lords has no exclusive powers of its own.

Table 6.2 The respective powers and functions of the Houses of Commons and Lords

Powers and functions of the Commons only	Powers and functions of both houses	Powers and functions largely of the Lords only
Examination and approval of the financial affairs of the government	Debating legislation and voting on legislative proposals	Examining secondary legislation and making recommendations for further consideration
Complete veto of legislation in certain circumstances	Proposing amendments to legislation	Delaying primary legislation for up to 1 year
Dismissal of a government by a vote of no confidence	Calling government and individual ministers to account	
Select committee examination of the work of government departments	Debating key issues of the day	
Final approval for amendments to legislation	Private members may introduce legislation of their own	

We can see from Table 6.2 that a large proportion of the powers and functions of Parliament are *shared* powers. Both houses appear to be doing the same thing. Indeed, the legislative process in each house is almost identical. It can be argued that the House of Lords examines legislation more thoroughly because all peers can be involved and because the party whips are less involved in forcing members to vote one way or the other. Otherwise, though, the same procedures apply.

If we scratch the surface, however, we can discover key distinctions. Above all, the House of Lords, since 1911, has been unable to interfere with the government's financial arrangements. Since the 1940s, too, it has been very much the junior half of the legislature, with the second Parliament Act in 1949 reducing the House's delaying power to 1 year. Finally, we have to consider the Salisbury Convention, which also dates back to the 1940s. This unwritten convention says that the House of Lords must not obstruct any legislative proposal that was included in the government's last election manifesto. The theory is that the government has a mandate to deliver its manifesto commitments and the *unelected* House of Lords has no authority to defy that mandate.

The Salisbury Convention also illustrates a basic truth about the relationship between the Commons and the Lords. The House of Lords stands in a weak position. Its members understand that it lacks democratic legitimacy. If, therefore, peers try to exceed their limited authority, they know that the House of Lords is likely to be reformed and replaced by a new elected chamber. They therefore have to restrain themselves, faced, as they are, by this permanent threat.

Table 6.3 summarises the relationship between the Commons and the Lords.

Table 6.3 The House of Commons and the House of Lords contrasted

The House of Commons	The House of Lords
Has sovereign powers	Lacks democratic legitimacy
Can veto legislation outright	Can only delay legislation by 1 year at most
Remains sovereign even when the government has a mandate from the electorate	Cannot obstruct the government's manifesto commitments
Can dismiss a government	Cannot dismiss a government with a vote of no confidence
Has potential control over public finance	Cannot regulate financial affairs
MPs can defy the party whips if they choose	Is constrained by the threat of reform or even abolition
Has the final say on legislative amendments	Can propose amendments but can be overruled by the House of Commons

However, despite the considerably higher status of the House of Commons it has to be said that the House of Lords did recover some of its former authority after the 1999 House of Lords Act. By removing most of the hereditary peers in that year, the Lords gained some additional legitimacy. Since then it has been more active and also more willing to challenge the Commons.

Legislation

The nature of legislation

There are three types of legislation.

1 **Private Bills** If an organisation, for example a local authority or a church, wishes to take some action which the law currently forbids it from doing, it can apply for a Private Bill to be passed by Parliament to allow it to go ahead. Often this concerns the building of roads or bridges or various new uses of land. The same process may also allow organisations to make compulsory purchases of land or buildings for a building project. Private Bills are not normally considered by either house as a whole but are considered by committees of one house or the other. Members of the public and other interested parties may give evidence to these committees, or present petitions. It is rare for such legislation to attract any publicity and the bills usually concern only private interests.

2 **Private Members' Bills** As the name suggests, these are presented by individual or groups of MPs or peers. At the start of the year, members who wish to present such a bill enter their names in a ballot. Usually seven bills are selected in this way. They are guaranteed at least one reading. Such bills have virtually no chance of being turned into law. This is either because it is difficult to persuade enough MPs or peers to turn up for a debate and **division** (a 'quorum' or minimum number is needed if the bill is to progress) or because it is opposed by the government. However, if a bill attracts the attention of ministers and seems to be desirable, it may receive government support. If it does, it will pass through the same procedures as a public or government bill, as shown below. MPs and peers know that their bills are unlikely to progress but use them to bring an issue to the attention of government in the hope that ministers might take it up later.

3 **Public Bills** Most bills fall into this category. They are presented by government and are expected to be passed without too much obstruction. Up to a year before they are drafted and announced, they are normally preceded by a **White Paper** which summarises the proposal. At White Paper stage a debate is held and a vote taken. Any potential problems are identified at this stage and, very occasionally, bills may be dropped if Parliament has serious concerns. Assuming all goes well, they follow the process shown below.

The legislative process

It is not necessary to grasp all the features of how laws are passed in the UK, but a basic knowledge is useful as it illustrates some of Parliament's roles. All Public Bills and Private Members' Bills must follow the procedure shown in Figure 6.5 to become Acts of Parliament.

> ### Key terms
>
> **Division** The name used in Parliament for a vote. It is so called because MPs or peers 'divide' between the 'Aye lobby' and the 'No lobby,' where they are counted by MPs appointed to be 'tellers'.
>
> **White Paper** A document outlining the main intentions and terms of a Public Bill. It is presented to Parliament up to a year before it is converted into a bill. Parliament normally debates a White Paper and votes on it. Any potential problems are identified at White Paper stage.

Figure 6.5 The passage of
a bill through Parliament

First reading
A bill is introduced in either the House of Commons or the House of Lords. This stage is purely formal, is never challenged and is designed to inform members that the bill is on the way.

Second reading
This is a crucial stage. It is the main parliamentary debate on the *principles* of the legislation. It is followed by a vote or division. The party whips will have requested or ordered the members of their own party to vote in a particular way. The details are not discussed at this stage. The government expects to win this vote and virtually always does. A government defeat on the second reading would create at least a political problem. If it is a major piece of legislation it causes a political crisis. For very major pieces of legislation, such as the annual government budget, the committee stage may involve the whole house.

Committee stage
In the House of Commons, a Public Bill Committee is formed for each piece of legislation. These committees usually contain 18 members, chosen by the party whips. Their job is to consider the detail of bills. In each committee the government side has a majority, reflecting its strength in the whole house. This ensures that the government can win any votes at committee stage if it is determined. Defeats for the government are not unheard of at this stage but remain rare. Committees can call witnesses from interested parties and consider written evidence when considering the details of a bill. Each proposed change or amendment is voted on.

In the House of Lords, the committee stage involves the whole house. The government whips try to ensure the government wins any votes, but there is no majority so this cannot be guaranteed. Governments often suffer defeats at the hands of the Lords at this stage. However, amendments proposed by the House of Lords can be overturned in the House of Commons.

It is hoped and assumed that amendments made at committee stage will improve legislation, ensuring that it is clear and fair and that it protects vulnerable minorities.

Report stage
The whole house debates the whole bill again with all the amendments included. This is usually a formality.

Transfer
If the bill started its life in the Commons, it is passed to the Lords and follows the same procedures. If it started in the Lords, it is passed to the Commons.

Royal assent
Finally, the monarch signs the bill, formally making it law. This stage is a formality. Royal assent has not been refused since 1707.

The interaction between the House of Commons and House of Lords

Most Public Bills start life in the House of Commons, although occasionally they may be introduced in the Lords, especially if the Commons is very busy. Whichever way they begin, they have to go through both houses if they are to become law. Normally the Lords will follow the lead of the Commons and pass a bill without obstruction. The only occasions when the House of Lords may be obstructive is if the government introduces a piece of legislation which is not part of its electoral mandate.

Nevertheless, in recent years the Salisbury Convention has become less important. In 2010–15 the government did not enjoy an electoral mandate as it was a coalition of two parties. Since 2015 Liberal Democrat peers have suspended the Salisbury Convention, largely because the government was elected on such a small popular vote. As a result the Lords have passed many amendments to legislation in defiance of the government.

If the House of Lords proposes an amendment to legislation, it must go back to the Commons, where it can be overturned. However, if the Lords digs its heels in and insists on an amendment, it may force the government and the Commons majority into submission. This occurred in 2015 when a government proposal to cut the payments of tax credits was rejected in the Lords and the government had to concede defeat.

As we have seen, the House of Lords can delay legislation for a year by forcing the House of Commons to pass the same legislation in two consecutive sessions. This rarely results in a government defeat but it does force government and the House of Commons to think carefully before introducing controversial legislation.

How Parliament interacts with the executive

A note on parliamentary privilege

The term 'parliamentary privilege' refers to the special protection that MPs and peers have when they are engaged in parliamentary business. It has a number of aspects:

- MPs and peers cannot be prosecuted or sued for liberal or slander for any actions taken with the Palace of Westminster. In effect this means complete freedom of speech. Representatives may say anything they wish without fear of being arrested or of being sued for defamation. It dates back to the time, before the seventeenth century, when Members of Parliament feared being arrested if their words were seen to be threatening to the monarch or to the state. Since the seventeenth century members have had no such fear. This is a vital principle as it means that members can call government and ministers to account more effectively; they do not feel at all constrained.
- This does not mean that members may act exactly as they please. Instead, parliamentary privilege means that both houses of Parliament regulate the behaviour of their own members. This means disciplining them for using provocative language, or for abusing their position. They should also not gain special financial advantage from their position as members. A key example of this principle occurred in 2009–10 when it was revealed that many members of both houses were abusing the system of expenses, which was loose and unregulated. In short they were 'fiddling their expenses'. A number of fines were levied and the whole system was overhauled. Several members were forced to resign over their behaviour. It was the leaders of the two houses who dealt with the problem, rather than the criminal law. Punishments for members vary from a reprimand from the Speaker through to suspension or loss of voting rights in the House of Lords.

- The fact that the government and the external legal system cannot interfere in Parliament means that members can feel secure and free to criticise government and other agencies of the state.
- The conduct of members is now regulated by the parliamentary commissioner for standards. Conduct is also regulated by committees on conduct and the speakers of both houses.

The importance of members of the Commons and Lords

The House of Commons: the election, role and importance of MPs

At the time of writing, there were 650 Members of Parliament (MPs), each one elected by a constituency with an average of about 75,000 voters. The number of MPs is shortly to be reduced to 600. MPs are of equal status unless they become government ministers or frontbench spokespersons for one of the opposition parties. It is an interesting practice that MPs never refer to each other by name in the chamber but usually as 'the member for...' followed by the name of the relevant constituency. This reflects the importance of constituency representation, as well as the highly traditional way in which Parliament operates.

Role of MPs

MPs at Westminster have had a generally poor reputation. Some of this has been self-inflicted but a great deal is also misplaced. The truth is that much of their work goes unnoticed. The performance of backbench MPs is also bound to vary from individual to individual, as in any profession. The list below is an uncritical review of some of the different roles any particular Westminster MP may play.

- Taking part in debates on legislation and voting in divisions
- Speaking in general debates on government business
- Speaking in backbench debates when national or constituency interests can be aired
- Scrutinising proposed legislation at committee stage
- Possibly being a member of a House of Commons select committee
- Active membership of a campaign committee of MPs on a particular issue
- Taking part in fact-finding missions, usually with groups of MPs and often abroad
- Membership of a committee formed by his or her own party to develop policy on a particular issue
- Campaigning, lobbying and speaking on behalf of an outside interest or cause
- Listening to grievances of constituents against a public body and sometimes acting to try to redress those grievances, including lobbying ministers and government officials
- Attending important events in the constituency, including listening to and perhaps joining local campaign groups

This is a formidable list but, even so, some MPs also take on outside work, often as journalists and writers or as members of outside associations.

As we have said, an assessment of the effectiveness of MPs is difficult to make because their work varies so much and every individual MP is different. Some attend the debates with great regularity; others may rarely be seen except when ordered to attend by the party whips. Committee membership also varies, as does the extent of constituency work undertaken. Table 6.4 summarises the common criticisms that are levied against MPs, alongside a defence of their work and importance.

Table 6.4 How effective are MPs in the UK Parliament?

Common criticisms	In defence of MPs
MPs are just 'lobby fodder' or 'party hacks', who simply do as the party whips tell them uncritically and hope their loyalty will one day be rewarded by promotion to ministerial office.	This may be true of many MPs but there are also numerous independent-minded MPs who are willing to put their beliefs and principles above narrow party interest.
Backbench MPs are actually powerless in the face of the domination of the party front benches. They have little or no influence over legislation and fail to bring government effectively to account.	This criticism may have been valid in the past, but it is less true today. Especially since 2010, Parliament has been more willing to defy government and the select committees are becoming increasingly effective in calling government to account.
Parliamentary debates are often sparsely attended, suggesting MPs lack interest in public policy.	Much of the work of MPs is carried out behind the scenes, often in committees.
Parliament has very long recesses, giving MPs excessively long so-called 'holidays'.	MPs often use the long recesses to catch up on constituency work.
MPs are self-seeking and sometimes corrupt, as exemplified by the 'expenses scandal' of 2009–10, when it was revealed that many MPs were claiming excessive, sometimes fraudulent expenses.	MPs have set up systems for controlling such excesses. They are paid a salary which is modest compared to similar professions.
MPs are often unknown in their constituencies.	Many, though not all, MPs actually undertake heavy workloads representing constituency interests, even if they are not well known.

Mhairi Black, MP for Paisley and Renfrewshire South, at the SNP spring conference, March 2017

Some examples

The backbench MPs listed below are examples of individuals who are playing a substantial role in politics in the 2015–17 UK Parliament, despite the fact that they do not hold any public office.

- **Mhairi Black (Scottish National Party, Paisley and Renfrewshire South)** The youngest member of the Commons, aged only 20 when she was elected in 2015, Black made an instant impact with a widely praised maiden (first) speech in the House. Despite her youth, she is already a member of the Work and Pensions Select Committee and specialises in issues concerning welfare and inequality.
- **Mike Freer (Conservative, Finchley and Golders Green)** Freer is known as a hard-working constituency MP. He has been a long-time champion of breast cancer screening and speaks often in the interests of the state of Israel. He is also a supporter of improved inter-community relations, encouraging links between the Jewish, Hindu, Sikh and Muslim communities in his constituency.
- **Maria Eagle (Labour, Garston and Halewood)** A former junior minister and former opposition frontbencher, Eagle is now a backbencher again. She was partly instrumental in persuading the government to pass the **Fur Farming (Prohibition) Act 2000** and has been a prominent campaigner for the rights of the LGBT community. She was a leading campaigner for the introduction of gay marriage. Her twin sister, Angela, is also an MP.

Discussion point

Think about these situations and decide whether you think a backbench MP should follow the party line, follow their own conscience, or do what they think their constituents would want them to do:

- A proposal to send UK combat troops to a Middle East war zone
- A proposal to decriminalise drugs
- A proposal to abolish zero hours contracts
- A proposal to build a nuclear power plant in the MP's constituency

The House of Lords: the selection, role and importance of peers

The House of Lords now numbers over 800 and is still growing, which is a cause for some concern. There are several ways of becoming a member of the House of Lords. They are as follows.

- Twenty-six members are archbishops or senior bishops in the Church of England. There are no *automatic* places for the leaders of other religions, though some have been nominated.
- Ninety-two are members of the aristocracy, known as hereditary peers. They have inherited their titles from their fathers. There used to be many more in the House, but, since the **House of Lords Act 1999**, the number is limited. When a vacancy arises, the surviving hereditary peers elect a replacement.
- **Life peers** are appointed for life only — their entitlement to sit in the Lords cannot be passed on to their children. They are usually given the title Lord, or Baron, or Baroness. Most appointments are 'political' in the sense that they are made by party leaders. Many political nominations are former government ministers whose main political career is over. Others have held prominent positions in public life, for example in the civil service, the police or the army. The number of peers appointed by each party every year normally reflects the party's relative strength in the House of Commons. Political peers normally support the party that nominated them (it is said that they 'take the party whip'). Large organisations, such as religious groups, trade unions and pressure groups, also make nominations and there are also suggestions from the general public. These are vetted for suitability by the House of Lords Appointments Commission.

Key term

Life peer A prominent member of society who is granted a peerage (becoming known as Lord or Lady, or Baron or Baroness). This entitles the holder to attend the House of Lords, take part in debates, and scrutinise and vote on legislation. The entitlement is for life unless they are convicted of serious misconduct. Life peers receive a generous daily attendance allowance as long as they attend regularly. They cannot pass their title on to their children.

Role of peers

There are three levels of participation by peers:

- **Non-working peers** These are individuals who have been granted the honour of a peerage but are not interested in political activity. They may appear in the Lords from time to time but rarely vote or take any active part. Some are never seen in the House.
- **Part-time politicians** Peers who are often not attached to any party, but do take part in debates and votes on issues that particularly interest them. A fair proportion of these are hereditary peers. Their attendance is irregular.
- **Working peers** Often these are members of a political party who consider themselves professional politicians. For various reasons they have not stood for election, but are often granted a peerage so that they can work for their party in the Lords. They may also be members of the government or the opposition front bench. As active members, they receive a modest income for their regular attendance.

The House of Lords was mildly reformed in 1999 through the **House of Lords Act**. This Act removed hundreds of hereditary peers from the House, leaving just 92. In the years since then the missing hereditary peers have gradually been replaced by new life peers. The effect of this has been to create a house which is more professional and active. The new life peers are much more likely to be active than the hereditary peers who have left. So, the House of Lords may still lack democratic legitimacy, but it is more active and effective than ever before.

Apart from the frontbench peers who are either ministers or opposition spokespersons, the backbenchers have a number of roles:

- From time to time the House of Lords is asked to debate a great national issue. This is an opportunity for peers, particularly those who are former government

Synoptic link

When discussing the nature and role of the House of Lords, re-consider the discussion of representative democracy in Chapter 1.

ministers or civil servants, or heads of major organisations such as pressure groups, businesses or trade unions, to influence such debates.

- The Lords is an important part of the legislative process. Before 2010 the Lords rarely had much impact on legislation, largely because governments normally enjoyed large Commons majorities and could claim a strong mandate for their proposals. Since 2010, however, governments have had either no secure majority or only a small advantage in the Commons. This has meant that the government has had to take potential opposition in the House of Lords seriously. Any controversial policy now needs assured support in both houses of Parliament. This inevitably gives peers increased influence over both the principles and detail of legislation. The government does not have a majority in the Lords, so it must win over the support of crossbench or opposition peers if it is to avoid obstruction.

- As we have seen, peers take part in the scrutiny of legislation, whether it be from the government or from backbenchers of either house. It is on these occasions that their experience and knowledge can be most useful in improving legislation and in ensuring that minorities are protected and that all sections of society are fairly treated.

- Each government department has a representative, in the form of a junior or senior minister, in the House of Lords. This enables peers to call government to account over its policies. However, it is acknowledged that this is a relatively minor role. In addition there are no adversarial select committees in the Lords as there are in the Commons, so the government does not need to fear excessively adversarial questioning.

Some examples

Many individual peers have carved out an influential role for themselves. Here are three examples:

- **Lord Adonis (Labour)** Andrew Adonis is a former academic and minister who is an expert on economics, education and transport issues. He continues to play a leading role in advising both main parties on these issues.
- **Lord Dannatt (crossbencher)** Richard Dannatt was formerly chief of the general staff and thus the UK's most senior soldier. He now lends his huge knowledge of military matters to the work of the House of Lords. In 2015–16 he campaigned for UK ground troops to be redeployed in Iraq to fight against ISIS (Daesh).
- **Lord Finkelstein (Conservative)** Danny Finkelstein is a prominent journalist on *The Times* and a regular broadcaster on political affairs. He is one of the highest profile peers in the House, known for his wit and moderate, balanced views despite his party affiliation.

The three peers described above, along with many others like them, are all full- or part-time parliamentarians. They are also as influential as any backbench member of the House of Commons. As well as their knowledge and experience, they have a high media profile, more so than most MPs, which alone gives them importance in the political system. Yet, for every active and influential peer, there are also many who are inactive and almost invisible. They are not accountable, so there is no check over the quality and quantity of their work.

Activity

Look up the websites of the following peers and identify what occupational experience they bring to the Lords and what committee roles they may have:

- Baroness Lane-Fox
- Baron O'Donnell
- Baroness Corston
- Lord Winston

The role and powers of select committees

Much of the work of Parliament in calling government to account is conducted by select committees. The whole house is a rather clumsy way of achieving this, so smaller committees are used which can focus on particular aspects of government work. Committees can also escape the rather formal, ritualised procedures of Parliament and operate in a less formal, but more effective manner. Departmental select committees were first set up in the Commons in 1979, though the Public Accounts Committee (PAC) dates back to the nineteenth century. There are many select committees in both houses, but in this section we concentrate on those committees whose specific role is calling government to account.

House of Commons select committees

We have seen that all MPs (other than government ministers) must serve on legislative (Public Bill) committees from time to time, but not all sit on important select committees. There are many kinds of select committee in both houses of Parliament, but here we consider the most important types, all in the House of Commons. These are the Public Accounts Committee and 19 departmental select committees, the Liaison Committee and the Backbench Business Committee. The first three of these committees exist to call government to account, while the Backbench Business Committee gives backbenchers some control over the parliamentary agenda.

The Public Accounts Committee (PAC)

The PAC is the oldest committee in the Commons, dating back to 1861. Arguably it is also the most influential of all parliamentary committees. Its role is to examine the public finances. In the words of Parliament's own website, the committee's job is as follows:

> This committee scrutinises value for money — the economy, efficiency and effectiveness — of public spending and generally holds the government and its civil servants to account for the delivery of public services.

Source: www.parliament.uk

This is a very wide remit. In effect, it also includes the collection (though not the rates) of taxation and how well that is done. Taxation and spending are fundamental activities of government, so their examination is crucial. The committee conducts investigations into various aspects of the government's finances, particularly how it allocates and spends money on public services. It can call witnesses, who are obliged to attend. Witnesses may be ministers, civil servants, government officials, outside witnesses and representatives of interested bodies as well as experts in a particular field.

It is powerful for a number of reasons:

- Its chair is always a member of the main opposition party.
- The chair has great prestige, not to mention a higher salary than other MPs.
- The chair and members are elected by all MPs and so are not controlled by party leaders.
- Its members, despite being party supporters, always tend to act independently, ignoring on the whole their party allegiance. This means the government has no advantage on the committee even though it has a majority of members on the committee.

Table 6.5 Membership of the Public Accounts Committee, 2015–17 parliament

Chair	Meg Hillier (Labour)
Conservative members	8
Labour members	5
SNP members	1'
Liberal Democrat members	1

- Its reports are often unanimous in their conclusions, so the committee stands above party politics.
- It has a high profile in the media. Many of its important hearings are broadcast as news items.

The committee rose to even greater prominence under its chair, Margaret Hodge, between 2010 and 2015. She introduced a new device, which was to call senior civil servants to give evidence, as well as ministers and outside witnesses. Above all, however, she was determined to publicise major issues and to question public policy where the committee felt that taxpayers were not getting value for money.

In the 2015–17 parliament, the PAC's membership was as shown in Table 6.5.

Recent reports from the PAC demonstrate its importance. They are shown in Table 6.6.

Table 6.6 Key PAC investigations

Date	Investigation	Conclusion and action
2010	Into the BBC's use of public funds	Highly critical of poor value for money and lack of accountability by the BBC Recommended government find ways of making the BBC more accountable for how it spends licence payers' money
2014	Into the financing of fast broadband for poorly served regions	Highly critical of the way in which government financed the programme and for the poor performance of organisations receiving public funds
2015	Into the effectiveness of cancer care by the NHS	Highly critical of variations in cancer treatment in different regions and for different age groups Criticised low cure rates and increased waiting times for treatment Publicity caused government to review cancer treatment.
2016	Into the tax affairs of Google	Google's payment of back tax of £130 million for 10 years was considered far too low. HMRC should investigate ways of better regulating the tax affairs of multinational companies and making them more transparent.

We can see that these and other investigations by the PAC deal with important aspects of public finance. The publicity achieved by the reports forces government to respond. Accountability is therefore achieved effectively.

Departmental select committees (DSCs)

DSCs have existed since 1979. Along with the PAC, they are a vital way in which Parliament — at least some groups of MPs — can call government to account. Each of the 19 committees investigates the work of a government department. Their features are as follows:

- The members are elected by MPs from the whole house.
- The chair, who receives an increased salary, is elected by the committee.
- Membership varies between 11 and 14.
- The governing party has a majority on each committee.
- The chairs may be from any political party.
- The small parties have a scattering of members.
- Like the PAC, they act largely independently of party allegiance and often produce unanimous reports.
- Also like the PAC, they can call witnesses who may be ministers, civil servants and outside witnesses such as pressure group representatives or experts.
- Their reports and recommendations are presented to the whole House of Commons and receive considerable publicity.

The impact and effectiveness of the departmental select committees is certainly growing alongside the PAC. The chairs of the committees have become important, influential parliamentarians, and governments now feel they need to respond to their criticisms and recommendations.

Some examples of important reports from DSCs are shown in Table 6.7.

Table 6.7 Key departmental select committee reports

Date	Committee	Investigation	Conclusion and action
2012	Home Affairs	Into the Independent Police Complaints Commission's (IPCC) role in the investigation into the 1997 Hillsborough disaster	The IPPC is investigating the Hillsborough disaster following the 2016 inquest.
2014	Defence	Into the circumstances when the UK should make military interventions in world conflicts	Among many recommendations, urged government to consider legislation about whether Parliament should control major armed interventions
2015	Treasury	Into proposals for stricter regulation of the banking sector	Insisted that government should implement the recommendations of the Parliamentary Commission on Banking Standards. This pushed policy forward on banking regulation.
2016	Business, Innovation and Skills	Into alleged bad working practices at Sports Direct	The company was forced to pay compensation to its workers for paying below minimum wage.
2016	Work and Pensions	Into the collapse of British Home Stores and the loss of much of the employees' pension fund	The company was reported to the Pensions Regulator.

The DSCs have now reached a point where they are an integral part of policy making and review, as well as a crucial way in which government and other public bodies can be held to account.

In recent years the DSCs have started to extend their work to consideration of matters of general public interest, not just the performance of government departments. Such investigations often take place in the hope and expectation that government will consider new legislation to deal with the problems revealed. Thus, in 2011, the Culture, Media and Sport Committee investigated the alleged widespread use of phone hacking by the press as well as the general conduct of journalists. And, as seen in Table 6.7, in 2016 the Business, Innovation and Skills Committee investigated alleged cases of unacceptable management practices at the Sports Direct company, while in the same year the events surrounding the takeover and subsequent failure of British Home Stores were investigated by the Work and Pensions Committee.

The Liaison Committee

This committee was created in its present form in 2002. It consists of the chairs of all the departmental select committees as well as several other committees. Apart from overseeing the work of House of Commons select committees, its main function is to call the prime minister to account. Twice a year the PM has to appear before the Liaison Committee. On the whole this committee had been a disappointment until the 2016 session when a Conservative, Andrew Tyrie, became its chair. He and the committee immediately decided that the conduct of UK forces in Syria and the way drones are used should be scrutinised more effectively than the rest of the Commons had done. It may be that, with the opposition fragmented and a small government majority, this committee will begin to have a greater impact.

> **Activity**
>
> Choose any three departmental select committees. Check their websites and identify and summarise their latest report.

The Work and Pensions Committee discussing the collapse of BHS, June 2016

The Backbench Business Committee

The committee was set up as part of the Wright Reforms of 2010. It is made up of elected backbench MPs. Its main role is to determine what issues should be debated on the one day a week allocated to backbench business. Before 2010 most of the parliamentary agenda was controlled by the government and the main opposition party leadership. Giving one day a week up to backbench business was, therefore, a major departure.

The subject matter of such debates comes from several sources. Among these are:

- when an e-petition on the Downing Street site achieves 100,000 signatures
- on the initiative of one of the select committees
- from a request by an MP or group of MPs
- requests emerging from national and local campaigns

In the 2014–15 parliamentary session, debates included the following examples:

- On International Women's Day
- On humane slaughter of animals for food (a result of an e-petition)
- On improving cancer care
- On the future of the BBC (from the Culture, Media and Sport select committee)
- On Harvey's law (the result of the police's poor handling of a dog killed in a road accident. An e-petition demanded a law requiring police to treat such incidents more seriously and to keep pet owners better informed following accidents.)

But the most celebrated example of the committee's work occurred in 2011. An e-petition had been held to order the publication of all the documents relating to the 1989 Hillsborough disaster. With over 100,000 signatures, the petition forced a parliamentary debate. As a result of this the government was forced to release previously secret papers about the disaster. The affair resulted in a new inquest and several inquiries into Hillsborough.

The impact of House of Commons select committees

All select committees in the Commons suffer the same basic weakness — they do not have the power to enforce decisions and recommendations. All they can hope to do is to bring publicity to issues, to call government to account and to recommend various courses of action. Nevertheless they are becoming an increasingly significant feature of parliamentary politics.

Knowledge check

Distinguish between the work of these select committees:

- The PAC
- The Liaison Committee
- Departmental select committees
- The Backbench Business Committee

On the other hand, the great strength of the select committees is that the MPs who make up their membership tend to be independent minded. They operate outside the normal constraints of party loyalty so that ministers and government officials increasingly have to take notice of what they say. Hearings are televised so that any controversy receives media coverage. While the questioning of ministers on the floor of the House of Commons tends to be weak and easily countered, the various select committees described above are playing a growing part in Parliament's role of demanding accountability. Questioning can be intense and prolonged, and MPs do not accept weak answers. Sometimes the hearings can resemble cross examination in a court of law. The investigations into the affairs of Philip Green (former owner of British Home Stores) and Mike Ashley, boss of Sports Direct, in 2016 became compelling TV viewing.

Study tip

Make sure you never confuse select committees with legislative committees (also called 'standing' or 'bill' committees). They have very different roles and statuses.

The role of opposition parties

It is often said that the democratic working of government in the UK depends on the existence of a strong, effective opposition in Parliament. Indeed, the 'official' opposition is recognised in the UK Constitution. The leader of the opposition receives a minister's salary and takes part in all official ceremonies. He or she also has the privilege of asking most of the questions at the weekly Prime Minister's Question Time. The opposition also has control over part of the parliamentary agenda. There are 20 days, known as 'opposition days', which are devoted to debates on issues chosen by the opposition. The largest opposition party is the official opposition, but other, smaller parties are also part of the opposition, though with less privileges.

The main roles of the opposition in Parliament (largely the House of Commons) include the following:

- To force the government to explain and justify its policies and decisions
- To highlight the shortcomings of the way the government is running the country
- To present alternative proposals to those of the government if appropriate
- To make itself ready to be an alternative government if the current government is defeated at the next general election

Before 2015 the interplay between government and opposition was relatively simple. The government presented one set of policies and the opposition challenged those proposals with which it disagreed and presented alternatives. When the next general election came round, the electorate was presented with a clear choice between the two. Even under coalition government between 2010 and 2015 the opposition played its traditional role.

Matters were less clear after 2015. In 2015 a weak government with a slim parliamentary majority was helped by the fact that opposition was fragmented. The Labour Party was split between right and left wings and, along with 56 Scottish National Party MPs plus assorted other small parties, it presented an incoherent opposition with little sense of what the alternative to government was. Opposition leader Jeremy Corbyn was hampered by the fact that he did not enjoy the support of a large proportion of his own party.

In 2017, however, the arrival of a minority government once again presented opportunities for the opposition parties to be an effective check on government. Unable to rely on the support of a parliamentary majority, the government was faced with the need to build a coalition of support for each policy initiative. Opposition members could now expect to have genuine impact on policy. At the same time the House of Lords could expect to exert its own influence over a weak government.

From a democratic point of view this is unsatisfactory as the Lords are unelected. Even members of the government admitted that they felt uncomfortable in these circumstances. They may have to get used to it. The advent of a multi-party system in the UK may well mean that the traditional government-versus-opposition model of parliamentary politics is over.

The role of the official opposition and opposition parties can be summarised by the following main functions:

- The main opposition party is a 'government in waiting'. It must be ready at all times to take over if a government falls or resigns, and it must be ready to fight for power at the next election.
- All opposition parties have the key function of calling the government to account by examining critically policies and decisions and by questioning ministers.
- Opposition parties often seek to defend the interests of sections of society they feel are being ignored or discriminated against in government policy. Thus, for example, Labour often defends the rights of workers, nationalist parties defend regional interests and the Greens defend those suffering environmental problems.
- The main opposition parties also have a ceremonial function at occasions such as visits by foreign heads of state, Remembrance Sunday and the like. The leaders of opposition parties are seen on these occasions in order to ensure all variations of political opinion are represented at national rituals.
- The main opposition party has a share in organising the business of the UK parliament. A significant minority of parliamentary time is given over to debates and business which they wish to hold.

Calling ministers to account

There are three main ways in which government ministers are called to account.

1 On 'questions to ministers days', every minister has to take their turn to appear on the floor of the House of Commons (or Lords if they are a peer) to face questions from members. They also have to respond to written questions. It is not just government policy that is under scrutiny; ministers may also have to answer questions about the way in which individuals and groups have been treated by an organ of the state. These are key occasions, when members pursue the grievances of their constituents or promote the interests of a group or association they may represent.

2 In departmental select committees or the Public Accounts Committee, ministers are subjected to close questioning, sometimes hostile, about their policies and about the performance of their department. This can be a challenging occasion for them and their civil servants and advisers. The select committees, have, indeed, largely taken over from 'questions to ministers days' as the main way in which government is called to account.

3 The prime minister must submit him- or herself to Prime Minister's Question Time (PMQT) every week. This is a largely ritualised occasion, conducted more for publicity than effective democracy. It says more about the personal qualities of the prime minister than the government's policies. Twice a year the prime minister also appears before the Liaison Committee containing the chairs of the main select committees. This is becoming more effective than PMQT but remains a somewhat obscure way of calling government to account.

Activity

Find an account of the most recent PMQT. What were the main issues raised by the leader of the opposition?

It remains true that ministers have a distinct advantage over MPs and peers when answering questions. On the whole, they have notice of questions and so can use their army of civil servants and advisers to help them with answers. Many ministers also become highly skilled in avoiding becoming trapped by difficult questioning. In contrast, MPs and peers lack a great deal of research back-up and may be seen as 'amateurs' competing with professionals. The select committee system, however, has gone some way to redressing this imbalance.

Theresa May during Prime Minister's Question Time

A general assessment of Parliament

How effective is the UK Parliament today?

We have seen that the relationship between government and Parliament is in a state of transition. However, it is possible to attempt an assessment of how effective Parliament is. In order to do this it is necessary to determine what 'effective' actually means. We can say that effectiveness implies the following:

- It holds government properly to account.
- It provides democratic legitimacy for government initiatives.
- It scrutinises legislation thoroughly and seeks to improve it.
- It prevents government from exercising power beyond its electoral mandate.
- It is an effective vehicle for the representation of constituencies.
- It represents the interests of various sections of society.
- It represents the national interest.
- It acts as a recruiting ground for potential ministers.

If we examine each of these requirements, we can determine how well Parliament is performing its functions. Table 6.8 summarises this assessment.

Parliament and a minority government

Before leaving this question we must consider the changed situation after 2017, when a government was elected with no parliamentary majority. The last time such a minority government existed was in the 1970s. The relationship between parliament and government is transformed in such circumstances. The government cannot guarantee a majority of support for any of its measures. An agreement with the Northern Irish DUP in June 2017 guaranteed a small government majority on votes of no confidence, but small parties or groups of like-minded MPs suddenly become powerful. The government must build support for every measure, both within its own party and among opposition parties. The government must fight for every vote in the House.

Table 6.8 How effective is Parliament?

Role	Positive aspects	Negative aspects
Holding government to account	The select committees are increasingly significant. Ministers must still face questioning in both houses.	MPs still lack expertise, knowledge, research back-up and time to investigate government thoroughly. PMQT remains a media 'event' rather than a serious session.
Providing democratic legitimacy	The UK's system is stable with widespread consent. Parliament provides strong legitimacy.	The House of Lords cannot provide this as it is neither elected nor accountable.
Scrutinising legislation	The House of Lords does an increasingly effective job, often improving legislation and blocking unfair or discriminatory aspects of proposals. Experts in various fields in the Lords use their knowledge to good effect.	As legislative committees in the Commons are whipped, this is largely ineffective.
Controlling government power	Increasingly both houses are checking the power of government, especially when the governing party does not have a commanding majority in the Commons.	The power of prime ministerial patronage and control by party whips still means that many MPs are unwilling to challenge government.
Representing constituents	This is an acknowledged strength of the Westminster system.	It is absent in the House of Lords. MPs' care of their constituencies varies from MP to MP. There is still no effective mechanism for removing poorly performing MPs.
Representing outside interests	Especially strong in the House of Lords Many MPs, too, support external causes and groups.	When there is clash between party policy and the interests of groups and causes, party loyalty often wins out.
Representing the national interest	When there is a free vote, both houses are seen at their best. MPs and peers take this very seriously.	When votes are whipped, party loyalty often wins out over national interest.
Acting as a recruiting ground for potential ministers	Parliament is a good training ground for future ministers, demonstrating their abilities well.	Being effective in parliamentary work does not necessarily mean a politician could manage a department of state.

How representative is the UK Parliament today?

This assessment can be viewed in four ways. This section looks at each in turn.

How well are different regions and localities of the UK represented?

As we have seen, the representation of constituencies is strong. Every constituency has its own MP whose duty it is to represent the interests of the locality. This is irrespective of which party the MP belongs to. He or she is expected to defend the constituency if proposals may threaten it, to publicise both the problems and the achievements of the constituency, and to raise the grievances of individual constituents with the relevant authorities. It also has to be said that many MPs have a regional outlook — that is, they see themselves as representing a specific part of the country, for example depressed industrial areas, rural farming regions or places of special natural beauty. This is, therefore, on the whole, a strength.

How well are various sections of society represented?

Turning to the House of Lords, the representation of interests is given great importance. When scrutinising legislative proposals, the Lords can take into account the interests of such groups as the professions, industrial and business groups, groups of workers in an industry, welfare recipients of various kinds, the elderly or the young, members of public services including the police and armed forces, as well as refugees and asylum seekers. All such groups claim formal or informal representation in the Lords, but less so in the Commons where the power of the party whips often holds sway. This is, therefore, another strength.

How *politically* representative of the whole nation is the UK Parliament?

Here we are looking at how well the UK Parliament reflects the strengths of the various parties in the country as a whole. There is no doubt that political representation is extremely distorted in the House of Commons. This is largely because of the way in which the first-past-the-post electoral system converts votes into seats in Parliament. This is nothing new. The outcome of general elections has always been distorted, but 2015 produced an especially unrepresentative outcome. Some of the most glaring examples are listed below.

Synoptic link

Consideration of how representative Parliament is should be undertaken in conjunction with the wider issue of representative democracy, discussed in Chapter 1.

- The UK Independence Party (UKIP) won 12.6% of the popular vote, yet only one seat.
- The Scottish National Party (SNP) won 50% of the popular vote in Scotland, but this converted to it winning 56 out of 59 seats available, i.e. over 95%.
- The Conservative Party won 36.9% of the popular vote, but secured 51% of the total seats.
- The Labour Party won 30.4% of the popular vote, converting to 35.7% of the seats.
- The Liberal Democrats only won eight seats on a popular vote of 7.9%. Thus the Liberal Democrats won many fewer votes than UKIP but secured eight times as many seats.
- The Green Party won 3.8% of the total votes but only one seat.

A good illustration of these distortions can be provided by an imaginary result where all the UK parliamentary seats were awarded in strict proportion to the votes cast for each party. This, together with the actual results and the actual party make-up in the House of Lords, is shown in Table 6.9.

Table 6.9 How the parliamentary seats would have been distributed on a strictly proportional basis in 2015

Party	Number of seats proportionally allocated	Actual seats won	House of Lords seats, May 2016
Conservative	240	331	247
Labour	198	232	211
SNP	30	56	1
UKIP	82	1	3
Liberal Democratic	51	8	109
Green	25	1	1
Others	20	21	240 (approx.)

Table 6.9 clearly shows the under- and over-representation of parties in 2015. The 2017 general election also distorted party representation, but to a lesser extent. The main anomalies from June 2017 were:

- The Conservative share of the national vote rose by 5.5% but it lost 13 seats.
- The Conservatives won 42.4 % of the votes but 48.9% of the seats.
- The Liberal Democrats won 7.4% of the votes but only 2.2% of the seats.
- Nevertheless, the parliament elected in June 2017 was much more representative of party support among the voters than the 2015 general election.

How *socially* representative of the whole nation is the UK Parliament?

We need to be careful when analysing the social make-up of the House of Commons elected in 2017. Take age, for example. We would expect that the

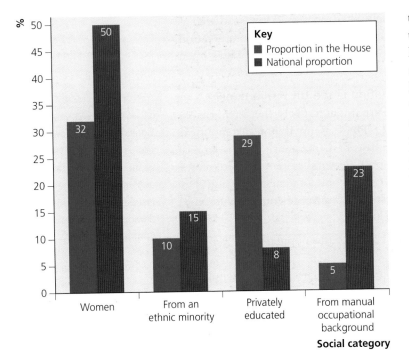

Figure 6.6 Social make-up of the 2017 House of Commons

Source: BBC, June 2017

typical age of an MP would be higher than that of the whole population. We would hope and predict that those who stand for election have considerable experience of life. Similarly, we would hope that MPs would be better educated than the average citizen. Nevertheless, there are some measures that can tell us more accurately how representative the Parliament is. Here we confine ourselves to gender, ethnic origin, whether privately educated and occupational background. Figure 6.6 shows how the Commons is made up in comparison with the general population.

Though there are social distortions in the make-up of the House of Commons, as Figure 6.6 shows, there was some improvement in social balance in June 2017. A record number of women were elected and ethnic minority membership rose from 6% in 2015 to 10% in 2017. More MPs than ever (over 50%) were comprehensive-educated and 45 LGBT members were in the House.

Knowledge check

Why is it important that Parliament should be 'socially representative'?

The House of Lords suffers similar distortion. In 2016, 26% of peers were women. As in the Commons, 6% were from ethnic minorities. The average age of peers is 69, compared to 51 in the Commons, again as one would expect. So, while there is a wide variety of occupational background represented in the Lords, it is more socially distorted than the Commons. This aspect of Parliament is a persistent weakness.

Reform of the House of Lords

There have been several attempts to reform the House of Lords since the 1960s when a concerted effort by the Labour government of the day failed in 1968. Since then there has been a growing consensus that reform is needed, but action has failed either because of a lack of political will or because there was no agreement on what should replace the existing arrangement.

The debate almost wholly centres on the *composition* of a reformed chamber. There has been relatively little appetite for any significant change in the *powers* of the second chamber. This is for two reasons:

1 An increase in its powers would, it is feared, lead to an American-style situation where legislating could become too difficult. In the USA the two legislative chambers have similar status and powers. This makes legislation complex, long-winded and very often too difficult. Furthermore, a more powerful second chamber would simply duplicate the work of the current House of Commons for no particular advantage.

2 If the second chamber had fewer powers than it currently exercises, the question would be asked, what is the point of it? So the present powers of a second chamber are broadly supported.

A reformed second chamber would therefore continue to act as a safeguard against a government abusing its authority and becoming an elective dictatorship without

The House of Lords in session

sufficient check by the House of Commons. It would also remain as a revising and delaying chamber. Three main proposals have been supported:

1 An all-appointed second chamber

2 An all-elected second chamber

3 A combination of the two

The problems associated with the current House of Lords have been well recognised. They include the following.

- An unelected legislature is simply not democratic.
- Without elections members are not accountable for what they do.
- Occasionally the House of Lords thwarts the will of the government and House of Commons without democratic legitimacy.
- The appointment of life peers is open to abuse by party leaders, leading to charges of '**cronyism**'. Party leaders use appointment to the Lords as a way of securing loyalty and rewarding their allies ('cronies').
- Too many members of the current House of Lords are not active or are only semi active.

Table 6.10 summarises the arguments for each of the three reform proposals.

> **Key term**
>
> **Cronyism** An accusation that party leaders often reward supporters and friends with a place in the House of Lords whether or not they are worthy of such an honour.

Table 6.10 Arguments for a reformed second chamber

All-appointed	All-elected	Part elected, part appointed
People with special experience and expertise could be recruited into the legislative process.	An elected second chamber would be wholly democratic.	Such a second chamber could enjoy the advantages of both alternatives.
The political make-up of an appointed body could be manipulated to act as a counterbalance to the government's House of Commons majority.	If elected by some kind of proportional representation (PR), it would prevent a government having too much power.	
Without the need to seek re-election members would be more independent minded.	Under PR, smaller parties and independent members would gain representation they cannot win through FPTP in the House of Commons.	

There does remain one other proposal. This is total abolition. The supporters of this idea are mostly left-wing thinkers who see the second chamber as a means of perpetuating privilege and spreading excessive patronage. They also point to its expense and to the fact that it has very limited democratic functions. But, despite the apparent logic of these reasons, abolition is unlikely to happen. Most democratic states are bicameral, with good reasons. There are always occasions when a special safeguard is needed against an alliance of government and a democratically elected legislature abusing their powers.

Discussion point

Should the second chamber be abolished or reformed? What kind of reform is preferable?

Key concepts in this chapter

Accountability A principle that is key to true democracy. Those who have been elected, including governments and MPs, are accountable to the people for what they do. This means they must explain what they do, face criticisms and perhaps be removed from office if they fail.

Backbencher A name given to MPs who do not hold any government post or are not senior members of the main opposition party. Backbenchers are typically more independent than frontbench MPs but are still 'whipped' by the whips to try to ensure that they support their party.

Bicameral An adjective describing a political system with two legislative chambers. If there is only one chamber, it is described as 'unicameral'.

Consent This is the idea that a proposed law or decision by the government is formally consented to by the people. This is vital in a democracy. However, in a parliamentary democracy, the elected Parliament can grant consent on behalf of the people.

Cronyism An accusation that party leaders often reward supporters and friends with a place in the House of Lords whether or not they are worthy of such an honour.

Crossbencher A name given to members of the House of Lords who are not formal members of any political party and so are independent minded.

Division The name used in Parliament for a vote. It is so called because MPs or peers 'divide' between the 'Aye lobby' and the 'No lobby,' where they are counted by MPs appointed to be 'tellers'.

Life peer A prominent member of society who is granted a peerage (becoming known as Lord or Lady, or Baron or Baroness). This entitles the holder to attend the House of Lords, take part in debates, and scrutinise and vote on legislation. The entitlement is for life unless they are convicted of serious misconduct. Life peers receive a generous daily attendance allowance as long as they attend regularly. They cannot pass their title on to their children.

Parliament The most common name for an elected body that forms the legislature. Strong parliaments can control both government and legislation, while weaker parliaments play a minor advisory role and are dominated by government.

Parliamentary vote of no confidence This is a vote that may take place in the House of Commons, usually called by opposition parties. It follows a debate during which the government will have been criticised by its opponents and defended by its supporters. Usually such votes fail, though they do call government to account. Occasionally (the last time this happened was in 1979), if opponents outnumber supporters, the government may lose and will normally resign to face a general election.

Party whip A party official appointed by the party leader whose role is to maintain party discipline and loyalty, to inform MPs about parliamentary business and to act as a communication between backbenchers and party leaderships. The term originates from fox hunting where a rider known as the 'whipper in' tried to keep the hounds in order.

Redress of grievances This is an ancient function of the House of Commons. It involves an MP pursuing a grievance that a constituent may have against a public body, usually claiming that they have been unfairly or unequally treated. MPs may lobby ministers and officials or raise the matter in the House of Commons.

Reserve powers Powers which exist and are very significant, but are only expected to be used in unusual or extreme circumstances. Instead they are held 'in reserve'. The UK Parliament has two key reserve powers — to veto legislation proposed by government and to dismiss a government in which it has lost confidence. The monarch also has such reserve powers but is even less likely than Parliament to use them.

Scrutiny A process conducted by both Houses of Parliament. It is the examination of proposed legislation, usually coming from government, to ensure that it is clear and fair, and that it protects minorities. In extreme cases, scrutiny may involve amending legislation to change its character completely. Government tries to control the process of scrutiny but MPs and peers may try to act independently.

Secondary legislation Laws, regulations and orders mostly made by government ministers. They require parliamentary approval but do *not* have to pass through the full procedure. Most secondary legislation is not discussed in Parliament, but passes through automatically or 'on the nod'. Only the occasional controversial piece of secondary legislation provokes debate and a vote in Parliament. The House of Lords pays more attention to secondary legislation than the Commons.

White Paper A document outlining the main intentions and terms of a Public Bill. It is presented to Parliament up to a year before it is converted into a bill. Parliament normally debates a White Paper and votes on it. Any potential problems are identified at White Paper stage.

Summary

Having read this chapter, you should have knowledge and understanding of the following:
- → How Parliament works and about the MPs and peers who make up both houses of Parliament
- → The main distinctions between the powers and functions of the House of Lords and House of Commons
- → The changing political and legal context within which Parliament is working
- → The status and effectiveness of MPs and peers
- → The ways in which the relationship between Parliament and the executive is changing
- → How well Parliament holds government to account
- → The work and growing importance of parliamentary committees
- → The degree to which Parliament is effective or ineffective
- → The degree to which Parliament is representative
- → The debate about whether and how the House of Lords should be reformed

Further information and web guide

Websites

The best website for information about all aspects of Parliament is **www.parliament.uk**.
Debates about the reform of Parliament can be found on such sites as
www.unlockdemocracy.org and **www.ucl.ac.uk/constitution-unit**.
The Hansard Society is also very useful: **www.hansardsociety.org.uk**.
For up-to-date information and statistics on parliamentary revolts, consult **www.revolts.co.uk**.
Lists of available books on Parliament can be found by accessing the website of the
parliamentary bookshop in Westminster: **www.shop.parliament.uk**.

Books

Philip Norton is perhaps the best-known author on Parliament. His latest book is Norton, P.
(2013) *Parliament in British Politics*, Palgrave.
The best general work on Parliament, which is reasonably up to date, is Rogers, R. and
Walters, R. (2015) *How Parliament Works*, Taylor and Francis.
An entertaining account of the work of MPs is Flynn, P. *How to be an MP*, Biteback.
A large reference book on the House of Lords is useful for information: Russell, M. (2013)
The Contemporary House of Lords, Oxford University Press.

Practice questions

AS

1 Describe the main distinctions between the House of Lords and the
House of Commons. (10)

2 Describe the importance of departmental select committees. (10)

3 Using the source, assess the importance and effectiveness of the Public
Accounts Committee. *In your response you must use knowledge and
understanding to analyse points that are only in the source. You will not be
rewarded for introducing any additional points that are not in the source.* (10)

> **The Public Accounts Committee**
>
> Under the chairmanship of Margaret Hodge between 2010 and 2015, the Public
> Accounts Committee became an effective and feared institution. It investigated such
> matters as tax avoidance and evasion, the expenditure of the BBC, the efficiency of Her
> Majesty's Revenue and Customs, and how much the NHS was providing value for money.
>
> The committee has shown a remarkable degree of independence and often produces
> reports which are unanimous. It has also attracted a great deal of public and media
> attention. The result of this is that government and Parliament cannot afford to ignore its
> recommendations and criticisms.
>
> After Hodge retired there was no change in the committee's status. Indeed, the Google
> case of 2016 demonstrated its importance. When Google paid £130 million in unpaid
> corporation tax, the committee argued that this was too little and directed HMRC to
> reconsider this and similar cases.

4 'The House of Lords is now an outdated institution and should be
abolished or replaced.' How far do you agree? (30)

5 'The House of Commons is a more important institution than the House
of Lords.' To what extent do you agree? (30)

A-level

1 Using the source, evaluate the arguments in favour of an elected second chamber. *In your response you must compare the different opinions in the source and use a balance of knowledge and understanding both arising from the source and beyond it to help you to analyse and evaluate.* (30)

Reform of the House of Lords

After most of the hereditary peers were removed from the House of Lords in 1999, the behaviour and status of the upper house began to change. In that year the house became largely an appointed body. Many of its members are experts in their field and take their role as legislation revisers very seriously. At the committee stage of a bill's passage through the Lords, many peers contribute to improving the legislation. So, although it remains an undemocratic body, it could be said to be more effective than ever before.

Nevertheless, calls for its replacement by an elected body remain strong. For democrats it is not acceptable that half the legislature should be unelected and unaccountable. Supporters of this reform ignore the fear that an elected house would fall under the control of party leaderships. As things stand, the Lords is extremely independent of party control and can therefore provide more meaningful opposition and call government to account more effectively. An elected chamber might also mean that many useful specialists and experts would be lost to politics.

A compromise position is to introduce a part-elected, part-appointed house. Such an option might provide the best possible solution.

2 Using the source, evaluate the effectiveness of the House of Commons. *In your response you must compare the different opinions in the source and use a balance of knowledge and understanding both arising from the source and beyond it to help you to analyse and evaluate.* (30)

Key debates in the House of Commons

2015 Debate on a proposal to start air strikes against Islamic State in Syria — approved

2015 Debate on whether to hold a referendum on the UK's EU membership — approved

2013 Debate on the UK's response to the use of chemical weapons by the Syrian government in the civil war in its country — the Commons refused to sanction direct military intervention

2003 Debate to approve the UK's involvement in a NATO attack on Iraq — approved, though the foreign secretary, Robin Cook, resigned from the Labour government

1993 Debate on whether the UK should approve the Social Chapter of the European Union, extending worker and social rights compulsorily to the UK — the vote was a dead heat. The Speaker (Betty Boothroyd) gave approval with her casting vote

1993 A vote of no confidence in John Major's Conservative government. Effectively a vote on whether the UK should sign the Maastricht Treaty, extending EU power over member states — treaty approved by a 40-vote majority

1969 Debate on whether to abolish capital punishment in the UK — abolished by a majority of 158

3 Evaluate the effectiveness of backbench MPs. (30)

4 Evaluate the effectiveness of the House of Lords. (30)

7 The prime minister and executive

On 13 July 2016, in the early evening, a grey limousine drew up outside Buckingham Palace. Out of it stepped an elegant 59-year-old woman, clearly dressed for a special occasion. Inside the palace the queen awaited her visitor. She knew who and what to expect. David Cameron, the prime minister, had announced his intention to resign on 24 June, the day after the referendum on the UK's membership of the European Union had gone against him. The ruling Conservative Party had held an internal election to find Cameron's successor. All this, the queen knew. She knew, too, that the winner, the former home secretary, Theresa May, would be coming to call.

An hour earlier, Prime Minister Cameron had come to tender his resignation and to advise the queen to appoint Mrs May as his successor. As a courtesy, a member of the royal household had called Mrs May, but she was already prepared to depart. Once in the queen's private receiving room, the new prime minister curtsied, kissed her monarch's outstretched hand and accepted her invitation to form a new government.

So power passed quietly from one pair of hands to another. It was all very civilised and understated. In one short ceremony, the queen's ancient prerogative powers were transferred to the new prime minister. Afterwards Theresa May returned to Downing Street, her new home, to begin the process of exercising the first of the queen's powers — that of patronage. She set about appointing a new set of ministers. It all happened without a general election or a vote in Parliament. Eleven months later the prime minister, having called an early general election to obtain a fresh mandate, found her position hugely undermined when her party lost its parliamentary majority. Such is the fragility of prime ministerial power.

Objectives

This chapter will inform you about the following:

→ The components and nature of the central 'executive' of the UK

→ The structure of the core executive

→ How party leaders come to be prime minister

→ The sources of prime ministerial power and authority, and the nature of the prime minister's powers

→ The nature, roles and limitations of the cabinet, and how the 'cabinet system' works

→ The nature and importance of collective responsibility, and whether it is a negative or positive principle

→ The nature and importance of individual ministerial responsibility

→ The nature of the relationship between the prime minister and the cabinet

→ How the power of the prime minister can be assessed

→ The extent to which the UK prime minister is effectively a president

The role, powers and structure of the core executive in the UK

The general role of the central executive

The term 'executive' refers to one of the three branches of government, standing alongside the legislature and the judiciary. The precise nature of an executive varies from one country to another, but we can identify a number of common roles for all executive bodies. The main roles of the executive are as follows:

- The development of government policy
- Conducting foreign policy, including relations with other states and international bodies
- Organising the defence of the country from external and internal threats
- Managing the finances of the state
- Responding to major problems or crises such as armed conflict, security threats, economic difficulties or social disorder
- Controlling and managing the forces of law and order, including the police, courts, armed forces and intelligence services
- Drafting and securing the passage of legislation
- Organising the implementation of legislation
- Organising and managing the services provided by the state

The structure of the executive

The UK is unusual in that many of the organs of the executive are described as being under the control of the monarch, for example 'Her Majesty's ministers' or 'Her Majesty's Treasury'. However, this is an illusion. In practice the executive branch is under the control of the prime minister (using his or her 'prerogative powers') and the cabinet. The civil service — the unelected permanent officials who serve the government — is expected to act in a neutral fashion, standing outside the party battle, and is forbidden from serving the *political* interests of the government, but it, too, is technically within the control of the prime minister, who is officially 'head of the civil service'.

> **Study tip**
>
> The terms 'executive' and 'government' can be used interchangeably. They mean almost the same thing.

We need not concern ourselves with these constitutional peculiarities. In fact the terms 'executive' and 'government' are virtually interchangeable. This is because the government — a political body — controls the executive, which is an organ of the state.

We will, from time to time, make comparisons with the USA in relation to the executive. In the USA the elected president heads the federal executive (he is often described as the 'chief executive') and controls the whole machinery of government, usually known in the USA as the 'Administration'. It shares all the same functions as performed by the UK executive. One key distinction, however, is that each of the 50 states has its own executive. This is because they have their own sovereign powers.

Many models of the UK executive branch have been constructed, but none is definitive. It is also unclear which individuals and bodies are actually part of the executive. For the purposes of this study, however, we need only consider what is often described as the **core executive**. This is the central hub of government in the UK. It is where key decisions are made and from which power is distributed to subordinate bodies. The main components of the core executive are as follows:

- The prime minister and his or her close advisers
- The cabinet — between 20 and 25 senior ministers appointed by the prime minister
- Various bodies that feed information and advice into the cabinet and to the prime minister
- Government departments — of these the Treasury holds a place of special importance as it controls government finances. Many heads of these departments are members of the cabinet. Others may not be in cabinet but are nonetheless influential.
- The senior **civil servants** who serve government ministers — of these the *cabinet secretary* is the most senior. The holder of this post serves both the prime minister personally and the cabinet collectively.
- Various advisers and policy-developing bodies (often called 'think tanks') that serve government departments
- There may also be a few very senior officials of the governing party who hold no official post but who are intimately involved in policy development.

Stating how large the core executive is would be very difficult. The total number of people who have *some* direct influence over government policy making is probably in the region of about 4,000. This is not the actual core, however. What we can say with some certainty is that the core executive numbers several hundred people.

Precisely how members of the core communicate and interact is extremely complex. Here, however, it is only necessary to consider one key relationship — between the prime minister and the cabinet. It is what has been described as part of the 'efficient secret' of government in the UK. Some have also called the prime minister–cabinet hub the 'cabinet system'.

Before looking at this relationship we can summarise the nature of the core executive, as shown in Table 7.1.

Key terms

Core executive The name given to the central part of government, the centre of power where key decisions are made. It is made up of a mixture of elected ministers and appointed advisers or civil servants.

Civil servant A civil servant is employed by a government department. The most senior civil servants are involved with presenting political decision makers with information, viable options and neutral advice. They are not politicians as they are not elected and not accountable, and so cannot be involved in party politics, but they do have influence. They are permanent and are expected to serve ministers of any party equally faithfully.

Table 7.1 The UK's core executive

Key individual or body	Role	Supporting elements
The prime minister	Chief policy maker and chief executive	Cabinet Cabinet secretary Private office of civil servants Policy unit
Cabinet	Approving policy and settling disputes within government	Cabinet committees Cabinet Office Cabinet secretary
Treasury	Managing the government's finances	Senior civil servants Special advisers Think tanks
Government departments	Developing and implementing specialised policies	Civil servants Special advisers Think tanks

We will now look at the key elements of the executive branch of government: the prime minister and cabinet, including ministers and their departments.

The prime minister

The key to understanding the position of prime minister is the nature of the **royal prerogative**. Before the powers of the monarch were curbed in the seventeenth century, the king or queen enjoyed what were known as 'prerogative powers'. These were powers that could not be controlled by Parliament or any other body. Arguably the courts exercised some sort of control, but it was clear that, in any dispute between the monarch and the Lord Chancellor (the head of the judiciary), the former would prevail. These powers were mainly to wage war, to make foreign treaties and to appoint ministers and other people to public office. It is worth noting that the monarch could not levy taxes without the permission of Parliament and also had to have his or her spending plans approved. As to other laws, including criminal law, the monarch could propose such laws, but needed parliamentary approval.

During the seventeenth to nineteenth centuries, as the political authority of the monarch began to wane, the question arose: what is to be done with the prerogative powers? If we no longer accept that the monarch can exercise them in a democratic system, who should exercise them? Parliament was much too big and too fragmented to do such things as conduct foreign policy or negotiate treaties or appoint ministers. The obvious candidate was government itself: the cabinet in particular, but even the cabinet was not capable of giving *singularity of purpose*. There needed to be a single figurehead. As a result, the position of prime minister gradually evolved during the eighteenth century.

The main role and powers of the prime minister today can be summarised thus:

- The prime minister has complete power to appoint or dismiss all government ministers, whether in the cabinet or outside the cabinet. The prime minister also has a say in other public appointments, including the most senior civil servants.
- The prime minister has power to negotiate foreign treaties, including trade arrangements with other states or international organisations.
- The prime minister is commander-in-chief of the armed forces and can commit them to action. However, it should be noted that this power has come under challenge in recent times (see pages 249–51). It is now accepted that the prime minister should only make major military commitments 'on the advice and with the sanction of Parliament'. Nevertheless, once armed forces have been committed to action, the prime minister has general control of their actions.

> **Key term**
>
> **Royal prerogative** The arbitrary powers formerly enjoyed by the monarchy, but gradually transferred to the government and then to the prime minister during the eighteenth and nineteenth centuries. The powers include patronage, conducting foreign policy, negotiating foreign treaties and conducting military affairs (as commander-in-chief).

- The prime minister conducts foreign policy and determines relationships with foreign powers. In this sense the prime minister represents the country internationally.
- The prime minister heads the cabinet system (see below), chooses its members, sets its agenda and determines what cabinet committees should exist and who should sit on them.
- It is generally true that the prime minister sets the general tone of economic policy. Usually this is done alongside the chancellor of the exchequer, who is normally a very close colleague.

The cabinet

The cabinet sits at the centre of power in the UK political system. Indeed, the UK system of government used to be commonly described as '**cabinet government**'. This is not to say that it is where all important decisions are made. It is not. Rather, it means that all official government decisions and policies must be cleared by the cabinet if they are to be considered legitimate. In that sense the cabinet holds a similar position to the UK Parliament. In order to be implemented and enforced, all laws must be approved by Parliament. In the case of policies and government decisions (which often lead to law making), they must be approved by the cabinet if they are to be considered *official policy*. In the case of both, Parliament and cabinet approval may well be brief and may require little meaningful debate, but such formal approval is essential. Occasionally, of course, conflict and real disagreement may occur in both Parliament and cabinet, but often such approval is merely ritualised. Cabinet is therefore sometimes described as a mere 'rubber stamp'.

The nature of the cabinet

The cabinet consists of between 20 and 25 senior government ministers. The precise number of members is in the hands of the prime minister. Indeed, the prime minister controls much of the work and nature of the cabinet. It is one of

Key term

Cabinet government
A term used to describe a situation where the main decision making of government takes place in cabinet. In modern history this is not normally the case. Its main alternative is the expression 'prime ministerial government'.

A cabinet meeting

their key roles. The prime minister also personally appoints all cabinet members and may dismiss them. He or she is not required to consult anyone else when making appointments or dismissals. Most of the members are senior ministers in charge of large **government departments**. A few may not have specific ministerial responsibilities but are considered important enough members of the party to sit at the centre of power. All cabinet members must be members of either the House of Commons (and are therefore also MPs) or the House of Lords (as peers). In practice, most are MPs.

Membership of the cabinet, as it was in June 2017 after the general election, is shown in Table 7.2. They are placed in approximate order of seniority.

Several other ministers are also invited to attend cabinet meetings and take part in discussions but are not cabinet ministers. When final decisions are being made, their view will not be invited. One of them will always be the chief whip of the governing party.

Individuals may also be invited to address the cabinet if they have special knowledge or important views, but they will not take part in full discussions. One civil servant always attends to record the minutes (what is agreed). This is the cabinet secretary, the UK's most senior civil servant. He or she is a key adviser to the cabinet and to the prime minister personally. In 2017 the cabinet secretary was Jeremy Heywood.

> **Key term**
>
> **Government department**
> The work of government is divided among a number of departments. In 2017 there were 19 major departments of state. Each department is headed by a senior, normally cabinet, minister. Departments are subdivided into sections, each headed by a junior minister, normally known as ministers of state. Each department and sub-department is staffed by a bureaucracy of civil servants and some other political advisers.

Table 7.2 Cabinet members, June 2017

Name	Post held
Theresa May MP	Prime minister
Damian Green MP	First secretary of state and cabinet office minister
Philip Hammond MP	Chancellor of the exchequer
Amber Rudd MP	Home secretary
Boris Johnson MP	Foreign secretary
Michael Fallon MP	Defence secretary
Liam Fox MP	International trade secretary
David Davis MP	Secretary for exiting the European Union
David Lidington MP	Justice secretary
Jeremy Hunt MP	Health secretary
Justine Greening MP	Education, women and equality secretary
David Gauke MP	Work and pensions secretary
Greg Clark MP	Business secretary
Michael Gove MP	Environment, food and rural affairs secretary
Karen Bradley MP	Culture, media and sport secretary
Priti Patel MP	International development secretary
Sajid Javid MP	Communities and local government secretary
Chris Grayling MP	Transport secretary
David Mundell MP	Scotland secretary
James Brokenshire MP	Northern Ireland secretary
Alun Cairns MP	Wales secretary
Baroness Evans	Leader of the House of Lords (manages government business in the Lords)

> **Activity**
>
> Table 7.2 shows the cabinet in February 2017. It shows eight female members. Research Margaret Thatcher's first cabinet in 1979. How many female members were there then?

A number of other features of the cabinet are also noteworthy:

- Only members of the governing party are cabinet members. The only exception is with coalition government, which occurred in 2010–15. In that case there were both Conservative and Liberal Democrat members.
- Cabinet normally meets once a week, usually on a Thursday, and a meeting lasts rarely more than 2 hours.
- Additional emergency cabinet meetings may also be called.
- The prime minister chairs the meetings unless abroad or indisposed, in which case his or her deputy may take over, though when this occurs cabinet may not meet at all.
- The proceedings of the cabinet are secret and will not be revealed for at least 30 years.
- Cabinet does not usually vote on issues. The prime minister always seeks a general consensus and then requires all members to agree to that consensus decision. Any member who wishes to dissent publicly will normally be required to resign and leave the cabinet.
- The prime minister sets the final agenda.
- The prime minister approves the minutes made by the cabinet secretary. These are a record of formal decisions made and key points raised for consideration.
- Cabinet decisions are released to a strictly limited number of civil servants and ministers. Media releases will also be sent out, but with no details of the discussions.
- Cabinet members receive an enhanced salary, well above that of junior (non-cabinet) ministers and MPs.
- Members of the cabinet are bound by the convention of *collective responsibility*. This is described below.

Knowledge check

How many ministers are there in the current UK cabinet? Are there any cabinet ministers who do not run a government department? Who are they?

The role of the cabinet

Perhaps surprisingly, the role of the cabinet is both changeable and unclear. Indeed, like the role of the prime minister, its existence is merely an unwritten constitutional convention. To some extent, what it does may vary from one prime minister to another. It may also depend on political circumstances. For example, when the UK was led by a coalition government from 2010 to 2015 the cabinet had a much wider role than usual. Following the 2016 decision to leave the EU, the cabinet had the additional role of overseeing the exit negotiations.

Some prime ministers may use the cabinet as an important sounding board for ideas and policy initiatives. John Major and David Cameron, for example, used it in this way. Other prime ministers, notably Tony Blair and Margaret Thatcher, had little time for cabinet discussion and tended to use it simply to legitimise decisions made elsewhere. Margaret Thatcher (1979–90), indeed, was notorious for downgrading cabinet to a rubber stamp for her own ideas. One of her ministers, Nicholas Ridley, expressed her style thus:

> *Margaret Thatcher was going to be the leader in her Cabinet. She wasn't going to be an impartial chairman. She knew what she wanted to do and was not going to have faint hearts in the Cabinet stopping her.*

Source: quoted in Hennessy, P., *The Prime Ministers*, Allen Lane, p. 400

Yet, despite the variability of the cabinet's position, it does have a number of functions which are common to all administrations in the UK. These are as follows:

- In some emergency or crisis situations the prime minister may revert to the collective wisdom of the cabinet to make decisions. They may take a leading role in the discussion but will also invite comments from their close colleagues. Military situations are the most common example, such as UK intervention in the Syrian civil war and in the war against the Taliban in Afghanistan. Even a determined prime minister will normally inform the cabinet of their intentions, as Tony Blair did before joining the US-led invasion of Iraq in 2003 and Margaret Thatcher before sending a task force to liberate the Falkland Islands in 1982. The fact that cabinet meetings are held in secret helps when military and security matters are at stake.

- Cabinet will discuss and set the way in which policy is to be *presented*, to Parliament, to the government's own MPs and peers, and to the media. It helps to present a united front when all ministers describe and justify decisions in the same manner.

- Occasionally disputes can arise between ministers, very often over how government expenditure is to be shared out. Normally the prime minister and cabinet secretary will try to solve such disputes, but, when this is not possible, the cabinet acts as the final 'court of appeal'.

- Most government business must pass through Parliament, often in the form of legislation. The cabinet will settle the government's agenda to deal with this. It is decided what business will be brought before Parliament in the immediate future, which ministers will contribute to debates and what tactics to adopt if votes in either house are likely to be close. The chief whip's presence is vital on these occasions.

In spite of the need to carry out these functions from time to time, most of cabinet's time is taken up with ratifying decisions reached elsewhere. Ministers are informed in advance of such proposals. Their civil servants prepare brief summaries of what is being proposed and any likely problems that might arise. If ministers decide they have some misgivings about proposals, they normally raise them with the prime minister or cabinet secretary before the meeting, not during it. Despite what the popular press often claims, cabinet 'rows' are rare. Any negotiations that need to be done will normally be settled outside the cabinet room.

So, the cabinet is a kind of 'clearing house' for decisions. Little discussion is needed. The prime minister will check that everyone can support a decision and it invariably goes through 'on the nod'. The origins of most proposals brought before cabinet are described in the next section.

The 'cabinet system'

As we have seen, most decisions are made outside cabinet and they only need to be formally approved in a full cabinet meeting. Therefore it is better to think of a 'cabinet system', rather than simply 'the cabinet'. Where do these decisions originate? The answer is from a variety of sources.

The prime minister

The prime minister — together with their advisers, policy units, close ministerial allies and senior civil servants — will develop proposals of their own. It is extremely rare for the cabinet to question seriously a prime ministerial initiative. When ministers intend to oppose the prime minister, they usually resign, an event which is invariably highly dramatic. Perhaps the most remarkable example was when Sir Geoffrey Howe resigned from Margaret Thatcher's cabinet in 1989, largely over her European policies. Howe's resignation and farewell speech

Study tip

Although it is often said that the cabinet is at the 'centre' of government, this does not mean it is where most decisions are made. Most decisions are made elsewhere, so be careful not to confuse these two realities.

Activity

Research Geoffrey Howe's resignation speech in 1989. Write a short account of the reasons behind his resignation, including observations about what his words tell us about Margaret Thatcher's style of leadership.

Key term

Cabinet committees
Small subcommittees of the cabinet formed to establish the details of government policies. Their recommendations are usually adopted by full cabinet.

in the Commons helped to bring Thatcher down the following year. Tony Blair lost two cabinet colleagues over his Iraq policy in 2003, Robin Cook and Clare Short. But such events are rare.

Cabinet committees

Most detailed policy is worked out in small committees consisting of cabinet members and other junior ministers. Most of these **cabinet committees** are chaired by the prime minister or a very senior minister, such as the chancellor. The committees present their proposals to full cabinet and they are usually accepted, though they may sometimes be referred back to committee for amendments and improvement.

The chancellor of the exchequer

Almost always supported by the prime minister, economic and financial policy is presented to the cabinet by the chancellor, often as a fait accompli. Indeed the annual Autumn Statement (in November) and the Budget (in March) are usually only revealed to the cabinet on the eve of their presentation in Parliament.

The budget must be passed by parliament in the months following its presentation. This is largely a formal process but occasionally there has been dissension. In March 2017, for example, Philip Hammond's proposal to increase national insurance for the self-employed was resisted by all opposition parties plus a number of Conservative rebels, so the measure was quickly dropped. Hammond has announced that the annual budget statement will be moved to November from 2018 onwards.

Individual ministers

Policies involving a government department specifically, but which require wider approval, are presented to cabinet by the relevant minister, aided by their civil servants. It is here that dissent is most likely — though if a minister is backed by the prime minister, they are in a good position to secure approval.

Chancellor of the exchequer Philip Hammond

Groups of ministers

Policies are often developed by various professional advisers, policy units and think tanks. These may be adopted by various ministers who then bring the ideas to cabinet, usually after securing the approval of the prime minister and chancellor. If other ministers have problems with such proposals, they are usually voiced well in advance.

We shall see below that the variety of sources of policy coming into cabinet helps the prime minister to control government in general. Prime ministers see all proposals in advance and have the opportunity to block policies of which they do not approve. They also control the cabinet agenda so they can simply avoid discussion of ideas they do not like. Most prime ministers, most of the time, can manage the cabinet system to promote their own policies and block those they wish to oppose.

Table 7.3 Who has the upper hand — prime minister or cabinet?

The powers of the prime minister	The powers of the cabinet
The prime minister is perceived by the public to be government leader and representative of the nation. This gives them great authority.	If the cabinet is determined, a majority of members can overrule the prime minister.
Prime ministerial patronage means the prime minister has power over ministers and can demand loyalty.	Ultimately the cabinet can remove the prime minister from office, as happened to Margaret Thatcher (1990) and Tony Blair (2007).
The prime minister now has a wide range of individuals or bodies to call on personally for advice.	Cabinet may control powerful ministers with a large following who can thwart the will of the prime minister. Tony Blair was rivalled by Gordon Brown in 2005–07, and David Cameron was by several influential Eurosceptics in 2010–15.
The prime minister chairs cabinet and controls its agenda, which means they can control the governing process.	If the prime minister leads a divided party, it is more difficult to control cabinet. This happened to John Major in 1992–97.
The prime minister enjoys prerogative powers and so can bypass cabinet on some issues.	

Wider government

The general nature of government

There is no universal definition of the term 'government'. It is a term often used very loosely. For the purposes of this study, we define government as the organisation that includes the following members.

Elected politicians
- The prime minister
- The cabinet
- Over a hundred junior ministers, who are either business managers for government, assistants to cabinet ministers or the heads of small departments

Unelected civil servants and other advisers
- The cabinet secretary
- The prime minister's private office
- The prime minister is helped by a Chief of Staff (Theresa May had two for her first year)
- The Cabinet Office, which advises the prime minister and cabinet. It consists of civil servants and advisers, not elected politicians.
- The prime minister's own policy unit, known as the Number Ten Policy Unit
- Various other policy units made up of civil servants and advisers
- Senior civil servants who give advice directly to their ministers

So, when we use the term 'government', we can mean all or part of the organisation described above. The prime minister and cabinet may be the 'public face' of government but they stand at the head of a vast machinery. Government, as we shall see below, is expected to speak with one voice, whether or not members are elected politicians.

The functions of government

Government, often described as the 'executive', has a number of key functions:

- To develop policy, guided by the policies of the ruling party and its leaders
- To draft legislation needed to implement policy. This includes major primary legislation and more detailed **secondary legislation** which sets out specific regulations and principles governing the operations of the state.

> **Key term**
>
> **Secondary legislation**
> This includes detailed laws and regulations passed by ministers under powers granted to them by primary legislation. Most secondary legislation does not concern Parliament, though Parliament reserves the right to debate and vote on such legislation if it is controversial.

- To manage the passage of legislation
- To negotiate with and regulate relations with external organisations and states
- To manage the operations of the state, including education, health, the welfare state, armed forces, the law enforcement establishment etc.

We also need to distinguish between the 'political' aspects of government and the 'administrative' aspects.

- The political aspects concern the development of policy. Although advice from unelected advisers may be taken, the final decisions are made by ministers as they alone are publicly accountable.
- The 'administrative' side, including the implementation of policy and organisation of the state, can be undertaken by unelected officials. Even so, ministers remain accountable for the quality of administration.

Ministerial responsibility

The nature and importance of collective responsibility

What is collective responsibility?

Governing in the UK is a collective exercise on the whole. While the prime minister does have their own prerogative powers, for example over foreign and security policy, decisions are taken *collectively* by the government. This means that *all* ministers (whether in the cabinet or not) are *collectively responsible* for all government policies and decisions. Even though most policy is created by the most senior members of government, there is a convention that all ministers will defend and publicly support all official policy. It is part of the 'deal' when they take office. This is known as the doctrine of collective ministerial responsibility. It has five principles:

1 Ministers are collectively responsible for all government policies.

2 All ministers must publicly support all government policies, even if they disagree privately with them.

3 If a minister wishes to dissent publicly from a government policy, he or she is expected to resign first.

4 If a minister dissents without resigning, he or she can expect to be dismissed by the prime minister.

5 As cabinet meetings are secret, any dissent within government is concealed.

Why is collective responsibility important?

We have seen that the principle of collective responsibility within government is a great support to prime ministerial power and this is perhaps its main significance. A prime minister's authority is greatly enhanced by the fact that they will not experience open dissent from within the government. It is also important that the government presents a united front to the outside world, including Parliament and the media. Specifically, the government knows it can rely upon the votes of all ministers in any close division in the Commons. This is known as the *payroll vote*.

It can also be said that collective responsibility reduces the possibility of open dissent. Critics will say that it 'gags' ministers and prevents them expressing their own opinions. Supporters of the principle, on the other hand, say that the secrecy of the system means that ministers *can* express their views honestly *within* cabinet, knowing that their disagreement is unlikely to be publicised.

Two key exceptions to collective responsibility

In recent years collective responsibility has been suspended for two different reasons.

The first occurred when UK government was a **coalition** between the Conservatives and Liberal Democrats in 2010–15. Clearly it would have been impossible for ministers from two very different parties to agree on every policy. Nobody would have believed them had they made such a claim. A special arrangement was therefore made. The coalition arrived at a Coalition Agreement, which included all the policies the two party leaderships decided should be common to both sets of ministers. Collective responsibility applied to the Coalition Agreement, but some areas of policy were not included. For example, the renewal of the Trident nuclear submarine missile system was excluded. Coalition ministers were allowed to disagree publicly on the issue. The same exception was applied to the question of intervention in the Syrian civil war.

The second suspension of collective responsibility became necessary when it was decided to hold a referendum on UK membership of the EU in June 2016. During the campaign, Conservative ministers were free to express views counter to the official government position — that the UK should remain in the EU. Several cabinet ministers, including former justice secretary, Michael Gove, and former leader of the House of Commons, Chris Grayling, openly campaigned against the official government line. A similar arrangement had been made the last time there was a referendum on UK membership of the European Economic Community (EEC) in 1975.

In summary we can say that collective responsibility can be viewed both negatively and positively. Table 7.4 summarises this question.

Key term

Coalition A type of government, rare in the UK but common in the rest of Europe, where two or more parties share government posts and come to agreement on common policies. Coalitions occur when no single party can command a majority in the legislature.

Table 7.4 The debate over collective responsibility: positive or negative?

Positive aspects	Negative aspects
It creates a government which is united, strong and decisive.	Some argue it puts too much power into the hands of the prime minister.
The public, Parliament and the media are presented with a clear, single version of government policy.	It means that ministers cannot be openly honest about their view on policies. This may stifle debate within government.
Though ministers cannot dissent publicly, the confidentiality of the cabinet means that ministers can engage in frank discussions in private.	Resignations under the doctrine are dramatic events which may seriously undermine government.

Individual ministerial responsibility

The nature of individual responsibility

As we have seen, ministers are collectively responsible for government policies. However, each minister is also *individually* responsible for matters that affect his or her department separately. Ministers are also individually responsible for their own performance as a minister and their conduct as an individual. The doctrine

Study tip

Students commonly confuse collective responsibility and individual ministerial responsibility in relation to UK government. Be careful to distinguish between the two.

of individual ministerial responsibility used to be a significant feature of governing in the UK but in recent year it has declined in importance. The features of the principle are these:

1 Ministers must be prepared to be accountable to Parliament for the policies and decisions made by their department. This means answering questions in the House, facing interrogation by select committees and justifying their actions in debate.

2 If a minister makes a serious error of judgement, he or she should be required to resign.

3 If a serious error is made by the minister's department, whether or not the minister was involved in the cause of the error, the minister is honour-bound to resign.

4 If the conduct of a minister falls below the standards required of someone in public office, he or she should leave office and may face dismissal by the prime minister.

The erosion of ministerial responsibility

The first principle — that ministers must offer themselves to be accountable to Parliament — certainly operates successfully and is a key principle of UK government. It is fully described in Chapter 6.

The second and third principles, however, have largely fallen into disuse. There is no specific way in which Parliament can remove an individual minister. Parliament and its select committees can criticise a minister and call for their resignation, but whether or not they go is entirely in the hands of the prime minister. There was a time, long ago, when ministers did resign as a matter of principle when a serious mistake was made, but those days have largely passed. The last time a minister resigned as a result of errors made was when the education secretary, Estelle Morris, left her post voluntarily. In her resignation letter to Prime Minister Blair she said, 'with some of the recent situations I have been involved in, I have not felt I have been as effective as I should be, or as effective as you need me to be'. This was a rare event indeed. Before and since, many ministers have experienced widespread criticism and have apologised for errors made, but have not resigned or been dismissed.

This erosion of the principle does not, however, extend to the fourth type of responsibility — that which concerns personal conduct. Here, when ministers have fallen short of public standards, they have been quick to resign or been *required* to resign by the prime minister. Some recent examples are shown in Table 7.5.

Table 7.5 Ministerial resignations following personal misconduct

Date	Minister	Position	Reason (actual or alleged)
2010	David Laws	Treasury secretary	Irregularities over his expenses claims
2011	Liam Fox	Defence secretary	Employing a personal friend as adviser at public expense
2012	Chris Huhne	Energy secretary	Convicted of a serious criminal offence
2012	Andrew Mitchell	Chief whip	Allegedly insulting a policer officer in Downing Street, using abusive language

We can see from Table 7.5 that ministers are vulnerable when it comes to their personal conduct. Perhaps ironically, it is more likely that a minister will lose their job because of personal conduct rather than the quality of their performance in office.

Synoptic link

The accountability of ministers is a key aspect of how democracy operates in the setting of UK parliamentary politics. You should therefore consider individual ministerial responsibility in the light of Parliament's role of calling government to account. See Chapter 6.

Chris Huhne arriving at court

The power of the prime minister and cabinet

The sources of prime ministerial authority and power

As we saw in Chapter 5, the UK has no codified constitution. It is therefore unclear how it has come about that the prime minister is the head of government. The office originated in the early eighteenth century but Parliament has never acknowledged the position in any of its statutes. However, in order to trace the history of the position, we only need to understand the sources of the prime minister's authority and power as they stand today.

The sources of authority of the prime minister

This is quite a complex set of circumstances. They are as follows.

Traditional

The monarch is no longer a political figure but *in theory* still has considerable powers, known as prerogative powers (also known as the 'royal prerogative'). As the monarch cannot exercise these powers, she delegates them to a prime minister. There is a ritual followed that *appears* to show the monarch summoning and appointing her chosen prime minister following each general election (the PM goes to the palace to 'kiss hands', as described in the introduction to this chapter) but this is an illusion. It is simply a representation of the reality that both the monarch and the new prime minister understand. Nevertheless, the new prime minister does inherit the **traditional authority** of the monarch. The monarch's approval, though merely formal, does grant the prime minister authority.

Party

The prime minister is always the leader of the largest party represented in the House of Commons following a general election. In this case, the PM's authority comes from the people through the leading party. If and when a party changes its leader, the

> **Key term**
>
> **Traditional authority** This refers to authority which is considered legitimate because it has existed for a long historical period. The authority of the UK prime minister is traditional because he or she inherits the traditional authority of the monarchy.

Discussion point

Is it democratically acceptable that the position of prime minister can change hands without any election taking place, as occurred in 2007 and 2016?

new leader will automatically become prime minister. The queen, or monarch, will summon that leader to the palace to confirm this. No election is necessary. This does occur from time to time, usually when the existing leader loses the confidence of their party. In 1990, for example, the Conservative Party replaced Margaret Thatcher with John Major, in 2007 the Labour Party replaced Tony Blair with Gordon Brown and, more recently, Theresa May replaced David Cameron after he resigned in 2016.

Parliament

Each new parliament, including the losing parties, recognises the authority of the prime minister to lead the government. There is no formal procedure to confirm this as there is in many other political systems; it is simply 'what happens'. Parliament has no formal procedure for replacing one prime minister with another. All it can do is to dismiss the whole government through a vote of no confidence.

The people

The prime minister is not directly elected, as we have seen. Nevertheless, during a general election campaign, the people are being asked to choose between alternative candidates for the position as well as for a party. We can therefore say that a prime minister does enjoy a degree of authority directly from the people. This causes a problem for prime ministers who rise to their position without a general election taking place.

Study tip

In the introduction to this book, we suggested you should try not to use 'power' and 'authority' interchangeably. They have different meanings. Use 'authority' when you are referring to the *right* to exercise power, and use 'power' when you mean the *ability* to achieve political ends. Note, however, that in the case of the UK prime minister, they actually come to the same thing.

> **Knowledge check**
>
> What do Alec Douglas-Home, James Callaghan, John Major, Gordon Brown and Theresa May have in common?

These four different sources of prime ministerial authority amount to a formidable range. As a result of this considerable authority, the UK prime minister is also able to exercise a great deal of personal power. The sources and nature of these powers are explored below.

The sources of power of the prime minister

We have established that any UK prime minister has impressive sources of authority and this translates into considerable power, but how else does the prime minister exercise their powers? Where do these powers actually come from? The answer is that they, too, come from a variety of sources.

Prerogative powers

We have seen that the traditional authority of the monarch has long been delegated to the prime minister. This authority is often described as the *royal prerogative*. When transferred to the prime minister, it becomes **prerogative powers**. These powers are not constrained and so can be freely exercised by the prime minister personally. When exercising these powers the PM is representing the whole nation, which means the prime minister is effectively the temporary head of state.

Party

The prime minister is the leader of the largest party in the House of Commons. There have been examples of a prime minister who was not leader of the largest party, but we have to go back to the 1930s to find one (Labour's Ramsay MacDonald). Being

Key term

Prerogative powers The powers formerly exercised by the monarch without constraint, now delegated to the prime minister of the day. They include powers of patronage, conducting foreign policy and commanding the armed forces.

party leader enables the prime minister to have the power to take the lead in policy making. For as long as the PM can carry their party with them, they therefore become chief policy maker.

Patronage

Patronage refers to the power an individual may enjoy to make important appointments to public offices. Having this ability grants power because it means that those who aspire to high office will tend to be loyal to the person who may appoint them. Once appointed, that loyalty remains, not least because disloyalty may end in dismissal. The prime minister enjoys patronage over hundreds of appointments, including government ministers, peers and the heads of various state bodies. It means that the majority of MPs and peers in the prime minister's party will tend to be loyal to them. This gives the PM great power.

Parliament

The prime minister is the leader of their party in Parliament. Clearly the larger the government's parliamentary majority, the more power the PM derives from this fact, but *all* prime ministers gain some power from it. If a government is unable to secure the passage of its legislation and financial plans through the House of Commons, it will lose power. MPs are always aware of this and so those who represent the governing party tend to support their prime minister most of the time to ensure the survival of their government. An illustration of this occurred in 1995. The Conservative prime minister, John Major, became concerned and angered by the disloyalty of a number his own backbench MPs. He therefore resigned (as party leader but not as prime minister). In the subsequent leadership election he was re-elected. This was a great boost to both his authority and his power. He had re-asserted his control over Parliament.

Collective cabinet responsibility

The prime minister is the senior member of the cabinet. This is not surprising as the prime minister has control over the cabinet's membership and its agenda. These are prerogative powers as described above. It has become a convention of the UK Constitution that all members of the cabinet should be *collectively* responsible for all the decisions the government makes. Under normal circumstances no individual member of the cabinet may publicly disagree with any government decision or policy (they may disagree privately). If they do, they face dismissal or must resign in order to have an independent voice. This endows the prime minister with great power as their central government body presents a united front. With no public opposition from colleagues, the prime minister gains considerable power.

The powers of the UK prime minister

We have now reviewed the sources of the UK prime minister's authority and power. However, it has to be stressed that both are variable. Every prime minister faces a different set of circumstances. Every holder of the office has a different personality, different abilities and their own distinctive style. It is therefore worth looking at the distinctions between the powers that all prime ministers enjoy and those that vary greatly according to circumstance.

Activity

Research the changes in the cabinet made by Theresa May when she became prime minister in 2016. Which ministers lost their cabinet posts, which new ministers were appointed to cabinet and which ministers changed jobs within the cabinet? In each case, note the position(s) the minister held or lost.

Activity

Research the careers of these politicians and identify the reason why each of them resigned under the doctrine of collective responsibility:

- Robin Cook
- Clare Short
- Iain Duncan Smith

Key term

Commander-in-chief This term describes the person who has ultimate control over the deployment of the armed forces including the security and intelligence services. In the UK the prime minister holds this position, delegated by the monarch.

Formal powers (the powers that all prime ministers enjoy)	Informal powers (the powers that vary from one individual to another)
• Patronage • Chairmanship of cabinet • Foreign policy leader • Commander-in-chief* • Calling elections as long as parliament agrees • Ability to call an early general election if parliament approves with a two-thirds majority or passes a vote of no confidence.	• Controlling government policy • Controlling the legislative agenda • Economic leadership • National leadership in times of crisis

*This power is now in a state of change. See below.

Before we consider these powers, we need to discuss the role of **commander-in-chief**. Until the twenty-first century it was generally accepted that the prime minister had the sole power to commit UK armed forces to action. While the prime minister might consult with their cabinet and invite a parliamentary debate, it was acknowledged that the final decision belonged to the PM. There have been several modern examples of this prerogative power being exercised, as shown in Table 7.6.

Table 7.6 Recent examples of the exercise of prerogative power

Date	Example
1982	Margaret Thatcher sent a task force to 'liberate' the Falkland Islands in the South Atlantic from Argentine occupation.
1999	Tony Blair committed British ground troops to intervene in the Kosovo war in the Balkans.
2000	Tony Blair sent troops to Sierra Leone in West Africa to save the elected government from an armed insurgence.
2003	Tony Blair committed UK forces to assist the USA in the invasion of Iraq to depose Saddam Hussein.
2011	David Cameron committed the Royal Air Force to air strikes in the Libyan civil war to save the 'democratic' rebels.
2017	Theresa May called an early general election and successfully secured the decision with a two-thirds majority vote in the House of Commons.

All this appeared to change abruptly in 2013. It was revealed that the Syrian government was using chemical weapons against civilian populations in the civil war there. In response Prime Minister David Cameron stated his desire to intervene, using UK air power. On this occasion, however, he sought the approval of Parliament. He did not need this approval constitutionally, but he felt it was politically important to do so. To Cameron's surprise, the House of Commons voted against such action. He respected the decision and cancelled any proposed intervention. It appeared that centuries of the prerogative power to command the armed forces had been set aside. Parliament seemed to be taking over military policy.

> Miliband: Can the prime minister confirm to the House that he will not use the royal prerogative to order the UK to be part of military action, given the will of the House that is expressed tonight?
>
> Cameron: I can give that assurance…I also believe in respecting the will of this House of Commons…It is clear to me that the British Parliament, reflecting the views of the British people, does not wish to see military intervention. I get that, and I will act accordingly.
>
> The exchange between opposition leader, Ed Miliband and Prime Minister David Cameron at the end of the debate on intervention in Syria, Hansard, 30 August 2013

Two years later, in December 2015, Cameron again asked Parliament for approval for air strikes in Syria, this time against ISIS/Daesh. Parliament gave its approval and the strikes began. However, the fact that Cameron felt the need to consult MPs demonstrated the vulnerability of his position.

Protesters against the government's proposal to commence bombing in Syria, November 2015

The powers of the UK cabinet

The cabinet has a number of important roles but, surprisingly perhaps, it has relatively few powers of its own. This is largely because the prime minister has her or his own rival powers. However, we can identify a number of powers that the cabinet has, whatever the prime minister may try to do. These are as follows:

- It is the cabinet that legitimises government policy and interprets what government policy actually is. The prime minister will have a say in this, but ultimately it is a cabinet power to organise the presentation of official policy.
- Again, though the prime minister has influence, it is a specific power of the cabinet to determine the government's legislative agenda — what policies are to be implemented first and which can wait.
- The cabinet does not have absolute power to remove a prime minister. There is no such thing as a 'vote of no confidence' in the cabinet. Nevertheless, cabinet can *effectively* drive a prime minister out of power by refusing to support them in public. The removal of a prime minister has two main procedures: either forcing the prime minister to resign through public criticism (as happened to Tony Blair in 2007) or provoking a leadership contest in the governing party which the prime minister may lose (as happened to Margaret Thatcher in 1990).
- The cabinet does have the power to overrule a prime minister if it can summon up enough political will and sufficient support for an alternative policy. In 2015, for example, Prime Minister David Cameron was forced by his cabinet to suspend collective responsibility in the EU referendum campaign to allow ministers to express their own personal views.

Apart from those described above, the cabinet does not really have any powers of its own. Government power is effectively shared between the prime minister and cabinet.

The relationship between prime minister and cabinet

The cabinet during coalition, 2010–15

Before we examine the relationship between the prime minister and the cabinet, it is important to understand what happened in the unique period when there was a coalition government in the UK between 2010 and 2015.

After the 2010 general election, no party enjoyed an overall majority in the House of Commons. It was therefore necessary to form a coalition which could command such a majority. The alternative would have been a minority government. Minority government is a daunting prospect. Such a government has to build a majority of support among MPs for each *individual* legislative proposal. This is extremely difficult and the government constantly faces the imminent prospect of defeat. Minority governments have survived in Scotland and Wales, and there was a brief period of minority (Labour) government in the UK from February to October 1974, but they are rare exceptions. So in 2010, when there was a **hung parliament**, a coalition was quickly agreed between the Conservative and Liberal Democrat leaderships. The arrangements for coalition were as follows:

- As leader of the larger of the coalition partners, David Cameron was to be prime minister. Nick Clegg, leader of the Liberal Democrats, was to be deputy prime minister.
- A period of negotiation followed during which an agreed set of policies was developed — the Coalition Agreement.
- Cabinet places were apportioned to the two parties in the ratio 22:5 Conservatives to Liberal Democrats. The Liberal Democrats were given five specific ministerial positions. Non-cabinet posts were apportioned on a similar basis.
- David Cameron would control appointments or dismissals to the 22 Conservative posts and Nick Clegg controlled the five Liberal Democrat posts.
- Collective responsibility applied to all policies included in the Coalition Agreement. On other policies, ministers from the two parties were permitted to disagree publicly.

Ironically, the coalition proved to be something of a brief 'golden age' for the cabinet. Suddenly, after years of becoming less and less significant, being increasingly marginalised within government and ignored by prime ministers, the cabinet was important again. This was largely because the cabinet now had roles it had never had before:

- Disputes within the coalition were inevitable. The cabinet was one of the key places where these could be resolved.
- Presentation of policy became difficult, so the cabinet had to develop ways in which agreements between the parties could be explained.
- If there was a dispute as to whether a policy had in fact been agreed between the coalition partners (and would therefore be subject to collective responsibility), cabinet would be called on to clarify the issue.
- David Cameron did work with a kind of '**inner cabinet**'. This consisted of himself, Chancellor George Osborne, the Liberal Democrat leader, Nick Clegg, and Danny Alexander, Osborne's Liberal Democrat deputy. They were collectively known as the Quad. Cabinet is too big to serve the prime minister constantly, so such inner groups of senior ministers are common.

Activity

Research the coalition cabinet appointed in 2010. Identify which positions were filled by Liberal Democrat ministers.

Key terms

Hung parliament This describes a situation where, after a general election, no one party has an overall majority of the seats in the House of Commons. It means either a minority government or a coalition must be formed.

Inner cabinet A small group of very senior ministers, including the prime minister, who dominate the development of government policy.

Eventually, as the 2015 general election approached, the coalition cabinet weakened and began to fragment. However, the government did, against many predictions, last for 5 years and it was the temporary restoration of cabinet government that helped to maintain stability.

How the prime minister selects the cabinet

Selecting the members of a cabinet is one of the key roles played by a prime minister. If they get this wrong, they will suffer difficulties ranging from poor policy making to constant threats to their own position. It may seem simple — to choose the best men and women for the job; but there is more to it than that. Essentially, prime ministers have three ways of constructing a cabinet:

1 To pack the cabinet with the prime minister's own allies. This ensures unity and bolsters the prime minister's power, but it may lack critical voices who can improve decision making. After 1982 this was the tactic adopted by Margaret Thatcher (1979–90), an especially dominant prime minister with a great singularity of purpose. Tony Blair (1997–2007) adopted a similar approach.

2 To pick a balanced cabinet that reflects the different policy tendencies in the ruling party. When Theresa May became prime minister in 2016 she chose such a cabinet, which included some of her former adversaries such as Boris Johnson, David Davis, Andrea Leadsom and Liam Fox. It was especially important for her to include members who were both in favour of and against leaving the EU. She did, though, keep some key allies close to her, including Chancellor Philip Hammond and Home Secretary Amber Rudd. John Major (1990–97) was forced into choosing a similarly varied cabinet.

3 To pick a cabinet of the best possible people. Such a cabinet has not been seen since the 1960s and 1970s when Harold Wilson (1964–70, 1974–76) and James Callaghan (1976–79) assembled a group 'of all the talents'.

Prime ministers have complete patronage powers so they can **reshuffle** their cabinets at will. Some prime ministers have changed the personnel in this way annually. Dismissing and appointing new ministers is a device prime ministers can use for asserting and re-asserting their authority, as well as ensuring the quality of government.

> ### Key term
>
> **Reshuffle** A reshuffle occurs when a prime minister changes the make-up of their government. A major reshuffle is when a number of cabinet members are dismissed, appointed or have their jobs changed.

Prime minister and cabinet: a changing relationship

We can divide the recent history of the relationship between prime ministers and their cabinets into three periods, as shown below.

Up to the 1960s

The prime minister was seen as 'first among equals', in other words the dominant member of cabinet but not able to command government completely. Prime ministers were aware that they had to carry their cabinets with them and so had to allow genuine debate among ministers. This was often characterised as 'cabinet government'.

1960s–2010

This period is often described as one of 'prime ministerial government'. Prime ministers were expected to dominate government completely. There had to be a cabinet and decisions had to be legitimised by the cabinet, but it was not expected that the cabinet would act *as a collective body*, but rather that it should collectively support the prime minister. Successive prime ministers found ways of dominating the cabinet or simply sidelining it so that it was relatively insignificant. This is not to say that *individual* ministers could not be powerful, but that the cabinet as a body was not powerful. Former Labour cabinet member, Mo Mowlem, summed this up in 2001 when describing how Prime Minister Blair managed the cabinet. 'Mr Blair makes decisions', she said, 'with a small coterie of people, advisers, just like the president of the United States. He doesn't go back to cabinet, he isn't inclusive in terms of other cabinet ministers' (*Guardian*, 17 November 2001).

Three styles of prime ministerial domination stood out in this period:

- Harold Wilson (1964–70 and 1974–76) manipulated cabinet by controlling the agenda and discussions, and by reaching agreements with ministers outside the meetings.
- Margaret Thatcher (1979–90) dominated the cabinet through the force of her will and by ruthlessly removing or marginalising her opponents.
- Tony Blair (1997–2007) marginalised cabinet. He adopted a style known as '**sofa politics**' whereby he would develop ideas with a few advisers and senior ministers outside the cabinet in informal discussions and the present the cabinet with a fait accompli.

2010–present

We have seen that the coalition cabinet of 2010–15 restored much of the importance of cabinet. Since 2010, too, the cabinet has become more significant. Lacking a decisive majority, the prime minister has had to seek consensus *within* government, and so 'prime ministerial government' is at an end for the time being. In 2016–17 Theresa May attempted to dominate the government machinery despite her small parliamentary majority but, having failed to retain that majority in the June 2017 election, it was clear that she would have to govern with the full co-operation of her cabinet.

In theory prime ministers have several levers they can use to control cabinet. These include the following:

- The use of patronage means the prime minister can promote supporters into cabinet, remove opponents and so demand loyalty.
- The prime minister has a large machinery of policy-making support within Downing Street, which they can use to support their own position against isolated ministers.
- The prime minister controls the cabinet agenda.

Nevertheless, as we have seen, the degree to which a prime minister can successfully use these powers can vary greatly according to circumstances.

An assessment of prime ministerial power

Now that we have examined the position of the UK prime minister, including the circumstances that determine how much authority and power the holder of the office may enjoy and their relationship with the cabinet, we can attempt an overall assessment of prime ministerial power. Having done that, we can also ask the question as to whether the UK prime minister is now effectively a president.

Key term

Sofa politics A style of governing, attributed to Tony Blair, but common to other prime ministers such as Gordon Brown. It refers to the practice of conducting informal meetings with colleagues outside cabinet, often with private advisers in attendance, so as to control policy making.

Table 7.7 categorises the types of power and associated limitations or weaknesses that prime ministers experience. The powers and limitations are each divided between those that are permanent, i.e. they apply to *all* prime ministers, and those that depend on short-term circumstances.

Table 7.7 A summary of UK prime ministerial power

Permanent powers	Permanent limitations	Short-term favourable circumstances	Short-term unfavourable circumstances
Patronage	Is forced to promote senior party members who may be rivals	Large parliamentary majority	Small or no majority in the Commons
Foreign policy leader	Must consult Parliament	Events may prove to be advantageous.	Events may prove to be disadvantageous.
Party leader	Can be removed if the PM loses party confidence	A healthy, growing economy	Economic recession
Parliamentary leader	May not be able to rely on the parliamentary majority	Good media image and personal popularity	Poor media and public image
Chair of cabinet	The PM can be removed by a majority in cabinet.	The PM may lead an ideologically united cabinet.	The PM's party may become ideologically divided.

Knowledge check

Study Table 7.7 and answer these questions:

1 What circumstances shown in the table might lead to the removal of a prime minister?

2 What are two limitations on the prime minister's position as foreign policy maker?

3 When is the prime minister likely to be most dominant in cabinet?

There are also a number of *external* factors that determine how much power the prime minister can exercise. These include the following:

- Devolution, as it develops further, gradually erodes the power of both the prime minister and the UK government as a whole. When Scotland and Wales develop legislative powers there will be large parts of the country outside central control.
- While the UK was a member of the EU the powers of UK government were limited as large areas of policy were in the hands of the Council of European Ministers. When the UK leaves the EU, however, these powers will be repatriated, offering a considerable boost to the prime minister and cabinet's ability to shape policy and determine the course of events.
- Similarly the UK's membership of the North Atlantic Treaty Organisation (NATO), and especially the country's close relationship with the USA, limit the UK's foreign policy options. Prime minister and cabinet must take into account the country's main allies when conducting foreign policy. The UK's involvement in Middle East affairs is an especially important example.
- Back at home, the extent to which the cabinet can shape policy independently of the prime minister varies according to the position of the prime minister her- or himself. A dominant prime minister, as we have seen above, narrows the cabinet's scope for policy determination. When prime ministers are weak, however, the cabinet can begin to dictate policy more effectively.
- Finally, as we have seen, events significantly affect the power of cabinet and prime minister. This is mainly true of economic policy. In the early 1980s, early 1990s and after 2008, for example, economic policy making was dominated by the problems of an economic recession.

Prime ministerial case studies

Margaret Thatcher, Conservative, 1979–90

Parliamentary majorities

1979: 43

1983: 144

1987: 102

State of the party

Up to 1982–83 the Conservative Party was fundamentally split. One section was described as 'traditional' or 'one-nation' Conservatives, who believed in centrist policies, taking into account the interests of business, workers and welfare recipients equally and trying to mediate between them. They were known by their opponents as 'wets' because they were seen as weak in dealing with the UK's economic problems. The other section was known as the 'dries'. They were neo-liberals who believed in free markets, low direct taxation, privatising large industries, reducing welfare benefits to a minimum and reducing the power of trade unions. Thatcher led the latter group. From 1982 she purged the leadership of the party of the 'wets'. She dismissed her opponents from the government and replaced them with her allies. This left her at the head of a united party, agreed on her political vision.

Examples of key policies

- Privatisation of major formerly nationalised industries
- Tight control over the government finances, avoiding excessive debt
- Curbing the power of trade unions
- Reducing direct corporate and personal taxes
- Reducing government regulation of business and finance
- Strengthening the rules governing who could claim welfare benefits
- Emphasis on national defence and an active foreign policy
- Strongly confronting the Soviet Union

Style of leadership

Thatcher was an extremely dominant personality who refused to compromise with her opponents. She believed that those who were not 'with her' were against her. Her supporters called her principled and visionary while her opponents called her stubborn and uncompromising

Prominent events

Thatcher was very unpopular until 1982. She introduced unpopular measures that did not seem to be having a beneficial effect on the ailing economy. Then her fortunes turned. First, the Argentine government invaded the British Falkland Islands. She ordered a task force, which soon liberated the islands. This created her reputation as the 'iron lady'. At the same time the economy began to improve. These events increased her authority and power, and she began to transform her party in her own image. Towards the end of the 1980s, the Cold War began to ebb and the USSR was weakening. She and American President Ronald Reagan were given much of the credit for 'defeating' communism. She also resisted moves to create a stronger political union in Europe, staunchly defending British interests.

Poll tax riot in Trafalgar Square, March 1990

Circumstances of loss of power

In 1988 Thatcher and her close advisers introduced the idea of a 'poll tax' to replace local property taxes (the rates). The idea of a flat rate poll tax was hugely unpopular as it did not take account of people's incomes and so broke a fundamental principle of taxation — that it should be based on ability to pay. Despite opposition from all sides including from inside her own party, Thatcher declared she was determined to introduce it. Her opponents were dismayed and a challenge was mounted against her leadership. Some of her close allies abandoned her and she lost the leadership election in 1990. John Major replaced her.

Case study

Tony Blair, Labour, 1997–2007

Parliamentary majorities

1997: 179

2001: 167

2005: 66

Tony Blair in 2007

State of the party

From the early 1990s onwards a tight-knit group of leading members of the Labour Party developed a new set of policies designed to challenge the Conservatives and to modernise the UK. They became known as 'New Labour' and their beliefs were collectively known as the 'third way'. The third way was a path somewhere between the radical right-wing, neo-liberal policies of Thatcher and the more socialist ideas of the left wing of the Labour Party, combining the best elements of each. The group was initially led by John Smith and contained such people as Tony Blair, Gordon Brown, Robin Cook and Peter Mandelson. In 1994, however, Smith died suddenly and Blair was elected leader of the Labour Party in his place. By then New Labour had taken over most of the party. The left-wingers (of whom Jeremy Corbyn was a leading member) were only a small minority. Blair, therefore, led a united party with a clear vision and strong determination to oust the Conservatives. It was to prove as cohesive and dynamic as the Conservative group that underpinned Margaret Thatcher's authority in the mid-1980s. New Labour remained united until events began to divide the party in 2003–04. By 2007 the split in the party was so severe that Blair had to go.

Examples of key policies

- An extensive programme of constitutional reform including devolution and the Human Rights Act
- Sharp, sustained increases in expenditure on health and education
- Increased welfare benefits for those genuinely unable to support themselves
- Introducing a national minimum wage
- Introducing tax credits, mainly to reduce child poverty
- Granting independence to the Bank of England to establish more rational financial policies
- Using government financial surpluses to reduce government debt
- An active foreign policy with major interventions in the Balkans war, the Sierra Leone civil war and Iraq
- Pursuing closer links with Europe but resisting joining the eurozone
- Reducing business taxes to promote economic growth

Style of leadership

Blair was as charismatic as Margaret Thatcher. However, unlike Thatcher, he was part of a collective leadership. The key policies adopted by the Labour government after 1997 were delegated to his leading cohort. Economic policy in particular was handled by Gordon Brown and domestic social policy by other senior ministers such as Jack Straw, David Blunkett, Harriet Harman and Frank Dobson. Blair himself concentrated largely on foreign policy. After 6 or 7 years, however, Blair's leadership became more singular and his popularity in the party waned. It was widely felt that he had over-reached his authority.

Prominent events

Rarely can the fortunes of a prime minister have turned so dramatically on a single event as happened to Tony Blair. Up to 2003 the UK had enjoyed a sustained period of economic growth, public services such as health and education were improving and Blair himself had initiated two successful overseas military campaigns in Sierra Leone and Kosovo. At the same time the peace process in Northern Ireland had come to a successful conclusion with the establishment of a power-sharing government in the province. Then Blair ordered the UK armed forces to join the USA-led invasion of Iraq. The war went reasonably well but the aftermath was a disaster. In particular it was revealed that the evidence that Saddam Hussein's regime had accumulated weapons of mass destruction was false. Saddam was deposed but Iraq fell into widespread sectarian strife. Blair's stock in the country and in the party began to fall. As violence in the Middle East grew, Blair was seen in an increasingly negative light. At the same time it appeared that inequality was growing in the UK. Those who believed the Labour Party's role was to reduce inequality were dismayed. Internal opposition gathered around Gordon Brown and the party fell apart.

Circumstances of loss of power

By 2007 the momentum in the party for a change of leadership became irresistible. Tony Blair resigned before a divisive leadership contest completely destroyed party unity. He recommended that Brown should succeed him.

Gordon Brown, Labour, 2007–10

Parliamentary majority

2007: 66

State of the party

Gordon Brown was elected unopposed as Labour leader in 2007. The party, however, was now divided between the centrist 'Blairites' and the left-of-centre 'Brownites'. Brown was unable to restore unity.

Examples of key policies

- Most attention given to dealing with the post-2008 economic crisis, investing in banks to save them from collapse
- Further increases in expenditure on health and education
- Raising income tax for the wealthier members of society

Style of leadership

Brown was not seen as a natural leader. He was viewed as austere on the one hand, but indecisive on the other. His media image was negative and it was felt that he lacked Blair's vision.

Gordon Brown in 2009

Prominent events

It was not an event, but rather a non-event, that set the tone of Brown's short period in office. He was urged to call a general election in the autumn of 2007. Labour was still ahead in the opinion polls (Brown enjoyed a brief 'honeymoon period', as most new leaders do) and there was a strong political argument in favour of an election.

Of the five prime ministers described in these case studies, Brown was the only one who had not led his party to election victory. He therefore lacked a mandate from the electorate. To make matters worse, he had been elected Labour leader unopposed, so the basis of his authority was generally weak. Leading his party to election victory (most commentators agree that Labour would have won in 2007) would have given him a mandate, enhanced his authority and given him 5 years to establish himself. But Brown dithered and finally rejected the idea of an election.

No sooner had he decided to carry on without a fresh mandate than a huge financial and economic crisis broke over the developed world. Brown struggled to fend off disaster, both at home and internationally. Ironically, Brown did act decisively in the crisis but received little public or media credit for doing so. Furthermore, as chancellor of the exchequer in the years leading up to the crisis, he was partly blamed. The crisis continued for several years and completely blighted Brown's premiership.

Circumstances of loss of power

Inevitably, after the economic crisis and the growing level of public debt in the UK, Labour lost the 2010 general election, even though no party won an overall majority. Brown resigned as party leader and was replaced by Ed Miliband.

David Cameron, Conservative, 2010–16

Parliamentary majorities

2010: no majority

2015: 12

State of the party

The party that Cameron inherited in 2005 when he became leader was both demoralised by its three consecutive election defeats and divided. It has remained divided since then and this was a major barrier to Cameron becoming a dominant leader. He is, by nature, a controller, but control often eluded him. The party did unite around the need for a programme of austerity (cuts in government spending) after the 2008 financial crisis so he was able to govern effectively. The internal divisions over the UK's relationship with the EU, however, constantly made his party difficult to lead and ultimately led to his downfall.

Examples of key policies

- A programme of austerity — higher taxes and reduced public spending — to reduce the government's financial deficit

David Cameron giving his resignation speech, June 2016

- Progressive social policies including the introduction of same-sex marriage
- Promoting more devolution, mainly to Scotland
- Reducing direct taxes on those with very low or very high incomes
- Targeted reductions in welfare benefits in order to encourage more people to find work
- Subsidies for pre-school childcare to help families with young children and encourage work
- Significant rise in the minimum ('living') wage
- Introducing sharp increases in university tuition fees
- Decision to hold a referendum on UK's membership of the EU

Style of leadership

Cameron had problems exerting the personal power he would have liked to wield. To combat the barriers to his leadership he formed a strong bond with his chancellor, George Osborne, and his home secretary and eventual successor, Theresa May. He kept his rivals close by avoiding the temptation to remove them from government. Thus such opponents as Michael Gove, Iain Duncan Smith and Boris Johnson remained near the centre of power.

Prominent events

Cameron's main achievement may well be seen as his government's success in bringing the UK out of recession and stabilising the financial system. He will also be notable for having kept together a coalition for a full 5 years and followed this with an election victory. However, he has been bedevilled by foreign policy setbacks, especially when Parliament restricted his freedom of action to intervene in the Syrian civil war. Despite this mixed picture, Cameron's term in office will probably be best remembered for one single event — the referendum on the UK's membership of the European Union. The fact that he lost that referendum will define his premiership in the same way the Iraq war defined that of Tony Blair.

Circumstances of loss of power

Having led the calls for a referendum on UK membership of the EU and campaigned strongly for the UK to remain a member, it was inevitable Cameron would have to resign following defeat in the referendum.

Activity

Study the prime ministerial case studies in this chapter. Establish the following:

● Which prime ministers especially benefited from large parliamentary majorities?
● Which prime ministers enjoyed a positive media image?
● Which prime ministers lost power through a general election loss?
● Which prime ministers were removed by their own party?
● Which prime ministers were undermined by adverse events?
● Which prime ministers were most active on the international stage?

Then make a general assessment of which prime minister was most dominant and why.

Study tip

Do not assume that, because a US president is head of state and a UK prime minister is not, the former is always more powerful. Sometimes the opposite is true. This is because a prime minister can normally command his or her own majority in Parliament, whereas a US president often faces a hostile, obstructive Congress.

What can we learn from the prime ministerial case studies?

The four prime ministers described in the case studies above experienced very different sets of circumstances, some of them random. However, some generalisations can be attempted. The common features that can be identified from recent history include these:

● The size of a prime minister's parliamentary majority seems to be critical. Blair and Thatcher both benefited from large majorities for much of their terms of office. A large majority helps them in two ways. One is that it gives them strong democratic legitimacy. The other is that it makes it easier for them to secure the passage of legislation.
● Events are crucial. However favourable or unfavourable the *political* circumstances may be, prime ministers can be made or broken by events outside their control.
● Prime ministers need to head a united party if they are to be truly dominant. David Cameron is a good example of a leader who was limited by splits in their party.
● The lesson of the premierships of both Thatcher and Blair is that prime ministers who seek to stretch their power too far can expect to be reined in. Prime ministers enjoy considerable authority and have great political and constitutional powers, but if they try to overstep their authority, powerful forces will act against them to prevent them becoming too dominant. This is sometimes described as the 'elastic theory'. The further prime ministers stretch their powers, the stronger the forces will be that restrain them.

Is the UK prime minister effectively a president?

Power at the top of the UK political system is unusual. This is because the head of state, the monarch, is totally apolitical. The queen cannot become involved in politics in any way. Her leadership of the nation is purely ceremonial. This means the prime minister must assume the roles that would normally be played by a president. In the democratic world, there are, effectively, four models of high leadership. These are as follows.

The US model
The popularly elected president plays the role of both head of state and head of government. It is unique to the USA. He or she governs the country in a *partisan* way — that is, he or she is either a Democrat (usually progressive, liberal) or a Republican (conservative). However, he or she represents the USA in a *non-partisan* way, uniting the people in their collective interests as he or she sees them.

The strong president model
The best example is France. The president is elected and has considerable power, close to those enjoyed by the US president. The president, however, is not head of government. There is also a prime minister. The prime minister runs the government with other ministers on a day-to-day basis and agrees policy with the president. The president and prime minister are, therefore, rivals for power.

The weak president model
This is common in Europe. Germany and Italy are examples. The president, often nominated by the legislature rather than popularly elected, is a weak figurehead but

does play some of the roles of head of state including ceremonial ones. The president can also become politically involved, especially when it becomes difficult to form coalitions to run the government or when a weak government needs to be removed from power.

The constitutional monarchy model

The UK is an example, as are Spain, the Netherlands and Belgium. The head of state is a monarch, but he or she is powerless and largely ceremonial. In such systems the prime minister plays all the roles of both head of state and head of government. He or she is *not* head of state (unlike the US president), but simply *acts like* head of state. This makes the question 'Is the UK prime minister effectively a president?' a difficult one to answer.

Here we attempt to present the arguments on both sides, but only comparing the UK prime minister's position with the US presidency.

Debate

Is the UK prime minister effectively a president?

No

- He or she is not head of state.
- The prime minister is not directly elected.
- The prime minister's conduct of foreign policy is subject to parliamentary approval.
- The prime minister cannot commit armed forces without parliamentary approval.
- A prime minister can be removed from office by Parliament or by his or her own party.
- The powers of the prime minister are not codified in a constitution but are conventional.
- Prime ministers cannot promote patriotic support for the state as presidents often do.

Yes

- The prime minister takes on many of the roles of head of state and speaks for the nation.
- The election of the governing party owes much to the prime minister's leadership.
- Despite parliamentary constraints, the prime minister is chief foreign policy maker.
- Once in action the prime minister makes strategic military decisions.
- The prime minister controls the intelligence services at home and abroad.
- The prime minister negotiates and agrees foreign treaties.
- Some charismatic prime ministers such as Churchill, Thatcher and Blair have adopted a presidential 'style'.

Key concepts in this chapter

Cabinet committees Small subcommittees of the cabinet formed to establish the details of government policies. Their recommendations are usually adopted by full cabinet.

Cabinet government A term used to describe a situation where the main decision making of government takes place in cabinet. In modern history this is not normally the case. Its main alternative is the expression 'prime ministerial government'.

Civil servant A civil servant is employed by a government department. The most senior civil servants are involved with presenting political decision makers with information, viable options and neutral advice. They are not politicians as they are not elected and not accountable, and so cannot be involved in party politics, but they do have influence. They are permanent and are expected to serve ministers of any party equally faithfully.

Coalition A type of government, rare in the UK but common in the rest of Europe, where two or more parties share government posts and come to agreement on common policies. Coalitions occur when no single party can command a majority in the legislature.

Commander-in-chief This term describes the person who has ultimate control over the deployment of the armed forces including the security and intelligence services. In the UK the prime minister holds this position, delegated by the monarch.

Core executive The name given to the central part of government, the centre of power where key decisions are made. It is made up of a mixture of elected ministers and appointed advisers or civil servants.

Government department The work of government is divided among a number of departments. In 2017 there were 19 major departments of state. Each department is headed by a senior, normally cabinet, minister. Departments are subdivided into sections, each headed by a junior minister, normally known as ministers of state. Each department and sub-department is staffed by a bureaucracy of civil servants and some other political advisers.

Hung parliament This describes a situation where, after a general election, no one party has an overall majority of the seats in the House of Commons. It means either a minority government or a coalition must be formed.

Inner cabinet A small group of very senior ministers, including the prime minister, who dominate the development of government policy.

Prerogative powers The powers formerly exercised by the monarch without constraint, now delegated to the prime minister of the day. They include powers of patronage, conducting foreign policy and commanding the armed forces.

Reshuffle A reshuffle occurs when a prime minister changes the make-up of their government. A major reshuffle is when a number of cabinet members are dismissed, appointed or have their jobs changed.

Royal prerogative The arbitrary powers formerly enjoyed by the monarchy, but gradually transferred to the government and then to the prime minister during the eighteenth and nineteenth centuries. The powers include patronage, conducting foreign policy, negotiating foreign treaties and conducting military affairs (as commander-in-chief).

Secondary legislation This includes detailed laws and regulations passed by ministers under powers granted to them by primary legislation. Most secondary legislation does not concern Parliament, though Parliament reserves the right to debate and vote on such legislation if it is controversial.

Sofa politics A style of governing, attributed to Tony Blair, but common to other prime ministers such as Gordon Brown. It refers to the practice of conducting informal meetings with colleagues outside cabinet, often with private advisers in attendance, so as to control policy making.

Traditional authority This refers to authority which is considered legitimate because it has existed for a long historical period. The authority of the UK prime minister is traditional because he or she inherits the traditional authority of the monarchy.

Summary

Having read this chapter, you should have knowledge and understanding of the following:

→ The position of the prime minister, including how an individual comes to be prime minister
→ The roles and powers of the UK prime minister compared with the weaknesses of the office
→ Why the prime minister is so powerful but also why some prime ministers have been more powerful than others
→ The position of the cabinet, together with its structure, its procedures and its relationship with the prime minister
→ The changing importance and power of the cabinet through recent history and circumstances
→ The importance of the doctrines of collective and individual ministerial responsibility and what distinguishes them
→ The position of four recent prime ministers, their strengths and weaknesses, and the reasons for those strengths and weaknesses
→ The relationship between the prime minister and the cabinet, and the extent of prime ministerial power
→ The role, powers and importance of the prime minister compared with those of a president

Further information and web guide

Websites

Factual and up-to-date information about the prime minister and the cabinet can be found on these official websites:

www.gov.uk/government/ministers
www.cabinetoffice.gov.uk

Books

Probably the best review of the office of prime minister is Hennessy, Peter (2001) *The Prime Minister: The Office and its Holders since 1945*, Palgrave.

A shorter book is Buckley, S. (2006) *The Prime Minister and Cabinet*, Edinburgh University Press.

If you want to read about individual prime ministers, the books of Anthony Seldon are ideal. They include:

- Seldon, A. (2015) *Cameron at 10*, Harper Collins
- Seldon, A. (2011) *Brown at 10*, Biteback
- Seldon, A. (2001) *The Blair Effect*, Little Brown
- Seldon, A. (1994) *The Major Effect*, Macmillan
- Seldon, A. (1989) *The Thatcher Effect*, Clarendon

Seldon also published a book (with others) about the coalition: Seldon, A. et al. (2015) *The Coalition Effect*, Cambridge University Press.

Another book on the coalition is D'Ancona, M. (2014) *In It Together: The Inside Story of the Conservative–Liberal Democrat Coalition*, Penguin.

Lee and Beech have compiled an interesting book on the coalition: Lee, M. and Beech, S. (eds) (2015) *The Conservative–Liberal Coalition*, Palgrave.

Practice questions

AS

1 Describe the limitations on prime ministerial power. (10)

2 Describe the main functions of the cabinet. (10)

3 Using the source, assess the limitations on prime ministerial power.
In your response you must use knowledge and understanding to analyse points that are only in the source. You will not be rewarded for introducing any additional points that are not in the source. (10)

> ### How prime ministers lose power
>
> The Conservative politician of the 1960s and 1970s, Enoch Powell, commented that 'all political careers end in failure'. This assertion seems particularly true of prime ministers. Several holders of the office have lost power under unfavourable circumstances.
>
> Margaret Thatcher, one the UK's most dominant prime ministers since the Second World War, was removed from office by her own party in 1990, even after winning three general elections in a row, two with strong majorities. Tony Blair lost the confidence of his party in 2007 and resigned, and David Cameron had to leave office after his defeat in the EU referendum of 2016.
>
> Prime ministers who lose general elections are almost inevitably destined to lose their position as party leader. Gordon Brown in 2010, John Major in 1997 and James Callaghan in 1979 all relinquished their position following an election loss.

4 'The UK prime minister is now effectively a president.' How far do you agree? (30)

5 'The appointment of ministers is the prime minister's most important role.' To what extent do you agree? (30)

A-level

1 Using the source, evaluate the importance of the cabinet in policy making. *In your response you must compare the different opinions in the source and use a balance of knowledge and understanding both arising from the source and beyond it to help you to analyse and evaluate.* (30)

> ### The core executive
>
> Although it cannot be precisely defined, the core executive contains the following elements:
>
> - The prime minister and her or his close advisers.
> - The cabinet — 20–25 senior ministers appointed by the prime minister.
> - Various bodies that feed information and advice into the cabinet and to the prime minister.
> - Government departments. Of these the Treasury holds a place of special importance as it controls government finances. Many heads of these departments are members of the cabinet. Others may not be in cabinet but are nonetheless influential.
> - The senior civil servants who serve government ministers. Of these the cabinet secretary is the most senior. He or she serves both the prime minister personally and the cabinet collectively.

- Various advisers and policy-developing bodies (often called 'think tanks') that serve government departments.
- There may also be a few very senior officials of the governing party who hold no official post but who are intimately involved in policy development.

We can see that a minority of the membership of the core executive is elected. It is also true that, although the cabinet is said to stand in the centre of the executive, it has many rivals in terms of policy formulation.

2 Using the source, evaluate the extent to which prime ministers dominate the UK political system. *In your response you must compare the different opinions in the source and use a balance of knowledge and understanding both arising from the source and beyond it to help you to analyse and evaluate.* (30)

The power of the prime minister

How much power does the UK prime minister really have? On the face of it, she or he dominates the political system, but the reality may be very different.

It is especially true that the power of the prime minister will vary according to circumstances. For example, it depends upon how large a majority the governing party enjoys. The media image of the prime minister can also change over time. Tony Blair, for example, began with a positive media and public image but was widely mistrusted when he left office in 2007.

But possibly the most serious limitation on prime ministerial power lies with events beyond his or her control. Gordon Brown, for example, faced a major financial and economic crisis within a few months of taking office.

So the ability of the prime minister to determine their own destiny is severely limited. Despite all the powers they have — over patronage, foreign policy and policy making, for example — they are at the mercy of forces outside their control.

One thing is for certain: virtually all prime ministers *appear* to be more dominant when they are conducting foreign policy abroad than when they face hostile forces at home. This was especially true of Margaret Thatcher (known internationally as the 'iron lady') and Tony Blair, who specialised in foreign policy initiatives, notably in Kosovo, Sierra Leone and Iraq. Of course, though, it was a military intervention that ultimately led to his downfall. After the aftermath of the 2003 Iraq war began to deteriorate and the uncertain legal basis for the war was revealed, Blair's position in the country and inside his own party became untenable.

3 Evaluate the extent to which prime ministers dominate cabinet. Use information about at least three prime ministers. (30)

4 Evaluate the importance of collective responsibility. (30)

8 Relations between institutions

At various ceremonial occasions, walking in procession across Parliament Square, between the Houses of Parliament and the Supreme Court building in London, we can see the senior judges of the United Kingdom. They will be wearing extravagant wigs, long robes, tights and buckled shoes. Depending on our perspective, they may look extremely dignified or faintly ridiculous. Yet this historical fancy-dress show hides a serious purpose.

Parliament Square stands in the middle of the three great branches of the UK political system — the executive (represented by Downing Street, including the Cabinet Office and the civil service), the legislature (represented by Parliament) and the judiciary, whose senior members we are describing here.

When the judges walk across the square, therefore, it is symbolic of the fact that they have a central role. Apart from dispensing everyday justice, the senior judges exist to ensure that neither of the other two branches of government exceeds its powers, threatens the liberties of citizens or breaks the principle of the rule of law.

The start of the legal year includes a service at Westminster Abbey

At their head walks the Lord Chancellor, whose position is the most ancient office of state in the land. He or she (Liz Truss, appointed in 2016, was the UK's first female Lord Chancellor) is also the government's secretary of state for justice, a cabinet minister and legal adviser to the prime minister and cabinet. But today, because the Lord Chancellor is part of the government, he or she is no longer the true head of the judiciary. Since the Constitutional Reform Act of 2005, the judiciary of the United Kingdom has finally become fully independent of government.

Objectives

This chapter will inform you about the following:

→ The nature and role of the UK Supreme Court
→ The extent to which the Supreme Court protects rights and freedoms in the UK
→ The extent to which the Supreme Court can control governmental power
→ The relationship between the judicial and the executive branches of government
→ The relationship between Parliament and government in the UK
→ The extent to which government controls Parliament
→ The extent to which Parliament controls government and calls it to account
→ The changing relationship between government and Parliament
→ The full nature of sovereignty, including its various meanings and applications
→ How the location of sovereignty has changed in recent history, and its current location in the UK

Background: the nature and role of the judiciary in general

Study tip

It should be noted that Northern Ireland and Scotland have separate legal systems, so the information in this section refers mostly to England and Wales only. However, the Supreme Court is still the highest court of appeal for the whole of the United Kingdom.

Before looking at the Supreme Court specifically, we need to examine the role of the **judiciary** in general. The Supreme Court stands at the apex of the legal system and dominates it, but below it there is a large organisation of courts and judges who dispense justice.

Key term

Judiciary The name given to the branch of government that enforces the law and interprets the meaning of laws, including constitutional law.

The nature of the senior judiciary

The term 'judiciary' refers to all the judges and courts that operate in the UK. At the lowest level we can find magistrates' courts and tribunals which are presided over by a mixture of amateur, semi-professional and fully professional lawyers. These courts and judges hear criminal cases and civil disputes, and deliver verdicts in accordance with law. Though important, we are not concerned with these courts here as they are not involved with political issues. The *political* role of the judiciary does not become significant until we look at the higher levels. We are here concerned with the three top levels:

- **The Courts of Appeal, Civil and Criminal Divisions** These courts hear appeals from lower courts, either questioning the outcome of cases or in order to clarify a difficult point of law.
- **The High Court** This is actually a collection of courts dealing with civil law disputes (not criminal law), such as family law, negligence cases, reviews of government decisions and, occasionally, constitutional issues.
- **The Supreme Court** As we shall see, this is the highest court in the UK. It only hears appeals from lower courts (usually from the High Court or the Courts of Appeal). It mainly deals with interpretations of the law, which will apply widely in society.

The reason why we have to concentrate on these courts is because they are involved not just in resolving cases, but also in interpreting the meaning of law. Furthermore,

The government develops and drafts legislation.

Parliament scrutinises and passes legislation, making it legitimate.

The senior judiciary reviews laws, interprets their meaning and determines how they should be applied in real-world situations. It can also determine whether government itself is acting lawfully and whether its actions conform to higher authorities, i.e. the European Union (until the UK leaves) and the European Convention on Human Rights.

Figure 8.1 The process of law making in the UK

Key term

Formal equality

A principle which is part of the rule of law. All citizens must be treated equally under the law. The courts and judges must not discriminate against individuals or groups on any grounds.

Activity

Research the following senior members of the judiciary. What is the role played by each of them?

- The Lord Chancellor
- The Master of the Rolls
- The Lord Chief Justice
- The President of the Supreme Court

the judges who sit in these courts are highly experienced and respected lawyers. They have been appointed on the basis of their good judgement, integrity and ability to understand the real meaning and application of law. In some way, we could say, they stand at the end of the law-making process. That process is shown in Figure 8.1.

The general role of the senior judiciary

As we have seen, the senior judiciary involves the top levels of the legal system and so includes not just the Supreme Court but also the High Court and the Courts of Appeal. All these courts share the same functions. These are listed below.

Dispensing justice

Though not of directly political importance, the lower courts — magistrates' courts, Crown Courts and county courts — do have a vital role in ensuring that legal justice is delivered. This implies that all citizens should be treated equally under the law and that the law is applied to them in a fair way. Trials and hearings should all be conducted in such a way as to ensure that all parties gain a fair hearing and that the law is applied in the spirit intended. All courts, at all levels, have the task of ensuring that the rule of law is maintained. All citizens must be treated equally under the law, a principle known as **formal equality**. However, decisions as to whether the rule of law has been abused will be left to the higher courts — the High Court, Court of Appeal and Supreme Court, the latter especially.

'Making' law

It may seem obvious that Parliament in the UK makes law. This is true but it does not tell the whole story. First, not all laws are clear, nor is it clear how they are to be applied in particular cases. Second, a great deal of law is *not* made by Parliament. This is common law or equity, which is unwritten law. The judges must declare the meaning of such law if they believe it exists. So, we can say that a good deal of law is 'judge-made'. This function is explained further below.

Interpretation of the law

All lawyers and judges have to interpret the meaning of law, but it is the three top levels of the judiciary that concentrate on this function.

The precise meaning of a statute (law) is not always clear, however well the drafters of legislation have done their job, and however much parliamentary legislative committees may have tried to make the law easy to understand. There will always be circumstances where those in court — disputants in a civil case, defenders and prosecutors in a criminal case — come into conflict over what the law is supposed to mean. In such cases it is for judges to interpret the meaning of law.

In cases involving the powers of government or its agencies, or the rights of citizens, such interpretations may be of great public significance. In a sense, interpretation can be seen as the final stage in the legislative process, tying up loose ends and unclear meanings. Here, **judicial precedents** become important. Once a senior judge has interpreted the law in a certain way, and if this is a new interpretation, other judges must follow the same interpretation. A judicial precedent can only be changed or overturned by a *higher*-level court.

Case study

Regina v *Jogee* (2016)

This case is a key example of the role of the Supreme Court in examining a judicial precedent, overturning it and so re-interpreting the law. The details of the case and the appeal are as follows:

- Jogee was convicted of murder even though he had not directly killed the victim, but had encouraged an accomplice to commit the killing. The precedent was known as 'joint enterprise'. It was assumed that, in similar cases, an accomplice could be found as guilty as the person who *actually* killed the deceased if he had encouraged the crime to be committed.
- Jogee appealed against his conviction for murder in a Crown Court. The Appeal Court, Criminal Division, refused the appeal on the grounds that there were judicial precedents which suggested this was joint enterprise, so the conviction was safe.
- Jogee appealed to the Supreme Court. The precedent was overturned. Jogee was not considered to be closely enough involved with the killing to be convicted of murder.
- Jogee was retried and found guilty of the lesser offence of manslaughter. His sentence was reduced from 20 years to 12 years.
- This judgement opened the door to many similar appeals by convicted murderers in joint enterprise cases. It also means that judges in similar cases will have to be more careful in deciding whether an accomplice should be found guilty of a crime if someone else actually committed it.

The Supreme Court had effectively rewritten the law on 'joint enterprise'.

Establishing case law

As with interpretations of statute law (made by Parliament), it is not always clear how the existing laws are to be applied *in a particular case*. For example, there are laws relating to racial prejudice, discrimination against women and against actions that are likely to incite people to commit crime or to indulge in race hatred. This is all very well, but how should the law operate in *specific* circumstances? It is for judges to decide this. Furthermore, when such a decision is made, it is expected that any similar cases that arise in the future should be dealt with in the same way. Here the concept of judicial precedent (see above) also applies. Once the application of law in specific kinds of case is established, the precedents are known as 'case law'. Case law is thus established by judicial precedent.

Declaring common law

Not all law is made by Parliament. Some law is known as **'common law'** — rules of behaviour that have developed solely by tradition. In other words, they are *common* ways of dealing with disputes of various kinds. This law typically relates to such matters as inheritance, commercial practices and, very occasionally, the rights of citizens. Much common law is well enough established for judges to be able to apply it relatively easily. However, from time to time there may be problems in settling disputes for which there is no relevant statute law and no clear common law. When this happens a judge must take evidence and decide what the common law is. This is the third example of 'judge-made law'. Once again the rule of judicial precedent applies.

Examples of common law — laws which are enforced because they always have been rather than because Parliament has passed them — include the following:

- Murder
- Manslaughter

Key terms

Judicial precedent
A principle that when a judge in a court declares an important point of law, which includes the meaning of law or how it should be applied, that declaration must be followed by all other courts and judges in similar cases. In other words, it is a precedent set by a judge. Only a judge in a higher court can change or overturn a judicial precedent.

Common law Laws which have not been passed by Parliament but which are declared by judges. Either they are laws which are commonly thought to be enforceable or they are applications of law to specific cases.

- Common assault
- Misconduct in a public office
- Many commercial practices and contract issues
- Laws relating to the rights of non-married cohabiting couples

At this stage we should summarise the various ways in which law is made, including the role played by the judiciary in this process. This is shown in Table 8.1.

Table 8.1 The nature of law in the UK

Type of law	How it comes about
Statute law	Laws passed by the UK Parliament or the Scottish Parliament
Administrative law	Regulations made by ministers under powers granted by Parliament
Case law	Interpretations by courts of how the law should be applied in particular types of case
Common law	Law that has not been written down or passed by Parliament but which comes about through traditional practices. It exists when judges declare that it exists.
Equity	Law declared by a court where no other kind of law can be found. It is based on the general concept of what most people understand as 'fairness'.
Judicial precedent	Interpretations of existing law or declarations of new law made by judges in difficult cases
Remaining EU law	After March 2019 all existing EU law will become UK law with the same status as statute law. Some of it may well be repealed at later dates.

Key term

Judicial review A process whereby the courts review decisions by the state or any public body in relation to its citizens. Where a review finds that a citizen has not been treated fairly, or that their rights have been abused, or that a public body has exceeded its legal powers, the court may set aside the decision.

Conducting judicial reviews

Citizens or groups of citizens may feel they have been mistreated by a public body, usually part of the state at central or local level. When this happens there is an opportunity to seek a **judicial review** by the courts. The review will examine whether the citizens' claims are justified. The purpose of the review for the citizens concerned is to establish the wrongdoing and may involve either compensation or simply the reversal of a decision. The quantity of cases involving judicial review has grown dramatically since the 1960s.

The Royal Courts of Justice, where the High Court and the Court of Appeal sit

Two cases led to a steady growth in the use of such reviews: *Ridge* v *Baldwin* in 1964 and *M* v *Home Office* in 1993. These cases extended the use of judicial review to claims that the government had not followed natural justice and to claims that the government may have acted above or outside the law.

Typical examples of judicial review more recently are cases where a minister or civil servant has not dealt equally with different citizens, or where there has been a clear injustice, or where government or a public body has exceeded its statutory powers. Judicial reviews increased after 1977 when the procedures for citizens who wished to call for a judicial review of a decision by the courts were simplified.

Judicial review is a critical role because it helps to achieve two democratic objectives. One is to ensure that government does not overstep its powers. The second is to assert the rights of citizens. The courts were given an enormous boost in this area when the **Human Rights Act 1998** came into force in 2000. This meant that courts could review actions by government and public bodies that might contravene the European Convention on Human Rights. At the same time, the **Freedom of Information Act**, which came into force in January 2005, gives citizens and the courts a right to see a much wider range of official documents than before. In this way there is considerably more scope for discovering whether injustice has been done and whether rights have been abused.

The number of judicial reviews being considered rose to a peak in 2013 when over 15,000 applications for review were made. However, most of these were refused. The number of judicial reviews has now settled down to a reasonable number. In 2014, 4,062 cases were heard, of which 36% were successful and led to a change in a decision by a public body. It is now expected that the number will settle at about 4,000 per annum with about one-third successful.

Holding public inquiries

Although it is not necessarily always the case, judges are often called upon to conduct public inquiries into matters of widespread public concern. The reason for using judges is twofold. First, as experienced judges, they are used to handling such issues. Second, they are independent of government so that an inquiry led by a judge can be seen to be politically neutral. Table 8.2 shows a number of such inquiries held in recent times. In each case, the chair was a current or former judge.

Synoptic link

The Human Rights Act and the Freedom of Information Act are discussed further in Chapter 5.

Activity

1 Research the two cases referred to above, *Ridge* v *Baldwin* (1964) and *M* v *Home Office* (1993). What was the case about, which court heard the case, why was it brought and what was the outcome?

2 Find out the same information about *R* v *Ministry of Justice* (25 June 2014).

Activity

Research these two reports and describe the main elements of their outcome:

● Leveson Inquiry
● Gibson Inquiry

Table 8.2 Examples of judge-led public inquiries

Inquiry name	Publication date	Detail
Macpherson Inquiry	1999	To examine the handling by the police of the case of the murder of black teenager Stephen Lawrence
Hutton Inquiry	2003	Into the circumstances surrounding the apparent suicide of civil servant David Kelly, a weapons expert, following questions over his role in the report on Saddam Hussein's 'weapons of mass destruction' in Iraq
Leveson Inquiry	2012	Into the conduct of the press following allegations of widespread 'phone hacking' by journalists in pursuit of stories
Gibson Inquiry (in suspension at time of writing)	2013	Into allegations that UK intelligence forces were involved with US forces in the torture of terrorist suspects

Sentencing issues

Judges have become increasingly involved in issues concerning sentencing in criminal cases. This is an intensely *political* issue and so has jeopardised the traditional neutrality of the senior judiciary. However, judges used to have a much freer hand in deciding what sentences to give out. The only major restrictions were homicide cases of various kinds, where a life sentence was mandatory, and the general use of maximum sentences determined by Parliament.

Since the mid-1990s, however, when growing crime rates became a major political issue, politicians have sought to take control away from judges and to force their hand in various ways. The judges have resisted on the grounds that they should be independent from government and that they are the best judges of each individual case. Politicians counter this by saying that judges are not accountable to the public. The public have shown a clear preference for more severe sentencing in general, so judges should be forced to respond to public opinion. The dispute goes on, but politicians appear to be winning by introducing *minimum sentences* for certain offences and for repeat offending. This takes away most of the flexibility that judges formerly enjoyed. This remains a current issue, especially with the treatment of offenders convicted of very minor drugs offences. The government is trying to keep such offenders out of prison.

The Constitutional Reform Act 2005

In 2005 Parliament passed the **Constitutional Reform Act**. Among other measures, the Act was designed to improve and guarantee the independence of the UK judiciary. Before the Act it had always been *claimed* that the senior judges in the UK were independent of political influences, but there was mixed evidence as to whether such independence was being upheld. After the Act, however, there were fresh guarantees in place which have largely removed those doubts.

The central feature of the Act was the establishment of the Supreme Court. The court became active in 2009. Before the Supreme Court was established, the highest court in the UK was situated in the House of Lords and was, therefore, a part of the legislature. This was a strange anomaly, almost unheard of in the democratic world.

The old system worked like this:

- Twelve 'Lords of Appeal in Ordinary', commonly known as the Law Lords, were members of the House of Lords. They were expected to be neutral crossbenchers but were free to take part in the business of the Lords.
- At the head of the Law Lords was the Lord Chancellor. He (all Lord Chancellors were men before 2016) had three roles. First he was Speaker of the House of Lords, i.e. the chairman of its meetings. This made him a member of the legislature. Second, he was also a cabinet minister, responsible for the direction and management of the UK legal system. This made him a political figure and a member of the executive. Third, he was the head of the judiciary, the most senior judge in the UK. Far from being an independent figure, therefore, he was a member of all three branches of government!
- The Lord Chancellor played a full part in advising the government on legal policy, in the appointment of senior judges and in deciding which of the Law Lords would hear each appeal case.
- When a case was brought to the highest court in the land, it would usually be heard by a group of Law Lords, normally five. So, when it was said that 'a case was heard by the House of Lords', it actually meant that it was heard by a small group of these senior judges, not the whole House.

Study tip

If you read a book published before 2005 or look at legal cases heard before 2009, when the Supreme Court started operating, you may see mention of the 'House of Lords' or 'Law Lords'. This is because, before the Supreme Court was established, the 12 senior judges, who also sat in the House of Lords, operated as the highest appeal court; in other words very much as the Supreme Court does today. So it carried out broadly the same functions.

- Not only did the Lord Chancellor play a leading role in appointing senior judges, but the prime minister him- or herself would have the final say if he or she felt so inclined.

Senior judges at the State Opening of Parliament

The Constitutional Reform Act changed all this in a number of key ways. These are described below.

The establishment of the Supreme Court

As we have said, the Constitutional Reform Act was mainly designed to reaffirm and guarantee the independence of the judiciary in the UK. Its main provisions were as follows:

1 The Lord Chancellor was no longer head of the UK judiciary as had been the case for centuries. This was now the Lord Chief Justice, a non-political figure and a senior judge. The Lord Chief Justice is also known as the President of the Courts of England and Wales (Scotland and Northern Ireland have their own chief judges).

2 The position of Lord Chancellor still exists and the holder combines the position with that of justice secretary in the cabinet. However, he or she is no longer an active member of the judiciary.

3 The Lord Chancellor was no longer to be the Speaker of the House of Lords and ceased to sit in the House of Lords.

4 The Supreme Court was established. It contains 12 senior judges known as Justices of the Supreme Court.

5 The head of the Supreme Court is known as the President of the Supreme Court.

6 When there is a vacancy in the court, a Selection Commission is established, consisting of a number of senior law officers from the whole of the UK. The commission recommends a candidate to the Lord Chancellor.

> **Study tip**
>
> Do not confuse the position of Lord Chancellor with that of the chancellor of the exchequer — a different post charged with handling the nation's finances.

7 In theory the Lord Chancellor can question whether a candidate is suitable but he or she does not have an absolute veto.

8 The Act reaffirmed the principle that a Supreme Court judge can only be removed by a vote in both houses of Parliament and only for misconduct, *not* as a result of their decisions. The salary of the judges is also guaranteed. This means they have security of both tenure and salary.

Thus the independence of the judiciary and the Supreme Court in particular were finally codified in law. Furthermore, the Lord Chancellor was charged with the task of guaranteeing and maintaining the independence of the Supreme Court and the rest of the judiciary from political or public pressure.

Knowledge check

Who were the 'Law Lords' and what replaced them?

The nature of the Supreme Court

The Supreme Court is made up of 12 of the country's most senior judges. The court is known as the highest appeal court in the country. During the UK's membership of the European Union, cases could be appealed to the European Court of Justice, but this will no longer apply after the UK leaves the EU. Cases concerning human rights can be taken to the European Court of Human Rights in Strasbourg, France, though there is no guarantee that the UK government or Parliament will obey its judgements.

The Supreme Court does not hear any cases in 'the first instance'. This means that the cases it hears have already been heard in a lower court. The court will only hear cases it believes are important. The reasons why the Supreme Court may allow a case to be brought to it include the following:

The Supreme Court

- It may be an important judicial review (see above) concerning the government or some other important body such as a school or a newspaper or the NHS. The court may need to establish what legal powers such bodies have.
- The case would have implications for other citizens and bodies — in other words, if it may create an important precedent to be followed elsewhere.
- It involves an important interpretation of law. It may be that lower courts have been unable to make a judgement about the meaning of law. The Supreme Court will examine what Parliament's *intention* was when it originally passed the law.
- It may be a case that has attracted a great deal of public interest.
- A key issue of human rights might be at stake.

Not all the Supreme Court judges hear the cases; there is normally a selection of five (though as many as 11 may sit on a key case). In such cases the judgement will need a majority (i.e. three) of the judges to agree. Once the case has been decided, the law is firmly established. Only the European Court of Human Rights might seek to reverse the judgement if human rights are at stake. The judgements are published, including the reasons for them.

Table 8.3 illustrates the variety of cases heard by the Supreme Court.

Knowledge check

Which body was responsible for establishing the terms of the European Convention on Human Rights?

Table 8.3 Recent Supreme Court cases of special interest

Case and date	Details	Principle at stake	Outcome
PJS v *News Group Newspapers* (2015)	An unnamed celebrity sought to prevent the media publishing details of his private life as it would infringe his privacy.	Extent of the right to privacy and freedom of expression	The Supreme Court ruled the celebrity's privacy should be upheld and took precedence over freedom of the press.
Vince v *Wyatt* (2015)	Ms Wyatt and Mr Vince divorced, after which Mr Vince became very wealthy. Ms Wyatt made a claim for considerable maintenance based on Mr Vince's new wealth, though the couple had been poor when married.	Interpretation of family law	It was ruled that Ms Wyatt did have a right to make such a claim after many years, opening the door to many similar cases.
Trump International Golf Club v *Scottish Ministers* (2015)	Donald Trump argued that a decision by the Scottish government to allow a wind farm to be built near his new golf course was beyond its powers.	**Ultra vires**. Trump argued the government was acting beyond its legal powers.	Trump lost the case. The Supreme Court agreed the Scottish government had acted within its powers.
Schindler v *Duchy of Lancaster* (2016)	Whether British citizens who have lived abroad for over 15 years should be able to vote in the 2016 EU referendum	Rule of law (equality under the law). Were such citizens suffering discrimination?	The court ruled the government had the right to deny them the vote for administrative reasons.

The judiciary (especially the Supreme Court) and Parliament

Parliament in the UK is *sovereign*. As we have seen, this is a fundamental feature of the country's constitutional arrangements. This means that the judiciary is a *subordinate* body. The judges are simply not in a position to defy the will of the UK Parliament. Furthermore, the UK Parliament is **omnicompetent**. This means it is able to do whatever it wants, to pass any law and to expect to have that law implemented and enforced. No matter how abhorrent or undesirable the judges may feel a law is, they must enforce it. They may pass an opinion on the law and they may recommend change, but that is as far as it goes.

Synoptic link

The powers of Parliament and its sovereignty are explored fully in Chapter 6.

Key term

Ultra vires A legal principle that literally means 'exceeding one's power'. When an action is ruled ultra vires by a court, it means the individual or body that takes a particular action was exceeding its legal power. Such actions will be set aside.

Key terms

Omnicompetence Literally this means 'ability to do everything'. In the context of the UK Parliament it means that nothing and nobody can constrain Parliament, whatever is being proposed.

Declaration of incompatibility
A declaration made by a judge that a particular UK law is in conflict with the terms of the European Convention on Human Rights. This does not make the law invalid, as Parliament is sovereign, but it advises Parliament and government to think again about the law and whether to make it compatible.

Habeas corpus A Latin term literally meaning 'you have the body'. It is a very old principle, dating back to before Magna Carta in 1215. It states that no individual or body, including government, shall detain a person against their will unless they can be charged and brought to trial quickly.

Activity

Research the Afghan hijackers' case, *S and others* v *Home Secretary* (2006). Describe what this case tells us about the relationship between the ECHR and parliamentary law.

Judges have to take into account the wishes of Parliament when interpreting law. When determining the real meaning of statute law, judges will look back at the original proceedings in order to establish what Parliament *intended*. It is not for the judges to decide what is desirable, but only what *Parliament thought* was desirable.

Of course, if judges make a ruling of which government and/or Parliament does not approve, Parliament always has the option of amending a statute or passing a new one in order to correct what the judges have done. Such a circumstance occurred in 2010. The Supreme Court ruled that the government did not have the power to freeze the bank assets of terrorist suspects. Prime Minister Brown was incensed but had to accept the judgement temporarily. In the event, though, a new statute was passed later the same year (the **Terrorist Asset-Freezing Act 2010**) granting such a power to the government. The will of Parliament ultimately prevailed. The Supreme Court could do nothing about it.

Parliament and the European Convention on Human Rights

The most important source of conflict between the judges and Parliament, however, occurs in relation to the European Convention on Human Rights (ECHR). The ECHR became part of UK law in 1998 through the **Human Rights Act**. This presents potential problems. What happens if a parliamentary statute conflicts with part of the ECHR? The ECHR is part of UK law but Parliament is sovereign. What are the judges to do? The answer is that the law made by Parliament shall be allowed to stand. All the judges can do is to make a **declaration of incompatibility**, stating that the law conflicts with the ECHR. It is then up to Parliament whether it sticks to its original intention or listens to the judges and changes the law to make it compatible with the ECHR.

The Belmarsh case of 2004 illustrated this problem. Nine suspected terrorists had been held for several years without trial in Belmarsh prison. This was under the terms of the **Crime and Security Act 2001**. They appealed against their detention. The Law Lords (this pre-dated the establishment of the Supreme Court) ruled that the 2001 Act was incompatible with the ECHR. As a result, the government chose to heed the judge's warning and released the prisoners. Detention for such suspects was replaced by control orders, restricting their movement, by the **Prevention of Terrorism Act 2005**. The UK Parliament and government did not have to do this, but it was viewed as essential if the UK was to preserve its reputation for respecting human rights. On this occasion the judges had their way — they asserted the ancient freedom of citizens not to be detained indefinitely without trial, a principle known as **habeas corpus**.

Perhaps fortunately, such declarations of incompatibility are rare. Between 2010 and 2015 there were only three such declarations. In each case, however, the government asked Parliament to amend the existing law to remove the conflict with the ECHR. Despite this small number, the principle is an important one. What is means is that those who draft legislation and those who scrutinise it in Parliament must take account of the ECHR. The mere threat of a declaration by judges is enough to influence law making. It is also a vital protection of human rights in the UK.

In summary, the relationship between the judiciary, especially the Supreme Court, and Parliament is dominated by the principle of parliamentary sovereignty. When the courts come to one conclusion and Parliament comes to another, Parliament will always prevail. This is because Parliament is elected and therefore accountable to the people. The courts and judges are, by contrast, not elected and therefore not accountable.

The judiciary (especially the Supreme Court) and the executive

Until the 1970s the relationship between the UK judiciary and the UK government was very different from what it has become. The judiciary was seen as a largely conservative body whose members came from the same social and political background as members of successive Conservative governments. The judiciary usually showed support for the power of the state in relation to its citizens. Judges were not expected to challenge the authority of government in any significant way. They saw themselves as servants of the state rather than an equal partner. This relationship has changed considerably for a number of reasons:

- The growth of judicial review since the 1960s (see *Ridge* v *Baldwin* (1964) and *M* v *Home Office* (1993) on page 271)
- The rise of liberal ideology in the UK from the 1960s onwards, including the growth of what is sometimes known as the 'rights culture'
- The appointment of a series of liberal–minded senior judges since the 1990s
- The passage of the Human Rights Act in 1998, giving judges a codified statement of human rights which could be used to protect citizens against state power
- The Constitutional Reform Act of 2005, which improved the independence of the judiciary in general

So the UK judiciary no longer sees itself as subordinate to the executive. Judges are no longer reluctant to challenge state power and to assert the rights of citizens. In short, the judiciary has become something of a counterbalance to executive power.

On the other hand, government does have a claim to greater authority than the judiciary. Furthermore, as long as it can control its majority in Parliament, it can use the sovereignty of Parliament to reverse any decisions made by the judiciary. However much they may protest, the judges must, by law, enforce the will of Parliament. Table 8.4 summarises the rival claims made by the executive and the judiciary to enforcing justice and the rule of law.

Study tip

You can use the terms 'the judges' and 'the judiciary' interchangeably. They mean the same thing.

Table 8.4 Who has the stronger claim to establishing justice and rights?

The claims of government	The claims of the judiciary
Government is elected and accountable. Judges are neither elected nor accountable.	Judges do not allow political considerations to interfere with their protection of rights.
Government has a clear mandate to run the country and to protect its citizens.	As qualified lawyers, judges bring a totally rational bearing to questions of law and justice.
Government can respond to public opinion.	Judges are expected to be immune to outside influences.
Government has an overarching responsibility to protect citizens even if it means setting aside individual rights in the interests of national security.	Because they are not elected, judges can take a long-term view while politicians have to consider their short-term re-election prospects.

R (Miller) v Secretary of State for Exiting the European Union (2016)

This case was heard originally in the High Court, Queen's Bench Division, in October 2016 and was brought to appeal in the Supreme Court later in the same year. It is possibly the most important constitutional case to appear in the courts in recent history and illustrates well the relationship between the judiciary and government, as well as the relationship between Parliament and government.

Gina Miller, a private citizen, requested a judicial review of whether the Secretary of State for Exiting the European Union (David Davis) had the prerogative power to trigger Article 50 of the EU which would start the process of the UK's departure. Her legal argument was that Parliament is sovereign and this stands above the claimed prerogative power to bring the UK out of the EU. The government's position was that it *did* have such a prerogative power.

The High Court ruled that the government did *not* have such a prerogative power and that the sovereignty of Parliament had to be exercised in this case. This was because departure from the EU would affect the rights of UK citizens in some cases. This ruling was later upheld in the Supreme Court. It forced the government to seek parliamentary approval to trigger Article 50 and begin the process of leaving the EU. Two extracts from the High Court's judgement are especially significant:

> The courts have a constitutional duty fundamental to the rule of law in the same way as the courts enforce other laws.

and:

> We hold the Secretary of State does not have the power under the Crown's prerogative [i.e. the royal prerogative] to give notice pursuant to Article 50 of the Treaty of the European Union for the UK to withdraw from the European Union.

The High Court decision was emphatically confirmed by the Supreme Court in January 2017.

The Miller case illustrates a number of constitutional realities:

- That it is for the judiciary to determine the limits of the government's prerogative powers
- That the rule of law is superior to political considerations
- That Parliament is sovereign over such matters in that the decision to leave the EU affects the rights of EU citizens and so the government must obtain parliamentary approval
- That referendums are not legally binding and their outcome must be confirmed by Parliament, not government

Following the case, several newspapers proclaimed that the judiciary was attempting to defy the will of the people, but politicians of all parties rushed to defend the judiciary, arguing that its independence from such pressures must be resisted.

Gina Miller talking to the press after the Supreme Court confirmed the High Court's decision in January 2017

Study tip

You should learn the details of the Miller case and use it to illustrate the relationships between the three branches of government.

The Supreme Court and rights

We have seen that the Supreme Court has a role in controlling the power of government and establishing the meaning of law alongside Parliament. But it has one other role. This is the protection of rights in the UK. It does this together with the European Court of Human Rights in Strasbourg. There are a number of ways in which the Supreme Court protects human rights:

Synoptic link

The protection of rights in the UK is a key political issue involving Parliament, the courts and pressure groups. It is discussed as a political issue in Chapter 5. Rights must therefore be viewed as both a political and a legal issue.

- Citizens or groups of citizens may appeal to the court on the grounds that a public body of some kind has abused their rights in some way. This might be central, regional or local government; a school or hospital; or any other agency of the state. In this regard the court will refer to both the European Convention on Human Rights, which is binding in the UK, and UK law, either statute or common.
- Through cases of 'ultra vires'. This is where appellants are claiming that a body, such as a government minister or local authority, has acted beyond its legal powers (ultra vires literally means 'beyond power'). If the court finds a body has acted ultra vires, it may set aside the action or even order compensation.
- An appeal may be based on a claim that the rule of law has not been applied in a case or a decision. The rule of law principle states that everyone must be treated equally under the law. Such cases revolve around a claim that a citizen or group of citizens has suffered unequal treatment.
- In common law cases, the court examines whether a common law right has been abused.

Table 8.5 shows examples of cases concerning rights that have been brought before the Supreme Court.

Activity

Research the following two cases and summarise the courts' decision and its significance. (Try the Supreme Court website **www.supremecourt.uk**.)

- *Regina* v *Hughes* (31 July 2013)
- *Regina* v *Ngango* (14 December 2011)

Table 8.5 Rights cases in the Supreme Court

Case	Issue	Principle involved	Outcome
Radmacher v *Granatino* (2010)	Whether pre-nuptial agreements can be enforced in law	Meaning of both common and statute law	Such agreements were ruled enforceable.
R v *Metropolitan Commissioner of Police* (2011)	Whether the DNA records and fingerprints of innocent people can be retained by the police	Meaning of right to privacy as declared in the European Convention	The Supreme Court ruled such records cannot be kept and should be destroyed.
Evans v *Attorney General* (2015)	An appeal from the Freedom of Information Tribunal — whether Prince Charles' letters to the government should be published	Meaning of the Freedom of Information Act	The court ruled the letters should be published under the Freedom of Information Act.

The European Court of Human Rights

Where there has possibly been a breach of the European Convention, the case may be taken to the European Court of Human Rights in Strasbourg, France. This court, made up of judges from different European countries, will examine cases in the light of their interpretation of the meaning and scope of the convention. Their decision is final. Table 8.6 shows a variety of cases in recent years to illustrate the breadth of its work.

Study tip

Be sure you understand the differences in the roles of the European Court of Human Rights and the European Court of Justice (ECJ).

Table 8.6 Cases brought from the UK to the European Court of Human Rights

Case	Year of decision	Details	Article of the ECHR concerned	Outcome
Shireby v *UK*	2009	Shireby (a man) had been refused the full 'widow's benefit' when his wife died. He claimed he was discriminated against on the grounds of his gender.	Article 14 (anti-discrimination on the grounds of sex)	The appeal was allowed. UK law was effectively changed.
McDonnell v *UK*	2014	McDonnell was a Northern Ireland terrorist suspect who died in custody in 1996. There was a delay of 17 years before the inquest into his death.	Article 2 (the right to life)	The appeal succeeded. McDonnell's mother was awarded 18,000 euros in costs and damages.
NJDB v *UK*	2015	NJDB (name withheld) appealed against a decision *not* to grant him legal aid for his child custody case.	Article 6 (right to a fair trial and fair access to justice)	The appeal was refused.
Voting rights for UK prisoners	2015	A group of over 1,000 prisoners appealed against a ban on their right to vote.	Article 3 (right to a free election)	The appeal was allowed but the UK government has refused to comply with the ruling, quoting the sovereignty of Parliament.

Activity

Research the following two cases in the European Court of Human Rights. In each case establish the basic facts of the appeal, which part of the ECHR was concerned, and the outcome of the case.

- *Abdi* v *UK* (9 April 2013)
- *Abu Qatada* v *UK* (17 January 2012)

European Court of Human Rights

It should be noted that any judgement made by the European Court of Human Rights applies to all 47 countries that have signed up to the ECHR, not just in the country from where the appeal was launched. So, the interpretations of law shown in Table 8.6 apply not only to the UK, but to all 47 countries which agree to the convention. Similarly, interpretations of law in cases from other countries apply in the UK, and all UK courts, including the Supreme Court, must apply those interpretations. That said, the UK can call upon the sovereignty of Parliament to defy the court. As long as the UK Parliament insists that one of its statutes should stand, even the European Court of Human Rights cannot enforce its judgement (this occurred when the UK refused to allow prisoners to vote in 2015 despite the court's ruling to the contrary).

So, the relationship between the European Court of Human Rights and the European Convention on Human Rights remains somewhat ambiguous. This is because the UK has never given up the principle of parliamentary sovereignty in the area of rights. The most appropriate version of the relationship is, therefore, that judgements of the European Court of Human Rights are morally and politically binding on the UK, but not constitutionally or legally binding.

Knowledge check

Outline two differences between the US Supreme Court and the UK Supreme Court.

The independence of the judiciary

An essential feature of any healthy democracy is that the judicial branch should be independent of the government. There are a number of reasons why this is so:

- If judges are not independent, there is a danger that the government will exceed its powers without legal justification. Without any effective check on government power, tyranny may result.
- Citizens need to feel certain that any legal cases with which they may become involved will be dealt with on the basis of justice and the rule of law. It may suit government to discriminate against individuals or groups in society for its own benefit. An independent judiciary can prevent such discrimination. The citizens of a democratic state must feel that their rights will be effectively protected.
- It is important that judges are not influenced by *short-term* changes in public opinion, reflected by politicians. Independent judges can take a long-term view. For example, following a terrorist atrocity, there may be calls for curbs in individual liberties. However, such curbs may harm the cause of human rights in the long term.
- In some political systems the judiciary may appear to be independent, but in practice the judges are specially selected by the government to ensure decisions that are friendly to that government. Independence, therefore, also implies that judges are selected on a neutral basis to prevent collusion between the judiciary and the government.

How is independence of the judiciary maintained?

There are four main ways in which **judicial independence** is guaranteed in the UK. These are: security of tenure, rules of sub judice (i.e. when something is the subject of an ongoing court case), the system of appointments and the background of senior judges.

Security of tenure

The first and key principle that attempts to ensure the political independence of the judiciary is security of tenure. This principle says that judges cannot be removed

Key term

Judicial independence
The principle that judges should be independent of government, Parliament, public opinion and media influence. It is a key principle of modern democracy in that it can protect human rights, maintain the rule of law and act as a check on the power of the state.

from office on the grounds of the kinds of decisions that they make. The only reason a judge can be removed is if they can be shown to be corrupt as a result of personal conduct incompatible with being a judge. It follows, therefore, that judges are free to make decisions without fear of dismissal, even if such decisions offend the government. For the same reason, judges are appointed on the understanding that their salaries cannot be reduced if they make contentious decisions.

Contempt
Second, it is a contempt of court for any servant of the government to attempt to interfere with the result of a court case or even to comment on such a case in public or in Parliament. This rule is designed to prevent any political pressure being placed upon judges. Any such interference would be strongly criticised in Parliament and could result in legal action against the government member concerned.

Independent appointments
The appointments system was reformed in 2005. Most judges are now appointed by a Judicial Appointments Commission. This is politically independent. Judges in the Supreme Court and Appeal Court (Civil Division) are appointed by a special committee comprising senior members of those courts and representatives from the Judicial Appointments Commissions in England, Scotland and Northern Ireland. This sounds complex, but the significance is simple — that there can now be little or no political influence on sensitive judicial appointments.

Training and experience
Finally, it should be pointed out that all senior judges must have enjoyed a lengthy career as lawyers. This means that they are accustomed to the principle that cases must be judged on the strict basis of law and not according to their personal opinions. Indeed, junior judges who gain a reputation for lack of impartiality are most unlikely to be put up for promotion.

In case one is tempted to be sceptical about these safeguards, there is a great deal of evidence to suggest that the UK judiciary is indeed politically independent. Under both Conservative and Labour administrations, senior members of the judiciary have made a large number of judgements that have been clearly contrary to government interests. This has been especially true since the implementation of the Human Rights Act in 2000. Indeed, it is significant that politicians of *both* the main parties have criticised the judiciary on the grounds that it is politically biased. This implies that there is little or no political bias among judges.

Are judges really independent and neutral?
The rule of law demands that judges be not only independent but also neutral. Neutrality implies that judges should have neither a bias towards any particular political philosophy (such as liberalism, socialism or conservatism) nor a bias in favour of or against any section of society. In the past, UK judges were often thought of as white, male conservatives from privileged backgrounds and therefore unlikely to be neutral. While the social profile of senior judges has changed little in recent times, the suspicions that they may not be neutral has receded. The main charge against them recently, indeed, has been that they are too liberal and they favour individual rights above the security of the state, but the evidence is unreliable. Table 8.7 shows the main arguments as to whether judges are independent and **neutral**.

> **Key term**
>
> **Judicial neutrality** The idea that judges should have no political bias and should not favour one section of society over another, but should always impose the rule of law whereby all are treated equally, including government.

Table 8.7 Are UK judges independent and neutral?

Arguments that they are independent and neutral	Arguments that they may not be independent and neutral
The Constitutional Reform Act 2005 removed most threats to their independence.	Ministers do have some influence over the final appointments of the most senior judges.
Judges cannot be removed by ministers as a result of their decisions. They have security of tenure.	The neutrality of judges is sometimes challenged on the basis that they come from a very narrow social background, being virtually all white males from comfortable backgrounds and privately educated.
Judges cannot be threatened with loss of income if politicians are unhappy with their decisions.	Some rights campaigners argue that some members of the judiciary tend to favour the establishment over citizens' rights.
Ministers have little or no influence over which judges are appointed. Appointments are largely independent of politics.	On the other hand, some conservative politicians claim the judiciary contains too many lawyers of a liberal disposition who tend to favour rights over state security and law and order.
There is no recent evidence of bias either in favour of or against governments. Both Labour and Conservative governments have equally been controlled by judicial decisions.	
Judges uphold the rights of all sections of society and so appear to be neutral.	

How powerful is the Supreme Court?

Since 2005, when it was set up, there has been much attention paid to the Supreme Court. For many rights campaigners and commentators who fear the rise of executive power, the court has largely been a success. As proof of this, many senior politicians have criticised the court for being *too* independent and for challenging the authority of government.

Nevertheless, the court still has its weaknesses. In particular, it has to recognise the sovereignty of Parliament. The UK has no entrenched constitution, so the court has no power to enforce constitutional principles against the wishes of Parliament. In the USA the Supreme Court in Washington *can* strike down legislation passed by Congress or decisions made by government if it believes they have breached the constitution.

Table 8.8 assesses the strengths and weaknesses of the UK Supreme Court.

Table 8.8 How much power does the Supreme Court have?

Powers	Weaknesses
The independence of the court is guaranteed in law.	It cannot activate its own cases but must wait for appeals to be lodged.
It can set aside executive actions that contradict the ECHR or the rule of law.	The sovereignty of Parliament means that its judgements can be overturned by parliamentary statute.
It can interpret law and so affect the way it is implemented.	The European Court of Human Rights can hear appeals from the court and overturn the decision, but this is not binding.
It cannot overrule the sovereignty of Parliament but it can declare proposed legislation incompatible with the ECHR, which is influential.	
With the UK leaving the EU, its judgements cannot be overturned by a higher court.	

The relationship between the executive and Parliament

Synoptic link

This section should be read in conjunction with Chapters 6 and 7, which explore the nature of Parliament and the executive.

How Parliament controls the executive

In past times, it was common to refer to the position of the executive in the UK as an **elective dictatorship**. This implied that, having been elected with a mandate, the government became all-powerful and there was little Parliament was likely to do to thwart its will. The House of Lords was weak and the majority of the House of Commons was obedient to their party's leadership and the whips. This reality has now all but disappeared. There is a greater balance between the power and influence of Parliament and the executive.

There is a natural conflict in the relationship between the executive and Parliament. It consists of these two constitutional principles:

1 Parliament is sovereign.

2 The government has an electoral mandate to carry out its manifesto commitments.

So, when Parliament exercises its right of sovereignty, it is threatening the democratic legitimacy of the government. This conundrum is normally solved by the fact that the government usually enjoys a majority of the members of the House of Commons. This means that Parliament — the House of Commons, at least — will not need to exercise its sovereignty as long as the government is operating within its mandate. In this sense, the sovereignty of Parliament becomes, effectively, the sovereignty of the elected government.

In addition to this reality, the powers of the House of Lords have been gradually brought under control. In particular, there are three limitations on the Lords:

1 The **Parliament Act 1911** prevented the House of Lords having any control over the government's financial arrangements (spending and tax). The Act also stated that, if a law is passed in 2 consecutive years in the House of Commons, the Lords cannot block it.

2 The **Parliament Act 1949** stated that the delaying power of the Lords, as first specified in 1911, should be reduced to only 1 year.

3 The **Salisbury Convention** was developed in the 1940s. This states that the Lords must not block any piece of legislation which was contained in the government's last election manifesto. This meant that the unelected House of Lords could not thwart the will of the elected House of Commons and government.

So, there are great limitations on the powers of Parliament in relation to the executive. This begs the question: what controls on the executive are there? There are a number of answers to this question:

- If the government lacks an electoral mandate for a policy, the Commons may exercise a veto if the government cannot persuade the majority of MPs to support it.

Key terms

Elective dictatorship
A phrase coined by Conservative minister Lord Hailsham in 1976 referring to the reality that, if it commands a majority in the House of Commons, the government has great power and can behave almost like a dictator.

Salisbury Convention
An unwritten aspect of the UK Constitution which means that the House of Lords cannot block any legislation for which the government has an electoral mandate from the last election.

Activity

Research the Salisbury Convention (or doctrine). How did it come about?

- Parliament — both houses — may amend legislation to change its character and to protect certain minorities.
- Parliament calls government and its ministers to account. This means they are constantly aware that errors or injustices will be exposed.
- In very extreme circumstances Parliament could dismiss a government by passing a vote of no confidence in the government, thus forcing a general election.

We must be conscious that government normally does dominate Parliament but we can see that there is something of a balance between the powers of each.

Activity

In the autumn of 2016 there was a major conflict between Parliament and government over who should have the final say on the terms of the UK's exit from the European Union. What form did this conflict take and what was the outcome?

How the executive controls Parliament

As we have seen, Parliament does enjoy great *potential* power. However, this is rarely exercised to the full. The normal reality in the UK is that the executive dominates Parliament. How does it do this? There are a number of devices:

- The government *normally* commands a **majority** of MPs in the Commons. As long as it does this, it can expect MPs to support it out of party loyalty.
- The patronage of the prime minister is a key factor. The PM has control of all appointments to government, as well as dismissals from it. This gives them power over the MPs in their own party. MPs who regularly cause problems for the government are likely to lose their chance of being promoted to ministerial office. This does tend to concentrate their minds on party loyalty.
- MPs dislike elections on the whole. It creates hard work for them, and there is also the danger they might lose their seat. MPs in the governing party are, therefore, unlikely to do anything that might bring down the government. The **Fixed Term Parliaments Act 2011** has, however, reduced this possibility.
- The party whips exercise control. In extreme circumstances, an obstructive MP can be suspended from their party, which will damage their career. Whips also remind MPs about prime ministerial patronage and how important party loyalty is. There is a variety of ways in which the whips can make life difficult for uncooperative MPs.

Key term

Parliamentary majority
A circumstance, which is normal in the UK, where the majority of MPs in the House of Commons are members of the largest party, which forms the government. In a hung parliament, no one party has such a majority, in which case there must be a minority government or a coalition.

The changing nature of the executive–legislature relationship

We have examined the political and constitutional relationship between government and Parliament. However, politics is not static. Circumstances are constantly changing. As the political landscape changes, so too does this relationship. Table 8.9 shows the circumstances which favour executive dominance and which favour parliamentary power.

Knowledge check

Study UK general elections since 1970. On which occasions did no party enjoy a parliamentary majority?

Table 8.9 The changing relationship between government and Parliament

Circumstances favouring executive power	Examples	Circumstances favouring parliamentary power	Examples
The government enjoys a very large majority in the House of Commons.	1983 1987 1997 2001	The government has no majority or a very small majority.	1992 (Conservatives elected with a 21-seat majority) 2010 (no overall majority) 2015 (Conservative majority of 12 seats) 2017 No overall majority
The government is united around a dominant ideology.	1983–89 (Thatcherism) 1997–2005 (Labour third way ideology)	The governing party is split on issues.	1992–97 (John Major's Conservative Party split over Europe) 2010–15 (coalition period and Conservative split over Europe)
The opposition is fragmented or weak.	1983–92 (Labour split on left–right ideas) 2015 onwards (Corbyn's leadership split the Labour Party)	The government faces a strong, united parliamentary opposition.	1994–97 (Conservative government faced a united 'New Labour')
The government is led by a dominant leader.	1979–89 (Thatcher) 1997–2003 (Blair)	The leader of the governing party has lost popular and parliamentary authority.	1989–90 (Thatcher) 1994–97 (Major) 2003–07 (Blair) 2008–10 (Brown)

Knowledge check

Table 8.9 indicates that dominant governments were elected in 1983, 1987, 1997 and 2001 with large parliamentary majorities. What were those majorities?

Discussion point

Key political decisions can be made by government, or by Parliament. In each of the following examples, which of the two is more appropriate and democratic?
- Whether to intervene in a major international conflict
- Whether to agree trade deals with foreign states
- Whether to reintroduce capital punishment
- Whether to replace the House of Lords with an elected second chamber
- Whether to reform the electoral system for general elections
- Whether to call a general election if the government loses its parliamentary majority

The current state of executive–Parliament relations

Notwithstanding the changing nature of executive–legislature relations, there are some trends and changes that have altered the relationship on a longer-term basis. Among these trends are the following. (See also Table 8.10.)

- Since 2010 there has not been a dominant government majority in the Commons. This is partly due to the emergence of a multi-party system, with the SNP, in particular, emerging as a major force. If this persists (it may not), the fragmented nature of Parliament makes it harder for the government to control MPs in general. This is especially true, given the persistent split in the Conservative Party.
- In recent years Parliament has insisted on taking over control of UK military intervention abroad. This is largely a legacy of the failed policy in Iraq after 2003. Since then Parliament has demanded that it approves major military adventures and directs military policy. For example, Parliament has been directing the nature of UK intervention in the Syrian civil war.

- The House of Lords has become increasingly active and obstructive since 1999. Measures which are not subject to the Salisbury Convention are vulnerable to problems in their passage through the Lords.
- The departmental select committees and the Public Accounts Committee in the House of Commons, led by powerful chairpersons with a good deal of status, have become increasingly aggressive and intrusive. The committees are now more willing to criticise government and to claim a role in policy making.
- The Backbench Business Committee now controls part of the parliamentary agenda and can order debates which may criticise or influence government.
- The backbench members now control membership of the select committees, which used to be controlled by party whips. This has enhanced their authority considerably.

Table 8.10 The changing balance of power and influence between Parliament and the executive

The growing influence of Parliament	Factors that retain executive power
Parliament is achieving considerable influence over foreign and military policy.	Governments still normally enjoy a Commons majority.
The select committees are increasingly influential and have come under backbench control.	The government still relies on a large 'payroll vote' where all ministers, numbering over a hundred, are bound by collective responsibility.
The Liaison Committee calls the prime minister increasingly to account.	Government still controls the legislative programme and the Public Bill Committees which propose amendments.
There has not been a decisive government majority in the Commons since 2005.	Prime ministerial patronage still creates loyalty among the government's own MPs.
The House of Lords has become increasingly proactive and obstructive.	Government still has a huge advantage in resources (advice and research) over Members of Parliament.

Knowledge check

We have seen that the behaviour of the House of Lords changed in 1999. What happened in 1999 to change the status of the Lords?

Governing with a parliamentary minority

In June 2017 the Conservative Party under Theresa May was returned to power but without a majority of seats in the House of Commons. The party was asked to form a government because it was the largest party. How can a government govern with a minority? The following factors emerge:

- Most proposals have to be negotiated individually with members of parliament from all parties to try to secure a majority of support.
- The government is constantly facing the possibility of defeat.
- To survive, the government must satisfy two conditions. First, it must survive any votes of no confidence. If it loses, it must resign. Second, it needs to secure the approval of the Commons for its overall financial budget proposal. Failing this would also require the government to resign, as it cannot govern without money. The June 2017 agreement with the DUP of Northern Ireland seemed to ensure a slim government majority on such votes.

The UK and the European Union

The functions of the EU

The European Union has several functions, all of which are linked to each other. These are as follows.

Nigel Farage, former leader of UKIP, in Brussels

- It is a **customs union**. This means that the member states can trade with each other without any tariffs (taxes on goods or services being imported), or any other artificial restrictions and regulations. However, members of a customs union cannot make separate arrangements with external countries.
- It is a **single market**. This means there is completely free movement of goods, services, money, workers (labour) and people across borders. It also means that goods and services must be produced and sold under the same regulations in every member country.
- It is an **economic union**. This means it is responsible for economic development throughout the EU but especially in those countries where national income is relatively low. There is a system of development grants and agricultural subsidies paid for from the EU budget. Most member states also use the same currency — the euro.
- It is a **political union**. The EU attempts to develop common foreign policy and negotiates with foreign powers as a single unit over issues of security and general diplomacy. It also seeks to promote common policies on human rights, economic and social rights, and international law enforcement.

The institutions of the EU

The European Union has five main institutions:

- **The European Commission** This is the civil service of the EU. It is staffed by non-elected officials. Their main role is to develop and propose policies which will further the aims of the EU, to draft European legislation and to organise the implementation of EU policies.
- **The Council of Ministers** In fact this is a number of councils, each one dealing with one aspect of the EU's activities, such as finance, economy, agriculture, transport or foreign policy. Ministers from the elected governments of member states attend meetings. Their role is to negotiate final legislation and to ratify new laws. In effect they are the legally sovereign bodies of the EU.
- **The European Council** The heads of government of member states meet, normally twice per annum, to form this council. They ratify important decisions and occasionally agree new treaties. Along with the councils of ministers described above, this is the sovereign body of the EU.
- **The European Parliament** MEPs are elected from member states. Most represent political parties. The Parliament has a veto on appointments to the European Commission and can amend or even block legislation in some circumstances. It calls the commission to account.
- **The European Court of Justice** Staffed by judges drawn from member states, the court is the highest court of appeal. It deals with disputes between member states, interprets EU law when it is disputed and can punish states which disobey EU law. Its rulings are binding on all member states.

The impact of the UK's exit from the EU

The constitutional impact

The position is clear. Upon leaving the European Union, the UK Parliament regains all its sovereignty. EU laws are no longer part of UK law and the UK is no longer subject to EU treaties. The European Court of Justice (not to be confused with the European Court of Human Rights) has no jurisdiction in the UK.

The political impact

Here the picture is less clear. The political repercussions of the UK people's decision to leave the EU will be felt for many years to come. However, a number of conclusions can already be reached. These include the following:

Campaigners for both sides of the 2016 EU referendum

- The top level of the Conservative Party who had supported the 'remain' side of the campaign lost power, notably David Cameron and George Osborne, the chancellor of the exchequer.
- The Conservative Party is seriously divided between those who wish to retain close relations with the EU and those who want a clean break (so-called 'soft' or 'hard' Brexit).
- The Labour Party is similarly divided.
- The referendum revealed deep divisions in UK society, between young and old, England and Scotland, the cities and the countryside, the well off and the poor. The vote to leave was seen as something of a protest against the 'political class' in Westminster and a populist movement against powerful vested interests in general.
- Because Scotland voted overwhelmingly to remain inside the EU but will be forced out, there are renewed demands for Scottish independence so that Scotland can remain in the EU.
- The UK will now have to undertake a long-term programme of developing new political and trade links with other countries. When the UK was a member it was not free to develop separate trading arrangements with states outside the EU.
- The issue of immigration control, which is now *potentially* in the hands of a newly independent UK, will be a key political issue for years to come.

What influence will the EU have after the UK leaves?

The UK will become a completely sovereign state after March 2019. However, at some stage there may well be a new treaty with the EU. If there is such a treaty it might have some of the following conditions:

- The UK may be obliged to allow workers to enter the workforce without hindrance.
- There may be reciprocal arrangements to allow people to move freely in and out of the UK from EU countries.
- If there is a trade deal, it may be that the UK will have to allow goods and services to be imported without any import taxes (tariffs), in return for tariff-free exports to the EU.
- There may be a reciprocal arrangement to allow the free movement of financial capital in and out of the EU.
- There may be other agreements governing international policing, security, drug enforcement, internet control etc.

The so-called 'four freedoms' of the EU are:

- Free movement of people.
- Free movement of labour.
- Free movement of financial capital.
- Free movement of goods and services.

Thus, even when the UK is no longer a member of the EU it may still be forced to accept one or more of these freedoms if it is to remain in the European single market or have special trading arrangements with the EU.

Despite any such agreements, the UK will remain sovereign and will be able to cancel such treaty agreements. In the absence of any agreements, the EU will cease to have direct influence over the UK.

Sovereignty

What is sovereignty?

Synoptic link

This section should be read in conjunction with Chapter 5 on the constitution, as parliamentary sovereignty is a key element of the UK Constitution.

Key terms

Sovereignty A convenient concise definition of this complex idea is that it means ultimate political power which cannot be overruled peacefully.

Legal sovereignty Where ultimate constitutional power lies. This is sovereignty that cannot be overturned or set aside without acting in an unconstitutional manner.

Political sovereignty Although Parliament is legally sovereign, political sovereignty relates to where ultimate power lies in reality. This is power that will not be denied except under the most extreme circumstances.

Sovereignty is a difficult concept, but one that must be mastered if we are to understand fully the relationships between different parts of the political system. A general description of the term is 'ultimate power', but this does not tell us enough. A better and fuller explanation should include the following principles:

- Sovereignty implies a power which cannot be overruled.
- It is the source of all other political powers. In other words, a sovereign body can delegate its powers to others, but reserves the right to recover those powers.
- Sovereignty can only be removed or transferred, at least in a democracy, by some special procedures which usually involve popular consent.

In the UK, the most important application of sovereignty is parliamentary sovereignty. The official parliamentary website describes this principle as follows:

Parliamentary sovereignty is a principle of the UK constitution. It makes Parliament the supreme legal authority in the UK, which can create or end any law. Generally, the courts cannot overrule its legislation and no Parliament can pass laws that future Parliaments cannot change. Parliamentary sovereignty is the most important part of the UK constitution.

Source: **www.parliament.uk**

The sovereignty of Parliament is the principal example of **legal sovereignty**. This is a constitutional reality which will be enforced in law. It may not, though, reflect **political sovereignty**. This refers to where real power lies as opposed to theoretical power. These two circumstances can be examined in the following way.

A constitutional reality: legal sovereignty

This refers to the single body — Parliament — whose laws will be supreme in all circumstances. It also means that political power can only be exercised if Parliament explicitly grants that power to a body. Parliament is also the single authority which can declare what the constitution is. The UK's exit from the European Union is the final confirmation of parliamentary sovereignty. The EU's laws were superior to parliamentary statutes, but this is now in the past.

A political reality: political sovereignty

Legal sovereignty is not the full story. It does not reflect what actually happens within the political system. For example, Parliament may be legally sovereign, but the Scottish Parliament makes laws that apply in Scotland. The UK Parliament can exercise its sovereignty by taking away the power of the Scottish Parliament, but it is unthinkable that it would do so. Similarly, we know in reality that it is the UK government that develops most national laws and not Parliament. The government is effectively sovereign, especially as it enjoys the democratic mandate granted by the electorate.

Sovereignty revisited

Some political commentators now argue that sovereignty is an outdated concept and that the distinction between legal and political sovereignty is meaningless. All that matters, they argue, is where real power lies. There are a number of examples which illustrate this philosophy:

- The key, strategic decisions concerning the constitution are now being made by referendum. In this sense it is the people who are sovereign. The fact that Parliament has to ratify the result of a referendum because it is legally sovereign does not matter. Realistically, Parliament will never overturn a referendum outcome.
- The devolution settlement is, in reality, a federal system. In a federation, sovereignty is divided between central authorities and regional authorities. This is the reality of the United Kingdom today, though it is power rather than sovereignty that is divided.
- It can be argued that, by winning a general election, the UK government has been granted sovereignty, certainly to implement its manifesto. The fact that Parliament can veto legislation is not relevant as it is such a rare event.
- The situation with the protection of rights is similarly clouded. In theory Parliament can set aside the rights of the citizens under its sovereign powers. However, the European Convention on Human Rights, and the European Court that enforces it, effectively control the protection of rights.

The distinctions between power and sovereignty are, therefore, extremely blurred. In these circumstances, it is suggested, we should abandon the distinction between legal and political sovereignty.

The changing location of sovereignty

There is no doubt that sovereignty is on the move in the UK. Now that sovereignty is returning from the European Union, attention has shifted back to parliamentary sovereignty. The old certainty, that Parliament was sovereign and nothing else matters, has gone. The location of sovereignty therefore varies:

- The people are sometimes sovereign — at elections and when a referendum takes place.
- The government is often sovereign — when it has such a decisive majority in the House of Commons, and therefore a very strong electoral mandate, that it dominates the political establishment.
- The courts may be sovereign — when they are enforcing the European Convention on Human Rights.
- The devolved assemblies of Wales and Northern Ireland and the Scottish Parliament may be sovereign — when they are passing laws under powers granted to them by the UK Parliament.

Knowledge check

Using information from this chapter or Chapter 5 on the constitution, identify examples of the following:

- The people being sovereign during a referendum
- The courts exercising sovereignty over a rights issue
- Parliament exercising its legal sovereignty over government
- A responsibility of government where the Scottish Parliament is sovereign

This is a situation which simply did not exist before 1997. Until that time, the only question was whether Parliament or government was truly sovereign.

Stormont, home of the Northern Ireland Assembly

Sovereignty today

The first observation we can make about sovereignty today — in the second decade of the twenty-first century — is that Parliament does appear to be restoring some of its past constitutional powers. It is claiming control over UK foreign and military policies, it has control over when general elections can be held, and it is increasingly determined to have its say over key political issues. These include agreements the UK makes with foreign powers and international organisations, and measures for which the government does not have a mandate.

The second current development is that sovereignty is increasingly being divided into different *functions*. In other words, sovereignty resides with whichever body or individual has ultimate power over a particular political issue. So, we may call this 'functional sovereignty'. This works like this:

- The people have sovereignty over key constitutional changes, such as devolution, the electoral system, the independence of Scotland and membership of the European Union.
- The courts, including the European Court of Human Rights, are sovereign when human rights and civil liberties need to be defined.
- The devolved administrations are sovereign when decisions and policies concern *only* Scotland, Wales or Northern Ireland.
- The prime minister is sovereign when determining who shall form the government.
- Parliament is sovereign when the government is proposing a major military initiative.
- The monarch *would be* sovereign if there were a major political crisis which could not be resolved by elected politicians.

As we have seen, all this can be changed if Parliament wishes, as Parliament remains *legally* sovereign. But political reality looks very different today.

Debate

How sovereign is the UK Parliament?

Sovereignty retained

- There has been no challenge to the legal sovereignty of Parliament.
- The Miller case (see page 278) confirmed that Parliament remains sovereign even after a referendum decision.
- The UK's departure from the EU restores parliamentary sovereignty.
- The UK does not have to conform to rulings by the European Court of Human Rights.
- Devolution can be reversed by Parliament.

Sovereignty threatened

- The executive continues to claim political sovereignty as long as it has a mandate.
- Devolution has been called 'quasi-federalism' in that it is unlikely that devolved powers will ever return to the UK Parliament.
- Though Parliament must confirm a referendum result, it is virtually unthinkable that Parliament would defy the will of the people.
- The European Convention on Human Rights is increasingly entrenched, making it difficult for Parliament to defy its terms.

Key concepts in this chapter

Common law Laws which have not been passed by Parliament but which are declared by judges. Either they are laws which are commonly thought to be enforceable or they are applications of law to specific cases.

Declaration of incompatibility A declaration made by a judge that a particular UK law is in conflict with the terms of the European Convention on Human Rights. This does not make the law invalid, as Parliament is sovereign, but it advises Parliament and government to think again about the law and whether to make it compatible.

Elective dictatorship A phrase coined by Conservative minister Lord Hailsham in 1976 referring to the reality that, if it commands a majority in the House of Commons, the government has great power and can behave almost like a dictator.

Formal equality A principle which is part of the rule of law. All citizens must be treated equally under the law. The courts and judges must not discriminate against individuals or groups on any grounds.

Habeas corpus A Latin term literally meaning 'you have the body'. It is a very old principle, dating back to before Magna Carta in 1215. It states that no individual or body, including government, shall detain a person against their will unless they can be charged and brought to trial quickly.

Judicial independence The principle that judges should be independent of government, Parliament, public opinion and media influence. It is a key principle of modern democracy in that it can protect human rights, maintain the rule of law and act as a check on the power of the state.

Judicial neutrality The idea that judges should have no political bias and should not favour one section of society over another, but should always impose the rule of law whereby all are treated equally, including government.

Judicial precedent A principle that when a judge in a court declares an important point of law, which includes the meaning of law or how it should be applied, that declaration must be followed by all other courts and judges in similar cases. In other words, it is a precedent set by a judge. Only a judge in a higher court can change or overturn a judicial precedent.

Judicial review A process whereby the courts review decisions by the state or any public body in relation to its citizens. Where a review finds that a citizen has not been treated fairly, or that their rights have been abused, or that a public body has exceeded its legal powers, the court may set aside the decision.

Judiciary The name given to the branch of government that enforces the law and interprets the meaning of laws, including constitutional law.

Legal sovereignty Where ultimate constitutional power lies. This is sovereignty that cannot be overturned or set aside without acting in an unconstitutional manner.

Omnicompetence Literally this means 'ability to do everything'. In the context of the UK Parliament it means that nothing and nobody can constrain Parliament, whatever is being proposed.

Parliamentary majority A circumstance, which is normal in the UK, where the majority of MPs in the House of Commons are members of the largest party, which forms the government. In a hung parliament, no one party has such a majority, in which case there must be a minority government or a coalition.

Political sovereignty Although Parliament is legally sovereign, political sovereignty relates to where ultimate power lies in reality. This is power that will not be denied except under the most extreme circumstances.

Salisbury Convention An unwritten aspect of the UK Constitution which means that the House of Lords cannot block any legislation for which the government has an electoral mandate from the last election.

Sovereignty A convenient concise definition of this complex idea is that it means ultimate political power which cannot be overruled peacefully.

Ultra vires A legal principle that literally means 'exceeding one's power'. When an action is ruled ultra vires by a court, it means the individual or body that takes a particular action was exceeding its legal power. Such actions will be set aside.

Summary

Having read this chapter, you should have knowledge and understanding of the following:
- ➜ The role of the judiciary in the UK
- ➜ The nature and importance of judicial review
- ➜ The interrelationships between the judiciary, the executive and Parliament
- ➜ A comparison between the role of politicians and the role of judges in the protection of human rights and civil liberties
- ➜ The nature and role of the Supreme Court
- ➜ The nature and importance of judicial independence, and how it is maintained
- ➜ The nature and importance of the European Convention on Human Rights
- ➜ The relationship between the Supreme Court and the European Court of Human Rights
- ➜ The nature of sovereignty, legal and political, and issues concerning the location of sovereignty

Further information and web guide

Websites

The best website to use for further information on the Supreme Court is its own website: **www.supremecourt.uk**.

For general information about judicial matters, look at the website of the Department of Justice: **www.justice.gov.uk**.

The issue of parliamentary sovereignty is explained in Parliament's website: **www.parliament.uk**.

The main pressure group in the field of human rights is Liberty. Its website contains information about issues which involve the courts, including some key rights cases: **www.liberty-human-rights.org.uk**.

Another rights pressure group is Rights Watch UK: **http://rwuk.org**.

Books

A reasonably up-to-date book is Paterson, R.N. (2014) *Final Judgment: The Last Law Lords and the Supreme Court*, Hart Publishing.

Expensive, but a useful reference book is Young, A. (2008) *Parliamentary Sovereignty and the Human Rights Act*, Hart Publishing.

Practice questions

AS

1 Describe the functions of the UK Supreme Court. (10)

2 Describe the main impacts of the UK leaving the European Union. (10)

3 Using the source, assess the importance of the government's prerogative powers. *In your response you must use knowledge and understanding to analyse points that are only in the source. You will not be rewarded for introducing any additional points that are not in the source.* (10)

> **Prerogative powers**
>
> *R (Miller) v Secretary of State for Exiting the European Union* in 2016/17 was one of the most important cases to come before the Supreme Court in modern times. The precise point of the case was whether the government could trigger Article 50, signalling the UK's notice to leave the European Union, without a vote in Parliament. The government lost the case and was forced to introduce legislation to start the process of leaving the EU.
>
> However, behind the detail of the case lay a basic principle. This was whether it is part of the prerogative powers of the government to withdraw from a treaty which would affect the rights of citizens. Nobody questions that the government may negotiate treaties as part of its prerogative powers, but it is not within its prerogative to establish or remove our rights.
>
> The case was also a landmark in the gradual erosion of the government's prerogative powers. The 2011 Fixed Term Parliaments Act took away the prime minister's prerogative power to choose the date of a general election without parliamentary approval, while the 2013 parliamentary vote forbidding the government from intervening militarily in the Syrian civil war challenged the prime minister's position as commander-in-chief.

4 'The UK Parliament is totally under the control of the executive today.'
To what extent do you agree? (30)

5 'Judicial independence is a cornerstone of the UK constitution.'
To what extent do you agree? (30)

A-level

1 Using the source, evaluate the idea that the House of Lords is a more effective check on government power than the House of Commons.
In your response you must compare the different opinions in the source and use a balance of knowledge and understanding both arising from the source and beyond it to help you to analyse and evaluate. (30)

> ### The House of Commons and the House of Lords
>
> When we think about the relationship between government and Parliament, we automatically tend to think of the House of Commons. This is natural. The Commons is more powerful than the House of Lords and enjoys more democratic legitimacy. But we should also be thinking about the government's relationship to the Lords.
>
> The traditional view of government–Commons relations is that the former is dominant. This is because the government normally enjoys the support of the majority of MPs and has various ways of controlling how they behave and vote. Of course, the extent of executive control does depend on how united the governing party is and on the size of its parliamentary majority. If the government has only a slim majority, as occurred in 2015, a small group of dissident MPs can thwart the will of the government by wiping away the majority.
>
> The government does not enjoy a majority of support in the Lords. At the same time, many peers are extremely independent and do not feel beholden to the party whips. This is largely because, being unelected, they are not accountable. In the 2010–15 coalition government period, the Lords was particularly active, especially in such fields as welfare reform and taxation policy.
>
> So we do need to differentiate between the Lords and the Commons when considering the relationship between government and Parliament.

2 Using the source, evaluate the role of judges in protecting rights in the UK. *In your response you must compare the different opinions in the source and use a balance of knowledge and understanding both arising from the source and beyond it to help you to analyse and evaluate.* (30)

Conflict between the judiciary and the government

In recent decades there has been an increasing level of conflict between the senior judiciary in the UK and the government. Three main areas can be identified:

1 The judges guard their role in determining sentences in criminal cases very closely. They are determined to impose the rule of law and assure every citizen a fair hearing and equal treatment. Government, on the other hand, constantly tries to control sentencing, mainly by imposing minimum prison terms for particular crimes such as murder and carrying offensive weapons.

2 While government sees the security of the state as its first priority, the judiciary sees the rule of law and the protection of human rights as its key role. The problem is that these two objectives often come into conflict. In particular, suspected terrorists, ministers often claim, should not be treated in the same way as other citizens because they represent a public danger. The judges, however, refuse to treat such suspects differently. They have the same rights as the rest of the population, they say.

3 With the increasing threat of religious extremism, the government wishes to curb freedom of speech in cases where it is believed that public words by religious figures may be encouraging terrorism. The judges, armed with the European Convention on Human Rights, seek to protect freedom of expression, even when the views expressed are distasteful.

This leads us to ask the question of whether unelected but independent judges are better placed to protect rights than the elected and accountable government and Parliament.

---

3 Evaluate the extent to which the Supreme Court can control governmental power. (30)

4 Evaluate the belief that the balance of power between the executive and parliament has markedly shifted towards parliament. (30)

Index

Page numbers in **bold** indicate key term definitions. Roman numerals as page numbers refer to the introductory chapter.

A

absolute majority **91**
abstention 129, **130**
accountability **4**
  calling ministers to account 224–25
  of government 205–06
Act of Settlement (1701) 155
Acts of Union (1707) 155
additional member system (AMS) 97–99
adversary politics, 1980s 76
age and voting behaviour 31, 122–24, 127, 129–30, 165
aggregation **44**
alternative vote (AV) system 102
apathy, political **129**, 131–32
ASH (Action on Smoking and Health) 28
asymmetric devolution **175**
authority **xii–xiii**
  of monarchy 55, 185–86, 247
  of prime minister 247–48
  provided by electoral mandate 8, 9, 109

B

Backbench Business Committee 164, 219, 222, 287
backbenchers **202**, 216
  peers, roles of 217–18
Barnett formula **182**
Belfast Agreement (1998) 179
bicameral political systems **202**
Bill of Rights (1689) **xvi–xvii**, 155
bills (proposed legislation) 212–13
Blair, Tony (1997–2007) (see also Labour Party) 65, 75–76, 254, 260
  Blairism/Blairites 67
  case study 257
  exercise of prerogative power 250
Blue Labour 67
broadcasting 138
Brown, Gordon (2007–10) 65, 134, 135, 258
Brown, Prof. Archie 136
Burke, Edmund (1729–97) 55, 56–57
'by-elections' 95

C

the cabinet 238–43
  collective responsibility 249
  during 2010–15 coalition 252–53
  features of 238–40
  powers of 243, 251
  relationship with recent prime ministers 253–54
  role of 240–41
  selection of 253
  'system' 241–43
cabinet committees **242**
cabinet government **238**
Cameron, David (2010–16) (see also Conservative Party) 68, 90, 136, 250–51
  coalition government (2010–15) 252
  case study 259
campaigning methods 25–26
case law 269
case studies
  court cases 269, 278
  general elections 144–46
  imaginary UK constitution 188
  pressure groups 28
  prime ministers 256–60
cash for honours **52**
celebrities, role in promoting causes 30
chancellor of the exchequer 242
charismatic authority xii–xiii
citizens
  appeals to the court 279
  and judicial reviews 270–71
  responsibilities 35
  rights and liberties 11, 162
city government/devolution **168**, 171–72, 173
civil liberties **31–32**
civil servants 235, **236**, 237, 239
  unelected 243
civil society **10**, 23
class see social class
class dealignment **121**
classical liberalism **68**
Clegg, Nick 68, 83, 134, 136, 138, 252
clickocracy **22**
coalition government 111, 146, 166, 170, **245**
  cabinet during 2010–15 coalition 252–53
codified constitution **153**, 155–56
  arguments for introducing 187–90
  case study of imagined 188
coercive power xi
collective responsibility 160, 244–45, 249

collective versus individual rights 35–36
commander-in-chief 237, **250**
committees 203
  cabinet 242
  legislative 206, 213, 219
  select 163–64, 219–23
committee stage of legislative process 213
common law **32**, 160, 161, **269**
  declaring 269–70
compulsory voting 21–22
conflict of ideas vii–viii
conflict of interests viii–ix
consensus politics **75–76**
consent **xi**, **205**
  reinforcing 47
conservatism 55
  New Right 58–60
  traditional (one nationism) 55–58
Conservative Party 50, 55–62
  case studies of leaders 256, 259
  factions 61–62
  funding 51, 52, 53, 54
  social classes voting for 120
Conservative Way Forward 62
constituencies 7–8, **91–92**
  representation 5, 206
the Constitution 152–95
  current debates on reform 182–90
  development of 154–55
  devolution 175–82
  functions of 153–54
  nature and theory of 155–59
  reform of 162–75
  sources of 159–61
constitutional conventions **154**
constitutionalism 12, 69
constitutional reform
  Conservative Party views 61
  current debates 182–90
  Labour Party views 66
  Liberal Democrats policy 70
  referendums, country comparisons 157–58
Constitutional Reform Act (2005) 169, 182, 272–73
constitutions
  codified and uncodified 159
  unitary and federal 158–59
contempt of court 282
conventions, constitutional **154**, 160
Corbyn, Jeremy 42, 46, 50, 66–67, 81
core executive **236**, 237
core values
  Labour Party 63–64, 75–76
  liberalism 68–69
core vote/core voters **132**, 133, 143
Cornerstone 62
courts (see also Supreme Court) 267–68, 271
cronyism **229**
crossbenchers **204**

D

Data Protection Act (1998) 167
debates in Parliament 207–08, 210, 222
decentralisation **7**, 162
declaration of incompatibility **276**
democracy 3–6
  direct 3–4
  representative 5–10
  in the UK 10–14
democratic deficit **12–13**
democratic legitimacy **xi**
democratic socialism **63**
democratic society 13–14
democratic system 10–12
Democratic Unionist Party (DUP) 8
  funding 52
democratisation 162
demographic factors and voting behaviour 119–32
departmental select committees (DSCs) 220–21
departments of state **239**
dependency culture **59**
deviant voting **120**, 121
devolution **175**, 175–82, 184
  assessment of 181–82
  cities **168**, 171–72
  differences made by 181
  in England 176–77
  English regions 176–77
  Northern Ireland 179
  Scottish 172, 177–78
  three types of 175–76
  in the UK (1979–2016) 180
  Welsh 172, 178–79
digital activists/democracy 15, 18
direct democracy **3–4**
  referendums as 208
disillusionment **129**
Disraeli, Benjamin 42, 55, 57, 61
division **212**
dominant-party systems 77, 78

E

ECHR see European Convention on Human Rights
economic voting **133**, 143
the economy
  Conservative Party 48, 60
  Labour policy 66
  left–right divide 49
  Liberal Democrats 69
  neo-liberalist views 59
e-democracy/e-petitions **18**
  digital activists 15
elections (see also voting behaviour)
  fairness of 109–11
  role and importance 109
  turnout 128–32
  versus referendums 105–06

elective dictatorship **284**
Electoral Commission 6–7, 53, 105, 138, 190
(electoral) mandate **8–9**
    doctrine of 47–48
Electoral Reform Society 94
electoral systems 90–117, **166**
    additional member system (AMS) 97–99
    alternatives to FPTP 96–97
    in different parts of the UK 101–02
    elections 109–11
    first past the post (FPTP) 91–96, 102–03
    and government 111
    and party systems 112
    referendums 102–09
    reforms 165–66, 173
    single transferable vote (STV) 99–100
    supplementary vote 100–01
    and voter choice 112
elitism **14**, 84
English votes for English laws (EVEL) 173, 177
entrenchment **156**
environmental issues
    Conservative Party 61
    Green Party 72, 73–74, 123, 124, 130
    Greenpeace 24–25, 26, 31
    Labour Party 66
    Liberal Democrats 69, 70
    SNP policies 73
equality (*see also* rule of law)
    formal **33, 268**
    Old Labour value 64
Equality Act (2010) 33–34
equity *see* common law
ethnicity
    Parliamentary 228
    and voting behaviour 125, 127, 143
European Communities Act (1972) 155
European Community (EC), Britain joins (1973) xix–xx
European Convention on Human Rights (ECHR) 32–33, 34, 164–65
    declarations of incompatibility 276
    and parliamentary sovereignty 201
    relationship with European Court of Human Rights 280–81
European Court of Human Rights 165, 279–81
European (Notification of Withdrawal) Act (2017) 155
European Union (EU) 287–88
    'four freedoms' of 289
    functions of 287–88
    institutions of 288
European Union (EU), UK leaving xxi
    2016 referendum on 106, 108, 117, 121–22, 139
    impact of 182, 288–89
    influence on UK after exit 289–90
    Miller court case 278
the executive xvi, 235–37
    interaction with Parliament 214–25
    relationship with judiciary 277
    relationship with Parliament 284–87
    role and structure 235–237

F

factions **61**
    Conservative Party 61–62
    Labour Party 66–67
    Liberal Democratic party 71
fair elections 11, 13, 109–11
Farage, Nigel, UKIP 82, 136, 287
Farron, Tim, Liberal Democrat leader 50
federal constitution 158
federalism **158**
    and devolution 175, 291
first past the post (FPTP) **91**
    case for and against 95–96
    compared to other systems 102–103
    working of 91–95
Fixed Term Parliaments Act (2011) 110, 156–57, 160, 170, 173, 285, 287
floating/swing voters **120**
    factors influencing 143
foreign policy
    Conservatives 61
    Labour 66
    Liberal Democrats 70
formal equality **33, 268**
franchise (suffrage) **19**
freedom of association 11, 13, 36
freedom of expression 11, 13, 36
freedom of information 11, 13, 110, **167**, 173
Freedom of Information Act (2000) 33, 160, 167–68, 183, 190, 271
free elections 10–11, 13
frontbench MPs 202
frontbench peers 204
functional representation 6
    pressure groups 9, 10
    sectional groups 23
functional sovereignty 292
funding of parties 51–54

G

gender
    representation in Parliament 228
    and voting behaviour 122, 127, 143
general election case studies 144–46
Glorious Revolution (1688–89) xvi–xvii, 186
Good Friday Agreement (1998) 179
governing competence **133**
government (*see also* the executive) 243
    branches of xv–xvi
    concepts related to xi–xiv
    functions of 243–44
    limits to power of 12
    representation 9
    versus the state xv

government by consent **104**
government departments 237, **239**
  civil servants 236
  House of Lords representative 218
  select committees 220–23
Government of Wales Acts (1998 and 2014) 178–79
Great Reform Act (1832) xvii–xviii, 19, 198
Green Party 72, 73–74, 123, 124, 130
grievances, redress of **5, 207**
group politics **27**, 31

H

habeas corpus **276**
hereditary peers **163**, 203, 204, 217
House of Commons
  election, role and importance of MPs 215–16
  functions of 205–08
  interaction with House of Lords 213–14
  origins 197–99
  reform of 163–64, 173, 183
  select committees 219–23
  social make-up 228
  structure of 202–03
  versus House of Lords 210–12
House of Lords 201
  functions of 208–10
  interaction with House of Commons 213–14
  reform of 163, 183, 228–30
  role in opposing Parliament 223–24
  selection, role and importance of peers 217–18
  structure of 203–04
  versus House of Commons 210–12
  versus US Senate 202
House of Lords Act (1999) 160, 163, 204, 217
Howe, Geoffrey, resignation 241–42
human rights (*see also* European Convention on Human
    Rights) 187
  European Court of 165, 279–81
  reform 164–65
  Supreme Court protection of 274–75, 279
  versus civil liberties 31–32
Human Rights Act (1998) 164, 165, 183
  and the ECHR 32–33, 189, 201, 276
  and judicial reviews 271
  and protection of rights in the UK 34
hung parliament **252**
hyperpluralism **27**

I

ideology **vii–viii**
  rejection of by traditional conservatives 58
inclusivity of parties 83–84
independence of the judiciary 12, **169**, 281–83
independence referendum, Scotland (2014) 16, 17, 74, 106,
    107, 130
Independent Labour Party (ILP) 63
individual ministerial responsibility 245–46

individual versus collective rights 35–36
influence, weak form of power xii
initiatives **105**
inner cabinet **252**
insider pressure groups 24, 31
institutions of the EU 288
instrumental voting **122**, 135
internet campaigns 15, 18–19
Ireland *see* Northern Ireland
issue voting 134–35, 143

J

judicial independence 12, **169, 281–83**
judicial neutrality **282–83**
judicial precedent 32, 170, 268, **269**
judicial review **270–71**
judiciary xiv, **267**
  codified constitution politicising 187
  and the executive 277
  independence of 12, 281–83
  and parliament 275–77
  reform of 169–70, 173, 272–74
  senior, nature and role of 267–71
  sentencing issues 272

K

Khan, Sadiq, mayor of London 100–01, 168

L

Labour Party 50, 62–67
  case studies of leaders 257–58
  creation of 62–63
  current ideas and policies 66
  factions 66–67
  funding 51, 52, 53, 54
  leadership issues 46, 135–37
  'left-wing' policies 76
  New Labour 64–66
  newspapers affiliated with 82–83, 138–40
  'Old' Labour 63–64
law (*see also* legislation)
  case law 269
  common law 32, 269–70
  interpretation of 268–69
Law Lords 169, 272, 276
law and order
  Conservative Party 60
  Labour policy 66
  Liberal Democrat Party 69–70
  Liberal Democrat policies 69–70
  neo-conservatism 59
leadership of a party 44, 46, 81–82
  effect on voting behaviour 135–37
  general elections 144, 145, 146
  satisfaction ratings 136
  televised debates 138
  valence issue 134

leadership style
  Blair, Tony 257
  Brown, Gordon 258
  Cameron, David 259
  Thatcher, Margaret 256
left-right divide 49–51
left wing **45**
legal-rational authority xiii
legal sovereignty **290**
legal sovereignty xiv 158
legislation 212–14
  amendment 208, 214
  constitutional statues 159, 160
  delaying by the Lords 209
  delegated 209–10
  process of passing 205, 212–13
  rights and equality laws 32–34
  scrutiny of 206, 209, 210, 218
  secondary 209–10
  stages of Constitution development 154–55
  suffrage timeline 19
  three types of 212
legislative committees 206, 213, 219
legislature xv–xvi
legitimacy xi
legitimation 205
Liaison Committee 221, 287
liberal democracy **69**
Liberal Democrats 50, 67–71
  coalition cabinet (2010–15) 252
  core values 68–69
  current ideas and policies 69–71
  factions 71
  funding 51, 52, 53, 54
  origins 67–68
liberalism
  core values 68–69
  neo-liberalism 59
libertarianism **73**
liberties
  civil liberties 31–32
  protection of 11, 13, 30
life peers 204, **217**
limited government **12**
lobbying **25**
lobbyists 29, 30
local government 7
  elections 79, 80, 99
  reform of 170–71, 173
London
  city government and devolution 168
  mayoral elections 100–01, 168
  and regional voting 126
Lord Chancellor 169, 266
  Constitutional Reform Act 272–74

M

Magna Carta (1215) xvi, 154–55
majority government **94**, 111, 200, 285
Major, John (1990–97), resignation 249
mandate (electoral) 8–9, 47–48
manifesto of a party **5–6, 47**, 48–49
  and mandate 8–9
marginal seats **94–95**
mayoral elections 170–71
  London 100–01, 168
  outside London 171
May, Theresa (2016–) 61, 81, 225, 234
media influence 82–83, 138–42
membership of political parties 14, 15
  decline in 15–16
members of parliament (MPs) (see also House of Commons) 202–03
  constituency representation 206–07
  expenses claims 167
  interests/causes, pursuit of 207
  Private Members' Bills 212
  recall of 172, 173
  role of 215–16
  selection of 203
Miliband, Ed 16, 136, 138, 250
military action 241, 250–51, 257, 286
Miller, Gina, Supreme Court case 278
ministers (see also the cabinet; prime minister)
  calling to account 224–25
  responsibility 244–46
minority government 48, **94**, 287
minor parties 71–74
  Greens 72, 73–74
  impact on major parties 74
  SNP 71–72, 73
  UKIP 72, 73
modernisation of constitution 162–63
modern liberals **68**
Momentum movement, Corbyn 67
the monarchy 155, 188, 197, 234, 261
  decline in power of 185–86
  role of xiv
  royal assent 213
  royal prerogative 237, 247
  and sovereignty 158
  traditional authority 247
multi-party systems 72, 77, 78, 79–80, 102–03, 112

N

national debate 207–08, 210
national interest 5, 44, 226
neo-conservatism 59–60
neo-liberalism **59**
neutrality of judges 282–83

New Labour **65–66**, 75–76, 257
New Right conservatism 76
  neo-conservatism 59–60
  neo-liberalism 59
New Right conservatism (Thatcherism) **58**
newspapers, political affiliations 82, 138–40
Northern Ireland
  devolution 179, 181
  electoral system 80, 99–100, 166
  political parties 92, 93

O

'Old' Labour 63–64
omnicompetence 275, **276**
one-nation conservatism **55**
one nationism (traditional conservatism) 55–58
one-party systems 77, 78
opinion polls 134–35, 140–42, 143
opposition parties
  funding for 53–54
  role of 223–24
Orange Book liberals 71
order (see also law and order)
  conservatism 56
organic society 57
Osborne, George 171, 252, 259, 289
outsider pressure groups 24–25, 31

P

Parliament 196–233
  bicameral structure of 201–04
  defined **197**
  functions and importance 204–10
  general assessment of 225–28
  government and sovereignty 199–201
  history and status 197–99
  interaction with executive 214–25
  legislation 212–14
  powers of House of Commons and House of Lords
    210–12
  reform of House of Commons 163–64
  reform of House of Lords 228–30
  relationship with executive 284–87
Parliament Acts (1911 and 1949) 155, 209, 284
parliamentary majority 260, **285**, 286
parliamentary privilege 214–15
parliamentary sovereignty **156**, 199–200
  erosion of 200–01
participation in politics 14–19
parties see political parties
partisan dealignment **132**, 143
party factions see factions
party funding 51–53
party leaders see leadership of a party

party manifestos **5–6, 47**, 48–49
party membership 14, 15
  decline in 15–16
party systems **72**
party whip **203**
patronage of the PM 243, 249, 253, 254, 285
peers see House of Lords
pluralism/pluralist democracy **14**, 28, 34
plurality (election system) **91**
police commissioners, election of 171
policies **44**
policy-making, party function 44
political authority, nature of xii–xiii
political opinion polls **140–41**
political participation 14–19
political parties 5–6, 8, 42–89
  consensus and adversary politics 75–76
  Conservative Party 55–62
  decline in membership 15–16
  defined **43**
  features of 43–44
  functions of 44–47
  funding of 51–54
  Labour Party 62–67
  Liberal Democratic Party 67–71
  mandate and manifesto 47–49
  minor parties 71–74
  party and electoral systems 77–80
  and pressure groups 31
  right- and left-wing politics 49–51
  role of 83–84
  success factors 80–83
Political Parties, Elections and Referendums Act (2000) 51,
    190
political power xi–xii
political sovereignty **290–91**
political sovereignty xiv
popular sovereignty xiv
politics, meaning of vii
populism/populist parties **45**
power(s)
  of the cabinet 243, 251
  devolved 175–76, 179, 185
  executive 186–87
  levels of xi–xii
  Parliamentary 210–12
  prerogative **248**
  of the prime minister 248–51
  reserve **200**
  separation of **170**
  struggle for x
  of the Supreme Court 283
  of the UK cabinet 251
pragmatism 57–58, 187
prerogative powers 161, 186, 237, 247, **248**

case study 278
recent examples 250
president models 260–61
the press 138–40
pressure groups 9–10, 18, 22–31
ASH case study 28
classifying 23–25
and democracy 28–29
failure factors 27–28
functions of 23
methods used by 25–26
success factors 26–27
primary legislation 210
prime minister (PM) (*see also* the cabinet; the executive)
237–38
assessment of power 254–55
authority and power 247–51
and the 'cabinet system' 241–43
case studies 256–60
and presidential leadership 260–61
relationship with cabinet 252–55
Prime Minister's Question Time (PMQT) 206, 224–25
Private Bills 212
Private Members' Bills 212
privilege, parliamentary 214–15
promotional (cause or issue) groups 18, **23**, 24, 25
property ownership 58
proportional representation (PR) 78, 96, **97**, 112, 166
additional member system (AMS) 97–99
single transferable vote (STV) 99–100
supporters of 103
Public Accounts Committee (PAC) 219–20, 232, 287
Public Bill (legislative) Committees 206, 213, 219
Public Bills 212
public campaigning 25–26
public inquiries, judge-led 271
public opinion polls 140–42

Q

quasi-federalism **175**
Queen's Speech 161
'questions to ministers days' 224

R

rational choice model **134**, 135, 143
Recall of MPs Act (2015) 172, 173
redress of grievances **5, 207**
referendums **103, 157**
case for and against 107–08
and constitutional reform 157–58, 174–75
impact of 106
operation of 103–06
and representative democracy 108–09
turnout in 17
reform
constitutional 162–75, 182–84, 190
electoral 165–66, 173, 183, 184

House of Commons 163–64, 183
House of Lords 163, 183, 228–30
human rights 164–65
judicial 169–70, 182, 272–74
local government 170–71
parliamentary 163–64
registration for voting 22
Regina v *Jogee* (2016) case 269
regions of the UK, voting bias 125–27
registration to vote, reforms 22
representation (*see also* proportional representation)
causal 6, 10
constituency 5, 7–8, 206–07, 226
elected government 9
functional 6, 23
House of Lords 226–27
of interests, MPs 207
levels of 7
mandate doctrine 8–9
parties 5–6, 8, 44–45
pressure groups 9–10
social 4
by UK parliament 227–28
Representation of the People Acts 19
representative democracy **3**, 4–6
nature of in the UK 6–10
political parties' role 83, 84
and referendums 108–09
reserve powers **200**
reshuffle **253**
responsibility
of citizens 35
collective 244–45
individual 245–46
ministerial 244–46
rights 31–36
citizens' responsibilities 35
civil liberties 31–32
collective versus individual 35–36
common law 32
equality laws 33–34
freedom of information 33
human rights 32–33, 279–81
protection of 11, 13, 162
Supreme Court cases 279
in the UK 34–35
right wing **45**
left-right divide 49–52
royal prerogative **237**, 247, 248, 250, 278
rule of law 12, 13, 279
equality principle 33, 160, 268
Magna Carta 154–55

S

safe seats **94**
salience **134**
Salisbury Convention 160, 208, 211, 214, **284**

Scotland Acts (1998 and 2016) 160, 177–78, 180
Scottish devolution 177–78, 180, 181
Scottish Elections (Reduction of Voting Age) Act (2016) 19
Scottish independence, 2014 referendum 16, 17, 74, 106, 107, 130
Scottish National Party (SNP) 71–72
    2015 general election 146
    concentrated support 92
    election results (2016) 98–99
    policies 73
    political stance 74
    Sturgeon, Nicola 81–82, 136, 137
secondary legislation **209–10, 243**
second chamber
    reform of 184, 228–30
    UK and USA comparison 202
sectional (interest) groups 18, **23–24,** 27
select committees 219–23, 287
    Backbench Business Committee 222
    calling ministers to account 224–25
    departmental (DSCs) 220–21
    impact of 222–23
    Liaison Committee 221–22
    Public Accounts Committee (PAC) 219–20
Senate (USA) versus House of Lords (UK) 202
senior judiciary
    appointment of 169, 282
    general role of 268–71
    nature of 267–68
    training and experience 282
sentencing issues, judges 272
separation of powers **170**
short money **53–54**
single transferable vote (STV) 99–100
social class **119**
    and turnout in UK general elections 130–31
    and voting behaviour 119–22, 127, 143
social democracy 60, 67, 68
social issues, left–right divide 49
social justice 61, 64, 66, 69, 71
social liberals **71**
social media 15, 18–19, 140
social representation 4
    UK Parliament 227–28
sofa politics **254**
sovereignty **xiv, 290**
    changing location of 291–92
    and constitutions 158
    current developments 292–93
    legal and political 290–91
    parliamentary **156**, 199–201, 283, 284
Speaker of the House of Commons 177, 203
the state versus government xiv–xv
statutes (see also legislation) 159, 160
Sturgeon, Nicola, SNP 81, 82, 136, 137
suffrage **xviii, 19–22**
supplementary vote system 100–01
Supreme Court 272

cases 269, 278
establishment of 273–74
and the executive 277–78
nature of 274–75
and Parliament 275–77
power of 283
reforms 169
and rights 279
swing (floating) voters **120**

T
tactical voting 95, **112, 137**, 138, 143
televised leadership debates 136, 138
tenure of the judiciary 281–82
terrorism 34–35, 183, 186, 276
Thatcherism ('New Right conservatism') 58–60
Thatcher, Margaret (1979–90)
    adversary politics 76
    cabinet stance 240, 254
    case study 256
    Conservative Way Forward 62
    post-Thatcher consensus 75–76
think tanks **29**
    examples of 29–30
'third way' (New Labour) **64–66**, 145, 257
three-party systems 77, 78
Tory Reform Group 62
traditional authority xii, **247**
traditional conservatism (one nationism) 55–58
traditional Labour Party ('Old' Labour) 63–64
traditions xi
    constitutional 161
    preservation of 56–57
turnout 16–17, **128**
    impact of age and class 130–32
    variability and long-term trend 128–30
    by young people 129–30
two-party system **71**, 78, 112
    decline in dominance of 78–79
    development of xviii–xix

U
UKIP (UK Independence Party) 51, 72, 227
    2015 election 91, 92, 93, 146
    class and voting 121, 122
    policies 73
ultra vires **275, 279**
unitary constitution 158
unity of a party 82, 134

V
valence issues, voting **133**, 134, 143
vote of no confidence **199**
voting (see also electoral systems) 15
    by 16- and 17-year-olds 20, 165–66
    compulsory 21–22
    franchise/suffrage 19–20

reform 166
registration reforms 22
right to vote (suffrage) 19–22
tactical 95, 112, 137–38, 143
voting behaviour 118–50
ethnicity 125
gender and age 122–24
general election case studies 144–46
the media and opinion polls 138–42
and perception of leaders 135–36
region 125–27
social class 119–22
summary of factors affecting 127–28, 142–43
turnout 16–17, 128–32

W

welfare
Conservative policy 60–61
Labour 66

Liberal Democrat policy 70
neo-liberalism 59
welfare state **xix**, 75
Welsh devolution 172, 178–79, 181
whips **203**, 285
White Paper **212**
women
suffrage movement 19–20
under-represented in Parliament 228
voting behaviour 122

Y

young people, voting behaviour
16- and 17-year-olds 20–21, 165–66
compulsory voting 22
party support 123–24
registration 22
social media use 140
turnout 129–30